Successful Emotions

Katharina Lochner

Successful Emotions

How Emotions Drive Cognitive Performance

With a preface by Prof. Dr. Michael Eid

Springer

Katharina Lochner
Hamburg, Germany

Dissertation at Freie Universität Berlin, 2015

ISBN 978-3-658-12230-0 ISBN 978-3-658-12231-7 (eBook)
DOI 10.1007/978-3-658-12231-7

Library of Congress Control Number: 2015959157

Springer

Printed on acid-free paper

Springer is a brand of Springer Fachmedien Wiesbaden
Springer Fachmedien Wiesbaden is part of Springer Science+Business Media
(www.springer.com)

I dedicate this book to my parents **Renate and Norbert Lochner**
who always supported me.

Preface

Intelligence is the most important general predictor for professional success and is one of the most often assessed abilities in personnel selection. Intelligence is considered a relatively stable trait and the assessment of intelligence should depend on one's ability and not on situational influences. In order to make valid decisions in personnel selection the result of an intelligence test should therefore not be prone to the momentary state of a candidate. However, psychological measurements always take place in a situational context. Test scores can be influenced by the outer situation such as the testing room but also by the inner situation of an individual such as the current mood or emotions.

In the present book Katharina Lochner analyzes the influence of mood and emotions on reasoning, an important facet of intelligence, in a complex experimental study that goes beyond previous research on this topic. She gives a very thorough overview of previous research on the influences of mood and emotions on intellectual performances, and describes different prominent theories in detail. Everyone who is interested in getting a current up-to-date overview of this important topic will find a concise discussion of the state of the art in research on affect and intelligence.

In her empirical study she focuses on a wide range of different emotions and hypothesizes that positive emotions have a stronger influence than negative emotions and that activating emotions are more important than deactivating emotions. Her hypotheses are scrutinized using the internet as scientific tool for conducting randomized experiments. Different emotional states are successfully induced by different movies and her hypotheses are analyzed in a longitudinal study. The results of this study show that her hypotheses cannot be confirmed. Because the statistical power of her study was strong enough, this result is of high importance for research on emotion, intelligence and personnel selection. It shows that the emotional quality of the current state of a candidate is of minor importance for the interpretation of reasoning scores. This result sheds new light on the emotional basis of intellectual abilities and will have important consequences for the interpretation of ability test scores. The book is therefore not only of interest for researchers but also for practitioners in the field of aptitude assessment. The clear and concise style in which the book is written makes it accessible to a broad audience and I am convinced that the book will find the attention that it deserves.

Michael Eid

Acknowledgements

First and foremost I would like to thank my supervisor, **Prof. Dr Michael Eid**, and my boss, **Dr Achim Preuß**, for giving me their support, trust, and patience. Without them, this thesis would not have been possible. During four years they were a source of inspiration, knowledge, and motivation to me.
I worked on this project outside of work and I would like to thank **Dr Achim Preuß** and **Andreas Lohff**, the managing directors of *cut-e*, the company I work with, for the time and resources they gave me for this thesis. Moreover, a big thank you goes to **Dennis Beermann**, with whom I spent innumerable hours on Skype discussing our PhD studies, for giving me a lot of valuable advice and thoroughly reading and commenting on my results section. I am very grateful to my colleagues **Carolin Lehmann** and **Mario Martella** who helped me tremendously with the editing of the film clips, and, even more importantly, programmed the online experiment for me which worked so extremely well and allowed me to gather the necessary data.
I would like to thank **Marie Pick**, **Mizzi Walker**, and **Dr Alexander Zimmerhofer** who gave me valuable input on my experiment in the pre-testing phase. A big thank you goes to **Fenne große Deters**, **Maike Wehrmaker**, and **Mizzi Walker** who thoroughly proof-read chapters of the manuscript and gave me valuable ideas and feedback on these.
I am very grateful to my colleagues **Anabela Costa**, **Anja Heins**, **Antje Exner**, **Diana Körner**, **Maike Wehrmaker**, **Nadja Mink**, **Nina Galler**, **Richard Justenhoven**, **Susan Dietz**, and **Tobias Castillo** who made sure I was free of obligations at work during phases that required me to concentrate on my PhD.
Finally, I would like to thank **Hetty Mainka** for her priceless support before and during my PhD disputation.

Content

ABSTRACT .... **XVII**

INTRODUCTION **1**

1 ONLINE ASSESSMENT AND ONLINE SURVEYS **7**

1.1 Definition, Advantages, and Disadvantages **8**

1.1.1 Advantages 8

1.1.2 Disadvantages 9

1.2 Quality of Online Data **10**

1.2.1 Equivalence of Paper-and-Pencil and Online Data 10

1.2.2 Fulfilment of Test Quality Criteria 13

1.3 Representativeness of Online Studies **15**

1.3.1 Sampling 16

1.3.2 Retention 17

1.3.3 Standardisation and Controllability of the Situation 18

1.4 Design of online studies **18**

1.5 Summary **20**

2 INTELLIGENCE AND INTELLIGENCE TESTING **21**

2.1 Models of Intelligence **23**

2.1.1 Two-Factor Theories 23

2.1.2 Primary factors 24

2.1.3 Integration of the models 25

2.1.4 Multidimensional Model 30

2.1.5 Other Theories of Intelligence 33

2.1.6 Summary 33

2.2 Intelligence tests 34
2.2.1 Raven's Progressive Matrices (RPM; Raven et al., 2003)................35
2.2.2 Woodcock-Johnson Test of Cognitive Abilities (Woodcock et al., 2001)..35
2.2.3 Berlin Intelligence Structure Test (BIS Test; Jäger et al., 1997) 36
2.2.4 Adaptive Matrices Test (AMT; Hornke et al., 2000).........................39

2.3 Summary..40

3 AFFECT, MOOD, AND EMOTIONS 43

3.1 Models of Affect 44
3.1.1 Structural Models...45
3.1.2 Models of Discrete Emotions 49
3.1.3 Hybrid Models..50
3.1.4 Domain-Specific Models 53

3.2 Measurement of Mood and Emotions 53
3.2.1 Assessment of the Physiological Component..................................53
3.2.2 Assessment of the Expressive Component 53
3.2.3 Assessment of the Affective Component...54

3.3 Elicitation of Mood and Emotions..58
3.3.1 Overview of Mood and Emotion Elicitation Methods......................59
3.3.2 Online Mood Induction...64
3.3.3 Reviews of Mood and Emotion Induction Procedures 65

3.4 Summary..66

4 AFFECT AND COGNITION 69

4.1 Affect and Cognition in the Brain...71
4.1.1 Neuropsychological Theory of Positive Emotions (Ashby, Isen, & Turken, 1999) 72
4.1.2 Affect and Information Processing 75

4.2 Cognitive Approaches: Mood-Induced Thinking Styles 76
4.2.1 The Theory of Personality Systems Interaction (PSI Theory; Kuhl, 1983a, b) 77
4.2.2 Feelings-as-Information Theory (Schwarz, 1990) 79
4.2.3 Somatic Markers Hypothesis (Damasio, 1994) 79
4.2.4 Empirical Findings on the Three Theories 80

4.3 Cognitive Approaches: Memory 81
4.3.1 Mood Congruency and State Dependency (Bower, 1981) 82
4.3.2 Cognitive Context (Isen, 1984) 82
4.3.3 The Broaden-and-Build Theory of Positive Emotions (Fredrickson, 1998, 2001) 84

4.4 Attention-Theoretical Approaches 86
4.4.1 Cue Utilisation (Easterbrook, 1959) 86
4.4.2 The Resource Allocation Model (Ellis & Ashbrook, 1988) 87

4.5 Activation-Theoretical Approaches 89

4.6 Motivational Approaches 91
4.6.1 Mood Maintenance and Mood Repair (Isen, 1984) 92
4.6.2 The Rubicon Model of Action Phases (Heckhausen & Gollwitzer, 1986, 1987) 93
4.6.3 Expectancy Theory (Vroom, 1964) 95
4.6.4 Seo, Barrett, and Bartunek's (2004) Theory 95

4.7 Task Demand-Based Approaches 99
4.7.1 The Multifactor-System Dynamics Theory of Emotion (Royce & Diamond, 1980) 99
4.7.2 Dual-Force Model (Fiedler, 1990) 101
4.7.3 Affect Infusion Model (AIM; Forgas, 1995) 104

4.8 An integrative Model: The Cognitive-Motivational Mediator Model of the Impact of Mood on Cognitive Performance (Abele, 1995) .. 108
4.8.1 Affect and Perceptual Speed 110
4.8.2 Affect and Creativity 110
4.8.3 Affect and Reasoning 112

4.9 Discrete Emotions and Cognitive Performance ... 116

4.10 Summary of Theories and Findings ... 120

5 THE PRESENT STUDY ... 125

5.1 Hypotheses on Emotions and Test Performance ... 125

5.2 Considerations about the Design of the Study ... 128
5.2.1 Selection of the Film Clips ... 129
5.2.2 Manipulation Check ... 130

6 PILOT STUDIES ... 133

6.1 Pilot study 1: Design of an Online Mood Questionnaire ... 133

6.2 Pilot study 1a: Validation of the Visual Analogue Scale ... 134
6.2.1 Method ... 134
6.2.2 Results ... 136
6.2.3 Discussion ... 140

6.3 Pilot Study 1b: Refinement of the Visual Analogue Scale ... 141
6.3.1 Method ... 143
6.3.2 Results ... 144
6.3.3 Discussion ... 147

6.4 Pilot study 2: Design of an Online Questionnaire Assessing Test-Related Emotions ... 148
6.4.1 Method ... 149
6.4.2 Results ... 150
6.4.3 Discussion ... 154

6.5 Manipulation Check using the Adapted Questionnaires ... 156
6.5.1 Expected Effects on the Mood Dimensions ... 157
6.5.2 Expected Effects on Motivation and Emotions ... 159

7 METHOD 161

7.1 Instruments Used 161
7.1.1 Mood..161
7.1.2 Test-Related Emotions and Motivation 163
7.1.3 IQ Test Performance..164
7.1.4 Induction of Emotional States..166

7.2 Procedure..167
7.2.1 Test Run..167
7.2.2 Experiment..168

7.3 Participants..176

8 RESULTS 179

8.1 Drop-Out Effects..180
8.1.1 Demographic Variables 180
8.1.2 Performance on the first test 182

8.2 Randomisation..183
8.2.1 Block Randomisation..183
8.2.2 Differences with Respect to Demographic Variables 185
8.2.3 Differences in Test Performance 188
8.2.4 Differences in Affectivity 191

8.3 Relations Between Mood, Emotion, and Performance Before the Emotion Induction 201
8.3.1 Intercorrelations of Mood and Emotion..201
8.3.2 Correlations of Mood and Emotion with Performance on the First Test 207

8.4 Manipulation Check 209
8.4.1 Changes in Affectivity after the Emotion Induction 209
8.4.2 Comparisons on Affectivity After the Induction 220

8.4.3 Change in Affectivity During the Test: After Induction versus After Test 230
8.4.4 Change in Affectivity During the Test: Before Induction versus After Test 236

8.5 Effects of Affective State on Test Performance 241
8.5.1 Test Performance After the Emotion Induction 241
8.5.2 Differences between the Scores on the Second Test 243
8.5.3 Effects of Emotion on Test Performance 246
8.5.4 Structural Equation Models 252
8.5.5 Summary 260

9 DISCUSSION 261

9.1 Impact of Emotions on Test Performance 262
9.1.1 Valence of Mood or Emotions and Reasoning Test Performance ..263
9.1.2 Activation of Mood or Emotions and Reasoning Test Performance 272
9.1.3 Task Type, Mood and Emotion, and Reasoning Test Performance 274
9.1.4 Impact of Emotions on Test Performance: Limitations 276
9.1.5 Summary 279

9.2 Online Emotion Induction 280
9.2.1 Affective State Before the Emotion Induction Procedure 281
9.2.2 Changes in Mood States due to the Emotion Induction Procedure .282
9.2.3 Changes in Emotional States due to the Emotion Induction Procedure 284
9.2.4 Changes in Mood States after the Test 285
9.2.5 Online Emotion Induction: Limitations 286
9.2.6 Online Emotion Induction: Summary 289

9.3 Unsupervised Online Experiments 290
9.3.1 Sampling and Retention 290
9.3.2 Data Quality 293
9.3.3 Unsupervised Online Experiments: Limitations 294
9.3.4 Unsupervised Online Experiments: Summary 298

9.4 Summary and Conclusions.....299

9.5 Outlook and Future Research.....300

REFERENCES..... 305

TABLES..... 341

FIGURES..... 345

APPENDIX A..... 347

APPENDIX B..... 349

APPENDIX C..... 363

APPENDIX D..... 375

APPENDIX E..... 385

APPENDIX F..... 407

APPENDIX G..... 423

Abstract

In personnel selection there is an ongoing trend towards the use of unsupervised online ability testing (Bateson, Wirtz, Burke, & Vaughan, 2013; cut-e Group, 2012; Lievens & Harris, 2003). The assumption is that the tests measure cognitive ability. However, performance on such tests has been found to be influenced by mood (Lyubomirski, King, & Diener, 2005). Results are contradictory because sometimes positive (Abele, 1995; Radenhausen & Anker, 1988) and sometimes negative mood (Melton, 1995) has been found to improve test performance. Specific emotions like joy or anger have only been studied in the context of academic performance (Pekrun, Elliot, & Maier, 2009), and there are no studies on the impact of mood or emotions on performance in unsupervised online testing.

Therefore, the purpose of the present study was to investigate the impact of specific emotions on performance on a reasoning test in an unsupervised online experiment. Hypotheses were that performance would be (1) better in joy than in anger, (2) better in contentment than in sadness, (3) better in joy than in contentment, and (4) better in anger than in sadness.

A diverse sample of 429 participants completed an online reasoning test, once before and once after the induction of one of the five emotional states of joy, anger, sadness, contentment, or neutral, respectively. The induction procedure successfully evoked distinct emotional states.

Contrary to the hypotheses, however, the experimentally manipulated emotions did not affect performance on the online reasoning test, which might be attributable to reasoning tests being less susceptible to the influence of emotions than other types of tests (Fiedler, 1990; Forgas, 1995; Royce & Diamond, 1988). There is also the possibility that the effects of affective state on test performance were too weak to be detected in the comparatively unstandardised situation and the diverse sample (Stanton, 1998). Another possibility is that participants entered a state of flow (Czikszentmihalyi, Abuhamdeh, & Nakamura, 2007) in which thoughts or feelings do not interfere with the task.

Introduction

A recent article in the Harvard Business Review (Bateson, Wirtz, Burke, & Vaughan, 2013) recommends using web-based psychometric tests as a first stage in the process of recruiting employees: “First Test, and Then Interview” (p. 34). The idea behind this approach is that online testing sifts out the least suitable applicants so that only those with the best qualifications will be allowed to pass through to the more costly stages of the recruitment process. In fact, there is a trend towards online assessment in personnel selection: In a 2012 survey of European companies, 83% of them indicated using online assessment in their recruitment processes (cut-e Group, 2012). This is an increase of 7% compared to 2 years prior (cut-e Group, 2012) and represents a continuing trend as even some 10 years ago, researchers had noted that the use of online assessment for recruitment was increasing (Lievens & Harris, 2003). Burke (2009) quotes Nancy Tippins from a 2008 symposium at the annual conference of the Society of Industrial and Organizational Psychology (SIOP): “The internet testing train has left the station!” (p. 35).

Online assessment refers to the measurement of aptitude, usually for a job, via the internet (Konradt & Sarges, 2003). It may comprise tests, questionnaires, and simulations that are often combined to make more accurate predictions (Hertel, Konradt, & Orlikowski, 2003). Aptitude tests that assess general mental abilities (GMA) are particularly good predictors of future job performance (Schmidt & Hunter, 1998) and are thus used in online testing. The assumption is that performance on such a test is largely determined by the test taker’s cognitive ability.

However, recent research findings suggest that applicants’ performance on ability tests is also influenced by factors other than ability, such as self-confidence (e.g., Stankov & Lee, 2008), cognitive training level (e.g., Jaeggi, Buschkuehl, Jonides, & Perrig, 2008), motivation (e.g., Duckworth, Quinn, Lynam, Loeber, & Stouthamer-Loeber, 2011), mood (e.g., Abele, 1995), and emotions (e.g., Pekrun, 2006). Whereas some of these factors are currently widely studied, mood and emotions and their impact on ability test performance have not yet received much attention from researchers despite the fact that there is an increasing body of research on emotions in the workplace (Seo, Feldman Barrett, & Bartunek, 2004). For example, there are studies investigating the effects of trait affectivity on individual performance (Cropanzano, James, & Konovsky, 1993) or the impact that moods or state emotions have on an organisation (Forgas & George, 2001).

Thus, it is important to ask how and to what extent moods and emotions impact performance in occupational testing. Whereas the study of emotions had previously not received much attention in work and organisational psychology, an increasing number of studies on emotions can now be found in those areas (Seo et al., 2004). However, the findings on moods and emotions and their impact on aptitude test performance are still scarce and contradictory. Particularly when it comes to tests that measure reasoning, "the core construct of intelligence" (Wilhelm & McKnight, 2002, p. 156), only a few studies exist.

Whereas one of these studies found that individuals in a positive mood outperform subjects in a negative or neutral mood on a syllogism test (Radenhausen & Anker, 1988), another found that individuals in a positive mood actually do worse on such a test than individuals in a neutral mood (Melton, 1995). A rather comprehensive study (Abele, 1995) that used verbal and nonverbal reasoning tests in several experiments found that individuals in a positive mood performed better on the tests than subjects in a negative mood. In a 2005 meta-analysis on the benefits of frequent positive affect, Lyubomirski, King, and Diener (2005) summarised their findings on mood and test performance: "The evidence shows that people experiencing happy moods have potential deficits when it comes to problem solving, but they can overcome these deficits if they are motivated to perform well at the task" (p. 840). Moreover, they noted that an important topic for future investigation would be to distinguish between positive and negative emotions on a general level and specific positive and negative emotions such as contentment or joy.

However, to date, there are no studies on discrete emotions and performance on classical IQ tests that measure reasoning, only studies on discrete emotions and academic performance. Here, again, it was shown that positive emotions are beneficial for performance on academic tests, whereas negative emotions usually impair performance unless they are activating emotions such as anger (Pekrun, 2006). Moreover, emotions and their impact on test performance have not been studied in online settings, although, as outlined in the beginning of this introduction, this mode of testing is increasingly being used by employers and researchers alike (van Selm & Jankowski, 2006).

From a scientific point of view, an impact of mood or emotions on IQ test performance would affect the construct validity of these tests: If there is an impact of mood and emotions on performance on IQ tests, then what do these tests measure? This question is particularly important in the field of unsupervised online tests where construct validity is frequently questioned because of the unstandardised environment they are taken in (Lievens & Burke, 2011). From a scientific as well as a practitioner's point of view, we should also ask if and to what extent criterion-related validity is also affected. How accurately can such a test predict job performance if it is affected by mood or emotions?

This is where the present study comes in. The present study tested the impact of different discrete emotions (joy, sadness, anger, and contentment) on performance on an IQ test assessing reasoning. It also measured mood to aid in comparing the current results to previous research and included not only the valence but also the arousal component in the analyses. The study was an unsupervised online study, the setting that is quickly increasing in popularity in the field of personnel selection. Moreover, a goal of this study was to make use of one of the opportunities that the internet offers: to reach out to a very diverse sample in terms of age, education, and current occupation and thus to find results that can be generalised across a wide range of people.

The following four chapters will provide an overview of research in the relevant fields. First, I will be briefly outline what online assessment and online studies are, the extent to which online data are comparable to paper-and-pencil data, whether data gathered online can be considered as reliable and valid, and what needs to be taken into account when designing online instruments or studies. This will provide some background for the study design and will later aid in comparing the current results with the results of previous studies, which have all been conducted in paper-and-pencil formats under supervision. The next chapter will provide an overview of what intelligence is, what models there are, and how intelligence can be measured. This background will provide a classification for the ability measured in the present study (i.e., reasoning) and the test used to measure it. The following chapter will summarise what mood and emotions are, what models of affect exist, and how affect can be measured. This background will later help the reader to understand how the emotions used in the present study were classified and how the hypotheses were derived. In addition, as the present study was experimental and the emotions were induced, I will present a section on the induction of mood and emotions. Subsequently, as the last part of the literature section, an overview of theories and models linking affect and cognitive performance will be given, along with empirical evidence supporting these models. After that chapter, the hypotheses for the present study will be presented, along with an overview of the present study. The empirical section will begin with two studies that needed to be conducted to adapt the instruments used to measure mood and emotions to the internet. After that chapter, the main study on emotions and IQ test performance will be reported and then, in the final chapter, they will be discussed.

1 Online Assessment and Online Surveys

As already mentioned in the Introduction, there is a move towards online assessment (cut-e Group, 2012). For survey research as well, the internet has been increasing in popularity (van Selm & Jankowski, 2006). Some even say that academic research data collection via the internet might replace paper-and-pencil-based studies in the future (Lefever, Dal, & Matthíasdóttir, 2007).

This trend is not surprising when one considers the advantages of this method of assessment and data gathering such as lower cost (Tuten, Urban, & Bosnjak, 2002) and larger samples (Wilhelm & McKnight, 2002). However, there are a few relevant questions that researchers have addressed in a large number of studies. Are online and paper-and-pencil tests equivalent, and are online tests and questionnaires reliable and valid? Can online studies be compared to laboratory studies? How does individual response behaviour change with the medium? And finally, what needs to be taken into consideration when designing online instruments and surveys? These questions will be addressed in the following paragraphs. First, I will provide a definition of the terms online assessment and online surveys along with a very brief overview of the advantages and disadvantages of conducting research online. Then, also very briefly, I will discuss some studies on the quality of online data consisting of the equivalence of online data to paper-and-pencil data, the fulfilment of test quality criteria, and representativeness. Finally, on the basis of the insights presented in the chapter, some recommendations for designing online studies will be given.

1.1 Definition, Advantages, and Disadvantages

Online assessment refers to the measurement of aptitude, usually for a job, via the internet (Konradt & Sarges, 2003). It may comprise tests, questionnaires, and simulations that are often combined to provide more accurate predictions (Hertel et al., 2003). In their Guidelines on Computer-Based and Internet-Delivered Testing (2005), the International Test Commission (ITC) distinguishes four different modes of computerised assessment: open mode, in which there is no supervisor present and no authentication of participants; controlled mode, in which there is no supervisor present, but the instrument is made available only to certain individuals; supervised mode, in which a supervisor is present, logs the participant in, and makes sure the instrument is completed properly; and managed mode, in which there is a trained supervisor present and the testing environment is highly controlled and standardised.

Online surveys are surveys conducted via the www. There are two modes of addressing potential participants: either via email or via a link on certain websites (van Selm & Jankowski, 2006).

1.1.1 Advantages

There are quite a few advantages to gathering data via the internet, such as lower cost, faster responses, and the opportunity to reach potential participants independent of geographical location and time zone (Tuten et al., 2002). This makes online assessment efficient and also provides the recruiting company with a high-tech image (Lievens & Burke, 2011). Furthermore, this mode of administration makes it possible to increase the statistical power of studies because larger samples can be procured more easily (Wilhelm & McKnight, 2002).

Online assessment and online studies are computer-based. This mode allows for adaptive testing, meaning that the test or questionnaire constantly adapts to the test taker's person parameter, always presenting the person with items that deliver the maximum amount of information. This not only allows for the use of shorter tests, but also ensures that the test taker is always administered items with appropriate levels of difficulty. Therefore, test takers are never bored or frustrated, thus contributing to the maintenance of their motivation (Kubinger, 2009), which is particularly important in online surveys. Furthermore, in adaptive testing, items are drawn from a large item pool or even generated according to a certain set of rules so that countless parallel versions of the same test can be generated (Klinck, 2002). This prevents test items from being spread amongst potential test takers and renders the test more resistant to this kind of tampering (Klinck, 2002), an issue that is particularly important when using such tests in high-stakes settings.

1.1.2 Disadvantages

Some disadvantages of online assessment consist of not knowing the identity of the candidate, cheating, problems with the security of the items, and hardware and software problems (Tippins et al., 2006). Likewise, when administering online surveys, the experimenter has no control over who participates in the experiment (Hertel, Naumann, Konradt, & Batinic, 2002; Tuten et al., 2002). All of this is a problem unless the assessment or study is conducted in a supervised or managed mode.

As mentioned previously, computerised adaptive tests save time and money during and after administration. However, the flip side of this coin is that such tests take much more time and money to construct than nonadaptive tests do because the item pool has to be large, and extensive testing and item calibration are necessary (Kubinger, 2009). Moreover, there are a few concerns with respect to the quality of the data gathered online. These concerns will be discussed in the following sections.

1.2 Quality of Online Data

1.2.1 Equivalence of Paper-and-Pencil and Online Data

Studies have shown that paper-and-pencil and computerised or online surveys are equivalent: As long as multiple choice questions as opposed to open question formats are used, the results of an online survey are essentially the same as the results of the same survey administered in paper-and-pencil format (Huang, 2006). This includes the completeness and quality of the data (Truell, 2003). Moreover, there are no differences between results administered in paper-and-pencil, computer, and smart-phone formats (Knapp & Kirk, 2003). Furthermore, reliability (Bosnjak, 1997), factor structure, and measurement error (Hertel et al., 2002; Stanton, 1998) have been shown to be equivalent between online and paper-and-pencil data. Additionally, studies have found fewer missing values in online data compared with paper-and-pencil data (Stanton, 1998) or the same amount of missing data (Hertel et al., 2002). Finally, there is evidence for less socially desirable responding on the web than in paper-and-pencil data (Rietz & Wahl, 1999). On the other hand, response patterns seem to differ between paper-and-pencil and online tests, with participants responding faster to online test questions than to questions on paper-and-pencil tests (Burke, 1993).

When considering the results of personality scales, research has consistently shown that there are hardly any or no differences between supervised paper-and-pencil and unsupervised online assessments using questionnaires that assess job-related competencies (Bartram & Brown, 2004; Meade, Michels, & Lautenschlager, 2007), and there are no differences between paper-and-pencil administration, supervised computer administration, and unsupervised internet administration of instruments assessing the Big Five (Chuah, Drasgow, & Roberts, 2006; Coyne, Warszta, Beadle, & Sheehan, 2005). This holds for both nonadaptive and adaptive questionnaires (Butcher, Perry, & Atlis, 2000). What needs to be kept in mind when visualising questionnaires presented on a screen is that the process of responding to online questionnaires differs from the one for paper-and-pencil questionnaires: The cursor has to be moved to a certain position using the mouse before the answer can be chosen with a mouse click. Particularly in matrix-like questionnaire formats in which the questions are written on the left side of the page and the reply has to be given by selecting between a wide range of options on the right side of the page, it is likely that users will show a uniform response pattern by selecting similar responses for all items (Gräf, 2002).

For ability tests, the results of comparisons between paper-and-pencil and computerised modes are a bit more complex. For example, a study on the equivalence of the paper-and-pencil and online versions of Raven's Advanced Progressive Matrices (APM; Raven, Raven, & Court, 2003) found no significant differences between the mean scores from the two versions, and individuals' scores were highly positively correlated ($r = .78$; Pearson Assessment, 2011). An older study (Neubauer, Urban, & Malle, 1991) found correlations between .70 and .82, depending on the test-retest interval. Thus, the authors of both studies viewed the test versions as equivalent. A meta-analysis by Mead and Drasgow (1993) found a high correlation of .97 between paper-and-pencil and timed online power tests but a lower correlation of .72 between paper-and-pencil and speeded online tests. However, a later study (Neuman & Baydoun, 1998) was not able to replicate these differences. Rather, the authors found both power and speeded tests to be equivalent across modes. A study with a within-subjects design (Lottridge, Nicewander, & Mitzel, 2011) found that the reliability and factor structure were the same for paper-and-pencil versus computerised algebra and English tests with computerised tests being slightly more difficult than paper-and-pencil tests. This finding was also reflected by a study that found that participants had significantly lower scores on an intelligence test battery given in a computerised format than in a paper-and-pencil format (Coyne et al., 2005). However, in this latter study, there were virtually no differences between formats for personality and interest scales that were administered in the same study.

Coyne and colleagues (2005) therefore concluded that performance differences were the result of the different entry modes on the timed tests (mouse vs. writing). Moreover, Mead and Drasgow (1993) indicated that low quality graphics might also be a reason for discrepancies between paper-and-pencil and online tests and concluded that such online tests therefore need to be designed carefully and that equivalence is affected when test takers are required to read large text passages. Wilhelm and McKnight (2002) suggested that discrepancies in ability test scores between the two modes of administration (computer vs. paper-and-pencil) may also result from the fact that participants do not read instructions and examples on screen properly and thoroughly. This is in line with the finding that internet users scan online material rather than reading it thoroughly (Gräf, 2002). Finally, Wilhelm and McKnight (2002) indicated that answer format is a problem that can be dealt with by using other designs.

From the suggestions made by Mead and Drasgow (1993), Coyne and colleagues (2005), and Wilhelm and McKnight (2002), it can be concluded that simply putting a paper-and-pencil test on a computer without making adjustments is not an adequate method for adapting a test to the computer. Rather, a good computer adaptation of a test seems to require certain design standards. Thus, Mead and Drasgow (1993) concluded their study by stating "Our results provide strong support for the conclusion that there is no medium effect for carefully constructed power tests" (p. 457).

1.2.2 Fulfilment of Test Quality Criteria

There is a wide range of studies on the reliability and validity of computer-based and online tests. There is also a lot of literature on the extent to which such tests conform to other test-quality criteria (economy, utility, opportunity to fake or cheat, appropriateness, norming). However, discussing them all would be beyond the scope of this chapter. Therefore, only a brief overview of the main findings on the main quality criteria—objectivity, reliability, and validity—will be given because these are the ones that are relevant for interpreting the results of the present study.

Objectivity. The objective administration, evaluation, and interpretation of online tests and questionnaires can be seen as a given (Kubinger, 2009): For computerised assessment, instructions are given in writing and not by the administrator, and for online assessment, most often an administrator is not even present. This favours administration objectivity. Evaluation and interpretation of the results are usually implemented automatically so that these processes are, like administration, independent of an administrator. Thus, the use of computerised and online assessment enhances objectivity.

Reliability. Reliability (Bosnjak, 1997) and measurement error (Hertel et al., 2002; Stanton, 1998) have been shown to be equivalent between online and paper-and-pencil data. In general, it can be said that measurement precision is higher for computer-based than for paper-and-pencil tests, particularly when such computer-based tests are adaptive (Huff & Sireci, 2001). Moreover, reliability may in some cases be higher for online assessment because the process of evaluating the results is less error prone than a manual process (Kubinger, 2009).

These claims are reflected by the reliabilities of some frequently used measures of intelligence. For example, in a study assessing the reliabilities of the online version of Raven's Advanced Progressive Matrices (APM; Raven et al., 2003), individuals completed both the paper-and-pencil and the online version in a counterbalanced design (Pearson Assessment, 2011). Split-half reliabilities were between .86 and .88, and internal consistencies were between .82 and .87 for both versions. The only exceptions were the split-half reliability and internal consistency of the online version when it was completed first: The split-half reliability here was .75, and the internal consistency was .70. The Adaptive Matrices Test (AMT; Hornke, Küppers, & Etzel, 2000), a test assessing reasoning specifically designed for use on the computer, had reliabilities between .70 and .86. The test scales lst (cut-e Group, 2008), which will be introduced in more detail later, had a split-half reliability of .89. These are just a few examples to illustrate that the reliabilities of computerised tests can be considered satisfactory.

Validity. With regard to construct validity, a study comparing the personality structure of participants on a Big Five measure in an online study with the one in a paper-and-pencil-based study found no differences (Hertel et al., 2002). Several studies have demonstrated that the factor structures were equivalent between online and paper-and-pencil data for questionnaires assessing job-related competencies (Bartram & Brown, 2004;

Meade et al., 2007) and the Big Five (Chuah et al., 2006; Coyne et al., 2005).

In their meta-analysis on the equivalence of paper-and-pencil and online ability tests, Mead and Drasgow (1993) found that the adaptivity of a test does not affect the construct assessed by the test. However, in general, there are only a few studies that have examined the factor structures of online tests or correlations with external criteria as evidence for validity (Mead & Drasgow, 1993). One such study found that paper-and-pencil and computerised ability tests measured the same construct and predicted job performance equally well (Neuman & Baydoun, 1998). Most studies on the validity of computer-based tests have focussed on cross-modal equivalence but have in fact found that computer-based tests were valid measures of a variety of abilities (Russell, Goldberg, & O'Connor, 2003). This can be attributed to higher measurement precision (which is a prerequisite for validity) and better construct representation, whereas computer proficiency (or lack thereof), speededness, and an inappropriate design can be seen as threats to validity (Huff & Sireci, 2001).

1.3 Representativeness of Online Studies

A question that often arises, particularly when research studies with voluntary participants are conducted online, is: To what extent is the sample representative of the population the study is aimed at? The response rates of online studies to which participants are explicitly invited can be seen as an indicator of how accurately an online study can estimate the underlying population parameters (Tuten et al., 2002). Two effects are of particular interest here: self-selection effects during the sampling phase and retention or systematic drop-out effects during the study.

1.3.1 Sampling

Sampling issues can result from a few different factors. First, different groups differ in their access to the internet and in their computer literacy. For example, the percentage of internet users differs across age groups such that the rate is significantly lower for people above the age of 40 than below the age of 40 (Bandilla, 2002). Internet users are also more likely to be educated, wealthy (Mossberger, Tolbert, & Gilbert, 2006; Tuten et al., 2002), and white (Hoffman & Novak, 1998).

Individuals who take part in online surveys differ in personality from those who do not. For example, online-survey participants have been found to be higher on extraversion, agreeableness, openness to experience, and narcissism (Marcus & Schütz, 2005). Motives that lead individuals to participate in an online study consist of curiosity, the opportunity to contribute to research, self-knowledge, and material incentives, with material incentives being the least important motive (Bosnjak & Batinic, 2002). However, these motives are likely to play a role in determining whether people will participate in laboratory experiments as well and thus are not specific to the online setting.

Another issue in sampling consists of how to capture the intended range of participants. Email invitations are a good method for preselecting people whom the researcher would like to participate in the study and for calculating the response rate (Lefever et al., 2007). The use of invitations has been shown to yield response rates that are comparable to mail surveys (Mehta & Sivadas, 1995); however, unused and incorrect email addresses are frequently encountered and thus pose a problem for this method of recruiting participants (Lefever et al., 2007). In addition, perceived anonymity is lower and might lead individuals to refrain from participating (Stanton, 1998). On the other hand, when posting a link on a website instead of inviting participants via email, frequent internet users might be overrepresented in comparison to infrequent users (Brenner, 2002) and a researcher has no control over who participates (Tuten et al., 2002).

1.3.2 Retention

Retention rates for online surveys seem to be impacted only by the level of personalisation of the invitation message but not by material incentives such as prize draws (Sánchez-Fernández, Muñoz-Leiva, & Montoro-Ríos, 2012). Furthermore, studies indicate that participants tend to quit online studies after 25 to 30 items (Krasilovsky, 1996). In general, the length of a questionnaire and the completion rates are associated: the longer the questionnaire, the lower the percentage of participants who complete it (Gräf, 2002). When asked how much time they would be willing to contribute to an online study, only 12% of respondents said they would dedicate more than 30 min to it (Bosnjak & Batinic, 2002). Furthermore, web users expect the contents of websites to be appealing, interesting, and diverse, which requires an online study to conform to these expectations to prevent drop out (Gräf, 2002). Therefore, it is recommended that an internet study be able to deliver "an optimal mixture of curiosity, challenge, and aptitude" (Gräf, 2002, p. 59).

Technical issues can be a problem in any study involving technology, but in unsupervised online assessments or studies, there is nobody who can resolve or even record the problem. People may be unable or unwilling to complete an online study if a server crashes or the pages load too slowly (Tuten et al., 2002).

1.3.3 Standardisation and Controllability of the Situation

In online assessments and experiments, there is no administrator present with whom participants can communicate; therefore, it is usually not known whether participants understand or follow the given instructions (Wilhelm & McKnight, 2002). Thus, a particular challenge for online studies is to ensure that participants know what their task is on an online questionnaire or test. Research on online assessment settings has shown that participants tend not to read the instructions, or more generally speaking, that they tend to scan rather than thoroughly read online material (Gräf, 2002). Furthermore, due to the rather unstandardised situation, participants' psychological states may vary more than they would in a laboratory setting (Stanton, 1998).

Thus, there are quite a few effects that may limit the generalisability of an online study. However, McGraw, Tew, and Williams (2000) collected data from online experiments across a period of 2 years and came to the conclusion that online experiments are able to deliver textbook results for both between- and within-subjects designs, meaning that the data from online experiments are just as interpretable as data from the laboratory. In addition, it is also worth noting that generalisability is not affected if sampling is biased along factors that are different from the factors that are being studied or along factors that do not affect the factors being studied (Brenner, 2002).

1.4 Design of Online Studies

Based on insights into the factors that affect data quality and the generalisability of online data, there are a few recommendations for how to gather high quality and generalisable online data.

Response rates for web surveys are about 10% lower than for telephone or mail surveys (Fan & Yan, 2010). However, researchers can improve response rates by pilot testing the survey with a small group of respondents, making it easy to access the survey website, adapting the survey to participants' (presumable) internet experience, and ensuring data safety (Fan & Yan, 2010). Furthermore, there are a few characteristics that increase respondents' willingness to participate in an online study (Bosnjak & Batinic, 2002): explaining the purpose of the study, explaining how the experimenter obtained a participant's email address, providing feedback on results, providing anonymity, and providing a personal request for participation from the researcher. In addition, the researcher can address participants' curiosity and interest in self-knowledge, stress the opportunity to contribute to research, and offer material incentives for participation (Bosnjak & Batinic, 2002).

Depending on the researcher's target, he or she will have to decide whether to use email invitations, post a link on a website or several websites, or combine the two. The use of email invitations is a good way to preselect participants (Lefever et al., 2007), but such invitations might also lead individuals to refrain from participating (Stanton, 1998). Anonymity is granted when using links on websites and, depending on where the link is posted, one might also reach a wider audience. On the other hand, one will have no control over who participates (Tuten et al., 2002).

As web users are not willing to expend a lot of time on web studies (Bosnjak & Batinic, 2002), and as they expect website contents to be appealing and interesting, it is recommended that an online study be challenging and interesting (Gräf, 2002).

Moreover, tests and questionnaires should be tested on screen with a lot of care. Graphics need to be of high quality (Mead & Drasgow, 1993). It is recommended that researchers avoid long matrix-like questionnaires and instead keep them short (Gräf, 2002). Furthermore, because internet users tend to scan rather than thoroughly read online material (Gräf, 2002; Wilhelm & McKnight, 2002), instructions on the www need to be short, and the important (but only a few) parts should be highlighted (Nielsen, 1995). Finally, a pilot test is highly recommended (Gräf, 2002). This means exposing a small sample of participants to the study prior to launching it and testing whether it works in the intended way.

1.5 Summary

The findings presented here indicate that online surveys and online questionnaires produce data that are comparable to paper-and-pencil data. Data from online questionnaires are objective, reliable, and valid. For online tests, the results are a bit more complex: The objectivity and reliability of online tests can be considered good; however, online tests are sometimes more difficult than paper-and-pencil tests, and their validity can be affected by test takers' lack of computer proficiency, speededness, or an inappropriate design. However, these discrepancies in difficulty and validity can be compensated for by carefully designing the test. The benefits of better construct representation and higher measurement precision also contribute to the validity of online tests.

With respect to the representativeness of online studies, it is possible that the sample may be biased by individuals' access to computers and the internet and by factors that drive people's willingness to participate in an online study. In addition, the risk of drop out is increased and standardisation is lower in online studies than in laboratory studies. However, most factors can be positively impacted by designing the study carefully so that the data gathered in online studies can be considered to be valid and generalisable.

2 Intelligence and Intelligence Testing

Most online tests measure intelligence or facets of intelligence. The most extensive research in personality has been applied to the area of intelligence (Holling, Preckel, & Vock, 2004). Intelligence tests have been shown to be amongst the most valid predictors of outcomes such as job performance (Schmidt & Hunter, 1998), academic performance (Watkins, Lei, & Canivez, 2007), health (Gottfredson, 2004), and socioeconomic status (Roberts, Kuncel, Shiner, Caspi, & Goldberg, 2007). Despite this fact, there is no universally valid definition of the term (Asendorpf & Neyer, 2012).

An early definition was offered by Alfred Binet (1905), one of the creators of the first general-purpose intelligence test (Gardner & Hatch, 1989). He considered being able to judge, comprehend, and reason to be at the core of intelligence. A few years later, William Stern (1912) suggested a slightly more concrete definition: "Intelligence is an individual's ability to consciously adapt his or her thinking to new requirements; it is a general mental ability to adapt to new tasks and conditions in life" (p. 3; translated by the author). Louis Leon Thurstone (1921) defined intelligence as "(a) the capacity to inhibit an instinctive adjustment, (b) the capacity to redefine the inhibited instinctive adjustment in the light of imaginally experienced trial and error, (c) the volitional capacity to realize the modified instinctive adjustment into overt behavior to the advantage of the individual as a social animal" (p. 201). David Wechsler (1939), the author of one of the most widely used intelligence tests, defined intelligence as "the global capacity of a person to act purposefully, to think rationally, and to deal effectively with his environment" (p. 229). Similarly, Gordon Allport (1961) referred to intelligence as the capacity to make judgments, learn from experience, and deal with novel problems. Finally, Robert Sternberg (1985) defined intelligence as "mental activity directed toward purposive adaptation to, selection and shaping of real-world environments relevant to one's life" (p. 45).

At the core of these definitions is the ability to comprehend one's environment, to reason and to judge on the basis of this understanding, and thus to deal with novel problems, to learn and adapt to one's environment, and to do all of this on purpose. Or, to shorten this definition, a constituting element of intelligence seems to be the quality and speed with which novel tasks are solved (Schuler & Höft, 2006).

There are also more general definitions such as the one presented by Eysenck (1976): Intelligence is an "innate, general, cognitive ability" (p. 115). In Howard Gardner's (1999) view, on the other hand, there is no universal notion of "the" intelligence. Rather, intelligence comprises abilities that are valued in certain periods of time (which were, e.g., different in ancient Greece than they are today) or in certain cultures. However, all of these definitions are vague and difficult to operationalise. It remains unclear what acting purposefully and effectively means because these words could easily be replaced by "intelligent"; thus, the definitions are tautological (Stemmler, Bartussek, Hagemann, & Amelang, 2011). Furthermore, it remains unclear what an adaptation to and an assimilation of environment looks like. Therefore, in a rather pragmatic approach, Edwin Boring (1923) stated: "intelligence is what the tests test" (p. 23).

As provocative as this may sound, it is in line with a 1921 symposium on intelligence and its measurement on which a special issue was published in the Journal of Educational Psychology (No authorship indicated, 1921): Although the concept of intelligence is controversial, there is wide agreement on how to measure it. This fact seems to reflect the view that is still held by researchers today. For example, Eysenck (1998) stated that a definition of intelligence is not necessary because the meaningful contribution of research on intelligence can be found in the fact that instruments that allow for the construct to be tested have been implemented. Thus, by looking at the tests and their designs, it becomes obvious what intelligence means.

Therefore, in this chapter, some tests assessing intelligence will be discussed. As such tests are always based on models of intelligence, some of the most influential intelligence theories will be introduced first.

2.1 Models of Intelligence

There are many models describing the structure of intelligence. Most of them are factor models that were created using the results of different intelligence test tasks to try to extract common factors. In the early days of intelligence testing, there was a controversy with regard to whether there was something like a general factor of intelligence or whether there were a number of distinct factors. Finally, a model with several levels subsumed the two opposing models, although it is still controversial whether something like a general factor of intelligence exists.

2.1.1 Two-Factor Theories

In 1904, Charles Spearman found intercorrelations between intelligence test tasks and therefore concluded that performance on these tasks could be predicted by two factors: a general ("g") factor that expressed general ability and a specific ("s") factor that was specific to the respective task (Spearman, 1904). He defined the test that best measured g as the one that showed the highest correlations with all other tests and considered g to be the essence of intelligence. At the core of his g factor, he placed operations such as problem solving, deduction, induction, and discovering rules, differences, and similarities; thus, operations that are commonly labeled “reasoning”.

Raymond B. Cattell (1941, 1943, 1950) also found that intelligence was comprised of two factors; however, he divided them into “fluid intelligence” (gf) and “crystallised intelligence” (gc). Fluid intelligence comprises reasoning, such as problem solving, deduction, induction, and discovering rules, differences, and similarities as in Spearman’s model, whereas crystallised intelligence refers to knowledge and learned structures. Thus, fluid intelligence is innate and begins to decline at a certain age, whereas crystallised intelligence increases as humans accumulate knowledge across the life course. Later, Horn (1965) extended the theory by adding some more specific factors: short-term memory (Gsm), long-term retrieval (Glr), processing speed (Gs), and visual-spatial thinking (Gv). Finally, auditory processing (Ga) was added to the model (Stankov & Horn, 1980). In contrast to Spearman (1904), Cattell and Horn did not assume one general factor of intelligence but rather saw Gf and Gc as the highest order factors (Horn & Cattell, 1966).

2.1.2 Primary factors

Louis Leon Thurstone (1938) did not agree with the idea of a general factor of intelligence. He claimed that there are seven domain-specific intelligence factors that he called primary mental abilities (PMA). These factors are:

- perceptual speed (P): the ability to quickly see differences and similarities between objects
- space (S): visual-spatial abilities
- numerical ability (N): the ability to deal with numbers

- word fluency (W): the ability to fluently use vocabulary
- verbal comprehension (V): the ability to deal with vocabulary and concepts
- memory (M): the ability to memorise
- reasoning (R): the ability to discover rules and relationships

However, due to the extraction method he used (i.e., an oblique one), his factors are moderately intercorrelated, which many see as evidence of a general factor of intelligence.

2.1.3 Integration of the models

John B. Carroll (1993) found that it was possible to integrate the above-mentioned models into one with several layers: at the bottom level or Stratum III, there are specific factors that converge to form the more complex factors of fluid and crystallised intelligence on the intermediate level or Stratum II and eventually to form one general factor on the top level or Stratum I. Therefore, the theory is called the Three-Stratum theory. Table 1 provides an overview of the stratum II factors and some examples of the respective stratum III factors (excerpt from McGrew, 2009, pp. 5–6):

Table 1
Stratum II Abilities and Descriptions and Examples of Stratum III Abilities in the Carroll (1993) Model (Excerpt of the Table in McGrew, 2009, pp. 5–6)

Stratum II Ability	**Stratum II Ability Description**	**Stratum III Abilities**
Fluid intelligence (Gf)	The use of deliberate and controlled mental operations to solve novel problems that cannot be performed automatically.	Deductive reasoning, induction, quantitative reasoning
Crystallised intelligence (Gc)	The knowledge of the culture that is incorporated by individuals through a process of acculturation.	Lexical knowledge, foreign language proficiency, oral production, and fluency
General memory and learning (Gy)	The ability to apprehend and maintain awareness of a limited number of elements of information in the immediate situation (events that occurred in the last minute or so).	Memory span, working memory
Broad visual processing (Gv)	The ability to generate, store, retrieve, and transform visual images and sensations.	Spatial relations, spatial scanning, imagery
Broad auditory perception (Gu)	Abilities that depend on sound as input and on the functioning of our hearing apparatus.	General sound discrimination, temporal tracking, sound localisation

Table 1 (continued)
Stratum II Abilities and Descriptions and Examples of Stratum III Abilities in the Carroll (1993) Model (Excerpt of the Table in McGrew, 2009, pp. 5–6)

Stratum II Ability	**Stratum II Ability Description**	**Stratum III Abilities**
Broad retrieval ability (Gr)	The ability to store and consolidate new information in long-term memory and later fluently retrieve the stored information (e.g., concepts, ideas, items, names) through association.	Associative memory, ideational fluency, originality/creativity
Broad cognitive speediness (Gs)	The ability to automatically and fluently perform relatively easy or over-learned elementary cognitive tasks, especially when high mental efficiency (i.e., attention and focussed concentration) is required.	Perceptual speed, number facility, writing speed
Processing speed (RT decision speed)	The ability to make elementary decisions and/or responses (simple reaction time) or one of several elementary decisions and/or responses (complex reaction time) at the onset of simple stimuli.	Simple reaction time, choice reaction time, semantic processing speed

McGrew (2009) proposed a few extensions to the model: He proposed general (domain-specific) knowledge (Gkn) such as knowledge of English as a second language, mathematical, or geography knowledge; however, most of his extensions refer to abilities that go beyond the classical cognitive ones such as tactile (Gh), kinaesthetic (Gk), and olfactory (Go) abilities as well as psychomotor abilities (Gp) and psychomotor speed (Gps). depicts the Three-Stratum Model (Carroll, 1993), the Cattell-Horn Model (Cattell, 1963; 1968; Horn & Cattell, 1966), and the Integrated Model (McGrew, 2009).

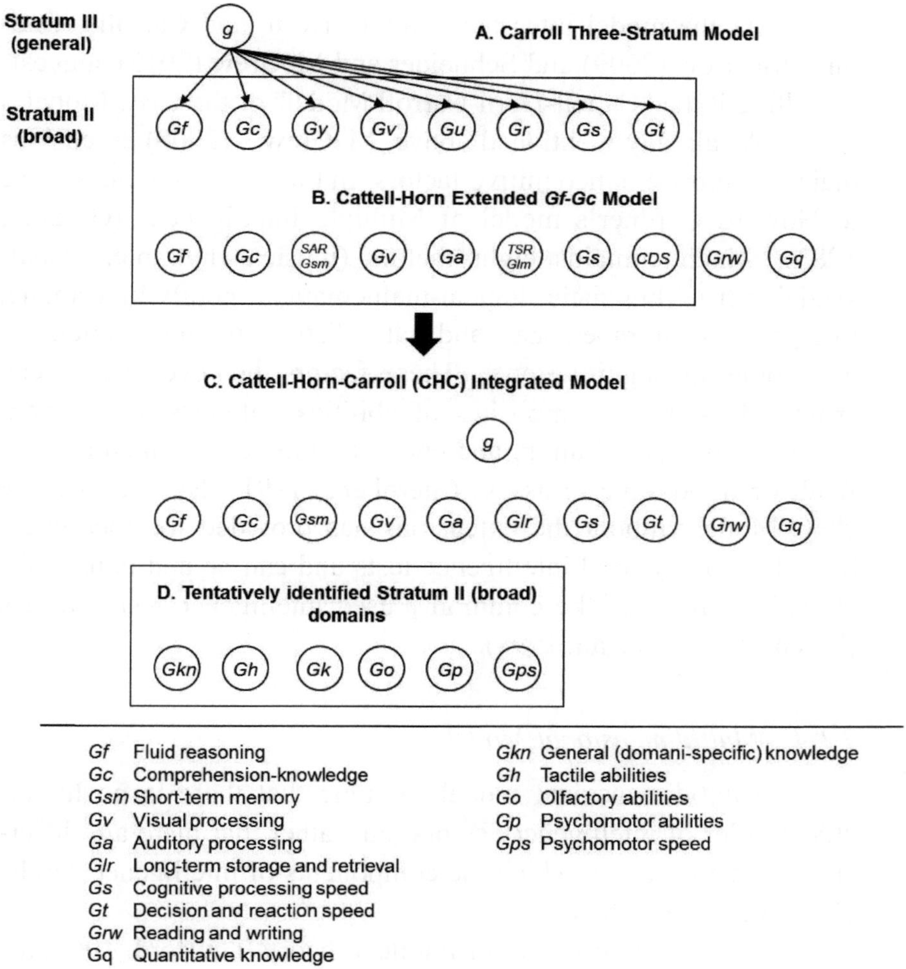

Figure 1. Integration of Carroll Three-Stratum Model into Cattell-Horn-Carroll (CHC) Model. Graphic from McGrew (2009) with slight changes. Printed with permission.

As the model integrates Cattell, Horn, and Carroll's findings, McGrew (2009) and Schneider and McGrew (2012) suggested calling it the "Cattell-Horn-Carroll Model" or the CHC Model.

As already mentioned above, McGrew's (2009) extensions mainly comprise noncognitive factors. In this sense, it comes close to Howard Gardner's model of Multiple Intelligences (Gardner, 1983), which contains eight factors (musical-rhythmic, visual-spatial, verbal-linguistic, logical-mathematical, bodily-kinesthetic, interpersonal, intrapersonal, and naturalistic), amongst which are also some noncognitive ones. These factors, however, have been criticised as being composites of abilities, interests, motivation, achievement, socialisation, and enculturation, all of which are difficult or impossible to assess (Sternberg, 1991). By contrast, the CHC Model without the extensions has provided the theoretical basis for widely used intelligence tests and can be and is used for classifying most of the commonly used intelligence test batteries (McGrew & Flanagan, 1998).

2.1.4 Multidimensional Model

Multidimensional models assume that there is no hierarchical order of intelligence factors, but rather that there are different dimensions along which the components of intelligence can be classified into clusters.

Guilford's Structure of Intellect theory (Guilford, 1967) assumes three dimensions: operations, content, and product. Operations are comprised of cognitive processes, cognition, memory recording and retention, divergent and convergent production, and evaluation. Content refers to the type of information that is processed and can be figural, semantic, symbolic, or behavioural. Finally, product describes the outcomes of operations made on the content and can be units, classes (sets of units), relations (links between units: associations, opposites, analogies, or sequences), systems (multiple relations), transformations (changes in knowledge), or implications (inferences or predictions).

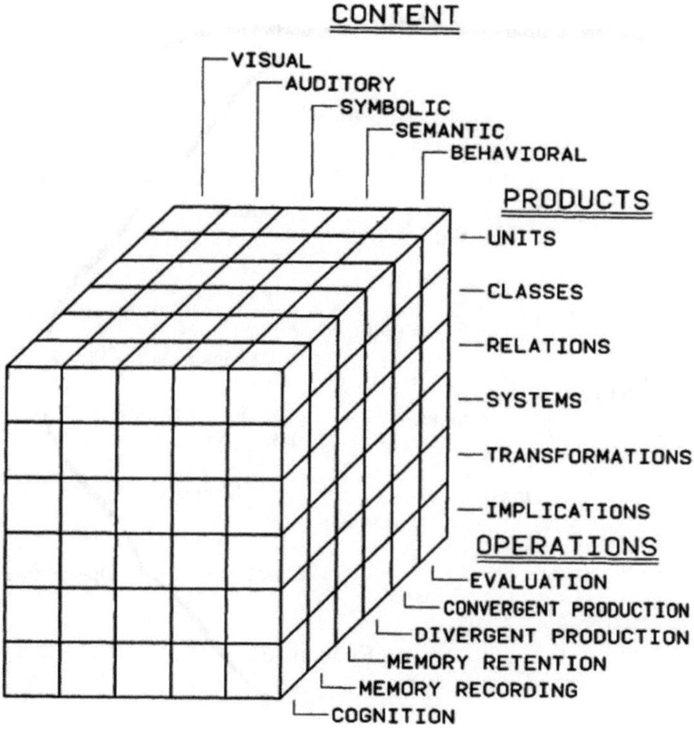

Figure 2. Guilford's Structure-of-Intellect Model (Guilford, 1967). Graphic from Guilford (1988). Printed with permission.

Similarly, the Berlin Model of Intelligence Structure (BIS; Jäger, 1982, 1984) has an operational and a content dimension. Operations in this model consist of processing speed, memory, creativity, and processing capacity. The contents are numerical, verbal, and figural. Along these two dimensions, intelligence test tasks can be classified into 4x3 “structuples”. The model is based on a review of 2,000 intellectual tasks.

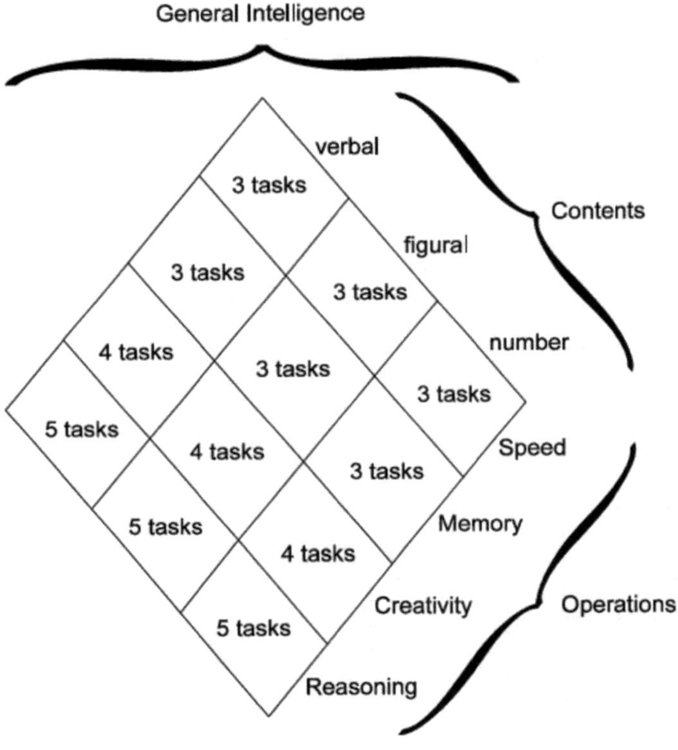

Figure 3. Berlin Model of Intelligence Structure (Jäger, 1982, Jäger, 1984) and how it is implemented in the corresponding test. Graphic from Süß, Oberauer, Wittmann, Wilhelm, and Schulze (1996). Printed with permission.

A study (Beauducel & Kersting, 2002) showed that processing capacity and memory were related to fluid intelligence and that processing speed and, to a lesser extent, processing capacity were related to crystallised intelligence. Thus, the multidimensional Berlin Model of Intelligence Structure can be integrated into Cattell and Horn's (Cattell, 1963; Horn, 1968; Horn & Cattell, 1966) model of Gf and Gc.

2.1.5 Other Theories of Intelligence

There are other theories of intelligence such as Sternberg's (1985) triarchic theory of intelligence or Das, Kirby, and Jarman's (1975) Planning, Attention-Arousal, Simultaneous and Successive (PASS) theory of intelligence. However, these are more cognitive or process theories of intelligence rather than structural or psychometric theories of intelligence and therefore cannot be used to measure abilities. Tests based on these theories are used to measure processes (e.g., the Cognitive Assessment System, CAS; Das, Naglieri, & Kirby, 1993, for the PASS theory).

2.1.6 Summary

All the structural models that were just mentioned have in common the factor "reasoning", which refers to induction, deduction, and problem solving. Apart from Spearman's (1904) model, all of the other models comprise factors such as processing speed and memory. Such factors are often connected to contents such as visual or auditory but also figural, numerical, and verbal. Some models also comprise knowledge. The BIS model is the only one that comprises creativity, which is viewed as different from intelligence by many researchers. In any case, there is wide consensus that reasoning is the "core construct of human intelligence" (Wilhelm & McKnight, 2002, p. 156) and thus is part of all major theories of intelligence structure and major tests of intelligence (Carroll; Jäger, 1984; Jäger, Süß, & Beauducel, 1997).

2.2 INTELLIGENCE TESTS

There are many intelligence tests that were constructed on the basis of the models described above or whose tasks can be classified using the outlined models.

In the English-speaking part of the world, some of the widely used intelligence tests for adults are the Wechsler Adult Intelligence Scale (WAIS; Wechsler, 1955; Wechsler, Coalson, & Raiford, 2008), the Stanford-Binet (Binet, 1905; Roid, 2003), and the Woodcock-Johnson Test of Cognitive Abilities (Woodcock & Johnson, 1977, Woodcock & Johnson, 1989; Woodcock, McGrew, & Mather, 2001). In Germany, there are adaptations of these tests, but there are also tests that were designed in Germany and that are frequently used such as the Intelligenzstrukturtest (IST; Test of Intelligence Structure, Liepmann, Beauducel, Brocke, & Amthauer, 2007), Berliner Intelligenzstrukturtest (BIS; Berlin Intelligence Structure Test, Jäger et al., 1997), or the Wilde Intelligenztest (WIT; Wilde Intelligence Test, Kersting, Althoff, & Jäger, 2008).

All of these tests measure various facets of intelligence. Sometimes there is an overall score indicating general intelligence. However, there are also tests that consist of only one scale and that are used as markers of general intelligence such as the Wonderlic Cognitive Ability Test (Wonderlic, 1992) or Raven's Progressive Matrices (RPM; Raven et al., 2003). A few of these tests will be described in more detail below. The aim of these detailed descriptions is to show how models of intelligence structure are implemented in a test and to provide an overview of the different types of tasks used in these tests and the different modes of administration these tests require.

2.2.1 Raven's Progressive Matrices (RPM; Raven et al., 2003)

Raven's Progressive Matrices (Raven et al., 2003) are based on Spearman's model with one general factor of intelligence. There are three different versions of the test: the Standard Progressive Matrices (SPM), which is the original form that was published in 1938; die Advanced Progressive Matrices (APM), which was designed for assessing above-average intelligence; and the Coloured Progressive Matrices (CPM), which was designed specifically for children. The test consists of matrices with 3x3 cubicles in which symbols are arranged according to a certain rule. The participant's task is to discover the rule and fill in the one cubicle that is left blank with one of eight options presented below the matrix. Split-half reliabilities are above r = .90, and test-retest reliabilities are between r = .80 and r = .90 (depending on the test-retest interval). Correlations with other nonverbal intelligence tests are high, whereas they are lower with intelligence tests involving language. There is also an online version that was already briefly mentioned in the chapter on Online Assessment and Online Surveys.

2.2.2 Woodcock-Johnson Test of Cognitive Abilities (Woodcock et al., 2001)

A test that is explicitly based on the CHC theory is the Woodcock-Johnson Test of Cognitive Ability (Woodcock & Johnson, 1977, Woodcock & Johnson, 1989; Woodcock et al., 2001). It consists of two parts: one for cognitive abilities and one for achievement. The former assesses the nine broad stratum II abilities: Comprehension-Knowledge (Gc), Long-Term Retrieval (Glr), Visual-Spatial Thinking (Gv), Auditory Processing (Ga), Fluid Reasoning (Gf), Processing Speed (Gs), Short-Term

Memory (Gsm), Reading-Writing (Grw), and Mathematics (Gq). Three subtests measuring Comprehension-Knowledge, Fluid Reasoning, and Processing Speed can be used as a short version for assessing general intelligence (General Intellectual Ability, GIA), whereas the long version can be used to assess all of the CHC facets as well.

The subtests require the test taker to, for example, have knowledge of synonyms and antonyms and complete verbal analogies (Gc), learn and recall pictures (Glr), complete shapes by choosing the missing piece from several options (Gv), synthesise language sounds (Ga), discover rules and relations (Gf), identify certain numbers in a set of numbers (Gs), reverse a set of numbers previously listened to (Gsm), find words in which phonemes are missing (Grw), and perform other tasks. Most of the tasks are completed orally; thus, this test is not suitable for group testing. Reliabilities (split-half reliabilities for most tests except for the speeded tests, for which Rasch analyses were calculated) are between $r = .76$ and $r = .94$. Test-retest reliabilities for the speeded tests are between $r = .81$ and $r = .97$. Factor analyses have replicated the structure of the underlying model, and correlations with other measures of intelligence have been shown to be satisfactory.

2.2.3 Berlin Intelligence Structure Test (BIS Test; Jäger et al., 1997)

The Berlin Intelligence Structure Test (Jäger et al., 1997) is based on the Berlin Model of Intelligence Structure (BIS; Jäger, 1982, 1984) and was designed on the basis of a review of 2,000 intellectual tasks. One hundred ninety-one of them assessing 98 different abilities were included in empirical analyses. The ones with the best properties were used for the current BIS Test (Beauducel & Kersting, 2002), which still comprises a large variety of different types of tasks (45 altogether). Therefore, it can be used to illustrate typical tasks that can be found in many intelligence tests.

- Processing capacity (figural): find the shape that can be made up using several pieces presented; complete figural analogies; complete series of symbols that are made up according to a certain rule; find the shape that can be folded using a certain flat plan; find the rule according to which patterns are made up and apply them to classify pattern extracts
- Processing capacity (numerical): solve math text problems; draw numerical information from a table; complete series of numbers that are made up according to a certain rule; estimate the result of an equation using logical reasoning
- Processing capacity (verbal): draw logical conclusions from statements; find similarities between words and cross out the one that does not fit; complete verbal analogies; decide whether a statement is a fact or an opinion; draw logical conclusions from syllogisms
- Processing speed (figural): assign symbols to digits using a certain key; find word pairs where one word is part of the other
- Processing speed (numerical): tick all numbers that are divisible by 7; tick all numbers that are 3 units greater than the previous number; find arithmetic operators for equations
- Processing speed (verbal): complete words in which a letter is missing; tick all “x”s in a series of characters; find letters of a certain font between letters of another font; find words that represent a certain category

- Memory (figural): encode and recall a certain route on a map; memorise and recall buildings on a map; encode and recall pairs of icons or shapes
- Memory (numerical): encode and recall a list of numbers; encode and recall pairs of numbers; encode and recall a list of large numbers
- Memory (verbal): encode and recall a list of words; write different sentences that contain certain words; encode a short story and recall some details from it; encode and recall word pairs
- Creativity (figural): complement certain shapes so that they turn into objects from the real world; design logos for a shop; compose single shapes into a larger shape; compose shapes into real-world objects and name them
- Creativity (numerical): write down different phone numbers that are easy to memorise; find combinations of numbers that result in a certain number; invent patterns of numbers; construct different equations from given numbers
- Creativity (verbal): write down words that begin with a certain syllable; find different ways of using a certain object; list abilities and traits an employee in a certain job is supposed to have; find several explanations for given facts

Due to the fact that all the subtests can be completed in a paper-and-pencil format, the test is suitable for group testing and for individual testing. Internal consistencies of the subscales are between $\alpha = .75$ and $\alpha = .89$, test-retest reliabilities are between $r_{tt} = .65$ and $r_{tt} = .90$. Factor analyses have confirmed the structure of the test, and school grades have been predicted from the test results ($r = .55$ to $r = .59$).

2.2.4 *Adaptive Matrices Test (AMT; Hornke et al., 2000)*

A test that was specifically designed for computer-based assessment of general intelligence is the adaptive matrices test (AMT; Hornke et al., 2000). It is language-free, and the task is to complete a grid of symbols whose composition follows a certain rule. Items are generated using a set of rules as the construction rationale. The test uses an item bank and constantly adapts the difficulty levels of the items to the test taker's aptitude. There are four versions of the test that differ in length: 24, 34, 54, or 64 min.

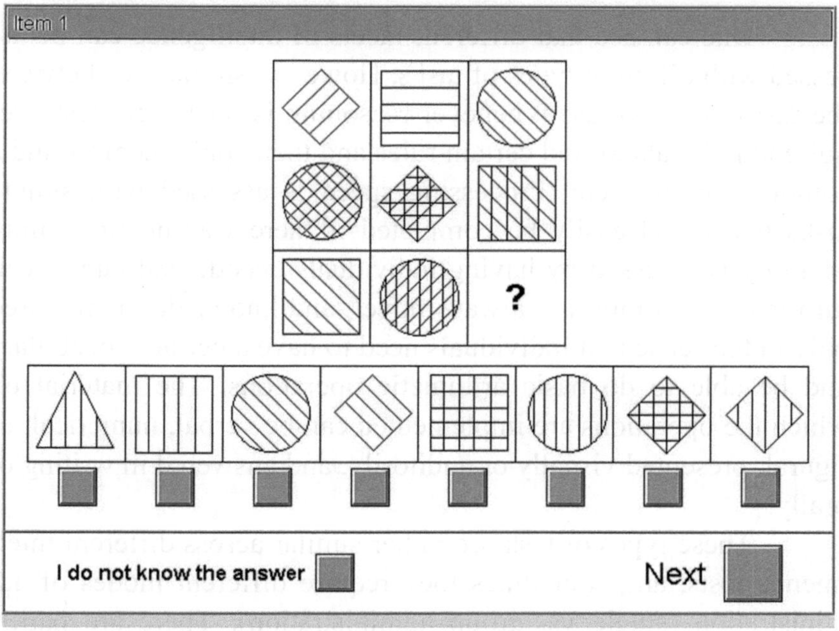

Figure 4. Sample item from the adaptive matrices test (AMT; Hornke et al., 2000). Retrieved from http://www.schuhfried.com/viennatestsystem10/tests-test-sets/all-tests-by-test-type/special-intelligence-tests/

Reliabilities for the test are .70, .83, or .86, depending on which of the four test forms are used. The test versions differ in the preset standard error of measurement, which is 0.63 for two of the versions and 0.44 or 0.39 for the other two versions. The construction rationale is correlated .72 with the difficulty parameter, which can be taken as evidence for the validity of the test. In addition, confirmatory factor analyses with other tests assessing reasoning have shown that the test measures this construct.

2.3 Summary

One can see that different facets of intelligence can be assessed with different types of tasks. However, similarities between the tasks are obvious: Whenever reasoning is measured, tasks require individuals to find certain rules and then apply them to find a solution for the item. Processing speed is assessed with simple tasks that could easily be completed if there was no time limit. Memory is assessed by having individuals encode and later recall information. Stimuli are always novel, and knowledge is required only in the sense that individuals need to have a certain vocabulary and be able to do basic arithmetic operations. The material on which the operations are implemented can be verbal, numerical, or figural, presented visually or auditorily, and answered in writing or orally.

These types of task are rather similar across different intelligence tests, and sometimes they require different modes of administration (single vs. group administration). There are paper-and-pencil and computer-based tests. An estimate of general intelligence can result either from a compound score of these different tasks or from using a single task type that is widely accepted as a marker of general intelligence, such as Raven's SPM or APM.

The summary of task types reflects Schuler and Höft's (2006) definition that a constituting element of intelligence is the quality and speed with which novel tasks are solved, and this can be taken as a working definition of intelligence.

3 Affect, Mood, and Emotions

Affect is commonly used as an umbrella term for emotions and moods (Frijda, 1994). However, emotions and moods are distinct phenomena. Whereas emotions usually have a stimulus event, are comparatively intense, short in duration, and have behavioural implications (Scherer, 2005); moods consist of rather global, undirected, and mostly unconscious background sensations that are more stable than emotions (Lischetzke & Eid, 2011). In addition, emotions evoke autonomic arousal (Diener, Scollon, & Lucas, 2009).

There is some consensus that emotions consist of some or all of the five components cognitive, physiological, motivational, expressive, and affective, and that each component is assigned to a certain subsystem of the body (Scherer, 1990). The cognitive component refers to the evaluation of an event; the physiological component comprises bodily changes due to the release of hormones or reactions of the autonomic nervous system; the expressive component is the nonverbal, bodily, or facial expression of the emotion; the motivational component refers to the action tendencies evoked by an emotion; finally, the affective component describes an individual's experience of the emotion (Lischetzke & Eid, 2011; Scherer, 2005).

Mood is defined as a purely inner experience—an individual's perception of his or her own inner state. It consists of subjective experience, behaviour, gestures, facial expressions, and physiological and biochemical variables (Steyer, Schwenkmezger, Notz, & Eid, 1997).

There is a state and a trait component of affectivity: the actual mood or emotion an individual experiences at a certain point in time (state), and an individual's disposition to experience certain moods or emotions (trait; Lischetzke & Eid, 2011). Thus, affective states are transitory conditions, whereas affective traits are stable across periods of time or even a lifetime (Mehrabian, 1996). A person's trait affectivity results from the frequency with which he or she experiences the respective affective state. A person's emotional or mood state results from a combination of his or her trait affectivity, the situation the individual is in, and the interaction between person and situation (Lischetzke & Eid, 2011).

3.1 Models of Affect

In the literature and in research, the polarity and dimensionality of affect are controversial subjects. The polarity debate refers to the question of whether positive and negative affect are independent and can be described as discrete categories (e.g., Diener & Emmons, 1984) or whether they represent a bipolar continuum (e.g., Green, Goldman, & Salovey, 1993). The dimensionality debate refers to the question of whether there are two (e.g., Larsen & Diener, 1992; Russell, 1980; Thayer, 1996; Watson & Tellegen, 1985) or three (e.g., Schimmack & Grob, 2000; Steyer, Schwenkmezger, Notz, & Eid, 1994) dimensions underlying affective experience or not (e.g., Diener, 2009; Ekman, 1992). On the basis of these two debates, models of affect can generally be classified into two categories: (a) structural models such as the circumplex model or three-dimensional models on the one hand and (b) models with discrete emotions on the other (Lischetzke & Eid, 2011). Some of the models are affect models and thus refer to mood and emotions, whereas others refer to either one or the other.

3.1.1 *Structural Models*

The model that posits that there are two dimensions that constitute affective experience is the circumplex model (e.g., Larsen & Diener, 1992; Russell, 1980; Thayer, 1996; Watson & Tellegen, 1985) with one dimension being valence and the other energy. Both dimensions are bipolar. On the basis of these dimensions, different models posit different axes along which mood can be described. All of these models are models of general affect.

One of the earlier circumplex models is the one by Russell (1980). The affective axis in this model is pleasure versus misery and the energetic one is arousal versus sleep. Along these axes, affect can be categorised into excitement, relaxation, depression, and distress.

The frequently used Positive and Negative Affect Schedule (PANAS; Watson, Clark, & Tellegen, 1988) questionnaire is based on the model by Watson and Tellegen (1985). The affective component is described by pleasantness versus unpleasantness, whereas the energetic one is engagement versus disengagement, and the two axes are uncorrelated. Along these two axes with their four poles, affect can be categorised as high positive (pleasant, engaged), high negative (unpleasant, engaged), low positive (unpleasant, disengaged), or low negative (pleasant, disengaged).

Similarly, the model by Larsen and Diener (1992) classifies mood along the axes pleasant versus unpleasant and high versus low activation. Consequently, moods are activated pleasant, unactivated pleasant, activated unpleasant, or unactivated unpleasant. Finally, Thayer's (1996) model presents the axes energy versus tiredness and tension versus calmness, such that moods are classified as tense-energetic, calm-energetic, calm-tired, or tense-tired.

An analysis by Yik, Russell, and Barrett (1999) found a large overlap between the four models (see Figure 5).

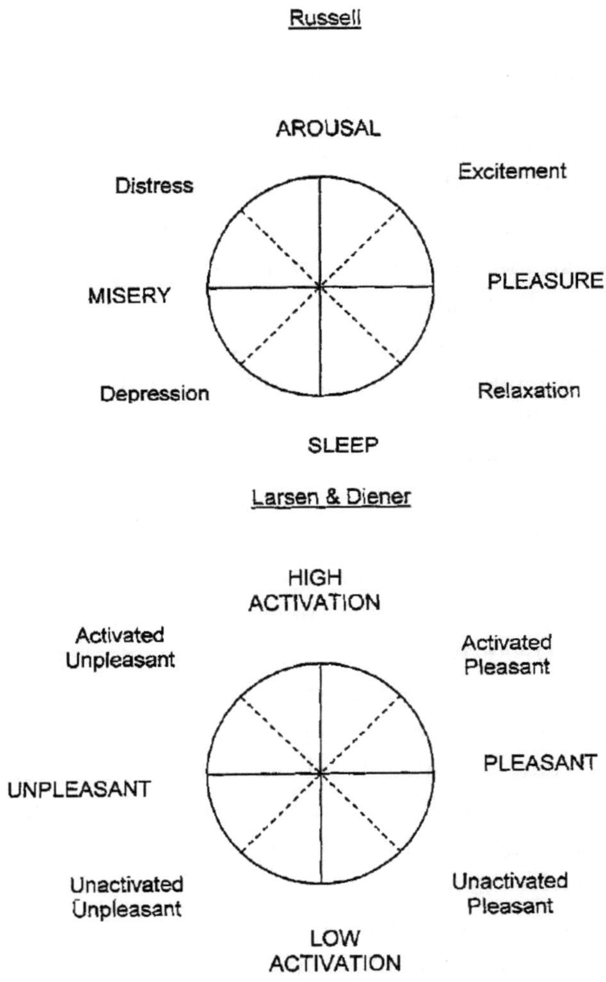

Figure 5. The four models by Russell (1980), Watson and Tellegen (1985), Larsen and Diener (1992), and Thayer (1996). Graphic from Yik, Russell, and Barrett (1999), p. 601. Printed with permission.

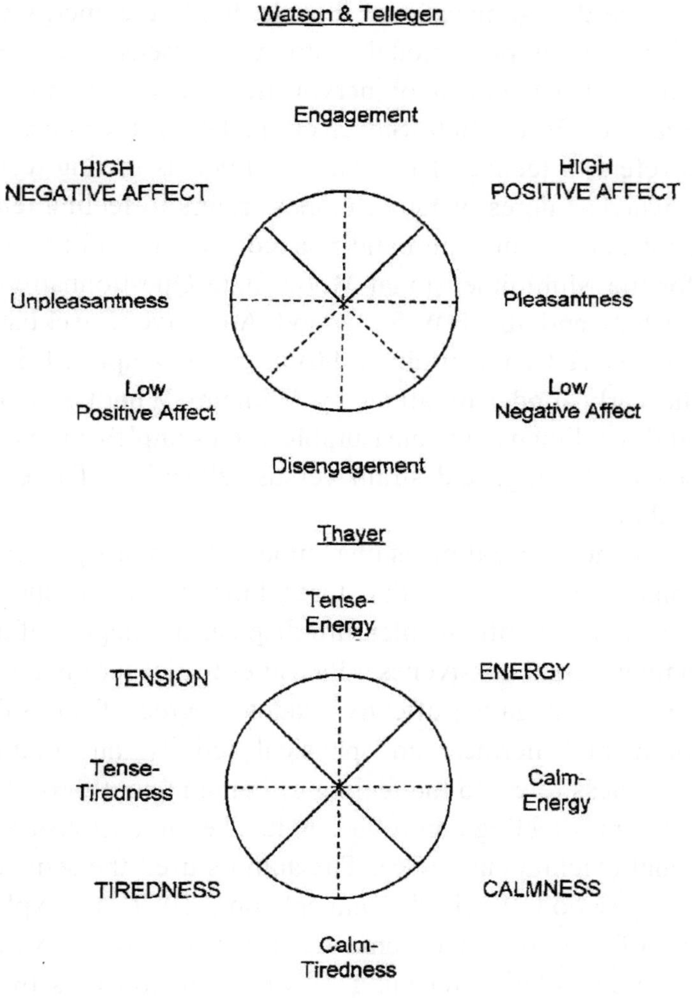

Figure 5 (continued). The four models by Russell (1980), Watson and Tellegen (1985), Larsen and Diener (1992), and Thayer (1996). Graphic from Yik, Russell, and Barrett (1999), p. 601. Printed with permission.

Some three-dimensional models divide the energy component of the circumplex models into two dimensions: sleepiness versus arousal and unrest or nervousness versus calmness (e.g., Schimmack & Grob, 2000; Steyer et al., 1994). Sleepiness versus arousal refers to feeling sleepy and tired versus feeling rested and awake, whereas unrest versus calmness refers to feeling tense and nervous versus feeling calm and relaxed. This model provides the basis for the Multidimensional Mood State Questionnaire (Steyer et al., 1997) and the UWIST Mood Adjective Checklist (Matthews, Jones, & Chamberlain, 1990) as two examples. It is in line with the early model of affect by Wilhelm Wundt (1896), who claimed three dimensions: pleasurable versus unpleasurable, arousing versus subduing, and strain versus relaxation. These models are mood models.

Another three-dimensional model, the one by Russell and Mehrabian (1977), claims that three bipolar dimensions can be used to describe emotions: pleasure-displeasure, degree of arousal, and dominance-submissiveness. Pleasure-displeasure is defined as positive versus negative affective states, degree of arousal is the level of mental alertness and physical activity, and dominance-submissiveness refers to the feeling of being in control of the environment versus feeling controlled by it. The dimensions are nearly orthogonal (Mehrabian, 1996). The authors used the semantic differential (Osgood, Suci, & Tannenbaum, 1957) to explore the structure of emotions. The semantic differential was developed to assess the connotative meaning of words or concepts by asking people to spontaneously provide associations with the word or concept using bipolar adjective scales. The semantic dimensions used are evaluation, activity, and potency, each of which usually has subdimensions.

3.1.2 Models of Discrete Emotions

As already mentioned, models of discrete emotions claim a number of basic emotions that are universal, innate, and have distinct characteristics. There seems to be a consensus that there are a finite number of distinct emotions, but how many there are and whether or not they have a biological basis are still under debate (Diener, 2009). These models usually assume unidimensionality of their components (Lischetzke & Eid, 2011).

Izard's (1977) Differential Emotions Theory (DET) "views emotion experience as a feeling state or motivational condition, a direct and immediate product of the particular neural processes associated with that emotion" (Izard, 1992, p. 561). Emotions have neural correlates, are innate and universal, and can be distinguished by facial expression and feeling. The basic emotions in this theory are thus based on facial expressions rather than analyses of verbalisations of feelings. Izard claims 10 basic emotions: anger, disgust, contempt, interest, joy, surprise, sadness, fear, shyness, and guilt. These emotions are also represented as scales in the Differential Emotions Scale (DES; Izard, 1991), a questionnaire designed to assess these emotions.

Ekman (1992) considered the dimensions of arousal, pleasure, and activity insufficient for describing the various emotions that are universal across cultures. He thus suggested 6 basic emotions: anger, disgust, fear, happiness, sadness, and surprise, with each of them having unique facial expressions, physiology, and evoking events. According to these features, the different emotions can be distinguished from each other, and by considering 6 more characteristics, they can be distinguished from other affective phenomena. These consist of presence in other primates, coherence in emotional response, quick onset, brief duration, automatic appraisal, and unbidden occurrence. On the basis of this classification of emotions, the Facial Action Coding System (FACS) was developed; among other things, the FACS allows emotional states to be assigned to facial expressions. The FACS will be discussed in more detail in the section on measurement of affect.

3.1.3 Hybrid Models

Finally, there are also models that combine the dimensional and discrete approaches. For example, in Tellegen, Watson, and Clark's (1999) model, there are three levels: at the bottom level, there are discrete emotions; next can be found positive and negative affect, which are largely uncorrelated; and at the top level, there is a bipolar happiness-versus-unhappiness dimension.

Similarly, the model by Diener, Smith, and Fujita (1995) has two levels: At the bottom level, there are the emotions love and joy as positive ones and shame, fear, sadness, and anger as negative ones. The positive and negative emotions constitute two factors, one representing the positive and one representing the negative emotions. They found positive and negative affect to be separate but related. Figure 6 depicts the model.

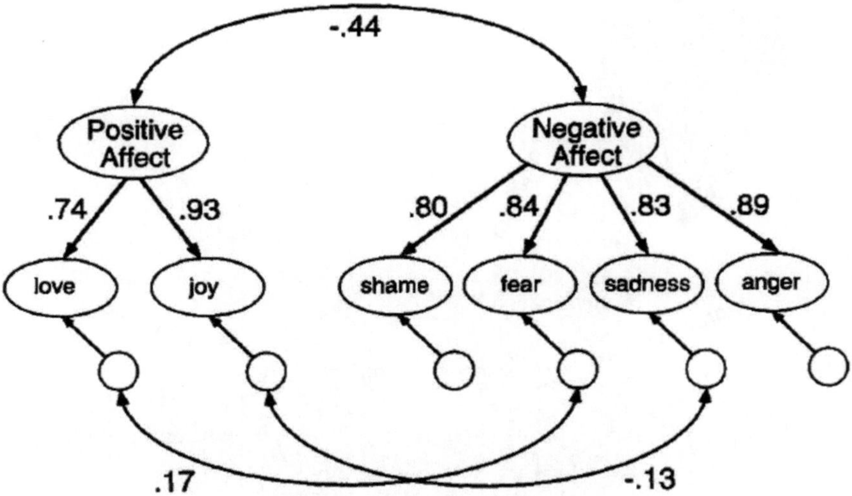

Figure 6. Two-factor model of affect structure for six emotions (Graphic from Diener et al., 1995, p. 137). Printed with permission.

Plutchik (2001) suggested 8 basic emotions: anger, fear, sadness, disgust, surprise, anticipation, trust, and joy, and arranged them as primary and bipolar emotions (joy vs. sadness; anger vs. fear; trust vs. disgust; and surprise vs. anticipation) in a circumplex with a third dimension, intensity of emotions. As emotions intensify, they turn into ecstasy, admiration, terror, amazement, grief, loathing, rage, and vigilance, and as they weaken in intensity, they turn into serenity, acceptance, apprehension, distraction, pensiveness, boredom, annoyance, and interest. Around these basic emotions, he arranged 8 advanced emotions, each of them a combination of the basic emotions (optimism, love, submission, awe, disapproval, remorse, contempt, and aggressiveness).

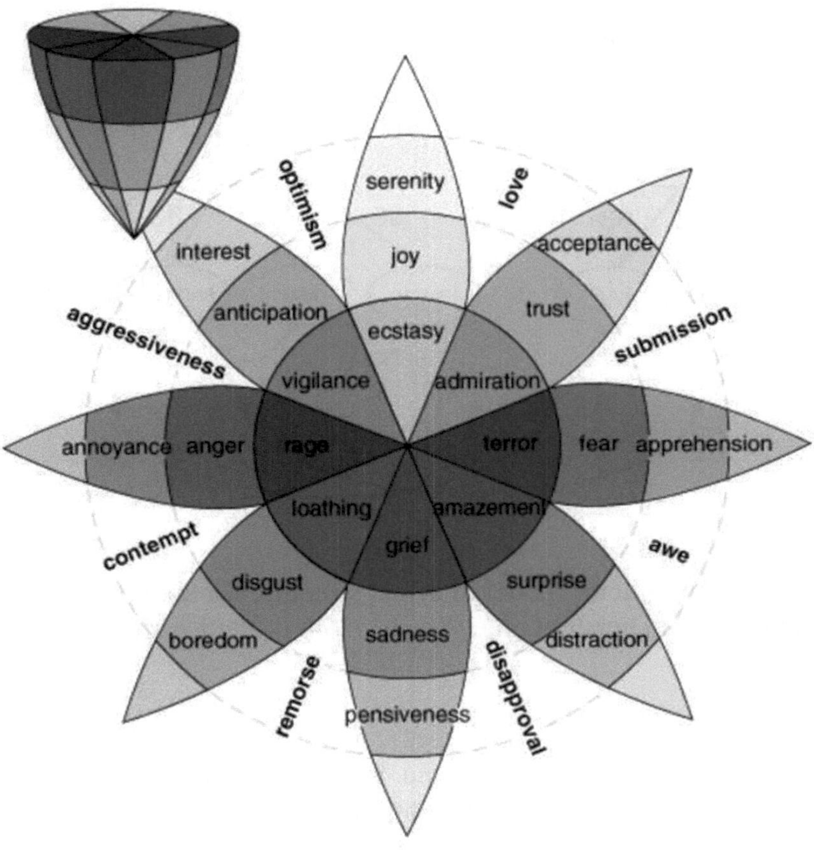

Figure 7. Plutchik's (2001) three-dimensional circumplex model of emotions. Retrieved from http://web.archive.org/web/20010818040222/http://americanscientist.org/articles/01articles/plutchikcap6.html

3.1.4 Domain-Specific Models

The models presented so far are general models of affect. However, there are also models designed specifically for certain domains such as testing. One such model is the Control-Value Theory of Achievement Emotions (Pekrun, 2006). It is based on the assumption that motivation, perceived control, goals, and their value as well as emotions jointly impact performance. It will be described in more detail in the section on affect and performance.

3.2 MEASUREMENT OF MOOD AND EMOTIONS

It was mentioned above that emotions are often seen as consisting of the five components cognitive, physiological, motivational, expressive, and affective. Theoretically, all of these components can be measured. However, very often only the affective component is assessed (Scherer, 2005).

3.2.1 Assessment of the Physiological Component

There are a number of indicators that can be used to assess the psychophysiological component of emotions such as facial electromyographic reactions (zygomatic and corrugator muscle activity), visceral responses (heart rate and skin conductance; e.g., Lang, Greenwald, Bradley, & Hamm, 1993), finger temperature, and somatic activity (e.g., Levenson, Ekman, & Friesen, 1990).

3.2.2 Assessment of the Expressive Component

The Facial Action Coding System (FACS; Ekman & Friesen, 1976, 1978) is a method that "can be used to describe any facial movement (observed in photographs, motion picture film or videotape) in terms of anatomically based action units" (Ekman

& Friesen, 1976, p. 56). It allows 44 different units of action to be classified and takes into account intensity, laterality, location, and timing. Research has shown, among other findings, that this technique in combination with video recording makes it possible to distinguish between true and simulated emotions (Ekman & Friesen, 1982). However, the system itself does not allow for emotions to be assigned to facial expressions. For this purpose, additional resources such as the FACS Investigators' Guide (Ekman, Friesen, & Hager, 2002) are required. Use of the FACS requires the observer to be trained, which can be done either by self-instruction or in groups with or without an instructor (Cohn, Ambadar, & Ekman, 2007). Learning the facial action codes takes about 40 h (Ekman & Friesen, 1976).

3.2.3 Assessment of the Affective Component

The affective component of emotions is usually assessed with self-report measures. For this purpose, individuals are usually confronted with words describing emotions and have to determine either which of them best describes their current state or the extent to which the words describe their current state, using either a Likert-type or a visual analogue scale (Scherer, 2005). Examples of such questionnaires are Watson, Clark, and Tellegen's (1988) Positive and Negative Affect Schedule (PANAS), which is based on the circumplex model; Steyer, Schwenkmezger, Notz, and Eid's (1997) Multidimensional Mood Questionnaire (MDMQ), which is based on the three-dimensional model of mood; or Izard's (1991) Differential Emotions Scale (DES), which is based on a model of discrete emotions.

The 20-item PANAS (Watson et al., 1988) measures positive and negative affect and can be used to assess present or past affective states. Its theoretical basis is the circumplex model of affect by Watson and Tellegen (1985). More recently, Watson and Clark (1994) developed the PANAS-X, an extended version that measures 11 specific affective states (fear, sadness, guilt, hostility, shyness, fatigue, surprise, joviality, self-assurance, attentiveness, and serenity) in addition to the higher order scales of positive and negative affect.

The MDMQ (Steyer et al., 1997) measures the three bipolar mood dimensions: bad mood versus good mood, sleepiness versus arousal, and unrest versus calmness. It consists of 24 items, with eight items measuring each dimension, four of them at each pole of the three scales. It will be discussed in more detail in Study 1 because a web adaption of it was used to assess mood in the main experiment.

On the basis of Izard's (1977) Differential Emotions Theory, the DES (Izard, 1991) assesses the discrete emotions of joy, surprise, anger, disgust, contempt, shame, guilt, fear, interest, and sadness using an adjective checklist with 30 adjectives.

All of the instruments use Likert-type response scales. However, there are also a number of instruments that use other response formats. The self-assessment manikin (Lang, 1980) measures pleasure, arousal, and dominance in a person's reactions to external stimuli using simple pictures (Mehrabian, 1996; Russell & Mehrabian, 1977). Figure 8 depicts this.

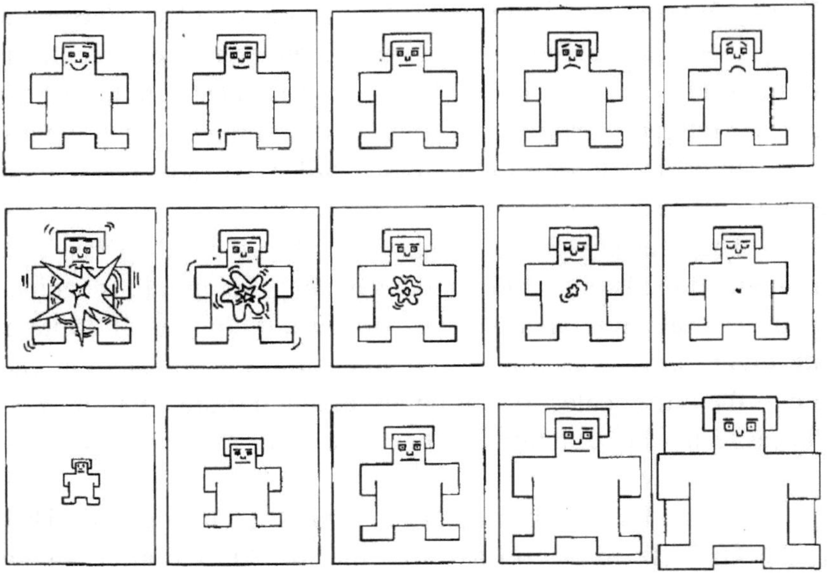

Figure 8. The self-assessment manikin (SAM; Lang, 1980). Top row: pleasure. Middle row: arousal. Bottom row: dominance (graphic from Bradley & Lang, 1994). Printed with permission.

Similarly, in the affect grid, individuals mark their mood state on a grid that has two dimensions: pleasantness versus unpleasantness and high versus low arousal. Figure 9 depicts this.

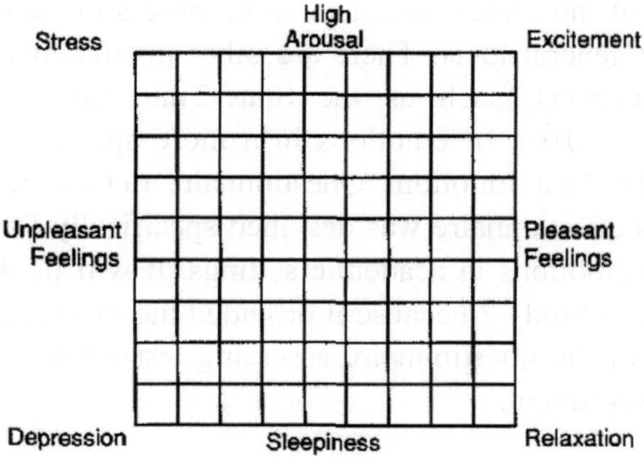

Figure 9. The affect grid (Russell, Weiss, & Mendelsohn, 1989). Printed with permission.

The website Trackyourhappiness provides a visual analogue scale for assessing individuals' current or general mood states (www.trackyourhappiness.org). Figure 10 depicts this response format.

Figure 10. Visual analogue scale for assessing state mood. Retrieved from the website www.trackyourhappiness.org.

All of the scales presented so far assess mood or emotions on a rather general level. There are other instruments that assess specific emotions, such as the State-Trait Anxiety Inventory (Spielberger, 2010), or emotions in a more specific context; for example, the Test Emotions Questionnaire (TEQ; Pekrun et al., 2004). This questionnaire was designed specifically for measuring test-related emotions in academic settings. It will be discussed in more detail in Study 2 because it provided the theoretical basis for the design of the questionnaire assessing test-related emotions in the main experiment.

3.3 Elicitation of Mood and Emotions

Earlier it was mentioned that there is a distinction between mood and emotion. This distinction also holds for elicitation methods. Some methods are used to elicit mood, some to induce emotional states. This does not mean that using a mood induction method does not have an effect on emotions and vice versa. However, researchers usually study either mood or emotion after the induction.

Eich and colleagues (Eich, Ng, Macaulay, Percy, & Grebneva, 2007) provided a number of desirable attributes of a mood induction technique as quoted here (p. 125):

- Technique has a high rate of success in altering participants' moods in predictable ways.
- Technique allows for individual differences in time taken to develop a particular mood.
- Induced moods are strong or intense.
- Induced moods are stable over time and across tasks.
- Induced moods seem real or authentic to the participants.
- One and the same mood can be reliably induced on more than one occasion.

In the following, different mood and emotion elicitation methods will be described. It is not always possible to evaluate the techniques against these standards, but it will be done as much as possible.

3.3.1 Overview of Mood and Emotion Elicitation Methods

There are many mood induction methods that have been studied by researchers. Many methods make use of individuals' imagination and trigger it with different techniques. One widely studied method is the Velten technique (e.g., Kenealy, 1986; Velten, 1968), which asks participants to read positive, negative, or neutral statements and instructs them to try to experience the mood. Other imagination techniques use pictures instead of words (e.g., Lang et al., 1993), have participants listen to music (e.g., Pignatiello, Camp, & Rasar, 1986), have them watch film clips (e.g., Gross & Levenson, 1995; Philippot, 1993; Rottenberg, Ray, & Gross, 2007), or ask them to recall happy or sad life events (e.g., Abele, 1990). Moreover, hypnosis (e.g., Weiss, Blum, & Gleberman, 1987) or primary reinforcers such as gifts (e.g., Isen, Daubman, & Nowicki, 1987) can be used. Finally, some techniques have the participant actively do something such as imitate a facial expression (e.g., Levenson et al., 1990) or engage in a social interaction (for an overview, see Harmon-Jones, Amodio, & Zinner, 2007; Roberts, Tsai, & Coan, 2007). Combinations of two or more techniques are possible (Gilet, 2008). All of these techniques will be described in more detail below.

Velten technique. As already mentioned above, the Velten technique (Velten, 1968) asks participants to read positive, negative, or neutral statements and instructs them to "try to feel the mood suggested" (Kenealy, 1986). An example of a positive statement is "This is great, I really do feel good, I am elated about things". A negative one is "I have too many bad things in my life". In the original study, Velten (1968) randomly assigned participants to one of five groups: positive, negative, neutral, and two role-play groups (a positive and a negative one) in order to control for effects of demand characteristics. He found that the statements successfully induced the respective mood states such that the demand characteristics groups had less extreme means on the mood scale than the experimental groups.

In a more recent study (Jennings, McGinnin, Lovejoy, & Stirling, 2000), participants were asked to rate a set of 84 Velten statements using the Self Assessment Manikin (SAM; Lang, Bradley, & Cuthbert, 1999). Fifty-two of these statements were consistent with the valence ratings by Velten (1968). This study also demonstrated a curvilinear relation between valence and arousal: High arousal was associated with positive valence, low arousal with neutral valence, and intermediate arousal with negative valence. There was no significant difference between men and women in the valence ratings of the stimuli, but there was a difference between their arousal ratings, with men rating low arousal stimuli as more arousing than women.

However, for this method, it is often debated whether the measured mood change is really due to the statements or rather due to demand characteristics (Kenealy, 1986; Polivy & Doyle, 1980). This caveat applies to all techniques that explicitly ask subjects to enter a specific mood state (Gilet, 2008).

Music. To avoid the demand characteristics problem, Sutherland, Newman, and Rachman (1982) used music instead of the Velten statements. Participants listen to music clips that are several minutes long and that range from classical to pop music. The method has been shown to successfully induce elated versus depressed mood and to work equally well for men and women (Pignatiello, Camp, & Rasar, 1986). The effect of the technique is thought to stem from various characteristics of music such as mode, tempo, pitch, rhythm, harmony, and volume, different combinations of which evoke different kinds of mood states (Västfjäll, 2002). This method is often combined with ideation or thought (Eich et al., 2007).

Pictures. When pictures are used, participants look at photos of people with certain facial expressions (e.g., happy or sad) and try to feel the emotion the person in the picture is experiencing at the moment (Schneider, Gur, Gur, & Muenz, 1994). With this procedure, happy versus sad mood was successfully induced in subjects: Individuals in the happy mood induction condition felt happier and less sad than individuals in the sad mood induction condition, whereas subjects in the sad mood induction group felt sadder and less happy than individuals in the other condition. Intensity for the two valences was about the same. The authors found a strong effect in 75% of participants (whereas the Velten technique was successful in only 60% of the subjects) and successfully replicated their results a month later.

Recall of happy and sad life events. In the recall of happy and sad life events method, also called the "autobiographical recollection methodology", participants are asked to write down important happy or sad life events (Abele, 1990). It has been found to successfully induce positive or negative mood and to last for about 15 min. The vividness and specificity of the events were positively correlated with the magnitude of the induction effect.

Hypnosis. Hypnosis is defined as "a social interaction in which one person, the subject, responds to suggestions offered by another person, the hypnotist, for experiences involving alternations in perception, memory, and voluntary action" (Kihlstrom, 1985, p. 385). For this method to be effective, the individual needs to be susceptible to hypnosis, and this susceptibility needs to be assessed in advance (Friswell & McConkey, 1989). To induce different moods, individuals are hypnotised. Afterwards, they are asked to relive past emotional experiences, and the contents of the experience are subsequently dissociated from the affective experience (Weiss et al., 1987). Research has shown that hypnosis changes psychophysiological responses, behaviour, and perceptual and cognitive processes; however, it is possible that these responses are influenced by social compliance (Friswell & McConkey, 1989).

Primary reinforcers. When using primary reinforcers as an emotion elicitation method, participants often receive a surprise gift such as a small bag of candy (Isen et al., 1987). Other methods have participants “find” coins in a phone booth or “release” them from a boring task. Finally, positive or negative feedback on a task such as performance on an intelligence test is used (for an overview of these techniques, see Otto, 2000).

Films. Emotion elicitation using films requires individuals to watch a film clip (Rottenberg et al., 2007). The films can be used not only to induce positive versus negative mood, but also to induce specific emotions such as amusement, sadness, anger, or contentment (Gross & Levenson, 1995; Philippot, 1993). Gross and Levenson (1995) conducted an extensive study and reviewed 250 films that were potentially suitable for eliciting emotions. They reduced the pool of films by applying several criteria (e.g., they had to be short and their content had to be understandable without additional explanation) and ended up with 78 films matching these criteria. They exposed individuals to these film clips and then asked them to fill out a 16-item emotion inventory. In the end, they created a list of films that were suitable for eliciting the emotions amusement, anger, contentment, disgust, fear, sadness, and surprise, and they additionally provided a neutral option. There are two film clips for each emotion, with a length between 9 s and 8 min. For these films, the authors also provided detailed instructions for editing the clips.

However, films pose high cognitive and attentional demands such that they might not be suitable for certain target groups. Examples are young children or individuals with cognitive impairments or certain experimental settings, such as when another task has to be implemented simultaneously (Rottenberg et al., 2007).

Facial expression. Techniques that use facial expression for mood induction make use of the finding that not only does mood trigger facial expression, but facial expression also impacts mood (e.g., Kleinke, Peterson, & Rutledge, 1998). Individuals receive precise instructions for how they have to use their facial muscles to generate various facial expressions of, for example, anger, disgust, fear, happiness, sadness, and surprise (Levenson et al., 1990). With this technique, it is possible to induce distinct emotions that are experienced by individuals as distinct and that are also reflected as distinct by objective measures such as heart rate, skin conductance, finger temperature, and somatic activity. However, this method requires instruction and training.

Social interaction. Mood induction via social interaction is often carried out in dyadic interaction tasks (i.e., asking two people to interact with each other; Levenson & Gottman, 1983). The task is usually to discuss an either positively or negatively valenced topic. The interaction is often videotaped to allow for further analyses later, and mood is assessed immediately after the conversation (Roberts et al., 2007). Major advantages of this technique are that it is ecologically valid, and it allows a wide range of emotions to be evoked. On the other hand, the task is hard to control (individuals may or may not comply with the experimental task; e.g., they may simply avoid the topic they are asked to discuss), and it requires a lot of resources (Roberts et al., 2007). Mood induction via social interaction is not restricted to dyadic interaction tasks. It can also be elicited by triggering social comparison in individuals, by asking them to take another person's perspective, or with other scenarios in which people interact with others (for an overview, see Harmon-Jones et al., 2007).

3.3.2 Online Mood Induction

Mood or emotion induction procedures that are suitable for mood or emotion induction in an unsupervised online study have to comply with certain restrictions. First, participants sit in front of their home computer by themselves; therefore, any methods that require an interaction partner, an instructor, or an observer are not suitable. The methods need to be self-explanatory or at least explainable in a few words, and it is not possible to train subjects in advance. Methods that fulfil these requirements are the Velten technique; techniques using photos, stories, films, or music; and recall of happy or sad life events. Gift-based procedures can be used if the gift is given online (e.g., a gift voucher that is sent via email).

In a series of five studies, Göritz (2007) compared the Velten technique, pictures (cartoons and photographs), texts (jokes and longer texts), and text-picture combinations in their effectiveness in inducing positive and negative mood states in an online setting. She found the Velten technique and photos to be effective only for negative but not for positive mood. Cartoons improved mood, but jokes did not. Positive and negative word association tasks failed to change mood, whereas picture-illustrated texts did so successfully. The findings were in line with an earlier study in which the Velten technique and photos deteriorated mood but failed to improve it and in which autobiographical recall did not work for either positive or negative mood (Göritz & Moser, 2006).

From her findings, Göritz (2007) drew a few general conclusions for online mood induction procedures: The effects of online mood induction are smaller than the effects of offline mood induction, and online mood induction is more error prone because the experimenter has less control over participants' other actions during the induction procedure.

3.3.3 Reviews of Mood and Emotion Induction Procedures

In their review of various mood induction procedures from 1979 to 1994, Gerrards-Hesse, Spies, and Hesse (1994) recommended that films or stories and gifts should be used to induce positive moods and imagination, whereas the Velten technique, films, stories, and success/failure methods should be used to induce negative moods.

These results are in line with another meta-analysis by Westermann, Spies, Stahl, and Hesse (1996) who compared the Velten technique, recall of happy or sad life events, watching films, reading or listening to stories, listening to music, receiving gifts or performance feedback, social interaction, and combinations of these methods. They came to the conclusion that the most effective methods for eliciting both positive and negative moods are the presentation of stories and films. In general, the effects are stronger for negative than for positive mood, and effects are particularly strong when individuals are explicitly asked to enter a certain mood state. For positive emotions, films and stories show the greatest effects, whereas facial expression provides only a small effect. For negative emotions, the effects of the Velten technique, imagination, listening to music, interactions, and feedback are as strong as the effects of stories and films, whereas facial expression does not have an effect. In general, effects are smaller when demand characteristics are controlled and when manipulation checks are conducted on the basis of behavioural indicators (as opposed to self-ratings).

It is recommended that manipulation checks be implemented after inductions and that—ideally—such manipulation checks should be multimodal and involve difference scores computed on measures taken before versus after the induction (Otto, 2000). To test whether the emotion or mood induction was successful, one can use the techniques that have been described above in the section on assessment of mood and emotions. However, when using self-report measures, this might make individuals think about the purpose of the experiment and the induction procedure and thus create characteristics of experimental demand (Parrott, 1991). For example, the effect of an emotion induction using facial expressions is stronger when individuals report which emotions they are experiencing (Levenson et al., 1990).

3.4 Summary

Mood and emotions are different phenomena. Whereas mood is a background sensation, emotions are more intense, directed towards a target, and shorter in duration than mood. There are different models of affect. Structural models usually consist of two dimensions, valence and arousal, with some of them further dividing the arousal component into an energetic and a tension component. Models of discrete emotions usually claim a number of distinct emotions (e.g., six or 10). Hybrid models integrate the two notions and classify emotions along dimensions such as valence or intensity.

Mood and emotions are mostly measured using self-ratings with different response formats (rating scales, visual analogue scales, or visualisations of the scales), thus assessing their affective component, but there are also ways of assessing the physiological or expressive components.

A wide range of techniques are available for inducing different mood states. Most of them have been shown to be successful at changing a person's affective state. The most effective methods for eliciting both positive and negative moods are stories and films, and effects are stronger for negative than for positive mood.

4 Affect and Cognition

The first ideas on the relation between cognition and emotion date back to the 1940s, when, for example, Cameron (1947) stated that emotion in general reduces cerebral competence. However, according to Bless (1999), the research programme on the relation between affect and cognitive performance did not begin until the 1970s when researchers began to systematically vary affective states under experimental conditions and assess the influence of these states on memory and social behaviour.

The present study's research question is whether discrete emotions have an impact on intelligence test performance, or more specifically, performance on a reasoning test. When I began my literature search, it quickly became apparent that there were only a few studies that had tested the relations between affect and reasoning. There is a wide range of literature on the influence of negative emotions—especially test anxiety—on test performance in academic settings. Researchers began studying test anxiety systematically in the 1950s (e.g., Mandler & Sarason, 1952) and consistently found that it impaired academic performance (e.g., Cassady & Johnson, 2002; Hembree, 1988). However, apart from test anxiety, emotions have been widely neglected in the literature on academic achievement (Pekrun, 2006). The literature on performance on classical IQ tests is also scarce. In fact, there were only three experimental studies that tested the effect of mood on performance on reasoning tests (Abele, 1995; Melton, 1995; Radenhausen & Anker, 1988), and these yielded partly contradictory results. With respect to discrete emotions, the only studies I could find were correlational studies that had been conducted in an academic setting and that investigated academic exams rather than intelligence tests (Pekrun, 2006; Pekrun & Hofmann, 1999).

Thus, to find research on the relation between affect and reasoning performance, it was necessary to extend my literature search to a broader realm of various cognitive outcomes such as information processing and complex problem solving and some of the components of intelligence described earlier: perceptual speed, memory, divergent thinking (or creativity), and finally, convergent thinking (or reasoning).

Whereas there are only a few findings on the relation between affect and reasoning test performance, on the other hand, there are quite a few theories that can be used to derive hypotheses. According to Abele (1995), theories on the relation between affect and cognition can be classified as follows.

Cognitive approaches consider the valence component of mood and assume that it impacts the encoding, processing, and recall of information. There are various assumptions about which processes are influenced. For example, mood impacts the encoding and recall of memory (e.g., Bower, 1981). An extension of this idea is that mood is interpreted as context, meaning that the context in which information is presented impacts the meaning or interpretation of the information (e.g., Clark & Isen, 1982; Isen, 1984; Schwarz, 1990). Approaches that consider mood-induced thinking styles posit that mood evokes a certain processing style, which is either sequential-analytic or intuitive-heuristic (e.g., Damasio, 1994; Isen, 1984; Kuhl, 1983a, Kuhl, 1983b; Schwarz, 1990).

By contrast, activation-theoretical approaches claim that activation and not the valence of affect impacts performance (e.g., Lambourne & Tomporowski, 2010; Onyper, Carr, Farrar, & Floyd, 2011; Yerkes & Dodson, 1908). Attention-theoretical approaches consider attention to be a limited resource that has to be divided between different tasks; some claim that performance on cognitive tasks is impaired by negative mood (e.g., Ellis & Ashbrook, 1988), whereas others posit that it is the intensity of affect that impairs performance on cognitive tasks (e.g., Easterbrook, 1959; Larsen & Diener, 1987; Schneider, 1987).

Moreover, motivational approaches posit that mood-contingent motives moderate the relation between affect and performance (e.g., Carver & Scheier, 1998; Erez & Isen, 2002; Gray, 1990; Schwarz & Bohner, 1996; Seo et al., 2004). Furthermore, demand-related approaches claim that the impact of mood on performance is moderated by the requirements of the task at hand (e.g., Fiedler, 1990a; Forgas, 1995; Royce & Diamond, 1980).

In the current chapter, theories on the relation between affect and cognitive performance will be reported according to Abele's (1995) taxonomy: cognitive approaches, attention-theoretical approaches, activation-theoretical approaches, motivational approaches, and demand-related approaches. Afterwards, Abele's (1995) integrative approach will be presented because it allows for the creation of testable hypotheses. In addition, two fields that were not covered in the above-mentioned taxonomy will be discussed: brain science and research on discrete emotions.

4.1 Affect and Cognition in the Brain

A number of connections in the brain suggest that there is in fact a connection between affect and cognition. Specifically, there are pathways between the limbic system and the neocortex. Klinger (1996) outlined a few of the connections reported by Derryberry and Tucker (1992). Pathways from the thalamus to the amygdala represent an interconnection between early cognitive and emotional processing. Furthermore, there are fibres from the amygdala leading to the neocortex, pointing to the fact that cognitive processing is influenced by emotions. Finally, there are fibres leading back from the neocortex to the amygdala, which might mean that emotional responses are influenced by cognition. Thus, connections in the brain suggest that there is a link between affect and cognition that go both ways: affect impacts cognition, but also cognition impacts affective experience. In the following theories and research on connections between affect and cognitive outcomes will be reported.

4.1.1 Neuropsychological Theory of Positive Emotions (Ashby, Isen, & Turken, 1999)

Ashby, Isen, and Turken (1999) proposed a neuropsychological theory that accounts for many of the effects that positive emotions have on performance by assuming that positive affect is associated with increased dopamine levels in the brain. The theory predicts influences of positive affect on olfaction, long-term (i.e., episodic) memory consolidation, working memory, and creative problem solving.

The basic assumptions of the theory are that positive affect is associated with increased dopamine levels in the brain and that these influence cognitive processing through a number of dopamine projections originating in the ventral tegmental area (VTA). Of special interest are the nigrostriatal and the mesocorticolimbic systems. The former consists of dopamine-producing cells in the substantia nigra pars compacta; such cells project to the striatum and are associated with motor activity. The latter consists of dopamine-producing cells in the VTA; these cells project to a number of limbic and cortical areas and are associated with motivation and reward.

Therefore, according to the theory, positive affect alters processing in any structure that receives a direct projection from the VTA but not in structures that do not receive a direct projection from that area. Figure 11 depicts these projections.

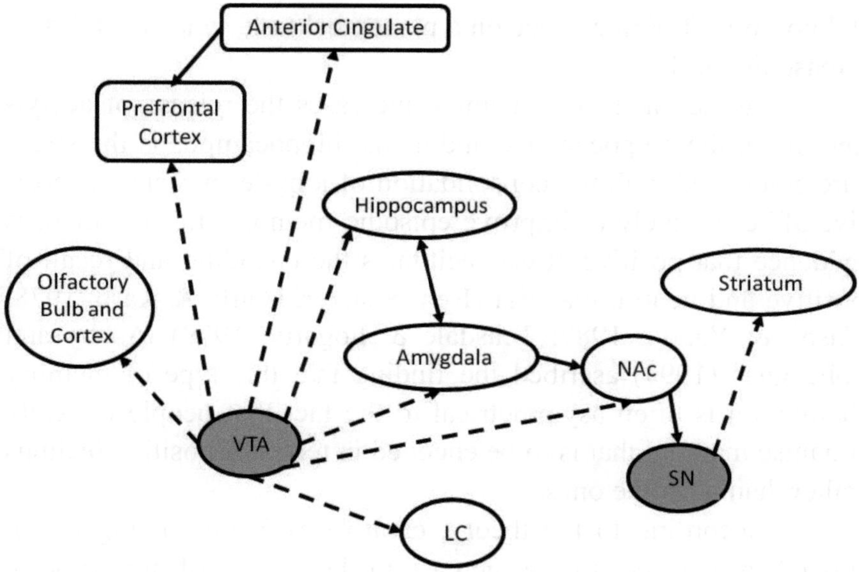

Figure 11. Some dopamine projections in the human brain. Dopamine-producing areas are shaded in grey, and dopamine projections are illustrated by dashed lines. NAc = nucleus accumbens; VTA = ventral tegmental area; SN = substantia nigra; LC = locus ceruleus (adapted from Ashby, Isen, & Turken, 1999, p. 533; printed with permission).

Consequently, as there are direct projections from the VTA to the olfactory bulb and the primary olfactory cortex, odour is likely to be closely linked to affect. However, there are no direct projections from the VTA to the other primary sensory areas (e.g., the primary visual or auditory areas). Therefore, it is less likely for affect to influence performance on perceptual tasks that involve, for example, the visual or auditory system. This idea is in line with a study by Radenhausen and Anker (1988) who found that mood did not impact performance on a perceptual task, whereas it did on a reasoning task.

Furthermore, as dopamine increases the release of acetylcholine in the hippocampus, and as the hippocampus is the structure associated with the consolidation of long-term memory, positive affect is likely to improve episodic memory. In fact, there is evidence that positive affect facilitates the encoding and recall of positive and neutral material (Isen, Shalker, Clark, & Karp, 1978; Nasby & Yando, 1982; Teasdale & Fogarty, 1979). Ashby and colleagues (1999) ascribed the finding that this type of memory facilitation is often asymmetrical to the fact that people typically organise material that is to be encoded in terms of positive feelings rather than negative ones.

According to the theory, creative problem solving is improved in part because an increase in the release of dopamine in the anterior cingulate improves cognitive flexibility and facilitates the selection of cognitive perspective. A meta-analysis of 25 years of research on affect and creativity confirmed that creative problem solving is better when a person is in a positive mood than when a person is in a neutral or negative mood (Baas, De Dreu, & Nijstad, 2008).

Finally, projections from the VTA to the prefrontal cortex, an area associated with working memory (Fuster, 1989; Goldman-Rakic, 1995), might facilitate working memory through increased dopamine levels. According to Ashby et al. (1999), working memory performance is optimal at an intermediate dopamine level. Therefore, the authors suggested that moderate levels of positive affect improve working memory, whereas extreme levels impair it. However, this hypothesis has not been tested so far.

What has been found so far is that increased activation or arousal is associated with the release of dopamine and noradrenalin, which in turn enhance working memory performance (Flaherty, 2005). Intermediate levels of dopamine are optimal for working memory performance (Kimberg, D'Esposito, & Farah, 1997), and this in turn would mean that an activation level that is too high is not beneficial for working memory, just as too low of an activation level is also not beneficial. Also, intermediate levels of noradrenalin are associated with better working memory (Chamberlain, Müller, Blackwell, Robbins, & Sahakian, 2006). Very high levels of noradrenalin are achieved only when a person is under massive stress, meaning that even fairly high activation can still yield optimal noradrenalin levels. This finding is supported by studies that found that working memory (Onyper et al., 2011) and performance on cognitive tasks in general (Lambourne & Tomporowski, 2010) were better in states of physical activation. Moreover, creativity has been shown to be better in activated mood states than in deactivated mood states (De Dreu, Baas, & Nijstad, 2008).

4.1.2 Affect and Information Processing

Studies have suggested that mood changes the alpha activity in the brain (Kuhbandner et al., 2009). Alpha activity in turn is associated with cognitive processing styles: Whereas an increase in alpha activity facilitates visual perception and enhances the processing of external stimuli, a decrease in alpha activity impairs visual perception and activates contents stored in memory (Ergenoglu et al., 2004; Hanslmayr et al., 2007; Thut, Nietzel, Brandt, & Pascual-Leone, 2006). Thus, positive mood leads to an activation of knowledge and negative mood to the processing of external stimuli (Kuhbandner et al., 2009). Therefore, positive mood leads to a top-down processing style in which stored knowledge is activated and the individual is less sensitive to bottom-up cues; whereas negative mood leads to a bottom-up processing style by which a person tends to focus on processing external information (Kuhbandner et al., 2009).

In line with this concept, studies have found that in positive moods, individuals tend to rely more on scripts and general knowledge when performing tasks than in negative moods (Bless et al., 1996). Furthermore, when judging the coherence of different concepts, individuals in positive moods are able to associate more distant concepts than people in negative moods because positive moods enhance the spread of activation in the brain (Bolte, Goschke, & Kuhl, 2003). The effect is also shown when individuals are asked to classify objects. In positive moods, they are more likely to do so on the basis of global concepts drawn from memory; whereas in negative moods, they rely more on local information (Gasper & Clore, 2002). Finally, individuals have a broader focus of attention in positive moods than in negative ones (Fredrickson & Branigan, 2005).

4.2 Cognitive Approaches: Mood-Induced Thinking Styles

Similar to the concepts of bottom-up versus top-down processing modes, mood-induced thinking style approaches posit that mood evokes a certain processing style, which is either sequential-analytic or intuitive-heuristic. Such approaches consist of the theory of personality systems interaction (PSI theory; Kuhl, 1983a, Kuhl, 1983b), the feelings-as-information theory (Schwarz, 1990), and the somatic markers hypothesis (Damasio, 1994).

4.2.1 The Theory of Personality Systems Interaction (PSI Theory; Kuhl, 1983a, b)

Kuhl (1983a, b) has argued that there are two different processes of problem solving: one that is sequential-analytic and one that is intuitive-holistic. The sequential-analytic process works with conceptually and semantically coded information, whereas the intuitive-holistic process uses cognitive-emotional schemes upon which attention in focused. The former process is more rigid and less open to different kinds of emotion, but it is also the less error-prone process. The intuitive-holistic processing mode has three features: (a) It enables the parallel processing of large amounts of information and therefore has a high processing capacity; (b) via emotional processes, it can also interlink information that is not logically connected; (c) as it evokes a certain mode of attention, it becomes more open to new information. The last feature also reflects Fredrickson's (1998, 2001) findings that one is more open in positive than in negative emotional states.

The two processing styles are evoked by different emotions. Kuhl (1983b) found explanations for these two different styles in evolutionary theory: Emotions that signal danger, such as fear, shame, guilt, and probably also sadness and surprise foster the analytic-sequential processing mode. This mode focusses attention on the one dominant piece of information—the present danger—thus making a quick reaction possible, and it also ensures a low risk of making mistakes. Therefore, it is the adequate processing style for dangerous situations. Intuitive-holistic processing, on the other hand, is evoked by emotions that are directed towards overcoming obstacles in the past or future, such as interest, joy, and anger. It has the advantage of being able to overcome barriers, an ability that is of the utmost necessity, for example, in complex problem solving.

What makes the intuitive processing mode the better one for complex problem solving is the fact that it uses schemes. The longer one works on a specific problem, the more items are added to the emotional set, thus making them all available at the same time. A solution to the problem is often achieved by the successive restructuring of all of this information. Kuhl (1983b) argued that upcoming emotions that signal danger cause the processing style to switch from intuitive-holistic to sequential-analytic.

He maintained that his hypotheses provide an explanation for the fact that anxiety leads to better performance on easy tasks but is detrimental to performance on more complex tasks: In an anxious state, the sequential-analytic processing mode prevails. Thus, a simple problem is solved quickly and with a low probability of making a mistake. More complex tasks, however, require consideration of many aspects at a time. Therefore, intuitive-holistic processing outperforms sequential-analytic processing for complex tasks. This is the reason why performance on complex tasks is impaired by anxiety.

However, research has not fully confirmed these findings. In a study by Abele (1995), individuals in a positive mood outperformed subjects in a negative mood on test items of intermediate difficulty, a finding that is in line with Kuhl's (1983b) ideas. However, individuals in a positive mood also scored higher on easy items and were more accurate than individuals in a negative mood. There was no performance difference on items of high difficulty. Similarly, in a study by Isen, Daubman, and Nowicki (1987), individuals in a positive mood outperformed subjects in a negative mood on items of intermediate difficulty but not on items of low or high difficulty. However, in both studies, the overall performance of individuals in a positive mood was superior to the performance of individuals in a negative mood.

4.2.2 Feelings-as-Information Theory (Schwarz, 1990)

Similar to Kuhl's (1983a, b) ideas, the feelings-as-information theory (Schwarz, 1990) posits that, depending on the respective mood state, there are different processing styles. The idea is that "rather than computing a judgment on the basis of recalled features of a target, individuals may … ask themselves: 'How do I feel about it?' [and] in doing so, they may mistake feelings due to a pre-existing state as a reaction to the target" (Schwarz, 1990, p. 529).

Thus, as Forgas (2002) put it, our judgements are based on an inferential error: Individuals in a positive mood ascribe their positive state to the fact that things are going well or that they are making the right judgement. Positive moods signal well-being and induce a relaxed and playful approach to tasks, whereas negative moods are perceived as indicators of danger or distress and thus evoke more effortful systematic processing styles. Forgas (2002) maintained that individuals use the heuristic processing mode when they lack the motivation, interest, or resources to process the information at hand in an elaborate manner.

Fiedler (1988) held a similar view: He differentiated between "tightening" and "loosening". The former is evoked by negative emotions and leads to a more systematic, rigid, and conservative processing, whereas the latter is triggered by positive emotions and results in a more intuitive and creative cognitive style.

4.2.3 Somatic Markers Hypothesis (Damasio, 1994)

In Damasio's (1994) theory, he posited that emotional processes guide or even bias behaviour, especially judgements and decision making. He introduced the concept of so-called somatic markers, which associate stimuli with affective physiological states. In situations in which decisions have to be made, the somatic markers create a certain somatic state. This state guides decision making by drawing attention to the alternatives that are more attractive than others.

Damasio (1994) posited that different affective states are combinations of perceived physiological states interacting with thoughts that are currently present. There is usually a thinking style that is congruent with the positive or negative physiological state. In a negative physiological state, the thinking style is slow and not very flexible; concepts come up slowly, they are not very diverse, and there is not much of a logical processing. Depressive states are extreme examples of these negative thinking styles in terms of slowness and irrationality of thinking. Euphoric emotional states, on the other hand, lead to the quick generation of concepts and make the associative process more flexible. In such emotional states, approach and exploratory behaviour are enhanced too. Extreme euphoric states are manic episodes in which there is an overflow of reactions.

What these three theories have in common is the notion that the valence of mood impacts the way individuals think and reflect: When in a negative mood, a person's thinking style is sequential-analytic, detail-oriented, slow, thorough, accurate, sometimes even rigid, and bottom-up; in a positive mood, a person is able to rely on schemata, and the person's thinking style is quick, efficient, sometimes shallow, more error-prone, flexible, and top-down. Depending on the task type, either thinking style may lead to improvements or detriments (Kuhl, 1983b).

4.2.4 Empirical Findings on the Three Theories

There are a few findings that support the idea that individuals in a positive mood process information based on heuristics:

For example, when making a (fictitious) decision about purchasing a car, individuals in a positive mood used a simpler strategy than individuals in a negative mood such that people in a positive mood selected one important criterion and then eliminated alternatives aspect by aspect (Isen & Means, 1983). However, they did not perform worse than the other group and were actually more efficient. By contrast, individuals in a positive mood tend to change their attitudes on the basis of peripheral cues such as the communicator's attractiveness rather than on the basis of the quality of the information delivered, whereas strong arguments are required to change a person's attitude when that person is in a negative mood (Bless, Bohner, & Schwarz, 1992).

Generally the findings suggest that in positive moods, individuals are more creative (Isen et al., 1987). They make decisions more quickly, rely more on things they learned in the past, use more heuristics (Bless et al., 1996), and thus generally process information more efficiently (Isen & Means, 1983).

On the other hand, negative mood leads to more systematic thinking (Sinclair & Mark, 1992) and to focussing on the details of the available information, thus leading to greater accuracy and less of a halo effect when making judgements (Sinclair, 1988).

4.3 Cognitive Approaches: Memory

Relations between affect and memory can be found in encoding and retrieval. Mood congruency and state dependency (Bower, 1981) describe the influence of mood on the encoding and recall of information. The concept of mood as context (Isen, 1984) widens the mentioned phenomena and can also be viewed as the basis for the later broaden-and-build theory of positive emotions (Fredrickson, 1998, 2001).

4.3.1 Mood Congruency and State Dependency (Bower, 1981)

Mood congruency and state dependency were first described by Bower (1981). Mood congruency refers to the fact that it is easier to retain contents that are congruent with one's current mood (e.g., Bless & Fiedler, 1999; Pekrun & Frese, 1992). State dependency describes an interaction between mood at the time of encoding and mood at the time of recall: Memories are easier to retrieve when the mood state at recall is the same as it was during encoding (e.g., Bless & Fiedler, 1999; Pekrun & Frese, 1992).

The effects of mood congruency and state dependency are stronger for positive moods than for negative ones (Leventhal & Tomarken, 1986). According to Pekrun and Frese (1992), there are two reasons for this: Encoding is less efficient for people in sad moods, and recall is impaired because individuals try to overcome sad moods when experiencing them. Moreover, Taylor and Brown (1988) considered it more difficult to encode negative information into semantic networks because nondepressed humans are normally in a positive baseline mood.

Another effect of mood congruency is expectancy motivation, which is higher for people in a positive mood (Cunningham, 1988; Erez & Isen, 2002) and thus has an impact on goal setting and goal striving. This will be discussed in more detail in the section on motivational approaches.

4.3.2 Cognitive Context (Isen, 1984)

The concept of cognitive context refers to affect functioning as a cognitive context in which information is processed and interpreted. Thus, affect influences the grouping, organisation, and relation of stimuli. For memory and retrieval, this means, as Isen (1984) put it: "material is simultaneously multiply encoded and therefore multiply retrievable" (p. 225). Thus, the meanings that subjects allocate to cues and stimuli differ according to the subjects' mood. It also means that during the process of encoding stimuli, affect can serve as a means for associating stimuli that otherwise would not be associated. Thus, affect can be seen as an additional cue for recalling content. In Isen's (1984) view, individuals in an elated mood have multiple cues available and thus have access to broader and richer contents in their memory.

Studies based on this notion have found that in positive emotional states, people have more unusual associations than when in sad moods (Isen, Johnson, Mertz, & Robinson, 1985). People are also more flexible in that they categorise objects into broader and less detailed categories than when in a neutral mood (Isen & Daubman, 1984). They have a more integrative and comprehensive style of thinking (Estrada, Isen, & Young, 1997; Isen, Rosenzweig, & Young, 1991). It is also easier for them to find similarities and differences between objects when they are in a positive mood than in a neutral mood (Murray, Sujan, Hirt, & Sujan, 1990).

Some of these findings provided the basis of the study by Isen, Daubman, and Nowicki (1987). They came to the conclusion that positive affect is beneficial for creative problem solving. They induced positive, negative, or neutral moods, and in addition, they induced arousal with physical exercise. Participants in a positive mood solved Duncker's candle problem (Duncker & Lees, 1945) more often and scored better on the Remote Associates Test (Mednick & Mednick, 1967) than participants in negative or neutral moods or those with elevated arousal. However, the effect on the Remote Associates Test held only for items of medium difficulty but not for easy or difficult ones. Furthermore, there were no differences in performance between negative and neutral affect and arousal. Thus, negative affect did not seem to be detrimental to performance compared with these conditions. The authors concluded that positive affect facilitates access to more as well as to more diverse contents (Isen & Daubman, 1984; Isen, Daubman, & Gorgolione, 1984) and attributed this effect more to cognitive processes occurring in different mood states than to differences in capacity.

However, mood as a context is more a concept than a theory. It is hard to derive testable and thus falsifiable hypotheses from it. For example, the concept does not specify exactly how affect influences the grouping, organisation, and relation of stimuli. Another question is how to test whether material is multiply encoded and retrievable. Thus, although the assumption that people can access broader and richer contents when in a positive mood seems to be testable and may appear to hold up, other aspects of the concept need clarification and specification in order to derive testable hypotheses.

4.3.3 The Broaden-and-Build Theory of Positive Emotions (Fredrickson, 1998, 2001)

The broaden-and-build theory of positive emotions (Fredrickson, 1998, 2001) posits that experiences of positive emotions broaden people's momentary thought-action repertoires, which, in the long term, build people's personal resources, such as their physical, intellectual, social, and psychological resources. Broadening repertoires of thought and action means that in a positive emotional state, the array of thoughts and actions that come to mind is greater than in negative or neutral emotional states as in the concept of cognitive context (Isen, 1984).

A study by Fredrickson and Branigan (2005) directly supported the broaden aspect of the theory: In their first experiment, they exposed individuals to a global-local paradigm and found that people saw more of the "big picture" when experiencing positive emotions but saw more details when experiencing negative emotions. In their second experiment, individuals experiencing positive emotions produced more ideas for completing open-ended statements than individuals experiencing negative emotions.

A 2008 meta-analysis of 25 years of mood-creativity research (Baas et al., 2008) confirmed that positive moods are beneficial for creative problem solving, whereas neutral and negative mood states are not. The study found no significant difference between the latter two. Moreover, the authors further differentiated within positive and negative mood states by finding that activating mood states with an approach motivation and a promotion focus such as happiness had the strongest positive impact on creativity, compared with deactivating mood states with an avoidance motivation and a promotion focus (e.g., relaxation). Negative activating moods with an avoidance motivation and prevention focus such as fear or anxiety, on the other hand, were found to be related to lower creativity. Finally, negative deactivating moods with an approach motivation and promotion focus such as sadness were not related to creativity.

One more aspect concerning the mood-creativity relation came from another 2008 meta-analysis (Davis, 2009). The conclusion was that there is a curvilinear relation between affect intensity and creativity. Intermediate levels of positive affect are most beneficial for creativity, whereas very low and very high levels are not. The authors saw the reason for this in the fact that if affect becomes too intense, it is brought into the individual's awareness and thus demands resources, whereas before, the person may not have been aware of it.

What hasn't been examined so far is the question of whether positive emotions also broaden the scope of working memory, and more generally, what basic cognitive processes underlie the phenomenon of broadened thought-action repertoires (Fredrickson, 2001).

4.4 Attention-Theoretical Approaches

The basis of attention-theoretical approaches is the notion that tasks require attention and that attention is a limited resource. Different processes share this resource; thus, when more of it is focussed on one process, less is available for the other ones.

4.4.1 Cue Utilisation (Easterbrook, 1959)

Early findings by Callaway and Thompson (1953) and Callaway and Dembo (1958) suggested that emotion or increased activity in the brain stem's reticular formation leads to a narrowing of the attentional field. Consequently, the number of cues an individual can process at a time decreases as emotional arousal increases; or to put it differently: Attention narrows with increasing arousal (Easterbrook, 1959). With respect to task performance, this effect may be beneficial or not. If task-irrelevant cues are ignored while attention is drawn only to relevant ones, task performance is likely to increase. However, if a wider array of cues needs to be utilised in order to perform well on a task (e.g., when working on a complex task), emotion is likely to be detrimental to task performance (Easterbrook, 1959).

More recently, there has been more research on this concept, indicating that elated mood leads to a broadening of attention, whereas depressed mood leads to a focussing of attention (Derryberry & Tucker, 1994). However, recent research has also found that task performance is not so much dependent on the focus of attention as the findings here might suggest and that rather motivation (performance vs. enjoyment goals) has an impact (Friedman & Förster, 2008). This will be further elaborated upon in the section on motivation.

4.4.2 The Resource Allocation Model (Ellis & Ashbrook, 1988)

In their resource allocation model, Ellis and Ashbrook (1988) referred to Kahneman (1973): They stated that information processing requires capacity and that the total available capacity is limited. This capacity can be allocated to different processes. In negative moods, some of the capacity is allocated to mood-relevant processes. These processes include mood-congruent and self-relevant information (see also Pekrun & Frese, 1992). Furthermore, time, effort and capacity are allocated to coping strategies in an effort to overcome the negative mood state (Isen, 1984). The capacity that is allocated to the mood-relevant processes is not available for the processing of a cognitive task. The more intense the bad mood, the more capacity is allocated to task-irrelevant processes. Thus, there is more capacity available in good moods than in bad moods, and for this reason, performance on tasks is better for people in good moods than in bad ones.

Fiedler (1990) criticised this model for being unable to explain and predict some of the phenomena that appear in the context of emotion and cognition, in particular, the effects of mood congruency and state dependency. For example, whereas the model explains the fact that memory deteriorates for people in depressed moods because their cognitive resources are occupied by thoughts about their depressed state, it does not account for phenomena such as selective memory (Fiedler, 1990).

On the basis of the resource allocation theory, Knapp (1986) conducted a study in which he compared performance on a complex problem-solving task for people in happy, sad, angry, or neutral moods. The task was a resource dilemma: Participants had to harvest as many fish as possible from a pond without endangering the propagation of the fish. Based on the model by Ellis and Ashbrook (1988), his prediction was that a negative mood would consume more capacity than a positive or neutral mood; in line with expectations, he found performance in the two negative groups to be worse than performance in the positive and neutral groups.

In a follow-up experiment (Knapp, 1988), he used the same task to compare the performances of people in negative versus neutral moods. This time he manipulated the processing capacity necessary for completing the task by changing the time-lag between the harvesting and restocking of the fish: The greater the time-lag, the greater the necessary processing capacity. Based on the model by Ellis and Ashbrook (1988) again, his prediction was that a negative mood would consume more capacity than a neutral mood and that the detrimental effect of the negative mood would increase with the intensity of the mood and the difficulty of the task. He found that subjects in a negative mood performed significantly worse than participants in a neutral mood, and he found an interaction between mood, intensity of mood, and the capacity requirements of the task: The more intense the negative mood and the more difficult the task, the greater the performance impairment.

Thus, Knapp's studies (1986, 1988) seem to support the idea that performance is impaired in negative moods and that the effect increases as the complexity of the task increases. However, it is unclear whether the effect he found in his second study (Knapp, 1988) is really due to the valence of mood and not to the fact that individuals in the negative condition simply experienced more intense affect than those in the neutral condition. Moreover, what has not been demonstrated so far is whether this effect is due to self-relevant thoughts and coping strategies to get out of the negative state. What has been demonstrated is that negative events consume more attentional resources than positive events (Larsen, 2009).

4.5 Activation-Theoretical Approaches

The impact of arousal on cognitive performance has been studied for over a century. In 1908, Yerkes and Dodson (1908) determined that performance increases with the level of arousal, but only to a certain point, beyond which performance begins to decrease (Yerkes-Dodson law). With respect to cognitive tasks, arousal theory generally considers moderate levels of arousal to be optimal (e.g., Sanders, 1983). However, this effect is mediated by task complexity.

Klinger (1996) reported two studies on the relation between emotional arousal and reaction time: Schneider (1987) found that when individuals were exposed to emotionally arousing distractor words during a reaction time task, their reaction times slowed down. Moreover, Larsen and Diener (1987) found that the reaction times of individuals who scored high on the Affective Intensity Measure were impacted significantly more by emotional arousal compared with the reactions times of other participants. Thus, reaction speed seems to be impaired by arousal, and this finding is not quite what the theory would predict as it predicts that high arousal will be beneficial for easy tasks and low arousal will be ideal for complex tasks.

In a series of experiments, Onyper and colleagues (Onyper et al., 2011) induced arousal by having participants chew gum prior to completing various cognitive tasks and found that gum-chewing individuals performed better on working memory and episodic memory tasks and that their perceptual speed on processing tasks was faster than participants who did not chew gum.

These findings are in line with a meta-analysis by Lambourne and Tomporowski (2010) in which they found that performance on cognitive tasks improved after physical exercise. This effect was largest for memory tasks and smaller for tasks assessing information-processing time or executive function. However, performance on all sorts of cognitive tasks was impaired when the tasks were performed during the first 20 min of exercise. If people continued exercising for more than 20 min, their performance increased again. Effects were again smaller for tasks assessing information processing and response speed than for memory tasks. The authors ascribed the detrimental effect of exercise on cognitive performance during the first 20 min to the fact that when a person begins exercising, some attentional resources are directed to the exercise, and only after the system has adapted to the task can the positive effect of arousal come into play.

These findings are supported by the already mentioned studies on activation, levels of dopamine and noradrenalin in the brain, and working memory: Activation or arousal is associated with the release of dopamine and noradrenalin, which in turn enhance working memory performance (Chamberlain et al., 2006; Flaherty, 2005; Kimberg et al., 1997).

Activation was also found to enhance creativity. De Dreu and colleagues (De Dreu et al., 2008) studied the impact of activating moods (e.g., angry, fearful, happy, elated) versus deactivating moods (e.g., sad, depressed, relaxed, serene) on creative fluency and originality. They found that performance on both fluency and originality was higher when a person experienced activating moods compared with deactivating moods.

This finding is in line with a meta-analysis on mood and creativity (Baas et al., 2008). The authors found that activating mood states such as happiness had a stronger positive impact on creativity than deactivating mood states such as relaxation. Negative activating moods such as fear or anxiety, on the other hand, were found to be related to lower creativity. Finally, negative deactivating moods such as sadness were not related to creativity.

By contrast, in the study by Isen, Daubman, and Nowicki (1987) mentioned above, there was no effect of arousal on creative problem solving. The authors induced positive, negative, or neutral moods as well as arousal through physical exercise. Participants in a positive mood solved Duncker's candle problem (Duncker & Lees, 1945) more often and scored better on the Remote Associates Test (Mednick & Mednick, 1967) than participants in negative or neutral moods or than participants who were aroused. Thus, aroused individuals did not perform any better.

Perhaps the different findings in the studies by Isen and colleagues (1987) and Baas and colleagues (2008) can be explained by the fact that the studies in the meta-analysis by Baas et al. (2008) did not assess pure physical arousal, but instead looked at activating versus deactivating emotions. Thus, it is possible that pure physical arousal does not have an impact on creativity, whereas arousal with a cognitive component does.

4.6 Motivational Approaches

There are two stages of motivation that mood impacts: selection and realisation motivation. Selection motivation refers to setting goals because they are desirable and realistic, whereas realisation motivation involves planning how to achieve them (e.g., calculating the amount of effort that needs to be invested; Achtziger & Gollwitzer, 2006). Moreover, two different types of task-related motivation moderate the influence of affect on performance: intrinsic and extrinsic motivation. The former comes from inside the individual and "refers to doing something because it is inherently interesting or enjoyable" (Ryan & Deci, 2000,

p. 55), whereas the latter comes from outside the subject and "refers to doing something because it leads to a separable outcome" (Ryan & Deci, 2000, p. 55).

4.6.1 Mood Maintenance and Mood Repair (Isen, 1984)

People seek to maintain or enhance their well-being (Isen, 1984). Thus, healthy individuals try to enhance positive affect and dampen negative affect (Larsen & Prizmic, 2010), thus determining their goal selection and goal striving. According to Isen (1984), the principle of "mood maintenance" typically applies when people are in positive moods, meaning that "positive affect gives rise to strategies designed to maintain that desirable state" (Isen, 1984, p. 198). For a person in a negative mood, the principle of "mood repair" applies, meaning that "negative affect results in strategies aiming to maintain that desirable state" (Isen, 1984, p. 198).

This is in line with the finding that positive affect leads to risk propensity when success is likely and to risk aversion when it is not. This finding can be explained by individuals seeking to maintain a pleasant status quo (Isen & Geva, 1987). This effect is moderated by the subjective value of success: When individuals are in a positive mood, they try to maintain this positive mood (Isen, 1984; Larsen & Prizmic, 2010). Thus, in a positive mood, people take risks only when the probability of success is rather high. However, averaged across mood, the propensity to take a risk does not depend on the probability of success (Isen & Geva, 1987; Isen, Nygren, & Ashby, 1988; Isen & Patrick, 1983).

4.6.2 *The Rubicon Model of Action Phases (Heckhausen & Gollwitzer, 1986, 1987)*

Schwarz and Bohner (1996) discussed some findings concerning mood and motivation against the backdrop of the "Rubicon" model of action phases by Heckhausen and Gollwitzer (1986, 1987). The model posits that there are four action phases that a person follows to meet a goal: forming a goal, planning the required steps, taking those steps, and finally, evaluating goal achievement. In the first phase, the predecisional one, individuals form goals and set priorities. In the second phase, the preactional phase, individuals plan their actions. In the third phase, the actional one, they focus on achieving their goals. Finally, in the fourth phase, the postactional one, they compare what they achieved to what they initially wanted.

Each of these steps is, according to Schwarz and Bohner (1996), influenced by moods. (a) Predecisional phase: In positive moods, goals appear more desirable and are viewed as more achievable than in negative moods. The process of achieving them is interpreted as more pleasant. However, this seems to hold only when people are not aware of the fact that they use their feelings as information. (b) Preactional phase: In positive mood states, people use less information to make a decision to engage in a certain action and are more likely to initiate an action. They use less effortful processing strategies, but also seem to be more flexible in their approach. (c) Actional phase: A task is perpetuated as long as it is perceived as enjoyable, and it is terminated when the goal is achieved (enjoyment goal vs. performance goal). As a default rule, people in positive moods are more likely to have enjoyment goals, whereas people in negative moods are more likely to have performance goals. When given an enjoyment goal (e.g., "work on the task as long as you enjoy it"), people in positive moods will expend more effort on the task and perform better than people in negative moods. When given a performance goal (e.g., "stop when you are satisfied with your performance"), people in negative moods will expend more effort and achieve better performance. (d) Postactional phase: Under a performance-related rule, people terminate their task when the standard is achieved (most likely when positive feelings tell them that this is the case), whereas under an enjoyment-related rule, they continue the task as long as their positive feelings persist. When evaluating their own performance, individuals also rely on moods: They judge their own performance better when they are in a positive mood and worse when they are in a negative mood.

The theory found support from a study (Cunningham, 1988) in which individuals in positive moods were more interested in pleasant activities than the control group. Thus, the positive-mood group had an enjoyment goal. Also in line with the theory, individuals in the positive mood condition had a higher expectancy of success and propensity to invest energy. This supports the idea that individuals in positive moods expend more effort when given an enjoyment goal. This is further supported by the finding that positive affect induces stable task-related (realisation) motivation (Pretty & Seligman, 1984).

Another study (Spieß, 1990) found that negative moods affected self-regulation such that individuals changed their goal structures: Subjects in negative moods preferred emotion-related goals over task-related ones. This applied to both selection and realisation motivation. Accordingly, Pekrun and Frese (1992) found that anxiety decreased intrinsic motivation while simutaneously increasing the external motivation to avoid failure.

4.6.3 Expectancy Theory (Vroom, 1964)

Vroom's expectancy theory (1964) conceptualises motivation as the product of a goal's perceived valence, the perceived instrumentality of the action leading towards the goal, and the perceived expectancy that the effort will lead to success. On the basis of this theory, Erez and Isen (2002) studied the impact that positive affect had on expectancy motivation and performance on an anagram task. Participants in positive moods performed better, persisted longer on the task, and reported higher motivation than subjects in neutral moods. The authors pointed out that this effect is due not only to the higher level of activation in positive affect, but can also be attributed to the cognitive processes underlying the generation of expectancy motivation: Positive affect influences valence, instrumentality, and expectancy, and therefore influences all three components of expectancy motivation.

Their findings were in line with findings reported by Schwarz and Bohner (1996) who concluded that, in positive moods, goals are more attractive, and the opportunities to achieve them are judged more optimistically. Besides, a larger number of ways to achieve them can be seen (due to greater flexibility in thinking).

4.6.4 Seo, Barrett, and Bartunek's (2004) Theory

The theory by Seo, Barrett, and Bartunek (2004) states that there are different direct and indirect paths through which affective feelings affect three dimensions of behavioural outcomes: direction, intensity, and persistence of behaviour. Their theory was tailored to the context of work and organisational psychology.

They presented the concept of "core affect", which they described as "momentary, elementary feelings of pleasure and or displeasure and of activation or deactivation" (Seo et al., 2004, p. 424). Thus, core affect is characterised by a subjective feeling and by activation. Core affect does not necessarily have to be linked to an object.

Core affect directly influences work motivation, but it also exerts an indirect influence on behaviour by influencing judgement components (expectancy judgements, utility judgements, and progress judgements) involved in conscious behavioural choices (e.g., goal setting). The three outcomes that are influenced are (a) direction (choice of alternatives), (b) intensity (effort invested), and (c) persistence (sticking with the chosen alternative).

Behaviour can be directed towards an approach goal or towards an avoidance goal. Seo, Barrett, and Bartunek (2004) referred to the research on the physiological basis of the approach-avoidance system (Gray, 1990) and on the relation between human emotions and the two different action orientations: approach and exploration for positive emotions and avoidance for negative emotions (Fredrickson, 2001).

The authors identified self-regulation (Carver & Scheier, 1998) as the basis of their theory. Self-regulation consists of two subprocesses: a discrepancy-producing process that is induced, for example, by setting a goal, and a discrepancy-reducing process that directs human effort towards discrepancy reduction. They also referred to goal setting theory (Latham & Locke, 1991), which assigns three properties to a goal: (a) Activity is directed towards actions that are relevant for reaching the goal. (b) The effort that is invested in achieving the goal is regulated and adjusted to the difficulty level of the goal. (c) When there are no externally set time limits, persistence is affected (i.e., the time people spend working towards their goal).

Within the process of goal setting, there is a strong influence of emotions. First, emotions influence outcome expectancies.

Positive moods lead to high expectations of positive outcomes and high utility judgements for these outcomes. Thus, the orientation in positive mood states is generative (i.e., directed towards an approach goal). However, negative moods lead to expectations of negative outcomes and high negative utility judgements, which in turn lead to defensive action orientations (i.e., avoidance goals).

Goal striving is also influenced by emotions: As positive moods lead to higher expectations and goal levels and also to greater utility judgements and goal commitment, the amount of effort invested in achieving the goal is greater than in negative moods. Furthermore, as in positive affective states, progress judgements are more favourable such that people in positive moods also persist in working towards their goals for longer periods of time than people in negative moods.

In summary, people in positive moods set higher goals, have a greater expectation of achieving them, and attribute higher values to them than people in negative moods (direction of behaviour). People also invest more effort in goal striving in positive than in negative moods (intensity of behaviour), and finally, after choosing their goal, people stick with their course of action for longer when in positive moods than in negative ones (persistence of behaviour).

In support of this theory, a study (Murray et al., 1990) found that task-related motivation was higher in people in positive moods compared with a control group. Task-related motivation was thus hypothesised to mediate the relation between mood and performance on a categorisation task.

Individuals in negative moods, on the other hand, change from task type to task type more often than those in positive moods (Saavedra & Earley, 1991). Moreover, Klauer, Siemer, and Stöber (1991) found that performance enhancement for people in positive moods was mediated by an elevated propensity to expend effort. Detriments to performance for people in negative moods, on the other hand, were mediated by reduced initiative.

However, negative emotions do not always seem to lead to performance impairments. Anger, for example, can lead to increased effort in sports (Sebej, Mullner, & Farkas, 1985) or when trying the task again the next time (Bandura & Cervone, 1983).

The findings reported here seem to reflect people's everyday notions. Abele (1992) surveyed individuals on their everyday notions of the impact of positive and negative moods on task-related motivation. Individuals reported that positive mood, as compared with negative mood, is related to higher interest in the task, to selecting higher levels of difficulty, and to a more task-related selection motivation. Thus, when selecting a task, individuals in positive moods base their decision on the task itself, whereas people in negative moods base their decisions on other aspects. Moreover, realisation motivation in a positive mood is guided to a greater extent by intrinsic motives, whereas in a negative mood, it is orientated towards the self. In negative moods, completing a task can distract an individual from their negative mood, but this works only for tasks that are fairly easy to complete.

This latter reverse effect was also what Matsumoto and Sanders (1988) were interested in. They found that before and during an intrinsically motivated task, mood was better than before and during an extrinsically motivated task. However, mood was equally good in both conditions after completing the task. Thus, there seems to be a mutual relation between mood and task-related motivation.

Finally, Erber and Tesser (1992) found that mood induction effects can disappear when individuals work on a task very intensely or when the task is very difficult.

4.7 Task Demand-Based Approaches

As outlined earlier, positive mood seems to induce creative, flexible, and holistic thinking styles, whereas negative mood seems to evoke more analytical, detail-oriented, and rigid processing styles (Damasio, 1994; Kuhl, 1983b; Schwarz, 1990). People in positive moods use heuristics more often than people in negative moods, whereas people in negative moods think more systematically (Bless & Fiedler, 1999). Thus, depending on the task demands, there might be an ideal affective state for each kind of task.

There are three theories that posit that the impact of affect on cognitive performance is moderated by task demands: the multifactor-system dynamics theory of emotion (Royce & Diamond, 1980), the dual-force model (Fiedler, 1990b), and the affect infusion model (AIM; Forgas, 1995).

4.7.1 The Multifactor-System Dynamics Theory of Emotion (Royce & Diamond, 1980)

According to this theory, emotion is the product of the interaction of the cognitive and affective systems. The cognitive system is "defined as a multidimensional, hierarchical system that transforms the information in order to detect environmental invariants" (Royce & Diamond, 1980, p. 268), and the affective system is "defined as a multidimensional hierarchical system that transforms information into arousal states" (Royce & Diamond, 1980, p. 268). The two systems are tightly coupled, and the purpose of their interaction is the transformation of information.

The cognitive subsystem is made up of three different subsystems: perceiving, conceptualising, and symbolising; the affective subsystem by the three subsystems emotional stability, emotional independence, and introversion-extraversion. The perceptual system detects physical invariance in the environment. It comprises abilities such as visualisation and spatial scanning. The conceptual system generates concepts and works on the basis of logical consistency. It comprises, for example, verbal and numerical comprehension and reasoning. Finally, the symbolising system creates ideas; it is responsible for fluency of expression and imaginativeness as two examples.

The three cognitive subsystems differ in the extent to which they are affect-laden: According to the authors, symbols are the most affect-laden, followed by percepts, and then concepts. The idea that percepts are less affect-laden than symbols is in line with the neuropsychological theory of positive emotions (Ashby et al., 1999). It assumes that, in comparison with creativity tasks as one example, perceptual tasks are not as susceptible to the influence of affect due to a lack of dopaminergic projections between the respective areas in the brain.

On the basis of Yerkes and Dodson's (1908) findings, the theory also states that there is an ideal arousal level for each kind of performance. This ideal arousal level varies with the kind of task: The easier the task, the higher the optimal arousal level. Royce and Diamond (1980) hypothesised that performance on perceptual tasks would be optimal at high levels of arousal, performance on conceptual tasks would be optimal at intermediate levels of arousal, and performance on symbolising tasks would be optimal at low levels of arousal. The optimum arousal levels should also differ within the three cognitive subsystems depending on the difficulty of the task.

Abele (1995) reported the results of a study by Blomquist (1982). This study was based on Royce and Diamond's (1980) taxonomy. Blomquist (1982) found that individuals performed best on perceptual tasks when the individuals scored low on a calmness scale (and thus high on arousal), whereas they achieved the best results on conceptual tasks when they were high on activation. However, the effects were small.

Abele herself (1995) compared performance on verbal and nonverbal tests requiring the conceptual system to performance on verbal and nonverbal tests requiring the symbolising system. On all the tests, individuals in positive moods outperformed individuals in negative moods. However, the effects were greater on symbolising tasks for both verbal and nonverbal tests. This can be seen as evidence that symbols are more affect-laden than concepts, meaning that the impact of affect on tasks that require the symbolising system is greater than on tasks that require the conceptualising system.

Altogether, however, there is little evidence to support the model. Testing it is likely to be challenging because a lot of parameters have to be taken into account: not only the task type but also the level of arousal. On the other hand, it might provide a promising approach because different levels of arousal can probably explain the seemingly contradictory results found so far on the impact of mood on performance on analytical tasks.

4.7.2 Dual-Force Model (Fiedler, 1990)

The Dual-Force Model (Fiedler, 1990) states that "psychological functioning at various stages (perception, encoding, organisation, recall or reconstruction, editing judgements or communications) can be conceptualised as a synthesis or rivalry of two forces: conservation and active transformation" (Fiedler, 1990, p. 19). At the first stage of information processing, information has to be conserved, but at later stages, it has to be actively transformed on the basis of knowledge from older sources. Conservation happens, for example, during perception or encoding tasks. A classical problem-solving task has conservation elements (there is "input" information that starts the problem-solving process), but the portion of active transformation is a lot larger. According to Fiedler (1990), different tasks allocate different weights to conservation and active transformation. He holds that active transformation, but not information conservation, is susceptible to emotional influences. This means that when the portion of active transformation in a task is larger, the processing of the task is influenced by emotions to a greater extent.

Fiedler (1990) did not classify different tasks according to the different amounts of conservation and active transformation they require, but he indicated that it is possible to do so by developing criteria for this. He offered a rough classification for ordering experimental tasks with respect to the involvement of productive task elements (see Table 2).

Table 2
Inequalities for Ordering Experimental Tasks with Respect to the Involvement of Productive Task Elements (adapted from Fiedler, 1990, p. 6, Printed With Permission)

Reproductive	⟷	**Productive**
Recognition	<	Recall
Cued recall	<	Free recall
Memory task	<	Judgment task
Unambivalent stimuli	<	Ambivalent stimuli
Experimenter-provided	<	Self-generated
Highly organized material	<	Poorly structured material
Pictorial representation	<	Symbolic representation
Restricted knowledge base	<	Large knowledge base
Automatic reactions	<	Controlled reactions

There are a number of empirical implications he drew from his hypotheses. As mentioned above, a greater amount of active transformation implies a greater influence of emotional states. This implies that emotions have a greater influence on the processing of newly acquired information that is only loosely tied to semantic memory compared with the processing of "old" information. The same holds for ambivalent stimuli when compared with clear information and memory-based judgements compared with memory recall or recognition tasks.

He suggested that the phenomenon of different cognitive styles in different moods could also be integrated into his model (Fiedler, Nickel, Asbeck, & Pagel, 2003): A person's thinking style in a negative mood is stimulus-driven and thus bottom up (accomodation). It is more exact and less prone to errors than a person's thinking style when in a positive mood. A person's thinking style in a positive mood, by contrast, is knowledge-driven and allows for more creativity and productivity when completing novel tasks (assimilation). In this respect, these ideas are in line with the findings from brain science reported earlier relating negative affect to bottom-up and positive affect to top-down processes (Kuhbandner et al., 2009). There is evidence from Fiedler and colleagues (Fiedler et al., 2003) supporting this part of the model. This part of the model is also supported by the studies that were reported earlier on knowledge versus stimulus-driven processing strategies (Bless et al., 1996; Isen & Means, 1983; Sinclair, 1988).

However, Fiedler (1990) remained vague about the other aspects of the model. As already mentioned, there is no classification of tasks on the continuum between reproductive and productive; merely some classification criteria. There is some evidence for the relevance of these criteria. For example, the effects of mood-dependent recall are stronger for self-generated than for experimenter-provided material (Fiedler et al., 2003). However, further evidence is lacking. What can be said so far is that the model has been validated only with respect to memory tasks (the context for which it was originally developed) but not for other tasks such as creative, analytical, or perceptual ones.

4.7.3 Affect Infusion Model (AIM; Forgas, 1995)

With his affect infusion model (AIM; Forgas, 1995), Forgas proposed that there are four different information processing strategies—direct access, motivated, heuristic, and substantive processing—that are arranged along a continuum. The degree to which affect infuses judgements depends on where on the continuum information processing takes place, with heuristic or substantive processing being more prone to the impact of affect than direct access or motivated processing.

He defined affect infusion as "the process whereby affectively loaded information exerts an influence on and becomes incorporated into the judgmental process, entering into the judge's deliberations and eventually coloring the judgmental outcome" (Forgas, 1995, p. 39). Similar to Fiedler (1990), he posited that affect infusion is more likely to occur on tasks that require active transformation than on ones that require mere reproduction. On the basis of this idea, he defined the aforementioned information processing strategies: (a) direct access processing: directly retrieving pre-existing information that appears when dealing with highly familiar material; (b) motivated processing: striving towards a predefined goal and using highly predetermined information search patterns and little generative processes; (c) heuristic processing: using simple rule-of-thumb strategies when accuracy or detailed considerations are not necessary; and (d) substantive processing: using a generative processing strategy. He posited that mood-congruent judgements should happen only in the latter two processing modes.

There are two ways in which affect infuses judgement: the affect-priming principle (Ellis & Ashbrook, 1988) and the affect-as-information principle (Schwarz, 1990). The affect-priming principle influences substantive processing through directing attention, encoding, retrieving, and associative processing. The affect-as-information principle has an impact on heuristic processing in that feelings are used to make judgements, thus applying a shortcut that avoids more elaborate processing.

One of the basic assumptions of the model is the notion that humans are "cognitive misers", meaning that, whenever possible, they use the simplest and least effortful information processing strategy. This notion is also at the core of a wide range of recent literature on human decision making (e.g., Kahneman, 2012; Stanovich, 2009).

The variables determining which processing strategy is applied are target features, judge features, and situational features. Figure 12 depicts the model.

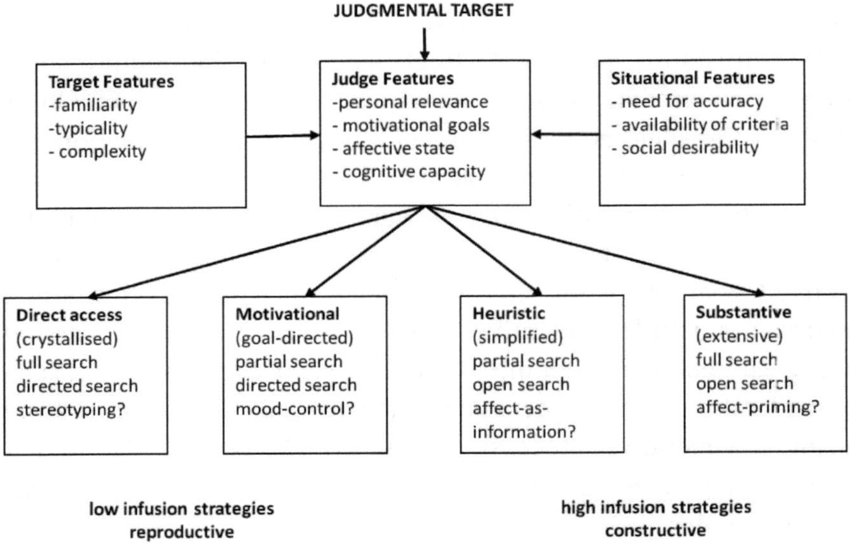

Figure 12. Outline of the multiprocess affect infusion model (Adapted from Forgas, 1995, p. 48). Printed with permission.

Target features are familiarity, typicality, and complexity. The more familiar the target, the more likely an individual will be to use the direct access strategy. Typical targets will be processed heuristically, whereas complex ones will be judged on the basis of substantive processing.

The judge features are personal relevance, motivational goals, affective state, and cognitive capacity. When the task is personally relevant and motivation is given, the individual will use the motivational processing strategy, whereas the person will use the substantive processing mode in the absence of motivation. When there is no personal relevance, the individual will use direct access processing when the target is familiar and heuristic processing when it is not.

A strong, pre-existing motivation will considerably reduce affect infusion. With respect to cognitive capacity, the model predicts that when individuals are under cognitive overload, they are more likely to use a heuristic processing strategy. Finally, affective state refers to the fact that processing strategies are impacted by an individual's current affect, meaning that information processing will be more heuristic and creative in positive moods and more careful and substantive in negative moods. Moreover, affect limits cognitive capacity (Ellis & Ashbrook, 1988).

Finally, the situational features are characterised by the need for accuracy, the availability of criteria, and social desirability. For example, when judgement outcomes are going to be evaluated by others, substantive processing is likely to occur. However, this is where the description of the model by Forgas (1995) becomes vague.

There is a fair bit of evidence supporting the model. For example, when Forgas (2002) compared cognitively demanding and not so demanding social judgement tasks, it became obvious that the effect of mood was greater on the more demanding tasks. In another study, individuals in positive moods rated their partners' video-taped behaviours more positively than individuals in negative moods (Forgas, Bower, & Krantz, 1984). In general, individuals in negative moods are less likely to fall for the fundamental attribution error, and their judgements are more accurate and based on facts compared with individuals in positive moods (for an overview of the findings, see Forgas, 2008).

The AIM has received much criticism from Isen (2002). For example, Isen wrote that the idea of superficial and lazy information processing in positive affect goes against the findings from the literature. Moreover, in her opinion, motivation is not something that is used to overcome the detrimental effects of positive mood on problem solving. Rather, in her opinion, one cannot say that motivation for effortful processing is generally low when a person is experiencing positive affect. However, in this respect, the model reflects the conclusion of a 2005 meta-analysis by Lyubomirski and colleagues (Lyubomirski et al., 2005): "the evidence shows that people experiencing happy moods have potential deficits when it comes to problem solving, but they can overcome these deficits if they are motivated to perform well at the task" (p. 840).

4.8 An Integrative Model: The Cognitive-Motivational Mediator Model of the Impact of Mood on Cognitive Performance (Abele, 1995)

Abele (1995) integrated several of the approaches described above into her model. She made two basic assumptions concerning the impact of moods on cognitive performance: (1) Mood-contingent (a) cognitive and (b) motivational processes mediate the relation between mood and performance. (2) The influences of mood on performance vary depending on the task requirements.

(1a) Cognitive processes comprise a number of different mechanisms: The actual mood state is used by the individual to assess the current match between the self and one's environment. A positive mood informs the individual that everything is going well, whereas a negative mood points to the fact that something is going wrong (Schwarz, 1990). Furthermore, mood influences the encoding and retrieval of information (mood-contingent encoding and recall; Bless & Fiedler, 1999; mood as context; Isen, 1984). Finally, mood-induced thinking styles influence the way in which information is processed: intuitive-holistically in a positive mood, sequential-analytically in a negative mood (Kuhl, 1983b).

(1b) Motivational processes comprise motivation for selecting and motivation for realising a task. According to Abele (1995), when people are to complete a cognitive task, selection motivation does not play a role because the goal is already set (the goal is to complete the test). Thus, only realisation motivation is relevant. This aspect of motivation expresses how much effort a person will expend on the task. Abele (1995) distinguished between intrinsic and extrinsic motivation such that individuals in a positive mood are intrinsically motivated and generally willing to expend effort, whereas subjects in a negative mood are motivated extrinsically with fluctuating willingness to expend effort.

(2) Finally, there is an interaction between type of task and the above-mentioned cognitive and motivational processes. For each type of task, there is a mood that is most appropriate for meeting the task's requirements. To classify the tasks, she used Royce and Diamond's (1980) model, which postulates three different kinds of tasks that call for different processing systems. These systems are the perceptual system, the conceptual system, and the symbol system.

On the basis of her model, she conducted several studies investigating performance on perceptual, conceptual, and symbolising tasks in positive versus negative versus neutral moods. She predicted that performance would be better on all types of tasks for people in positive moods. In addition, she predicted that impaired performance on symbolising tasks for people in negative moods would be compensated by high levels of extrinsic motivation.

These studies will be reported in the following sections, along with other studies supporting or contradicting her findings.

4.8.1 Affect and Perceptual Speed

In the first study on processing speed, Abele (1995) found no main effect of mood. When she used a repeated-measures design—first having participants complete the test, then inducing different moods, and then having them re-do the test—she found that performance improved most in participants in positive moods, followed by the control group, and then by the participants in negative moods.

This finding is contrasted by a study by Kuhbandner and colleagues (Kuhbandner et al., 2009) in which they studied how the temporal threshold for access to conscious perception changes with different moods. They found that this temporal threshold decreased with negative mood and increased with positive mood, indicating that the perceptual system was more sensitive to incoming cues when people were in negative than in positive moods. Thus, individuals in negative moods outperformed individuals in positive moods in their study.

4.8.2 Affect and Creativity

Abele (1995) used Duncker's candle problem (Duncker & Lees, 1945) in one of her studies and found that participants in positive moods solved the problem more often and more quickly than participants in negative moods. The control group had the worst performance. However, the differences between negative and control group were not significant.

On two verbal creativity tests, participants in positive moods produced a higher number of ideas and more original ideas than the control group. Individuals in positive moods even produced more ideas with negative valence (which contradicts the notion of mood congruency; Bower, 1981). When she used a creativity task in which positive or negative associations had to be made, she found that participants in negative moods performed better than the control group when positive associations had to be made, but they performed worse when negative associations had to be made. This finding is in line with the finding that people in negative moods try to improve their mood (Larsen & Prizmic, 2010). She also found that participants in positive moods showed more intrinsic interest in the task, whereas participants in negative moods showed more extrinsic interest in the task. The latter saw the task as a means for improving their mood. A reward had no impact on positively tempered individuals' task motivation, but decreased the task motivation of negatively tempered individuals (overjustification effect; Lepper, Greene, & Nisbett, 1973).

Abele (1995) investigated this effect more closely using a repeated-measures design and assessed the number and originality of words produced in the first versus second trial when there was a reward versus when there was none. With respect to the number of words produced, she found that participants in the positive mood condition improved from the first to the second trial no matter whether there was a reward or not. The performance of participants in the control group decreased when there was a reward but improved when there was none. In the control condition, there was a slight deterioration in performance, but the presence or absence of a reward had no effect. With respect to the originality of the words, there was only a main effect of mood: improvement in the positive mood condition, no change in the control group, and deterioration in the negative mood condition. She also found an inverse relation between the number of mood-related thoughts and performance.

These findings are in line with the other findings on mood and creativity: Performance on creativity tasks is better when people are in positive than in negative or neutral moods (Baas et al., 2008; Davis, 2009; Isen et al., 1987).

4.8.3 Affect and Reasoning

Abele (1995) found that positive mood was beneficial for performance on a verbal reasoning test (finding similarities). She chose a repeated-measures design because of high interindividual differences in test performance and found that participants in the positive mood condition increased their numbers of correct solutions from the first to the second trial, whereas the performance of individuals in the negative mood condition decreased, and there was no significant change in the control condition. Specifically, positive mood led to improvements on items of easy and medium difficulty compared with the negative mood and control conditions, whereas the performance impairment found in the negative mood condition was due to decreased performance on items of high difficulty. There was no difference in performance on easy items between the negative mood group and the control group. Generally speaking, the effect was due to an increase in the number of correct solutions in the positive mood condition and decreases in speed and the number of correct solutions in the negative mood condition.

In two follow-up experiments, one with a verbal and one with a figural reasoning task, Abele (1995) replicated the findings described above: Participants in a positive mood performed better than participants in a negative mood and the control group on a reasoning test. The effect was due to the higher number of correct solutions (higher accuracy) for items of low and medium difficulty in the positive mood condition (compared with the negative mood group and the control group) and fewer correct solutions for items of medium and high difficulty in the negative mood condition (compared with the positive mood group and the control group).

By contrast, Melton (1995) hypothesised (a) that people in positive moods expend less effort on a task than people in negative or neutral moods and thus use more effort-saving heuristics or (b) that positive thoughts and feelings distract people in positive moods from their task. He based his hypotheses on a number of previous findings. First, people in positive moods are motivated to maintain this mood (Isen, Means, Patrick, & Nowicki, 1982). From this, he concluded that they would not be willing to expend effort on a task that they considered to be "no fun". Second, people use positive mood as an indicator that everything is fine (Schwarz & Clore, 1988). On the basis of this idea, he reasoned that they tend not to critically evaluate the conclusions they come to. Rather, because of their positive mood, they consider their conclusions to be appropriate. Third, people in positive moods judge information more superficially and tend to base their judgements on characteristics of the communicator rather than on the contents of the information (Mackie & Worth, 1989).

In his study, he compared subjects in a positive mood to individuals in a neutral mood. Positive mood was induced either by reading a comic strip or by listening to a comedian. Afterwards, he assessed mood. Subjects in the control group only completed the mood assessment. Then all participants were given 10 min to complete 10 syllogism tasks. He found that people in a positive mood performed significantly worse on the syllogism tasks than participants in the control condition. Compared with controls, the people in a positive mood made more universal judgements that actually required more careful processing according to Melton (1995). He also found that the subjects in a positive mood had more of a tendency to evaluate the information on the basis of the "atmosphere heuristic". In summary, he concluded that individuals in a positive mood were not willing to expend effort on the task and that maybe they were also distracted from the task.

There are several problems with this study. Subjects in the positive mood condition either read cartoons or listened to a comedian as induction procedures and then completed a short questionnaire assessing their mood. Subjects in the control condition, however, were not exposed to a comparable procedure before filling out their mood questionnaire. Therefore, individuals in the positive condition had already been placed under cognitive load, whereas individuals in the control condition were still fresh. Moreover, his results do not clearly indicate whether the performance deficit in the positive condition was really due the valence of the mood or just due to the fact that individuals experienced affect versus no affect.

In favour of the latter idea, there is evidence that the intensity of affect impacts performance beyond its valence: Riediger and colleagues (Riediger, Wrzus, Schmiedek, Wagner, & Lindenberger, 2011) had individuals complete working memory tasks after assessing their current mood and found nonlinear relations between the intensity of affect and working memory performance. Moderate positive or negative affect was associated with better working memory performance than high positive or negative affect. The valence of the affect did not make a difference. However, effects were small for people with a pro-hedonic orientation (i.e., the tendency to pursue positive affect), which applies to individuals in most cases. Effects were greater for people with a contra-hedonic orientation (i.e., the tendency to strive for or to maintain negative affect), which is sometimes necessary because it is socially appropriate or otherwise instrumental.

In another study, Radenhausen and Anker (1988) induced positive, negative, or neutral moods using the Velten technique.

They found that individuals in positive moods performed better on a syllogism task than individuals in negative moods. There was no significant difference between the negative mood group and the control group, indicating that negative mood has a limited effect on performance on such a task, whereas positive affect does have an impact. Subjects performed better on neutral than on positive or negative syllogisms, but the authors did not find interaction effects between mood and syllogism type.

Thus, whereas it is not clear whether the results from Melton's (1995) study can really be ascribed to the valence of the mood, other studies have indicated that positive mood is beneficial for performance unless it becomes very intense.

Abele's (1995) model integrates many of the previous findings on mood and performance. Her results show that the predictions made from the model are accurate and testable, and the results she found are in line with the predictions. However, the model does not explain the somewhat contradictory results found for reasoning performance. A possible explanation could be that she did not consider one of the factors from Royce and Diamond's (1980) model: arousal. The theory states that for each type of task (symbolic, conceptual, perceptual), there is an ideal state of arousal. Melton (1995) reasoned that individuals in a positive mood were not willing to expend a lot of effort on their task and were likely to be distracted from the task. In the study by Radenhausen and Anker (1988), on the other hand, individuals in a positive mood were apparently willing to expend effort and were able to concentrate enough to perform well. This could be due to their higher level of arousal. Radenhausen and Anker (1988) used the Velten technique to induce mood, and a study by Jennings et al. (2000) showed that the Velten technique leads to higher arousal in people in a positive mood. Arousal in turn was shown to narrow the focus of attention (Easterbrook, 1959). Thus, perhaps different levels of arousal explain the contradictory findings. This would provide an alternative to the previous explanation, which was that it was not possible to determine whether the performance deficit in the positive condition was really due to the valence of the mood or just due to the fact that individuals experienced affect versus no affect.

Therefore, perhaps hypotheses on the relation of mood and performance need to be more specific such that not only the valence of mood has to be taken into consideration but also arousal. For creativity, Baas et al. (2008) showed that activating positive affective states enhance performance on creativity tasks more than deactivating positive affective states do.

This finding is also in line with the conclusions Lyubomirski and her colleagues (Lyubomirski et al., 2005) drew in their meta-analysis after reviewing the literature on the benefits of positive affect: They saw an important topic for future investigation in distinguishing between positive and negative emotions on a general level as well as between specific positive and negative emotions such as contentment and joy or sadness and anger. According to them, the question is whether the results found so far apply to all positive emotions or only to those high in arousal. They also stated that the studies they reviewed hardly ever made a distinction between emotions and moods, so the authors wondered whether emotions and moods differ in the impacts they have on cognition and behaviour.

4.9 Discrete Emotions and Cognitive Performance

All the research reported so far has been on mood, and there have been no studies on discrete emotions. To date, emotions seem to have been studied only in academic settings. Thus, to obtain some background information on how discrete emotions (beyond test anxiety) impact performance, a theory and a few studies from academic settings will be reported in the following section.

The control value theory of achievement emotions (Pekrun, 2006) was developed for predicting learning and achievement in academic settings. It is based on the assumption that motivation, perceived control, goals, and their value as well as emotions jointly impact performance.

According to the model, emotions can be classified along three dimensions: valence, activation, and point in time at which they occur. Along the valence and activation dimensions, emotions can be classified into four categories: (a) positive-activating emotions (e.g., enjoyment), (b) positive-deactivating emotions (e.g., relief), (c) negative-activating emotions (e.g., anger), and (d) negative-deactivating emotions (e.g., hopelessness; Feldman Barrett & Russell, 1998).

Brehm (1999) proposed a similar classification of emotions in which happiness (which he did not differentiate further) and sadness are passive emotions, whereas anger is an active emotion. Similarly, Carver (2004) associated eagerness (positive emotion) and frustration and anger (negative emotions) with high engagement and elation (positive emotion) and sadness and depression (negative emotions) with low engagement.

Moreover, classifications along the point-in-time dimension have resulted in three categories: Prospective outcome emotions occur prior to the performance situation and refer to future performance. Activity-related emotions occur during the performance situation. Finally, retrospective outcome emotions occur after the performance situation and refer to its outcome (i.e., success or failure).

According to the model, the emotions that an individual experiences before, during, and after a performance situation can be predicted by how the person evaluates the situation (positively vs. negatively) or its result (approach vs. avoidance goal), respectively, and by the person's perceived control. For example, for an individual who has high perceived control and expects success, the model predicts anticipatory joy. By contrast, for an individual who is low on perceived control and expects failure, it predicts hopelessness.

Performance emotions in turn impact motivation and effort as well as a person's use of learning strategies and self-regulation (Pekrun, Elliot, & Maier, 2009). Positive emotions such as joy, hope, and pride have a positive impact on motivation, use of flexible learning strategies, self-regulation, and availability of cognitive resources. By contrast, negative-activating emotions such as anger, anxiety, or guilt reduce a person's use of flexible learning strategies, self-regulation, and cognitive resources. On the one hand, such negative emotions reduce intrinsic motivation, but on the other hand, they enhance a person's extrinsic motivation to avoid failure. Thus, negative-activating emotions do not necessarily impair performance; rather, the effects are complex. Negative-deactivating emotions such as boredom or hopelessness, however, have a negative impact on a person's use of learning strategies, self-regulation, and availability of cognitive resources and thus always impair performance.

Another factor that needs to be considered when looking at emotions and performance is the individual's goals. In academic settings, one can distinguish between mastery goals and performance goals (Pekrun et al., 2009). Mastery goals focus attention on the current activity and its positive value, thus evoking positive and preventing negative emotions (Pekrun et al., 2009). Performance goals focus attention on the outcome of the activity and can be further divided into performance-approach and performance-avoidance goals (Pekrun et al., 2009). Performance-approach goals (achieving success) focus attention on the controllability of the situation and the positive value of the outcomes and are thus likely to evoke positive outcome emotions (e.g., pride) once the task is finished. Performance-avoidance goals (avoiding failure), on the other hand, focus attention on the uncontrollability of the situation and the negative value of the outcomes and are thus likely to evoke negative outcome emotions (e.g., disappointment) once the task is finished.

The studies by Pekrun and colleagues (Pekrun et al., 2009) confirmed the hypotheses that emotions mediate the impact of performance goals on performance. The relation between performance-approach goals and performance was mediated by the emotions hope and pride. The relation between performance-avoidance goals and performance was mediated by the negative emotions hope, pride, anger, anxiety, hopelessness, and shame. Thus, emotions mediate the relations between both performance-approach and performance-avoidance goals and performance.

The authors concluded that emotions substantially impact academic achievement beyond ability and motivation (see also Pekrun, 2006; Zeidner, 1998). They maintained that the relations are clearer when looking at distinct emotions instead of positive versus negative affect (see also Linnenbrink, 2007).

This idea is in line with studies on emotions and academic performance: In a literature review, Yasutake and Bryan (1995) found that positive emotions led to more accurate math performance and better learning of vocabulary. Negative-deactivating emotions, on the other hand, led to the selection of less difficult goals and to taking less action and were thus detrimental to performance (Turner, Thorpe, & Meyer, 1998).

4.10 Summary of Theories and Findings

This chapter presented different theoretical approaches for predicting and explaining how affect and cognition interact to impact performance outcomes and the empirical findings supporting or questioning them. The key points will be summarised in the following sections.

Results from brain science support the idea that there is a close connection between affect and cognition (Klinger, 1996). More specifically, affect and arousal impact memory, working memory, and creative problem solving via dopaminergic and noradrenergic pathways (Ashby et al., 1999; Flaherty, 2005; Kimberg et al., 1997). Moreover, information processing in positive moods is top-down, whereas it is bottom-up in negative moods (Kuhbandner et al., 2009).

This is in line with what cognitive approaches and their findings suggest: Thinking is intuitive-heuristic for people in positive moods and sequential-analytical for people in negative moods (Damasio, 1994; Isen, 1984; Kuhl, 1983a, b; Schwarz, 1990). This implies that problem solving is faster and more efficient in positive moods, particularly when dealing with previously learned material because, in this case, efficient heuristics may be used, and when dealing with difficult or complex tasks that require the processing of several stimuli or pieces of information at the same time. On the other hand, negative mood implies a more thorough problem-solving approach that is less superficial and slower but also less error-prone.

Aside from mood-dependent encoding and state-dependent recall (Bower, 1981), memory approaches predict that encoding and recall are better in positive moods than in negative moods (Clark & Isen, 1982; Isen, 1984; Schwarz, 1990). The concept of cognitive context (Isen, 1984) and the broaden-and-build theory of positive emotions (Fredrickson, 1998, 2001) also suggest that individuals experiencing positive affect have access to a wider array of thoughts and actions than individuals in a negative mood. In addition, individuals experiencing positive affect have a more holistic as opposed to a detail-oriented view of things (Fredrickson & Branigan, 2005). These approaches predict better performance on creativity tasks for people in positive moods, a finding that has been consistently demonstrated in research and has also been confirmed by some more recent meta-analyses (Baas et al., 2008; Davis, 2009).

Attention-theoretical approaches consider attention to be a limited resource that needs to be divided between different tasks (Easterbrook, 1959; Ellis & Ashbrook, 1988). When a person experiences negative affect, self-relevant thoughts and strategies that are applied to overcome the bad mood consume part of this limited capacity (Ellis & Ashbrook, 1988). Moreover, in intense emotional states, not taking into account valence, capacity for the task at hand is limited (Easterbrook, 1959). This approach predicts that performance on tasks that require a lot of capacity (e.g., complex tasks) will be impaired in people in negative or intense affective states. It also predicts that attention will narrow with increasing arousal.

Activation-theoretical approaches (Yerkes & Dodson, 1908) claim that different tasks have different ideal levels of arousal. For reaction-time tasks, arousal has been found to be detrimental (Larsen & Diener, 1987; Schneider, 1987), whereas it is beneficial for information processing, working memory, and memory tasks (Lambourne & Tomporowski, 2010; Onyper et al., 2011). Pure physical arousal does not seem to be beneficial for creativity tasks (Isen et a., 1987), whereas activating emotions seem to be (Baas et al., 2008).

Motivational approaches (Carver & Scheier, 1998; Erez & Isen, 2002; Gray, 1990; Schwarz & Bohner, 1996; Seo et al., 2004) claim that individuals in positive moods set higher goals, see those goals as more desirable, and are more optimistic about achieving them than subjects in negative moods. Subjects in positive moods are intrinsically motivated, and thus the best motivator for them is an enjoyment goal; whereas individuals in negative moods are extrinsically motivated, and the best motivator for them is a performance goal (Erez & Isen, 2002). This idea is also in line with the concept of mood maintenance and mood repair (Isen, 1984): Individuals in a positive mood strive to maintain this mood state, whereas subjects in a negative mood try to overcome their negative state. In general, individuals in a positive mood invest more effort in the task and stick with it for longer than individuals in a negative mood.

Task-demand-based approaches (Fiedler, 1990; Forgas, 1995; Royce & Diamond, 1980) posit that the degree to which affect impacts performance depends on the type of task. Its impact is highest on tasks that require active transformation of information or creating ideas, whereas it is lower on tasks that require only automated processing or the mere reproduction of contents. In addition, some researchers have claimed that for different types of tasks, different levels of arousal are optimal: high levels for perceiving, intermediate levels for conceptualising, and low levels for symbolising (Royce & Diamond, 1980).

The integrative model (Abele, 1995) integrates most of the above-mentioned approaches in that it predicts access to broader cognitive contents and an intuitive-heuristic processing style for people in positive moods and a sequential-analytic processing style for people in negative moods. Selection motivation does not play a role in test completion because the goal is already selected; however, realisation motivation is higher in positive than in negative moods. Finally, there are differential impacts of mood on performance, depending on which type of task is completed.

The only approach linking discrete emotions and performance comes from an academic setting (Pekrun, 2006). It distinguishes between positive and negative emotions on the one hand and between activating and deactivating emotions on the other hand. A third distinction concerns the point in time: before, during, or after taking the test. Positive emotions increase motivation and thus increase performance. Negative-deactivating emotions impair motivation and thus decrease performance. Negative-activating emotions, however, increase performance motivation and therefore are not detrimental to performance.

5 The Present Study

5.1 Hypotheses on Emotions and Test Performance

Hypotheses on the impact of discrete emotions on test performance were derived from the circumplex model of affect (Larsen & Diener, 1992; Russell, 1980; Thayer, 1996; Watson & Tellegen, 1985) and its two dimensions valence and activation.

With respect to valence, Abele's (1995) comprehensive model claims two pathways by which mood impacts cognition: a cognitive one and a motivational one. There is evidence for performance enhancement and performance impairment through both paths. The processing style of a person in a positive mood is intuitive-heuristic, and this allows the person to process several stimuli at a time, thus leading to less thorough and therefore more efficient information processing. The processing style of a person in a negative mood is sequential-analytical, thus enabling the person to apply a more thorough and less error-prone processing style but also one that is slower and less efficient. Proponents of mood-induced thinking styles (Damasio, 1994; Isen, 1984; Kuhl, 1983a, b; Schwarz, 1990) posit that the latter processing style leads to better performance on easy tasks because it is less error-prone, whereas the former yields improved performance on tasks of medium and high difficulty because it allows for the simultaneous processing of several stimuli. Isen, Daubman, and Nowicki (1987), however, found that individuals in positive moods performed significantly better only on items of medium difficulty on the Remote Associates Test. Abele's (1995) results in turn demonstrated that individuals in positive moods outperform subjects in negative moods on items of all three levels of difficulty. Radenhausen and Anker (1988) and Melton (1995) executed studies in which they did not differentiate between difficulty levels. The results by Abele

(1995), Radenhausen and Anker (1988), and Isen, Daubman, and Nowicki (1987) suggest that the overall performance of individuals in positive moods is better than the performance of individuals in negative moods.

In addition, there is the notion that positive affect provides access to more and broader content in memory (Clark & Isen, 1982; Isen, 1984; Schwarz, 1990). However, this finding may be more relevant for creativity tasks and thus not relevant for deriving hypotheses about IQ test performance.

Attention-theoretical approaches predict that performance should be worse for people in a negative mood compared with positive and neutral moods (Ellis & Ashbrook, 1988). According to these theories, this decline can be explained by the attentional capacity that is directed to task-irrelevant processes in negative moods.

The neuropsychological theory of positive emotions (Ashby et al., 1999) posits that working memory is best when affect is moderate and positive. Many researchers consider working memory to be at the core of reasoning performance (Ackerman, Beier, & Boyle, 2005); therefore, this theory would predict that reasoning test performance would be best for people experiencing moderate positive affect.

With respect to the motivational pathway, on the one hand, researchers have found that individuals in positive moods set higher goals, are more optimistic, experience higher self-efficacy, and invest more effort into achieving their goals (Erez & Isen, 2002; Schwarz & Bohner, 1996; Seo et al., 2004), all of which in turn positively impact performance. On the other hand, they are not as motivated to use effortful processing strategies as individuals in negative moods (Forgas, 2002; Schwarz & Clore, 1988). Enjoyment goals act as motivators for individuals in positive moods, whereas performance goals motivate subjects in negative moods

(Schwarz & Bohner, 1996). The majority of studies have found that individuals show higher motivation when they are in positive moods than in negative moods (Abele, 1995; Erez & Isen, 2002; Schwarz & Bohner, 1996; Seo et al., 2004). Thus, it seems that positive moods enhance performance more than negative moods do.

Therefore, when comparing emotions with opposite valences but with comparable levels of activation, I hypothesized:

> **Hypothesis 1:** Performance on an IQ test will be better for participants experiencing a positive-activating emotion than for participants experiencing a negative-activating emotion.
>
> **Hypothesis 2:** Performance on an IQ test will be better for participants experiencing a positive-deactivating emotion than for participants experiencing a negative-deactivating emotion.

What Abele's (1995) model does not take into account is the arousal component of mood. Studies that have reported on arousal and performance point to the fact that increased arousal leads to more focused attention (Easterbrook, 1959). In addition, it leads to improved memory and working memory (Lambourne & Tomporowski, 2010; Onyper et al., 2011). Evidence for this fact comes from brain science studies in which higher arousal was found to be associated with increased dopamine and noradrenalin levels, both of which are associated with memory and working memory capacity (Chamberlain et al., 2006; Flaherty, 2005; Kimberg et al., 1997). Moreover, studies that have induced arousal in individuals have repeatedly shown that performance on memory and working memory tasks improves after people are exposed to physically arousing stimuli (Lambourne & Tomporowski, 2010; Onyper et al., 2011).

Moreover, Pekrun (2006) classified emotions into activating (e.g., joy and anger) and deactivating (e.g., contentment and sadness) emotions and found that motivation and consequently performance were higher when people experienced activating emotions than deactivating ones. This is backed by the finding that anger can lead to increased effort (Bandura & Cervone, 1983; Sebej et al., 1985).

Therefore, when comparing emotions with different activation levels but the same valence, I hypothesized:

> **Hypothesis 3:** Performance on an IQ test will be better for participants experiencing a positive-activating emotion than for participants experiencing a positive-deactivating emotion.
> **Hypothesis 4:** Performance on an IQ test will be better for participants experiencing a negative-activating emotion than for participants experiencing a negative-deactivating emotion.

The emotions that were used as positive-activating, negative-activating, positive-deactivating, and negative-deactivating emotions will be discussed in detail below.

5.2 Considerations about the Design of the Study

The purpose of the present study was to investigate discrete emotions on an unsupervised online test. Abele (1995) had worked with a repeated-measures design that allowed her to control for interindividual differences in the underlying ability. Therefore, I chose to use a repeated-measures design here as well. The intelligence test that was used was adaptive, with items generated automatically at run-time so that the second test would provide a parallel version of the first test, and thus, training effects would be minimized.

To choose an emotion induction method, I considered Göritz's (2007) conclusions about online mood induction: The effects of online mood inductions are smaller than the effects of offline mood inductions. Therefore, I decided to use the strongest method available. According to the meta-analysis by Westermann and colleagues (Westermann et al., 1996), the most effective methods for eliciting both positive and negative moods are stories and films. As internet users tend to scan rather than thoroughly read online material (Gräf, 2002), I decided to use film clips as the stimulus material. These were also the only stimuli that had previously been shown to evoke discrete emotions.

5.2.1 Selection of the Film Clips

Gross and Levenson (1995) had identified several films that evoked the emotions amusement, anger, contentment, disgust, fear, sadness, surprise, and a neutral emotional state. All of them are comparable in intensity according to Plutchik's (2001) model. I had to decide which film clips to use in the current study. It was obvious that a clip inducing a neutral state was to be included. For the other emotions, again, the circumplex model of affect was used. It combines the two dimensions of valence and activation into four emotion quadrants: pleasant-activated (e.g., excited, elated), pleasant-deactivated (e.g., calm, relaxed), unpleasant-activated (e.g., tense, nervous), and unpleasant-deactivated (e.g., tired, bored; Yik et al., 1999). After comparing these emotions to the emotions resulting from the above-mentioned models, I decided to use amusement (or joy) as the positive-activating emotion, contentment as the positive-deactivating emotion, anger as the negative-activating emotion, and sadness as the negative-deactivating emotion.

On the basis of this selection, the hypotheses were concretised as follows:

> **Hypothesis 1:** Performance on an IQ test will be better for participants in the emotional state of joy than for participants in the emotional state of anger.
> **Hypothesis 2:** Performance on an IQ test will be better for participants in the emotional state of contentment than for participants in the emotional state of sadness.
> **Hypothesis 3:** Performance on an IQ test will be better for participants in the emotional state of joy than for participants in the emotional state of contentment.
> **Hypothesis 4:** Performance on an IQ test will be better for participants in the emotional state of anger than for participants in the emotional state of sadness.

For each emotion, there were two clips. From those, five that were about equivalent in length were chosen: "When Harry Met Sally" (Joy), "The Champ" (Sadness), "Cry Freedom" (Anger), "Waves" (Contentment), and "Abstract Shapes" (Neutral).

5.2.2 Manipulation Check

Otto's (2000) recommendation was followed for conducting manipulation checks directly after induction. The Multidimensional Mood Questionnaire (MDMQ; Steyer et al., 1997) was used to assess moods because it has three dimensions and thus provides the most differentiated measurement of mood. The Test Emotions Questionnaire (TEQ; Pekrun et al., 2004) was used to assess emotions because it assesses test-related rather than general emotions. However, because internet users are not willing to expend a lot of time and effort in filling out questionnaires and tend to display uniform response patterns when completing long matrix-like questionnaires (Gräf, 2002), both tests were too long for use on the internet. In addition, the TEQ is not suitable for a nonacademic setting because many items refer to exams or marks (e.g., "I look forward to exams" or "My marks embarrass me"). Therefore, I decided to design internet adaptations of both questionnaires. This was done in two pilot studies that will be described in detail in the following chapter.

6 Pilot Studies

6.1 Pilot Study 1: Design of an Online Mood Questionnaire

The Multidimensional Mood Questionnaire (MDMQ; Steyer et al., 1997) was used to assess mood. As the questionnaire consists of 24 items assessing three bipolar dimensions, it is too long for an internet administration. Internet users are not willing to expend a lot of time and effort to fill out questionnaires and tend to display uniform response patterns when completing long matrix-like questionnaires (Gräf, 2002). Thus, online instruments have to be short and entertaining (Gräf, 2002). Therefore, a shorter version of the MDMQ was developed: Participants were asked to indicate their actual state on the three dimensions using a visual analogue scale that allowed them to move a slider between the two poles of each dimension. This method allowed a shorter questionnaire to be administered but still yielded interval-level data (Funke, 2010).

The three MDMQ dimensions are: pleasure versus displeasure, wakefulness versus tiredness, and relaxation versus tension. The questionnaire consists of 24 items that are answered on a 5-point rating scale (ranging from 1 = not at all to 5 = very much). Each of the three dimensions is represented by eight items, four of them with a positive valence and four of them with a negative valence. The theoretical basis for the MDMQ is a three-dimensional model of affect (Steyer et al., 1994) that splits the arousal component of the circumplex model of affect (Larsen & Diener, 1992; Russell, 1980; Thayer, 1996; Watson & Tellegen, 1985) into two dimensions: wakefulness versus tiredness and relaxation versus tension. The third dimension is pleasure versus displeasure as also found in the circumplex model.

Internal consistencies for the questionnaire were calculated by Steyer et al. (1997) for four different measurement occasions. They were between .91 and .94 for pleasure versus displeasure, .92 and .96 for wakefulness versus tiredness, and .86 and .91 for relaxation versus tension. Test-retest reliabilities for the same four measurement occasions (with a test-retest interval of about 3 weeks) were between .24 and .43 for pleasant versus unpleasant, .21 and .30 for wakefulness versus tiredness, and .29 and .51 for relaxation versus tension. The coefficients indicate that the three mood dimensions indeed vary over time and that the instrument is sensitive enough to capture these fluctuations. A latent-state-trait model confirmed these notions.

Content validity was seen as given. Factor analyses confirmed three dimensions plus one additional dimension that could be interpreted as an individual's tendency to agree or disagree with statements.

6.2 Pilot Study 1a: Validation of the Visual Analogue Scale

The purpose of the first pilot study on the online mood questionnaire was to design three visual analogue scales, each representing one bipolar dimension of the MDMQ, and to validate it with the original MDMQ.

6.2.1 Method

Instruments. Three online mood sliders were designed. For each dimension, there was a bar with the two adjectives describing its two poles at each end of the bar. To describe the two poles, one of the four adjectives that best described the respective pole was chosen from the original questionnaire. A blue circle that could be moved using the computer mouse was depicted in the middle of the bar. Above the bar was a text field presenting the initial value of 50. This value could be changed accordingly by moving the slider. The instructions were: "How are you feeling at this moment? Please use your mouse to move the blue slider to show a value between 0 (*bad/tired/tense*) and 100 (*good/alert/relaxed*) in the text field". Figure 13 depicts the three mood sliders.

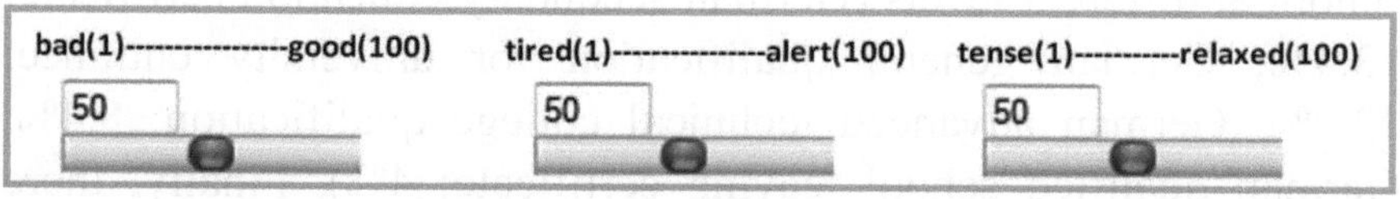

Figure 13. First version of the visual analogue scales.

Participants could move the slider along the bar to represent values ranging from 1 (very left end of the slider) to 100 (very right end of the slider). Each slider was shown on a separate page so that the responses given for each dimension would not influence each other.

Procedure. To assess whether the mood sliders measured the same constructs as the original questionnaire, they were administered to a number of participants together with the original questionnaire.

Participants of the mentaga GYM programme (N = 3,354) were contacted via email. They were asked to participate in a study with the purpose of testing a new instrument for the programme. Using the link in the email, they could directly access an online questionnaire. They gave some demographical data and then completed the three visual analogue scales, followed by the original

MDMQ questionnaire. The participants were not paid for their participation in the study, but they could ask for the study results.

Participants. $N = 202$ participants completed the questionnaire between July14 and July 31, 2011 (response rate: 6%). Of those who indicated their sex (13 participants did not), 40.2% were male and 59.8% were female. They were between 14 and 73 years old ($M = 40.48$, $SD = 15.56$). Most of them had completed vocational training (17.8%) as their highest degree or had a master's degree from a university (17.3%); the rest had graduated from high school at different levels (German secondary education certificate: 13.4%; German general qualification for university entrance: 12.9%; German advanced technical college qualification: 8.4%; German qualified school leaving certificate: 4%). Finally, there were some participants who held a master craftsman certificate (4.5%) or a Ph.D. degree (3%). Thirty participants did not specify their highest degree. When asked for their current primary occupation (which 17 participants did not indicate), 28.7% indicated being white collar workers, 16.8% were high school students, and 10.4% were self-employed. The rest were university students (5.4%), blue collar workers (5.4%), civil servants (5.9%), freelance professionals (1.5%), retired (9.4%), housewives or -husbands (5.9%), or unemployed (2%). Most of the participants were married (55%), and the rest were unmarried (28.7%), divorced (4%), or widowed (1.5%). Of those who were unmarried, 22.6% lived in a partnership, 70.7% were single. Twenty-two participants did not indicate their marital status.

6.2.2 Results

Table 3 depicts the descriptive statistics for the visual analogue scales. Participants used the full range of the scale (from 1 to

100). Altogether, their mood was rather positive, alert, and relaxed.

Table 3
Descriptive Statistics for the Visual Analogue Scale

	N	*M*	*SD*	Range
Slider bad versus good	200	70.68	23.43	1-100
Slider tired versus alert	199	62.46	26.67	1-100
Slider tense versus relaxed	195	68.26	25.01	1-100

Note. The poles of the scales were: “bad versus good”: bad = 1, good = 100; “tired versus alert”: tired = 1, alert = 100; “tense versus relaxed”: tense = 1, relaxed = 100.

Table 4 depicts the descriptive statistics for the three MDMQ dimensions as assessed by the full questionnaire. Here, the possible range (from 8 to 40) was used to its full extent only for the dimension “tired versus alert”. On this version of the questionnaire, individuals also described themselves as in a rather good mood, alert, and relaxed. Cronbach’s alpha was between .90 and .92 for the three dimensions and thus could be considered high.

Table 4
Descriptive Statistics for the MDMQ Dimensions

	N	*M*	*SD*	Range	α
Scale bad versus good	172	30.65	6.65	12-40	.92
Scale tired versus alert	173	25.98	7.13	8-40	.91
Scale tense versus relaxed	175	29.97	6.33	15-40	.90

Note. The poles of the scales were: "bad versus good": bad = 8, good = 40; "tired versus alert": tired = 8, alert = 40; "tense versus relaxed": tense = 8, relaxed = 40; α = Cronbach's alpha.

Corrected item-total correlations were between .68 and .79 for the scale "bad versus good", between .59 and .77 for the scale "tired versus alert", and between .61 and .75 for the scale "tense versus relaxed". Complete items statistics can be found in Appendix A.

Table 5 depicts the intercorrelations of the visual analogue scales (mood sliders) and the mood scales. All intercorrelations were significant at the 1% level. The correlations between the slider and the scale were $r = .74$, $p < .01$, for "bad versus good", $r = .71$, $p < .01$, for "tired versus alert", and $r = .66$, $p < .01$, for "tense versus relaxed". The correlations between the visual analogue scales and the scales measuring the different dimensions were also high and significant at the 1% level, but they were lower. Only the correlation between the two visual analogue scales "bad versus good" and "tense versus relaxed" were higher than all of the other correlations, $r = .74$, $p < .01$.

Table 5
Intercorrelations between the Visual Analogue Scales (Mood Sliders) and the Mood Scales

		Mood slider			Mood scale	
		Bad versus good	Tired versus alert	Tense versus relaxed	Bad versus good	Tired versus alert
Mood slider	Tired versus alert	.600**				
	Tense versus relaxed	.755**	.573**			
Mood scale	Bad versus good	**.739****	.465**	.524**		
	Tired versus alert	.480**	**.709****	.433**	.444**	
	Tense versus relaxed	.564**	.462**	**.661****	.579**	.389**

Note. Listwise, $N = 166$.
* $p < .05$. ** $p < .01$.

An examination of the score distributions for the sliders indicated that the default value of 50 (on which the slider was initially set) was over-represented. The suspicion was that this was due to the fact that the slider was already in this position and remained there if the participant decided not to answer the question. Therefore, the value 50 could mean either that participants had decided that this value accurately mirrored their current state or that they had not responded to the item. Figure 14 demonstrates this.

Slider "bad versus good" | Slider "tired versus alert" | Slider "tense versus relaxed"

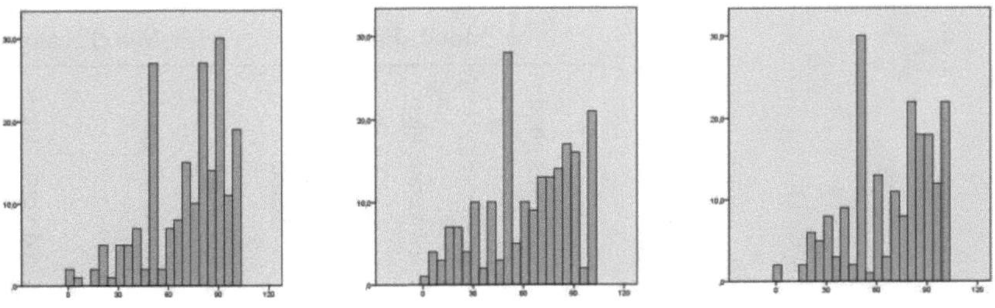

Figure 14. Score distributions for the three mood sliders "bad versus good", "tired versus alert", and "tense versus relaxed".

6.2.3 Discussion

The MDMQ (Steyer et al., 1997) showed good psychometric qualities when used in an online setting. It was possible to use three visual analogue scales to assess the three bipolar dimensions of the questionnaire. The only aspect that needed to be considered with some caution was the high correlation between the dimensions "bad versus good" and "tense versus relaxed" because it was fairly high when assessed with the visual analogue scales. However, this correlation was also fairly high for the two respective dimensions when measured with the original scales. Therefore, I concluded that the visual analogue scales could be used to assess the three dimensions of the MDMQ.

However, it also became obvious that the design of the visual analogue scales needed some refinement: The initial setting of the slider at the value 50 made it impossible to determine whether this number was deliberately chosen by the subject or whether it was a missing value. Therefore, a new mood slider was created in which only the bar was visible initially. The slider did not appear until the participant clicked on the bar. This allowed nonresponses to be separated from responses reflecting a value of 50.

Moreover, I decided to rename the "tired versus alert" dimension "tired versus energetic" because feedback from some participants indicated that they had trouble with the pole "alert" ("wach" in German). Therefore, another adjective that better mirrored the meaning of the pole was chosen: "energetic" ("munter" in German).

6.3 Pilot Study 1b: Refinement of the Visual Analogue Scale

In the follow-up study, two versions of the visual analogue scale were compared to determine which of them would yield more reliable and interpretable results. One version was the original mood slider with 50 as the default value; the other version was a new mood slider for which participants had to click on the slider bar to make the slider appear. Figure 15 depicts the two versions of the visual analogue scales.

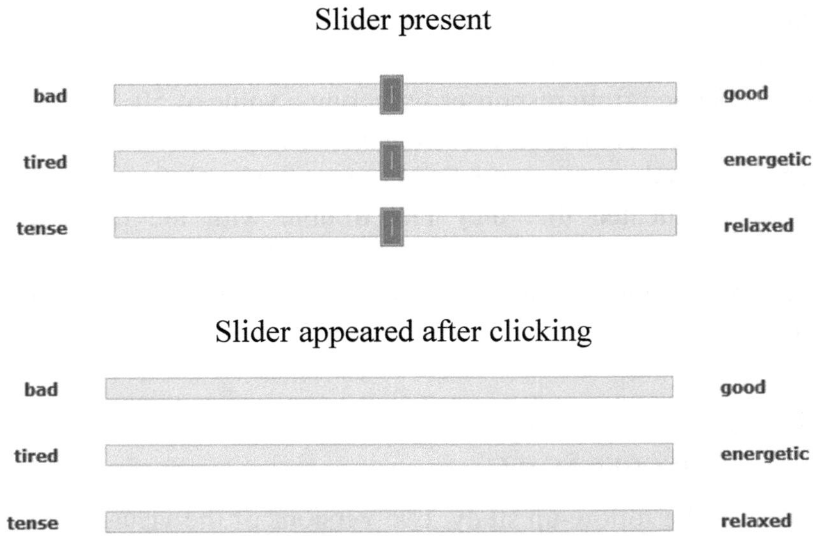

Figure 15. The visual analogue scale versions that were compared in the study.

After clicking on the bars, the two versions of the mood sliders worked in the same way: Subjects could move the sliders by dragging them with the mouse as depicted in Figure 16.

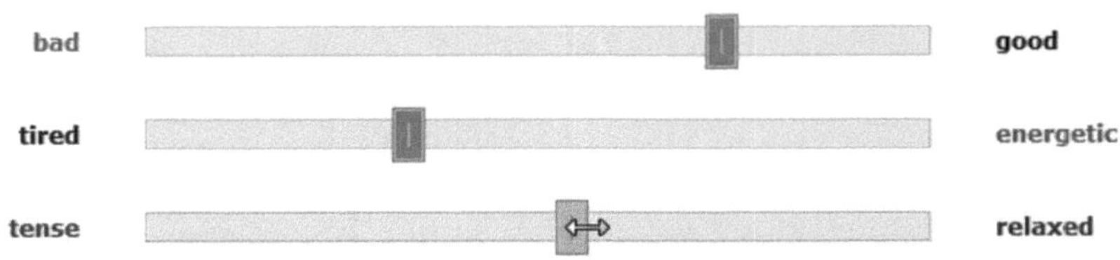

Figure 16. The visual analogue scales with the slider present. The colour of the terms on the left and right hand side of the slider changes depending on the slider position.

German and English versions of the visual analogue scales were developed. I translated the German version into English myself because of my knowledge of what was meant by each word. A colleague who is bilingual in German and English back-translated and revised the questionnaire.

The downside of the original version of the visual analogue scale was that the format made it impossible to separate ratings of 50 from missing values. However, for the new version of the visual analogue scale, it was not known whether the participants would understand how to operate the slider given that web users tend not to read instructions.

6.3.1 Method

The two types of visual analogue scales were integrated into the mentaga GYM portal. After logging in, the participants were randomly shown either the original mood slider with 50 as the default value or the new mood slider for which they had to click on the bar to make the slider appear. Data were collected between February 2 and April 24, 2012.

Participants. The two types of visual analogue scales were used 1,636 times. As it was possible for the mentaga GYM participants to log into the system anytime and as often as they wanted, many participants used the sliders a number of times (a few logged in up to 50 times). Therefore, the total of 1,636 times the sliders were used came from a total of 519 participants.

Participants of the programme were required to provide their date of birth and gender. Therefore, these data were available for all participants. Females comprised 53.9% of the sample, and 46.1% were male. They were between 8 and 80 years old (M = 31.32, SD = 16.50). Data on marital status, education, and current occupation were available for 161 of the participants. Of these,

41.6% were single, 6.8% were unmarried but living with a partner, 45.3% were married, 3.7% were divorced, and 2.5% were widowed. For educational background, most of the participants had a high school diploma (26.1%), held a degree from a university (14.3%) or a university of applied sciences (11.2%), or had undergone professional training (26.1%) or secondary education (14.3%). The rest held a Ph.D. degree (3.1%), a master craftsman's diploma (1.2%), had completed primary education (3.7%), or had not completed primary education (4.3%). As their current occupation, most participants stated they were high school students (31.1%) or white collar workers (28.6%). The rest were university students (3.1%), blue collar workers (7.5%), civil servants (6.8%), free-lancers (4.3%), self-employed (5.6%), retired (6.2%), housewives or -husbands (5.0%), or unemployed (1.9%).

6.3.2 Results

Table 6 depicts the descriptive statistics for the two versions of the mood sliders. For the version in which the slider was present, the computer recorded whether or not the slider was moved. The results of this tracking showed that 161 individuals (19.4%) did not move the slider at all. In the version in which the slider appeared after clicking, 215 individuals (26.7%) did not click and thus did not use the slider at all.

Table 6
Descriptive Statistics for the Two Slider Versions

	Slider present				Slider appeared upon clicking			
	N	*M*	*SD*	Range	*N*	*M*	*SD*	Range
Bad versus good	831	60.48	21.01	0-100	541	62.11	24.36	0-100
Tired versus energetic	831	51.12	21.22	0-100	542	46.56	24.63	0-100
Tense versus relaxed	831	55.71	21.02	0-100	532	54.76	24.75	0-100

Note. The poles of the scales were: "bad versus good": bad = 0, good = 100; "tired versus alert": tired = 0, alert = 100; "tense versus relaxed": tense = 0, relaxed = 100.

Figure 17, Figure 18, and Figure 19 depict the comparisons between the score distributions for the instrument in which the slider was initially present versus the instrument in which the slider appeared after the bar was clicked. Again, it was obvious that the value 50 was over-represented for the version in which the slider was initially present ("bad versus good" slider: 316 participants; "tired versus energetic" slider: 314 participants; "tense versus relaxed slider": 321 participants). For the sliders that appeared after the bar was clicked, the missing values were removed before creating the graph. For the "bad versus good" slider, there were 263 missing values, for the "tired versus alert" slider, there were 263 missing values, and for the "tense versus relaxed" slider, there were 272 missing values.

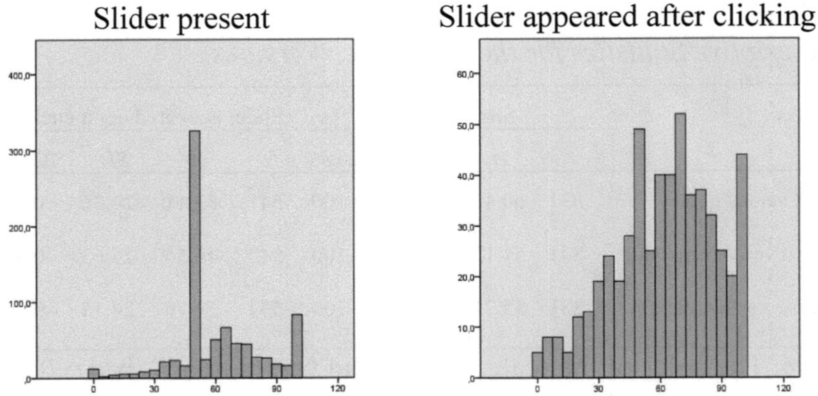

Figure 17. Slider "bad versus good": comparison of the score distributions for when the slider was present (left) and when the slider appeared after the bar was clicked (right).

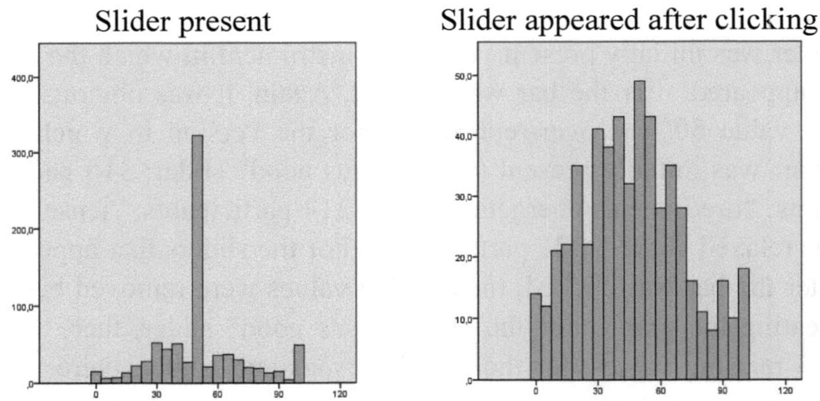

Figure 18. Slider "tired versus energetic": comparison of the score distributions for when the slider was present (left) and when the slider appeared after the bar was clicked (right).

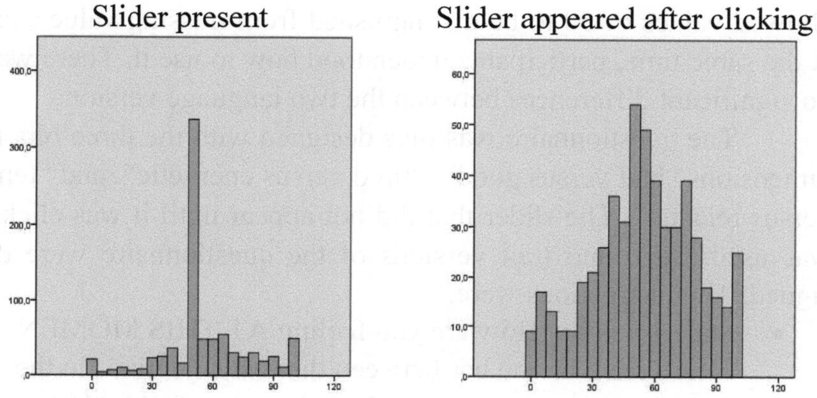

Figure 19. Slider "tense versus relaxed": comparison of the score distributions for when the slider was present (left) and when the slider appeared after the bar was clicked (right).

To compare the two language versions, multiple completions were excluded so that there would be only one completion per participant. For those who had completed the questionnaire multiple times, only the first completion was included in the analysis. For both versions, there were no significant differences between the two language groups; slider present: "bad versus good": $t(256) = 0.27, p > .05$; "tired versus energetic": $t(256) = 0.74, p > .05$; "tense versus relaxed": $t(256) = -0.59, p > .05$; slider appeared after clicking: "bad versus good": $t(181) = -0.35, p > .05$; "tired versus energetic": $t(180) = -1.22, p > .05$; "tense versus relaxed": $t(176) = 0.42, p > .05$.

6.3.3 *Discussion*

The purpose of this study was to determine which of the two versions of the visual analogue scales would yield more reliable and interpretable results. The study clearly indicated that the version in which the slider appeared after clicking was better. It allowed values of 50 to be distinguished from missing values, and at the same time, participants understood how to use it. There were no significant differences between the two language versions.

The questionnaire was thus designed with the three bipolar dimensions "bad versus good", "tired versus energetic", and "tense versus relaxed". The slider that did not appear until it was clicked was used. State and trait versions of the questionnaire were designed. The instructions were:

- State version: "How are you feeling AT THIS MOMENT? Please click on the bar between the two adjectives in the spot that most accurately reflects how you feel at this moment. You can move the slider as you wish after clicking on the bar."
- Trait version: "How do you feel IN GENERAL? Please click on the bar between the two adjectives in the spot that most accurately reflects how you feel in general (not at the moment, but generally, most of the time). You can move the slider as you wish after clicking on the bar."

6.4 Pilot study 2: Design of an Online Questionnaire Assessing Test-Related Emotions

A literature search for a questionnaire assessing the full range of test-related emotions (and not only test anxiety) yielded only one instrument: the Test Emotions Questionnaire (TEQ; Pekrun et al., 2004). The model represents two orthogonal dimensions, valence and activation, according to which emotions can be classified into four categories: (a) positive-activating emotions (e.g., enjoyment), (b) positive-deactivating emotions (e.g., relief), (c) negative-activating emotions (e.g., anger), and (d) negative-deactivating emotions (e.g., hopelessness; Feldman Barrett & Russell, 1998). The authors also classified test-related emotions into prospective and retrospective ones. The questionnaire comprises the emotions joy, hope, pride, relief, anger, anxiety, shame, and hopelessness. All of them can be classified along the dimensions valence (positive vs. negative), activation (activating vs. deactivating), and time (prospective vs. retrospective).

The questionnaire was developed for assessing test-related emotions, but it turned out to be unsuitable for a nonacademic setting because many items refer to exams or marks (e.g., "I look forward to exams" or "My marks embarrass me"). In addition, there are several items per emotion, which would have made it too long to be used on the internet or as a manipulation check (which is not supposed to take too long). However, the model on which the questionnaire was based has been developed and validated in a number of studies and seemed to be suitable for the purposes of studying test-related emotions in a nonacademic setting.

Therefore, based on the model, a short questionnaire assessing test-related emotions was designed. The intention was to design state and trait versions of the questionnaire, both of them assessing emotions that people experience before and after taking a test. To make the questionnaire as short as possible for use on the internet, I decided to use a single adjective to describe each of the respective emotions. In addition, an adjective describing test-related motivation was added because motivation has been found to mediate the relation between emotions and performance (Pekrun, Elliot, & Maier, 2006).

6.4.1 Method

Procedure. First, five different adjectives for motivation and each emotion from the TEQ model were assembled using the online portal http://wortschatz.uni-leipzig.de. The website automatically gathers data on words including descriptions, meanings, subject areas, morphology, grammar, and synonyms.

An expert rating was conducted to determine which adjectives would best describe the emotions. *N* = 22 experts who were very experienced in designing and reviewing test and questionnaire items were invited via email to complete an online questionnaire. After a short introduction to the background of the study, they were asked "How well do these adjectives describe the emotion ...?" and had to indicate on a 4-point rating scale (1 = *very poorly* to 4 = *very well*) how well the adjective represented the respective emotion in their opinion. Five different adjectives were presented per emotion.

Participants. *N* = 20 experts completed the questionnaire (response rate = 91%). They were between 28 and 68 years old (*M* = 44.75, *SD* = 12.47); 45% were female, 55% male; 55% indicated having a Ph.D. as their highest degree, 35% a master's degree, and 10% a German general qualification for university entrance. When asked for their years of experience in item construction, 55% indicated more than 10 years, 15% said 6 to 10 years, 25% declared 3 to 5 years, and 5% stated that they had 1 to 2 years of experience. Finally, they were asked to rate their own expertise on a scale from 1 (*low*) to 100 (*high*) using a slider. The ratings ranged from 1 to 100, with a mean of *M* = 72.60 (*SD* = 26.68).

6.4.2 Results

The following tables show the descriptive statistics for the five adjectives rated by the experts for each emotion and for motivation. The words were presented to the experts in German; therefore, the tables contain the German words with an English translation for each.

Table 7

Descriptive Statistics for the Adjectives for "Motivation"

	M	*SD*	Range
herausgefordert (challenged)	2.80	0.89	2-4
motiviert (motivated)	3.90	0.31	3-4
beflügelt (quickened)	2.20	0.77	1-4
leistungswillig (dedicated)	2.70	0.92	1-4
angespornt (encouraged)	3.05	0.69	2-4

Note. $N = 20$. "How well does the adjective describe the emotion?" 1 = *very poorly*, 4 = *very well.*

Table 8

Descriptive Statistics for the Adjectives for "Joy"

	M	*SD*	Range
voller Vorfreude (full of positive anticipation)	3.70	0.57	2-4
begeistert (enthusiastic)	2.50	0.61	2-4
inspiriert (inspired)	1.95	0.69	1-3
freudig (joyful)	2.70	0.80	1-4
erfreut (pleased)	2.10	0.72	1-4

Note. $N = 20$. "How well does the adjective describe the emotion?" 1 = *very poorly*, 4 = *very well.*

Table 9

Descriptive Statistics for the Adjectives for "Anxiety"

	M	*SD*	Range
besorgt (worried)	3.10	0.79	2-4
ängstlich (anxious)	3.85	0.37	3-4
aufgeregt (agitated)	2.10	0.79	1-4
zittrig (shaky)	1.90	0.85	1-4
unsicher (unconfident)	2.35	0.81	1-4

Note. $N = 20$. "How well does the adjective describe the emotion?" 1 = *very poorly*, 4 = *very well.*

Table 10
Descriptive Statistics for the Adjectives for "Hope"

	M	*SD*	Range
optimistisch (optimistic)	3.35	0.67	2-4
hoffnungsvoll (full of hope)	3.50	0.61	2-4
zuversichtlich (confident)	3.60	0.68	2-4
erwartungsvoll (eager)	2.20	0.89	1-4
mutig (courageous)	1.45	0.51	1-2

Note. *N* = 20. "How well does the adjective describe the emotion?" 1 = *very poorly*, 4 = *very well.*

Table 11
Descriptive Statistics for the Adjectives for "Hopelessness"

	M	*SD*	Range
hoffnungslos (hopeless)	3.75	.72	1-4
pessimistisch (pessimistic)	3.30	.57	2-4
mutlos (discouraged)	2.50	.83	1-4
niedergeschlagen (depressed)	1.95	.69	1-3
skeptisch (skeptical)	1.95	.83	1-3

Note. *N* = 20. "How well does the adjective describe the emotion?" 1 = *very poorly*, 4 = *very well.*

Table 12
Descriptive Statistics for the Adjectives for "Anger"

	M	SD	Range
ärgerlich (angry)	3.65	0.49	3-4
wütend (furious)	3.70	0.57	2-4
gereizt (irritated)	2.42	0.61	2-4
sauer (annoyed)	2.65	1.04	1-4
zornig (irate)	2.70	0.87	1-4

Note. *N* = 20. "How well does the adjective describe the emotion?" 1 = *very poorly*, 4 = *very well.*

Table 13
Descriptive Statistics for the Adjectives for "Shame"

	M	SD	Range
verlegen (embarrassed)	3.15	0.67	2-4
beschämt (ashamed)	3.60	0.82	1-4
betreten (abashed)	2.35	0.81	1-4
zerknirscht (contrite)	2.05	0.95	1-4
kleinlaut (subdued)	1.90	0.72	1-3

Note. $N = 20$. "How well does the adjective describe the emotion?" 1 = *very poorly*, 4 = *very well.*

Table 14
Descriptive Statistics for the Adjectives for "Relief"

	M	SD	Range
erleichtert (relieved)	3.90	0.31	3-4
befreit (freed)	3.25	0.55	2-4
erlöst (redeemed)	2.80	0.77	1-4
heilfroh (delighted)	2.65	0.88	1-4
froh (glad)	2.25	0.79	1-3

Note. $N = 20$. "How well does the adjective describe the emotion?" 1 = *very poorly*, 4 = *very well.*

Table 15
Descriptive Statistics for the Adjectives for "Pride"

	M	SD	Range
stolz (proud)	3.89	0.32	3-4
erfolgreich (successful)	2.33	0.92	1-4
zufrieden (satisfied)	2.53	0.84	1-4
beglückt (highly delighted)	2.11	0.74	1-3
froh (glad)	2.05	0.85	1-4

Note. $N = 20$. "How well does the adjective describe the emotion?" 1 = *very poorly*, 4 = *very well.*

Table 16
Descriptive Statistics for the Adjectives for "Disappointment"

	M	SD	Range
enttäuscht (disappointed)	3.90	0.31	3-4
frustriert (frustrated)	3.20	0.77	2-4
ernüchtert (disillusioned)	2.40	0.75	1-4
deprimiert (depressed)	2.60	0.94	1-4
unzufrieden (dissatisfied)	2.45	0.61	2-4

Note. $N = 20$. "How well does the adjective describe the emotion?" 1 = *very poorly*, 4 = *very well*.

6.4.3 Discussion

The purpose of the study was to find the verbs that most appropriately described the test-related emotions in the TEQ model (Pekrun et al., 2004). The ratings were very clear in most cases. Thus, for almost every scale, the item with the highest rating was chosen. The chosen items were:

- Motivation: motiviert (motivated; $M = 3.90$, $SD = 0.31$)
- Joy: voller Vorfreude (full of positive anticipation; $M = 3.70$, $SD = 0.57$)
- Anxiety: ängstlich (anxious; $M = 3.85$, $SD = 0.37$)
- Hope: zuversichtlich (confident; $M = 3.60$, $SD = 0.68$)
- Hopelessness: hoffnungslos (hopeless; $M = 3.75$, $SD = 0.72$)
- Anger: ärgerlich (angry; $M = 3.65$, $SD = 0.49$)
- Shame: beschämt (ashamed; $M = 3.60$, $SD = 0.82$)
- Relief: erleichtert (relieved; $M = 3.90$, $SD = 0.31$)
- Pride: stolz (proud; $M = 3.89$, $SD = 0.32$)
- Disappointment: enttäuscht (disappointed; $M = 3.90$, $SD = 0.31$)

The only scale for which the adjective with the second highest instead of the highest rating was selected was “ärgerlich” (angry) for anger. The difference between the two means was not large: 3.65 for “ärgerlich” (angry) versus 3.70 for “wütend” (furious). This choice was made for two reasons: The first reason was content-related: “Wütend” (furious) describes a more intense emotion. For example, in Plutchik’s (2001) model, an emotion of such intensity would be on a different level than the other emotions described here. Conversely, “ärgerlich” (angry) is on the same level of intensity as the others are. The second reason was consensus between the raters: There was a smaller standard deviation for “ärgerlich” (angry) than for “wütend” (furious), and the minimum rating was higher for “ärgerlich” (angry; *Min* = 3) than for “wütend” (furious; *Min* = 2).

The questionnaire was thus designed with the above-mentioned adjectives with a 5-point rating scale (strongly disagree to strongly agree). Motivation is assessed before participants take the test. Five of the emotion scales are prospective emotions and are thus assessed before the test as well (joy, anxiety, hope, hopelessness, anger); five of them are posttest emotions and are thus assessed after the test (anger, shame, relief, pride, disappointment). The instructions are:

- Emotions before the test:
    - Trait version: “How do you feel BEFORE taking a test IN GENERAL (not at the moment, but usually; e.g., aptitude tests during a selection process, an exam at school, vocational training, or university)? I feel…”
    - State version: “In the following, you will complete a test to assess your logical thinking. How does this make you feel? I feel…”
- Emotions after the test:

- Trait version: "How do you feel AFTER taking a test IN GENERAL (e.g., aptitude test during a selection process, exam at school, vocational training, or university)? I feel…"
- State version: "You have just completed a test. How do you feel? I feel…"

Over the course of designing of the experiment, I presented the questionnaire to three volunteers who were asked to complete the entire experiment under supervision (one at a time) and verbalise their thoughts while doing so. During this trial phase, it turned out that the posttest emotions were difficult to rate. Participants said that they could not say how they felt after a test in general because their emotional state after a test depended too much on what the test had been like. Therefore, the trait version of the emotion posttest was not used.

The original version of the questionnaire was in German. I translated it into English myself because of my knowledge of what was meant by each word. A colleague who is bilingual in German and English back-translated and revised the questionnaire.

6.5 Manipulation Check using the Adapted Questionnaires

Before using the two internet-adapted questionnaires for the manipulation check, it was necessary to generate some hypotheses on the effects that the emotion-induction procedure would have on the three mood dimensions, motivation, and the test-related emotions.

6.5.1 *Expected Effects on the Mood Dimensions*

The Control condition was chosen as the reference condition; therefore, it was necessary to first generate hypotheses on what a person's mood state would be after the induction in this condition. The question was what a neutral affective state after the induction would be in comparison with the state before the induction. On the one hand, this could be trait mood as an individual baseline because trait mood is the state that is experienced most frequently. In this case, the neutral condition would not be expected to deviate from trait mood after the induction. On the other hand, in the study by Gross and Levenson (1995), a neutral emotional state meant that individuals rated themselves low on all emotions. In terms of the three MDMQ dimensions, this would mean that individuals would rate themselves as being at the centre of the scale on all three dimensions, neither feeling bad nor good, neither tired nor energetic, and neither tense nor relaxed. Because the emotion induction was implemented according to Gross and Levenson's (1995) work, the latter option was followed with one exception: Because human baseline mood is elevated above a neutral point and is thus positive (Diener & Diener, 1996; Diener, Lucas, & Scollon, 2006), it was hypothesised that a "neutral state" would deviate towards the positive end of the "bad versus good" scale; for "tired versus energetic" and "tense versus relaxed", individuals would provide ratings that would fall in the centre of the scale.

The following mood states would thus be expected after the induction:

In the two positive conditions (Joy and Contentment), individuals will feel good, whereas in the two negative conditions (Sadness and Anger), they will feel bad. Because in the two positive conditions, the current state signals to the individuals that everything is going well (Schwarz, 1990), they will feel relaxed in these two conditions. By contrast, because individuals in the two negative conditions are likely to be striving for mood repair (Isen, 1984), they will feel tense. Finally, in the two activating conditions (Joy and Anger), individuals will feel energetic (Pekrun, 2006), whereas in the two deactivating ones (Sadness and Contentment), they will feel tired (Pekrun, 2006).

Consequently, the following specific mood states were expected after the induction:

- In the Control condition, individuals will feel good, neither tired nor energetic, and neither tense nor relaxed.
- In the Joy condition, individuals will feel good, energetic, and relaxed.
- In the Sadness condition, individuals will feel bad, tired, and tense.
- In the Anger condition, individuals will feel bad, energetic, and tense.
- In the Contentment condition, individuals will feel good, tired, and relaxed.

Whether or not there would be a change from the initial state to the state after the induction would depend on the mood state of the individual before the induction. For example, if a person is in the Joy condition and is already feeling good before the induction, then no change in this mood dimension would be expected. If the person is already feeling bad before the induction, a change would be expected.

For comparing the mood states of the four experimental conditions to the Control condition after the induction, the following predictions were made:

- In the Joy condition, individuals will feel better, more energetic, and more relaxed than in the Control condition.

- In the Sadness condition, individuals will feel worse, more tired, and more tense than in the Control condition.
- In the Anger condition, individuals will feel worse, more energetic, and more tense than in the Control condition.
- In the Contentment condition, individuals will feel better, more tired, and more relaxed than in the Control condition.

6.5.2 *Expected Effects on Motivation and Emotions*

As was done for mood, to derive the hypotheses on motivation and test-related emotions, I followed Gross and Levenson's (1995) idea that a neutral state is indicated by low scores on all emotions. Motivation was hypothesised to be neither high nor low in this condition. For the four experimental conditions, there were no hypotheses for all test-related emotions, but only for those that corresponded to the induced emotion: "full of positive anticipation" in the Joy condition, "hopeless" in the Sadness condition, "anxious" and "angry" in the Anger condition, and "confident" in the Contentment condition. Consequently, the following hypotheses were derived for participants' motivation and emotional states after the induction:

- In the Control condition, individuals will be neither motivated nor unmotivated and will be low on all test-related emotions.
- In the Joy condition, individuals will feel motivated and full of positive anticipation (positive-activating emotion).
- In the Sadness condition, individuals will feel unmotivated and hopeless (negative-deactivating emotion).
- In the Anger condition, individuals will feel motivated, anxious, and angry (negative-activating emotions).
- In the Contentment condition, individuals will feel unmotivated and confident (positive-deactivating emotion).

Here, it was also assumed that whether or not a change in emotions was to be expected would depend on individuals' initial emotional states.

For comparing the motivational and emotional states of the four experimental conditions to the Control condition, the following predictions were made:

- Joy condition: Individuals will rate themselves higher on motivation and full of positive anticipation than in the Control condition.
- Sadness condition: Individuals will rate themselves lower on motivation and higher on hopelessness than in the Control condition.
- Anger condition: Individuals will rate themselves higher on motivation, anger, and anxiety than in the Control condition.
- Contentment condition: Individuals will rate themselves lower on motivation and higher on confidence than in the Control condition.

7 Method

In this section, first, the instruments that were used will be introduced, followed by an overview of the procedure and then the sample description.

7.1 Instruments Used

7.1.1 Mood

The internet-adapted version of the MDMQ (Steyer et al., 1997) that had been developed in Pilot Study 1 was used to assess mood. It measures the three dimensions of affect "good versus bad", "tired versus energetic", and "tense versus relaxed" using three bipolar scales and applies a visual analogue scale as the response format. Trait and state versions of the questionnaire were used. They were identical except for the instructions. For the trait version, the instructions were: "How do you feel IN GENERAL? Please click on the bar between the two adjectives in the spot that most accurately reflects how you feel *in general* (*not* at the moment, but generally, most of the time). You can move the slider as you wish after clicking on the bar." The instructions for the state version were: "How are you feeling AT THIS MOMENT? Please click on the bar between the two adjectives in the spot that most accurately reflects how you feel at this moment. You can move the slider as you wish after clicking on the bar." The slider did not appear on the bar until the participant clicked on the bar. The slider could then be moved by dragging it with the mouse (see Figure 20 andFigure 21). The three dimensions are measured on a scale ranging from 0 to 100, with 0 representing "bad", "tired", or "tense", respectively, and 100 representing "good", "energetic", or "relaxed", respectively.

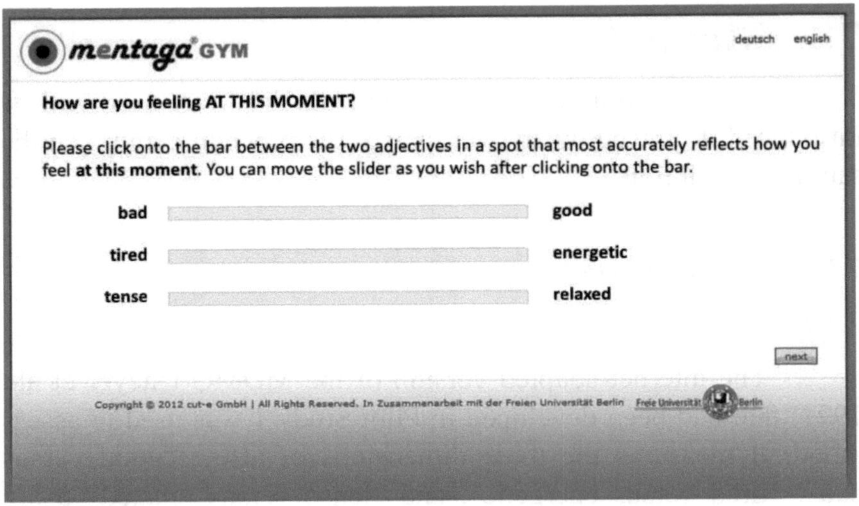

Figure 20. The mood questionnaire (state version) before the participant had clicked on the slider bar.

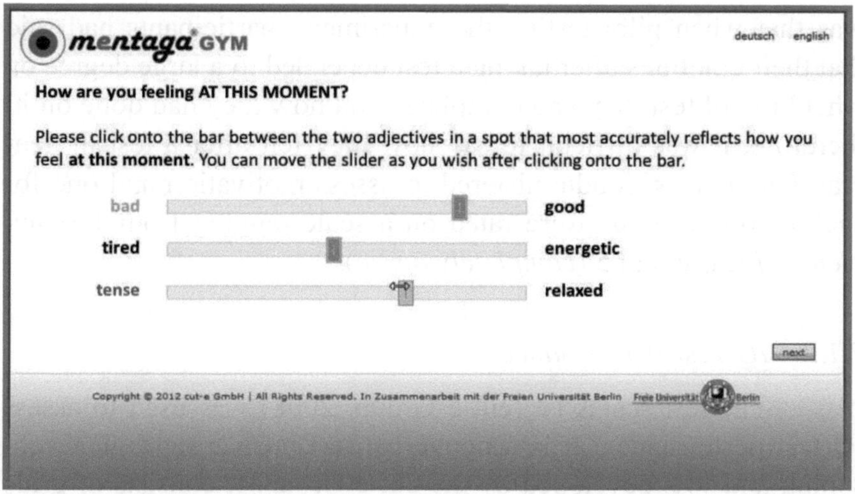

Figure 21. The mood questionnaire (state version) after the participant had clicked on the slider bar.

7.1.2 Test-Related Emotions and Motivation

The questionnaire based on the model by Pekrun et al. (2004) described in Pilot Study 2 was used to assess test-related emotions and motivation. The first part of the questionnaire assesses motivation and the prospective test-related emotions positive anticipation, anxiety, confidence, hopelessness, and anger, and the second part measures the retrospective test-related emotions anger, shame, relief, pride, and disappointment. The first part was administered before the participants took the test, and the second part was administered after they completed the test. I used trait and state versions of the questionnaire for assessing prospective test-related emotions but only a state version of the questionnaire for assessing retrospective test-related emotions. The reason for this was that when pilot testing the experiment, participants had said that their emotions after taking a test depended to a large degree on what kind of test they had completed and how they had done on it; therefore, it was difficult to say how they felt after a test in general. One item was administered to assess motivation and one for each emotion. Items were rated on a scale ranging from 1 (*completely disagree*) to 5 (*completely agree*).

7.1.3 IQ Test Performance

The test scales lst (cut-e Group, 2008) was used to assess IQ test performance. It is a nonverbal test measuring logical reasoning and was developed by the cut-e Group. It consists of grids of 4x4 or 5x5 cubicles that contain different symbols, each of which must appear only once in each row and each column. On the test, incomplete grids are depicted in which one cubicle contains a question mark. The participant has to find the symbol to replace the question mark and select it by clicking on one of the four or five alternatives provided. Figure 22 presents a screen shot of an easy test item.

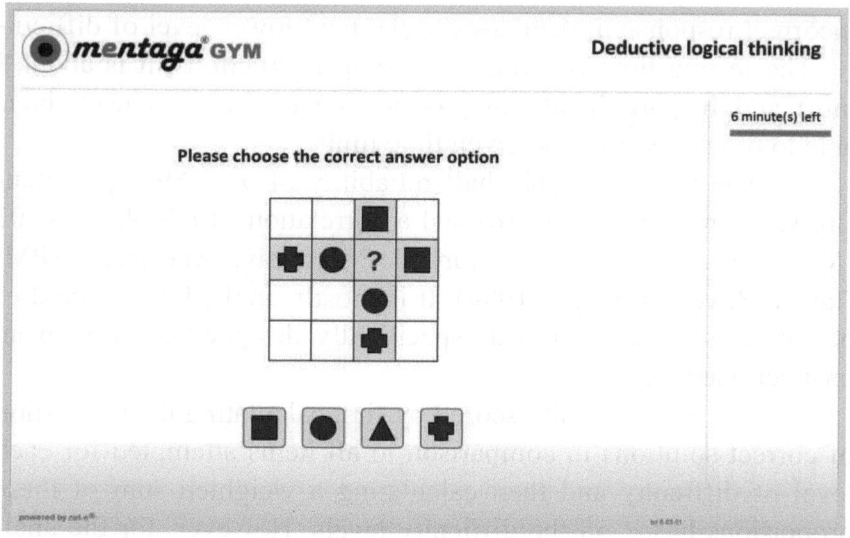

Figure 22. Screen shot of an item from the test scales lst.

Each test is generated at run-time by an item generator according to a certain set of rules. The test has six different levels of difficulty that are generated on the basis of Relational Complexity Theory (Halford, 1993; Halford, Wilson, & Phillips, 1998). The theory posits that it is the complexity of relations between single elements that determines the difficulty of an item. This complexity of relations between single elements is constituted by how many variables have to be processed in parallel to solve the item. On the test, this principle is implemented by using the size of the matrix (4x4 or 5x5) and the number of rows and columns that need to be taken into account to solve the item. This kind of test has been shown to be a valid indicator of processing capacity (Birney, Halford, & Andrews, 2006). The test is adaptive. It begins with an item in the easiest category. Upon a correct response, the difficulty level increases to the next higher level of difficulty, and upon an incorrect response, it decreases to the next lower level of difficulty. The testing time is 6 min (including instructions, it is about 8 min), and the participant may process as many items as he or she is able to process within the given time limit.

The test has a split-half reliability of $\alpha = .89$ (Spearman-Brown corrected; $N = 3{,}216$) and a correlation of $r = .48$, $p < .01$ ($N = 90$) with Raven's Advanced Progressive Matrices (APM; Raven, Raven, & Court, 1998). It is mostly applied in the field of personnel selection and was specifically designed for use in an unsupervised setting.

The test is usually scored by first calculating the proportion of correct solutions in comparison to all items attempted for each level of difficulty and then calculating a weighted sum of these proportions based on the difficulty levels. However, for the analyses in the present study, the number of correct solutions (absolute number of items for which the correct solution was selected) and the number of incorrect solutions (absolute number of items for which one of the distractors was selected) was used as the dependent variable. This was the same scoring model that had been used in the other studies on affect and test performance; thus, this scoring method was chosen so that the results would be comparable to the other studies.

The test is language-free and has been in use in multiple languages for many years. Therefore, it was not considered problematic to use it in German and English for the current experiment.

7.1.4 Induction of Emotional States

Five short film clips were used to induce the four discrete emotions and a neutral emotional state. They were shown to evoke the discrete emotions amusement ("When Harry Met Sally"), contentment ("Waves"), anger ("Cry Freedom"), sadness ("The

Champ"), or a neutral emotional state ("Color Bars") by Gross and Levenson (1995). Gross and Levenson studied more than 250 movies and also included results previously found by Philippot (1993). Three of the five film clips that were used were commercial ones ("When Harry Met Sally," "The Champ," and "Cry Freedom"); thus, permission had to be obtained from the rights holders. Film clips were edited according to the instructions on James Gross' homepage at http://spl.stanford.edu/resources.html. The other two film clips ("Waves," "Abstract Shapes") were noncommercial ones that had been made available on the same website. However, the quality was not good enough to display them on the web, and thus, new versions of them that contained all the features of the original ones were created.

7.2 Procedure

7.2.1 Test Run

Before the experiment was launched as an unsupervised online study, a test run was conducted. Three people, one at a time, completed the instrument under supervision and were asked to verbalise their thoughts while completing the experiment. One of them was an expert in the field of tests and testing; the other two were laypersons in this field. The test run showed that there were no technical problems, that the experiment in general was easy to understand and to follow, and that it was diverse enough to capture and maintain participants' attention. A few minor corrections to some of the instructions were made before the experiment was launched for data gathering.

7.2.2 *Experiment*

Participants could access the starting page of the experiment via the link provided in the email or on the respective website. In the introductory text, the true purpose of the experiment was obscured, and participants were told that it was designed to "expand and improve the choice of instruments in mentaga GYM, our online brain training programme". On this page, participants could also select their language by clicking on one of the two options in the top right corner of the page.

The instruction text was:

"Thank you for participating in our scientific survey. Its purpose is expanding and improving the choice of instruments in mentaga GYM, our online brain fitness programme. We are conducting this research in collaboration with Prof. Dr. Michael Eid of the Freie Universität Berlin.

"We are testing a number of different instruments and to check whether we can use them in the programme. The instruments include a new test version assessing logical reasoning, a number of videos and a number of assessments of affectivity. We will assess your affectivity several times. Please note that some of the videos are scenes from films with an age rating of 16 years.

"Completing all instruments will take less than half an hour. Please switch on the sound on your computer.

"Your data will be used anonymously and for scientific purposes only. We will not disclose your information to any third party.

"You will find the user agreement and information on data protection here [link].

"There will be a prize draw for three vouchers worth 50 Euros each for Amazon.com. Terms and conditions apply and can be reviewed here [link].

"If you would like to participate in the raffle, please enter your email address here: [text field for entry of email address]"

Via http links, participants could access Prof. Eid's website, the user agreement for the study, and the terms and conditions for the raffle. The links opened in separate windows.

After participants clicked on the "next" button, they were assigned to one of the five conditions. For this, a block randomisation algorithm was used. The first participant was randomly assigned to one of the five conditions. The second participant was randomly assigned to one of the remaining four, and so on. After five participants, the loop began again. This was done separately for German- and English-speaking participants. Figure 23 provides an overview of the steps of the experiment after participants had clicked on the "next" button.

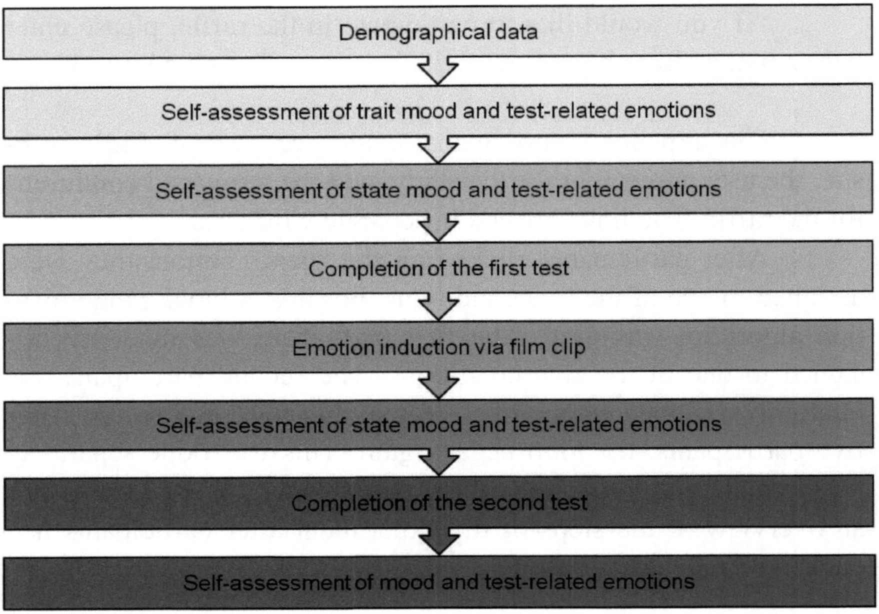

Figure 23. Overview of the steps of the experiment.

On the next screen, participants gave their biographical data: sex, year of birth, marital status, highest educational attainment, and current occupation. Providing this information was voluntary as was the case for all ratings on the questionnaires throughout the experiment, and participants were told so.

On the following screen, participants rated the three trait mood dimensions (bad vs. good, tired vs. energetic, and tense vs. relaxed) using the visual analogue scale that had been developed in Pilot Study 1. The instructions stated: "How do you feel IN GENERAL? Please click on the bar between the two adjectives in the spot that most accurately reflects how you feel in general (not at the moment, but generally, most of the time). You can move the slider as you wish after clicking on the bar." On the next screen, they rated their trait test-related emotions (motivated, full of positive anticipation, anxious, confident, hopeless, and angry) using a 5-point rating scale. The instructions stated: "How do you feel BEFORE taking a test IN GENERAL (not at the moment, but usually; e.g., aptitude tests during a selection process, exam at school, vocational training, or university)?"

On the following two screens, they did the same for their state mood (bad vs. good, tired vs. energetic, and tense vs. relaxed; instructions: "How are you feeling AT THIS MOMENT? You have just described how you feel in general. Now we would like to know how you feel at this moment. Please click on the bar between the two adjectives in the spot that most accurately reflects how you feel at this moment. You can move the slider as you wish after clicking on the bar.") and test-related emotions (motivated, full of positive anticipation, anxious, confident, hopeless, and angry; instructions: "In the following, you will complete a test assessing your logical thinking. How does this make you feel?"). The following screen shots illustrate the assessments of mood and test-related emotions (given here for state mood, but trait mood looked similar).

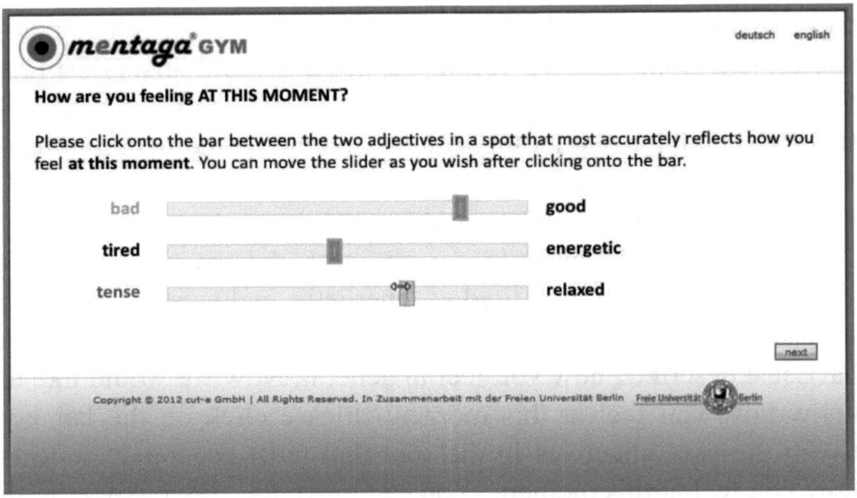

Figure 24. Assessment of mood.

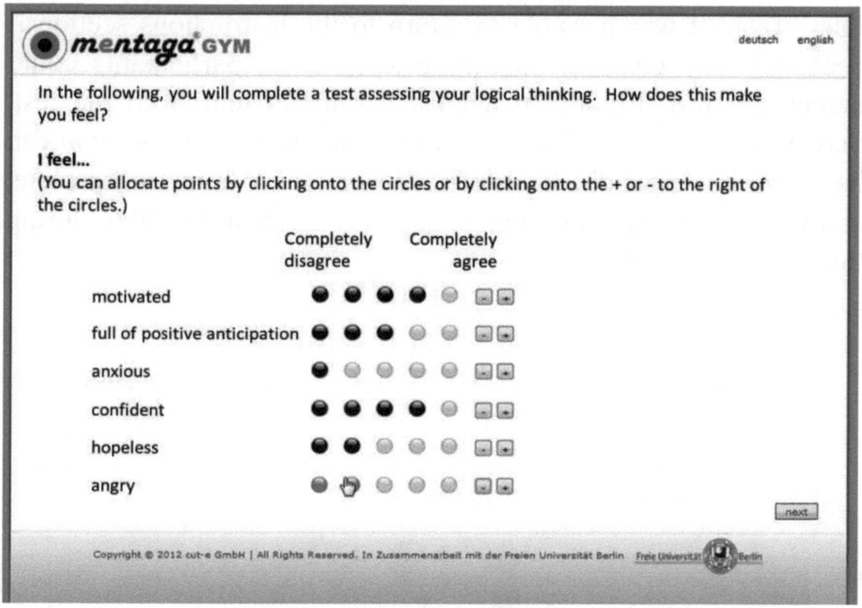

Figure 25. Assessment of test-related emotions.

On the next screen, participants were asked to complete the test and instructed that their sincere effort was required. The test could be launched by clicking on a link that said “Please click here to start the module”. Participants were then taken through a step-by-step instructions section that explained the structure and operation of the test. To ensure participants knew what to do, at some points, they had to do what the instructions told them before they could proceed. They were asked to mark responses, and they also had to mark interim solutions in the grid. Afterwards, they completed an example that gave them instant feedback on their solution, and they were not allowed to proceed to the real test until they had found the correct solution for the example. Then a final screen provided a short overview of the most important points. On this screen, it was possible to return to the instructions section if necessary. By clicking on the “next” button, participants could launch the test. Figure 26 depicts a sample item from the test. Screen shots of the entire instructions and the example section can be found in Appendix B. The test itself took 6 min to complete, and participants could complete as many items as possible during this time.

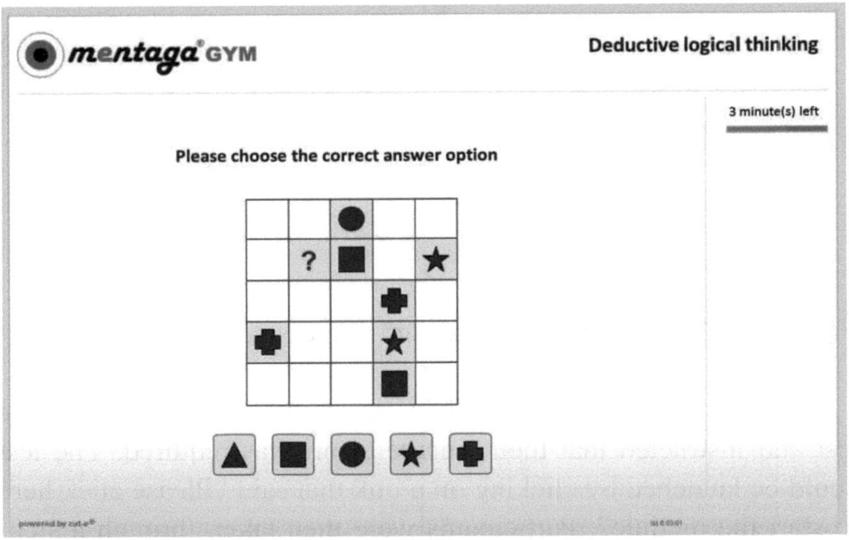

Figure 26. Screen shot of a test item.

After completing the test, participants watched the film clip. They could launch the film by clicking on an arrow on the screen. They were instructed to observe closely because they would be asked questions about the film later. This was to ensure that participants would concentrate on the film clip.

After watching the film clip, they were asked for their current mood (bad vs. good, tired vs. energetic, and tense vs. relaxed) and test-related emotions (motivated, full of positive anticipation, anxious, confident, hopeless, and angry) again. They then completed the test once more. This time, the first screen informed them that they were to complete the test they had worked on previously once more. There were no instructions or example section this time because participants had already read the instructions; thus, another section like this would have bored or annoyed them, and it was necessary to begin the test quickly in order to make sure that the effect of the induction procedure would not be lost before participants even began the test. Participants were shown only the key points on the screen from which they could launch the test. The test was a parallel version of the one they had completed before and took 6 min to complete.

After the test, participants rated their current mood (bad vs. good, tired vs. energetic, and tense vs. relaxed) again and additionally their test-related retrospective emotions (angry, ashamed, relieved, proud, and disappointed).

Finally, participants were asked a few questions about the film clips. These questions were not meant to be further evaluated; they were asked just because it had been announced that there would be questions about the film. However, this announcement had been made only to motivate participants to concentrate on the film clips.

On the very last screen, participants were thanked for their participation and given a contact email address in case they had questions. There was a cartoon on this final page that was supposed to rehabilitate their mood if necessary.

7.3 Participants

To determine the sample size that would be necessary to yield a significant effect if an effect was in fact present, effect sizes from the studies by Isen, Daubman, and Nowicki (1987), Abele (1995), and Radenhausen and Anker (1988) were used as the effect size estimates in power analyses. Appendix C provides a table depicting the effect sizes from these studies along with a second table summarising the key results for these studies. For the studies that had investigated processing capacity and for the comparison between positive and negative mood, an average effect size of d = 0.60 was calculated (difference in means between the positive and negative experimental groups). This is a medium effect according to Cohen (1992). For such an effect to yield a significant result, a sample size of 50 participants per group was required (Bortz & Döring, 2006).

Participants of the mentaga GYM brain fitness programme (*N* = 22,696; 17,537 of them German-speaking and 5,159 of them English-speaking) as well as my family, friends, acquaintances, and (former) colleagues (*N* = 300; 230 of them German-speaking and 70 of them English-speaking) were invited via email to participate in an unsupervised online study. Furthermore, the link was posted on social media websites (Facebook, Twitter, LinkedIn, Xing) and some psychology-related websites. Participants could access the online experiment via a link. They were not paid, but it was announced that they could participate in a raffle for one out of three Amazon vouchers.

Of the mentaga GYM programme, 531 participants began the experiment (response rate = 2%), of my social contacts, 225 did (response rate = 75%). In addition, 32 participants accessed the experiment via a link that had been posted on social media sites, and 52 accessed the experiment via a link posted on other websites. For the last two sources, it was not possible to provide a response rate.

Thus, a total of 840 participants began the experiment at least to the extent that they clicked on the link and were assigned a participant ID. Assignment to one of the five conditions took place when participants clicked on the "next" button after reading the introduction page. At this point, the language they chose to take the experiment in was also recorded. A total of 770 out of the 840 participants clicked on the "next" button. Those 770 participants were equally distributed across the five conditions. Of those, 339 participants dropped out at some point during the experiment, whereas 431 completed the entire experiment. Of these remaining 431, two participants were excluded from the final analyses because it was obvious that they had merely clicked through the two tests. This became apparent when examining their response patterns on the tests. Their percentage of correct answers was below chance. Therefore, these two participants were excluded from the analyses on emotions and test performance.

The 429 participants who had completed the entire experiment and whose data were used for the present study were between 12 and 86 years old (M = 36.14, SD = 15.50); 35.4% were male, 65.6% were female; 50.3% were unmarried, 41.4% were married, 6.2% were divorced, and 2.2% were widowed. Altogether, 53.5% were living with a partner. Their education (highest educational attainment) was as follows: primary education (2.4%), secondary education (12.8%), A-levels (31.4%), vocational qualification (10.7%), bachelor's degree (9.3%), master's degree (26.3%), doctoral degree (5.6%). Their current occupation was as follows: high school student (14.1%), university student (20.9%), blue collar worker (2.5%), white collar worker (35.8%), civil servant (3.8%), self-employed (10.1%), retired (6.3%), housewife/-husband (5.8%), unemployed (0.8%). Percentages were always calculated out of the number of participants who had provided the respective data. Twenty-eight participants (7%) did not provide their age; 16 participants (4%) did not provide their sex and marital status; 53 participants (12%) did not provide their education, and 32 participants (7%) did not provide their current occupation. A total of 352 (82.1%) were German-, and 77 (17.9%) were English-speaking.

8 Results

As the data wsere collected in an unsupervised online experiment, it was necessary to determine whether there were systematic drop-out effects and whether the randomisation had worked. Drop-out effects were studied on the basis of demographic variables and performance on the first test. For randomisation to be considered successful, it was necessary that the block randomisation algorithm had worked and that the five groups were equal with respect to affectivity, test performance, and all variables that could impact performance (e.g., age, sex, education, and occupation). Therefore, drop-out effects and randomisation will be presented first. In the following section, the relations between mood and emotions as well as between mood and emotions and performance on the first test will be described.

It was not until after the first test that the emotion induction took place. Thus, in the next section, the emotion induction procedure will be described. Then the results for whether the induction successfully changed mood and emotions from the initial state to the state after the induction and whether there were significant differences in affectivity between the groups after the induction will be presented. For the manipulation to be successful, the affective state after the induction would need to be different from the initial affective state. Furthermore, the groups would need to differ in affectivity after the induction.

Finally, the study's research question will be addressed: whether differences in affective state produced differences in test performance.

8.1 DROP-OUT EFFECTS

As mentioned above, drop-out effects were studied on the basis of demographic variables and performance on the first test. If the demographic variables do not predict drop-out and if there are no differences in performance on the first test between those who dropped out and those who completed the entire experiment, drop-out effects can be concluded to be nonsystematic.

8.1.1 Demographic Variables

To investigate systematic drop-out effects on the basis of demographic variables, participants were divided into two groups: those who had completed the entire experiment versus those who had dropped out at some point during the process. When the criterion or dependent variable is measured on a nominal scale, a logistic regression is appropriate. The independent variables may in this case be nominally or metrically scaled (Bortz, 2005). Alternatively, one can calculate a MANOVA, using the criterion variable as an independent variable and the predictor variables as dependent variables (Bortz, 2005).

A logistic regression with "completed the experiment yes versus no" ("yes" coded as 1, "no" as 0) as a dichotomous dependent variable and the demographic variables (age, gender, marital status, living with a partner, education, and occupation) as independent variables showed that only the variable education had a p-value smaller than .05. However, to control the familywise error rate, a Bonferroni correction was applied. As a result, this effect was not considered significant. A likelihood ratio test revealed that the model containing all demographic variables as predictors was not significantly better than the null model ($\chi^2 = 22.76$, $p > .05$).

Taking all demographic variables into account at the same time, none of them was a significant predictor of drop out (Table 17).

Table 17

Logistic Regression for Predicting Completion of the Experiment (Yes vs. No) from the Demographic Variables

Predictor	β	$SE\ \beta$	$Wald\ \chi^2$	p	e^β
(Intercept)	14.58	622.46	0.001	0.981	
	0.00	0.01	0.039	0.844	1.003
Gender (reference cat. = male)					
Female (1 = yes)	0.40	0.21	3.523	0.061	1.491
Marital status (reference cat. = widowed)					
Unmarried (1 = yes)	0.51	0.73	0.493	0.483	1.672
Married (1 = yes)	0.47	0.71	0.442	0.506	1.599
Divorced (1 = yes)	0.54	0.74	0.537	0.464	1.722
Living with partner (reference cat. = no)					
With partner (1 = yes)	0.14	0.29	0.242	0.622	1.154
Education (reference cat. = PhD)					
Primary Education (1 = yes)	-1.89	0.79	5.669	0.017	0.151
Secondary Education (1 = yes)	-1.10	0.62	3.190	0.074	0.333
A-Levels (1 = yes)	-0.88	0.61	2.045	0.153	0.416
Voc. Qualification (1 = yes)	-1.43	0.60	5.664	0.017	0.240
Bachelor Degree (1 = yes)	-0.97	0.62	2.462	0.117	0.378
Master Degree (1 = yes)	-0.76	0.57	1.769	0.184	0.469
Occupation (reference cat. = unemployed)					
High School (1 = yes)	-13.70	622.46	0.000	0.982	0.000
University (1 = yes)	-13.59	622.46	0.000	0.983	0.000
Blue Collar Worker (1 = yes)	-13.67	622.46	0.000	0.983	0.000
White Collar Worker (1 = yes)	-14.01	622.46	0.001	0.982	0.000
Civil Servant (1 = yes)	-13.51	622.46	0.000	0.983	0.000
Self-employed (1 = yes)	-13.98	622.46	0.000	0.982	0.000
Retired (1 = yes)	-14.52	622.46	0.001	0.981	0.000
Houswife/-husband (1 = yes)	-13.76	622.46	0.000	0.982	0.000

Note. $SE\ \beta$ = standard error for β; e^β = odds ratio, effect size for β; reference cat. = reference category. Null deviance: 630.05 on 486 degrees of freedom. Residual deviance: 607.30 on 466 degrees of freedom. AIC: 469.3.

8.1.2 Performance on the first test

To study whether there was a systematic drop-out effect on the basis of performance on the first test, performance on the first test was compared between those who dropped out at some point after completing the first test but before completing the second test (N = 74) and those who completed both tests (N = 431). There were two different test scores that were investigated: Number Correct (number of items to which the participant had responded correctly) and Number Wrong (number of items to which the participant had responded incorrectly). Table 18 depicts the descriptive statistics for the two groups.

Table 18
Descriptive Statistics for Performance on the First Test for the Two Groups (Only First Test Completed vs. Both Tests Completed)

		N	*M*	*SD*	Range	Skew	Kurtosis
Number Correct	Only test 1	74	11.84	8.16	3-46	1.97	4.43
	Both tests	431	9.73	6.96	1-64	3.43	16.44
Number Wrong	Only test 1	74	7.58	13.96	0-92	3.80	18.56
	Both tests	431	4.44	9.70	0-131	7.49	79.01

However, a logistic regression with “completed the experiment yes versus no” (“yes” coded as 1, “no” as 0) as a dichotomous dependent variable and Number Correct and Number Wrong on the first test as independent variables showed that test performance was not a significant predictor of drop out (Number Correct: β = -0.02, p > .05; Number Wrong: β = -0.01, p > .05). A likelihood ratio test showed that the model was not significantly better than the null model, $\chi^2 = 2.94$, $p > .05$. Thus, there was no systematic drop out on the basis of performance on the first test.

8.2 Randomisation

There were five conditions (Joy, Sadness, Anger, Contentment, Control) to which participants were randomly assigned using a block randomisation algorithm. A number of steps were necessary to test whether the randomisation was successful. First, the block randomisation algorithm was checked to determine whether it had worked correctly and thus whether all five conditions had been equally distributed across the participants. Then I tested for differences in demographic variables across the conditions. Finally, I tested for differences between the five groups in performance on the first test, mood, and emotionality before the emotion induction.

8.2.1 Block Randomisation

As already mentioned, 770 participants were assigned to the five conditions. Table 19 depicts how many participants were assigned to each condition and how many of them completed the entire experiment. Each condition contained an almost equal number of participants, leading to the conclusion that the block randomisation algorithm was successful. However, when examining the number of participants who completed the entire experiment, one can see that there were considerable differences between the Sadness condition and the other four conditions.

Table 19
Number of Participants Assigned to Each of the Five Experimental Conditions and Number of Participants who Completed the Entire Experiment

Group	Film clip	Emotion	No. assigned	No. completed
1	When Harry met Sally	Joy	153	88
2	The Champ	Sadness	154	72
3	Cry Freedom	Anger	154	90
4	Waves	Composure	155	87
5	Abstract Shapes	Neutral	154	92

Note. No. assigned = number of participants assigned to each condition; No. completed = number of participants who completed the entire experiment.

There were two hypotheses about what could have caused this drop out. One was that maybe a disproportionately large share of participants who were assigned to the Sadness condition came from one and the same data source (mentaga GYM, my social contacts, social media, web sites). The other was that maybe the film clip had caused participants to abort the experiment.

To test whether participants from all data sources had been assigned equally across all of the five conditions, a $\chi2$ test was calculated. It showed that there were no significant differences across the data sources, $\chi^2(12) = 5.86$, $p > .05$. In Appendix D, there is a table containing the number of participants who came from each data source in each condition. Thus, coming from different data sources was not the reason for the different drop-out rates.

The other hypothesis was, as mentioned, that perhaps the Sadness film clip had caused more people to drop out. For this to be the case, the number of participants dropping out after the induction would need to be significantly higher in the Sadness condition than in the other conditions. Thus, in order to determine exactly when the drop out had occurred, each step of the experiment was investigated. A detailed description of this investigation can be found in Appendix D. To summarise the findings: Most participants dropped out during the first test when the five conditions were still the same for all participants. The emotion induction did not take place until after the first test. This means that there was no evidence for systematic drop out caused by the film clip and thus by the condition.

In addition, a χ^2 test revealed that the conditions did not differ significantly with respect to number of participants who completed the entire experiment, $\chi^2 = 2.95, p > .05$.

8.2.2 Differences with Respect to Demographic Variables

Testing for differences in demographic variables was necessary because age, sex, education, and occupation/socioeconomic status are variables that account for differences in performance on intelligence tests.

An ANOVA showed that there were significant age differences between the groups, $F(4, 396) = 3.12, p < .05$. Table 20 depicts the descriptive statistics. A Scheffé test showed that there was a significant difference between the Sadness and Control conditions, Mean difference = 7.65 years, $p < .05$. This difference would be problematic if it resulted in performance differences on the first test. This was tested in the section on differences in test performance.

Table 20
Descriptive Statistics for Age across the Five Groups

					95% CI		
	N	*M*	*SD*	*SE*	*LL*	*UL*	Range
Joy	85	34.92	15.78	1.71	31.51	38.32	12-77
Sadness	69	40.74	16.39	1.97	36.80	44.68	13-68
Anger	84	34.80	15.33	1.67	31.47	38.13	15-70
Contentment	75	38.39	15.15	1.75	34.90	41.87	12-78
Control	88	33.09	14.17	1.51	30.09	36.09	13-71
Total	401	36.14	15.50	0.77	34.62	37.66	12-86

Note. SE = standard error; CI = confidence interval; *LL* = lower limit; UL = upper limit.

With respect to sex a χ^2 test shows that there are no significant differences between the five groups, $\chi^2(4, N = 413) = 5.83, p > .05$.

To test whether education was equally distributed across the five conditions, another χ^2 test was calculated. However, one of the assumptions of this test is that no more than 20% of the expected frequencies are smaller than five (Bortz, 2005). Alternatively, an exact test can be calculated or groups can be aggregated so that the expected frequencies in each cell equal five or more (Eid, Gollwitzer, & Schmitt, 2010). The latter recommendation was followed, and thus primary and secondary education were collapsed into one category (no significant difference between the two groups in Number Correct, Mann-Whitney U test, $Z = -0.44$, $p > .05$, and Number Wrong, Mann-Whitney U test, $Z = -0.04$, $p > .05$) and so were bachelor's and master's degree (no significant difference between the groups in Number Correct, Mann-Whitney U test, $Z = -0.66$, $p > .05$, and Number Wrong, Mann-Whitney U test, $Z = -0.51$, $p > .05$). A Mann-Whitney U test was chosen to test whether there were significant differences between the categories that were to be collapsed into one because the data were not normally distributed (Kolmogorov-Smirnov test; Number correct: $Z = 4.51$, $p < .01$; Number Wrong: $Z = 6.04$, $p < .01$).

There were no significant differences between the five groups with respect to education, $\chi^2(16, N = 397) = 8.77$, $p > .05$.

To test whether all occupations were equally distributed across the five groups, one more χ^2 test was calculated. For the same reason as mentioned for education, some of the occupation categories were aggregated so that the expected frequencies would total five or more in 80% of the cells. All the participants who were working were collapsed into one group (i.e., blue and white collar workers, civil servants, self-employed people); no significant differences between these groups in Number Correct, Kruskal-Wallis test, $\chi^2(3) = 1.59$, $p > .05$, and Number Wrong, Kruskal-Wallis test, $\chi^2(3) = 1.83$, p > .05. All those who were at home were collapsed into another group (i.e., housewives/-husbands, retired people, and unemployed people); no significant differences between these groups in Number Correct, Kruskal-Wallis test, $\chi^2(2) = 1.77$, $p > .05$, and Number Wrong, Kruskal-Wallis test, $\chi^2(2) = 1.36$, $p > .05$. A Kruskal-Wallis test was chosen to test whether there were significant differences between the categories that were to be collapsed into one because the data were not normally distributed (Kolmogorov-Smirnov test; Number correct: $Z = 4.51$, $p < .01$; Number Wrong: $Z = 6.04$, $p < .01$).

The χ^2 test showed that there were no significant differences between the five groups with respect to occupation, $\chi^2(12, N = 397) = 20.41$, $p > .05$.

Finally, both languages (German and English) were distributed equally across the five groups, $\chi^2(4) = 2.56$, $p > .05$.

Thus, there were no significant differences between the five groups on the demographic variables (sex, education, occupation) except for age, for which there was a significant difference between the Sadness and Control conditions.

8.2.3 Differences in Test Performance

Conditions for the five groups did not differ until the emotion induction via the film clips. Thus, no differences in the performance on the first test were to be expected. Table 21 depicts descriptive statistics for performance on the first test for the five experimental groups and for the entire sample.

Table 21
Descriptive Statistics for Performance on the First Test by Experimental Group and for the Entire Sample

		N	*M*	*SD*	Range	Skew	Kurosis
Joy	Number Correct	88	9.58	5.96	4-49	3.90	21.91
	Number Wrong	88	3.76	6.05	0-41	3.65	17.16
Sadness	Number Correct	72	9.08	7.59	1-47	3.08	11.30
	Number Wrong	72	4.17	7.76	0-49	3.98	18.36
Anger	Number Correct	90	9.46	6.00	3-38	2.58	8.43
	Number Wrong	90	3.59	6.74	0-53	5.22	34.02
Contentment	Number Correct	87	9.66	7.08	2-44	2.84	9.52
	Number Wrong	87	4.84	10.02	0-81	5.69	39.68
Control	Number Correct	92	10.18	5.86	3-44	2.67	11.73
	Number Wrong	92	4.12	6.28	0-42	3.52	15.94
Total	Number Correct	429	9.62	6.46	1-49	2.97	11.74
	Number Wrong	429	4.09	7.46	0-81	5.13	36.75

Note. Number Correct = Number of items solved correctly; Number Wrong = Number of items solved incorrectly.

To test whether there were significant differences between the five groups, an analysis of variance was computed. For an analysis of variance, there are three assumptions that have to be fulfilled: independence of residuals, homoscedasticity, and normality (Eid et al., 2010). Independence of residuals is given when individuals have been randomly assigned to the conditions (Eid et al., 2010) as was the case here. Therefore, the first assumption could be seen as given. To test for homoscedasticity, or equality of variances within the five groups, a Levene test was calculated. The test showed that the variances between the five groups were equal; Number Correct: $F(4, 424) = 0.46$, $p > .05$; Number Wrong: $F(4, 424) = 0.61$, $p > .05$.

However, the test scores were not normally distributed (Kolmogorov-Smirnov test; Number correct: $Z = 4.51$, $p < .01$; Number Wrong: $Z = 6.04$, $p < .01$). The distributions for these scores are depicted in Appendix F. However, the test statistic for analyses of variance, the F test, is quite robust against violations of the assumption of normality when sample sizes are large due to the central limit theorem (Eid et al., 2010).

Thus, a one-way multivariate analysis of variance (MANOVA) was calculated to test for whether there were significant differences between the groups. The MANOVA was not statistically significant; Pillai's Trace = .02, $F(8, 848) = 0.96$, $p > .05$.

To test the robustness of the MANOVA results, the scores were transformed using the Box-Cox transformation (Box & Cox, 1964) so that they would more closely resemble a normal distribution. This transformation is a power transformation that may be used to find the optimal normalising transformation for variables (Osborne, 2010). The syntax used to calculate different values of the lambda parameter and corresponding transformed scores along with the corresponding values for skewness and kurtosis can be found in Appendix F.

The score that was closest to a normal distribution was used to calculate another MANOVA in order to check the results of the previously conducted analysis. In line with the results of the first MANOVA, the second MANOVA was also not significant, Pillai's Trace = .03, $F(8, 848) = 1.77$, $p > .05$. It was obvious that the F value was larger here compared with the one for the untransformed scores, and consequently, the p-value was different as well. Thus, the differences were analysed once again using a Kruskal-Wallis test (Kruskal & Wallis, 1952). The Kruskal-Wallis test is a nonparametric test that has greater power when the scores are not normally distributed (Eid et al., 2010). The test yielded the same results: no significant differences between the groups for Number Correct ($\chi^2 = 8.96, p > .05$) or Number Wrong ($\chi^2 = 2.50, p > .05$).

Thus, as expected, there were no significant differences between the five groups in performance on the first test.

8.2.4 Differences in Affectivity

The last thing to be done for the randomisation check was to determine whether the five groups were equal with respect to their trait affectivity and state affectivity before the emotion induction procedure. After the participants were randomly assigned to the conditions, the expectation was that there would be no differences between the five groups. This is particularly important with respect to trait affectivity because trait affectivity can be considered the state individuals always eventually return to. State affectivity is also important, but state affectivity is the variable that the emotion induction procedure is designed to change.

Differences in trait affectivity. Table 22 and Table 23 depict the descriptive statistics for trait mood and emotion, respectively. Mood was measured using a visual analogue scale (ranging from 0 to 100), whereas motivation and the emotions were measured with only one item each on a 5-point rating scale. Thus, trait mood was measured on an interval level, whereas the trait motivation and emotions were ordered categories.

Table 22
Descriptive Statistics for Trait Mood

	N	*M*	*SD*	Range	Skewness	Kurtosis
Bad versus good	426	74.05	17.96	6-100	-0.92	0.79
Tired versus energetic	426	60.07	21.69	1-100	-0.18	-0.71
Tense versus relaxed	426	58.81	21.96	4-100	-0.03	-0.61

Note. The poles of the scales were: "bad versus good": 0 = bad, 100 = good; "tired versus energetic": 0 = tired, 100 = energetic; "tense versus relaxed": 0 = tense, 100 = relaxed.

The trait moods "bad versus good" and "tired versus energetic" were negatively skewed. "Bad versus good" was leptokurtic, whereas the other two mood dimensions were platykurtic. A Kolmogorov-Smirnov test showed that only the trait mood "tense versus relaxed" was normally distributed ($Z = 0.89$, $p > .05$), whereas "bad versus good" ($Z = 1.87$, $p < .01$) and "tired versus energetic" ($Z = 1.60$, $p < .05$) were not.

Table 23
Descriptive Statistics for Trait Emotions

			Percentiles		
	N	Range	25	*Mdn*	75
Motivated	423	1-5	3.00	4.00	5.00
Full of pos. anticipation	421	1-5	2.00	3.00	4.00
Anxious	415	1-5	2.00	2.00	3.00
Confident	423	1-5	3.00	4.00	4.00
Hopeless	402	1-5	1.00	1.00	2.00
Angry	403	1-5	1.00	1.00	2.00

The emotions "motivated" and "confident" had medians of 4, whereas "anxious" had one of 2, and "hopeless" and "angry" had medians of 1. Overall, trait affectivity was rather positive in tendency.

A one-way multivariate analysis of variance (MANOVA) was calculated to test for whether there were significant differences between the groups with respect to trait mood. The MANOVA was not statistically significant, Pillai's Trace = .04, $F(12, 1263) = 1.25$, $p > .05$. Thus, there were no significant differences between the five groups on the three mood dimensions "bad versus good", "tired versus energetic", or "tense versus relaxed".

Trait motivation and trait emotions were measured with one item each and thus had to be considered ordered categories. Therefore, an ordinal regression was calculated using the five levels of motivation and the respective emotions as dependent variables and the dummy-coded conditions as predictors (the Control condition was used as the reference category). There would be no differences between the groups unless one or several groups were significant predictors of motivation or emotion. In this latter case, the regression model would be significantly different from the null model. If the randomisation procedure was successful, we would expect no differences between the five groups; thus, none of the groups would be a significant predictor of the rating on trait motivation or trait emotions, and there would be no significant difference between the regression model and the null model.

Before calculating an ordinal regression, however, it is necessary to look at frequency tables. Each individual in this current study could be classified along two dimensions: his or her response to the respective trait motivation or emotion item (1-5) and the groups he or she was assigned to (1-5). Thus, for the entire sample, a 5x5 frequency table could be created to indicate how many individuals there were in each combination of level of trait motivation or trait emotion and condition. Many cells with zero or small frequencies can lead to problems in parameter estimation (Eid et al., 2010). Furthermore, one assumption of ordinal regression is that the conditional probability functions are parallel at all levels of the dependent variable (Eid et al., 2010). Therefore, before calculating the ordinal regression, I had to determine whether there were cells with zero or small frequencies and whether the conditional probability functions were parallel. If the functions are not parallel, accumulating categories is recommended (Eid et al., 2010). Finally, for each model, a likelihood ratio test was calculated to determine whether the model was significantly better than the null model.

Thus, for trait motivation and trait emotions, the following steps were performed: (1) display contingency tables of group x rating on motivation or the respective emotion; (2) calculate the test of parallel lines; (3) if necessary, accumulate categories; (4) calculate the ordinal regression; and (5) calculate the likelihood ratio test to compare the model against the null model. The entire procedure can be found in Appendix E. Here, only the results of the likelihood ratio test will be displayed along with the three effect sizes: the Cox-Snell, Nagelkerke, and McFadden indexes. The detailed results of the analysis will be presented only when the likelihood ratio test was significant. The likelihood ratio test indicates whether the regression model fits the data significantly better than the null model; thus, $p < .05$ indicates that the null model has to be rejected. This would indicate that the regression model is significantly better than the null model and that one or several conditions predict the trait motivation or trait emotion ratings.

As can be seen in Table 24, this was the case only for "angry (trait)" here ($\chi^2 = 14.10$, $p < .01$), indicating that there was a difference between the conditions.

Table 24

Ordinal Regression Predicting the Ratings on Trait Motivation and Trait Emotions from the Conditions: Results of the Model Fit Test

				Pseudo R^2		
	χ^2	*df*	*p*	CS	NK	MF
motivated (trait)	1.65	4	.799	.004	.004	.002
pos. anticipation (trait)	2.09	4	.719	.005	.005	.002
anxious (trait)	1.04	4	.903	.003	.003	.001
confident (trait)	2.56	4	.634	.006	.007	.002
hopeless (trait)	8.50	4	.075	.021	.025	.011
angry (trait)	14.19	4	.007	.035	.044	.022

Note. χ^2 = test statistic resulting from the likelihood ratio test of the regression model and the null model; CS = Cox-Snell index; NK = Nagelkerke index; MF = McFadden index.

Table 25 shows that the conditions "Joy" and "Contentment" were significant predictors of participants' level of trait anger. This means that these two conditions were different from the other three with respect to trait anger. For these conditions as predictors of the ratings for "angry (trait)", the effect sizes e^β were 2.44 ("Joy") and 2.45 ("Contentment"); see Table 25.

Thus, individuals in the Joy and Contentment conditions differed from the others in their level of trait anger. They were slightly higher on trait anger.

Table 25
Ordinal Regression Predicting Angry (Trait) from the Five Experimental Conditions

							95% CI for β		
		β	SE β	Wald test	*df*	*p*	Lower	Upper	e^{β}
Threshold	Angry = 1	1.54	0.28	29.89	1	<.001	0.99	2.09	4.67
	Angry = 2	2.77	0.31	77.69	1	<.001	2.15	3.38	15.91
	Angry = 3	3.88	0.39	101.10	1	<.001	3.13	4.64	48.60
Location	Joy	0.89	0.36	6.09	1	.014	0.18	1.60	2.44
	Sadness	-0.15	0.43	0.12	1	.730	-1.00	0.70	0.86
	Anger	0.28	0.38	0.55	1	.460	-0.47	1.04	1.33
	Contentment	0.90	0.37	6.01	1	.014	0.18	1.61	2.45

To summarise the results so far, in most cases, the five conditions were not significant predictors of the motivation and test-related trait emotion ratings. The only exception was trait anger, on which individuals in the Joy and Contentment conditions were slightly higher. However, the effects were very small. Thus, randomisation with respect to test-related trait motivation and emotions could be considered successful.

State affectivity. Table 26 and Table 27 depict the descriptive statistics for state mood and emotion before the induction and before the first test. State mood was measured using a visual analogue scale (ranging from 1 to 100), whereas motivation and the emotions were measured with only one item each with a 5-point rating scale. Thus, state mood was measured on an interval level, whereas state motivation and the state emotions were ordered categories.

Table 26
Descriptive Statistics for State Mood

	N	*Min*	*Max*	*M*	*SD*	Skew	Kurtosis
bad vs. good	426	4	100	72.07	21.32	-0.71	-0.14
tired vs. energetic	426	1	100	53.35	26.46	0.04	-0.95
tense vs. relaxed	426	1	100	67.95	24.13	-0.64	-0.29

Note. The poles of the scales were: "bad versus good": 0 = bad, 100 = good; "tired versus energetic": 0 = tired, 100 = energetic; "tense versus relaxed": 0 = tense, 100 = relaxed.

The mood dimensions "bad versus good", "tired versus energetic", and "tense versus relaxed" were negatively skewed. All of them were slightly platykurtic. Only "tired versus energetic" was normally distributed (Kolmogorov-Smirnov test, $Z = 1.32$, $p > .05$), whereas "bad versus good" (Kolmogorov-Smirnov test, $Z = 1.96$, $p < .01$) and "tense versus relaxed" (Kolmogorov-Smirnov test, $Z = 1.90$, $p < .01$) were not.

Table 27
Descriptive Statistics for State Emotions

			Percentiles		
	N	Range	25	*Mdn*	75
motivated	426	1-5	3.00	4.00	5.00
full of pos. anticipation	424	1-5	3.00	3.00	4.00
anxious	408	1-5	1.00	1.00	2.00
confident	426	1-5	3.00	4.00	4.00
hopeless	400	1-5	1.00	1.00	1.00
angry	400	1-5	1.00	1.00	1.00

Table 27 shows that, similar to the trait emotions, "motivated" and "confident" had medians of 4, whereas "anxious", "hopeless", and "angry" had medians of 1. Thus, the state emotions were also rather positive in tendency.

A one-way multivariate analysis of variance (MANOVA) was calculated to test for whether there were significant differences between the groups in state mood. The MANOVA was statistically significant, Pillai's Trace = 0.06, $F(12, 1263) = 2.22$, $p < .01$. Therefore, three one-way ANOVAs were computed for each of the dependent variables "bad versus good (state)", "tired versus energetic (state)", and "tense versus relaxed (state)". The analysis showed that there were no significant differences in trait mood between the five groups, "bad versus good": $F(4, 421) = 0.47$, $p > .05$; "tired versus energetic": $F(4, 421) = 1.48$, $p > .05$; "tense versus relaxed": $F(4, 421) = 1.51$, $p > .05$.

As mentioned above, for state motivation and state emotions, an ordinal regression was calculated using the five levels of state motivation and the respective emotions as dependent variables and the dummy-coded conditions as predictors (the Control condition was used as the reference category). Here as well, only the table with the model fit information and the effect size for the entire model will be displayed. Table 28 shows that the likelihood ratio test did not show significant results for any of the emotions, meaning that there were no significant differences between the conditions with respect to the state emotions.

Table 28
Ordinal Regression Predicting State Motivation and State Emotion Ratings from Condition: Results of the Model Fit Test

				Pseudo R^2		
	χ^2	*df*	*p*	CS	NK	MF
motivated (state)	0.50	4	.947	.001	.001	.000
pos. anticipation (state)	6.72	4	.151	.016	.017	.005
anxious (state)	9.19	4	.056	.022	.026	.012
confident (state)	5.40	4	.248	.013	.013	.005
hopeless (state)	9.06	4	.060	.022	.031	.018
angry (state)	7.44	4	.115	.018	.035	.025

Note. χ^2 = test statistic resulting from the likelihood ratio test of the regression model and the null model; CS = Cox-Snell index; NK = Nagelkerke index; MF = McFadden index.

In summary, with respect to state affectivity, there were no differences in mood and emotions between the groups.

Overall, there were no differences in trait and state mood as well as in state motivation and emotions, as expected. Only with respect to trait emotions, there were some slight differences in anger. In summary, the randomisation with respect to trait and state mood, motivation, and emotions was successful.

8.3 Relations Between Mood, Emotion, and Performance Before the Emotion Induction

8.3.1 Intercorrelations of Mood and Emotion

Table 29 shows that there were highly significant correlations between almost all affective traits. The correlations between the three mood dimensions were, according to Cohen's (1992) taxonomy, medium (r = .48 between "tired vs. energetic" and "tense vs. relaxed") to large (r = .55 between "bad vs. good" and "tense vs. relaxed" and r = .67 between "bad vs. good" and "tired vs. energetic"). The correlations between the mood dimensions and motivation were between .13 and .24; thus, they were positive and small. The correlations between the mood dimensions and positive test-related emotions were between .22 and .36; thus, they were positive and small to medium. The correlations between two of the negative test-related emotions, "hopeless" and "angry", and mood were negative and small to medium. Thus, individuals who feel hopeless or angry also tend to feel worse, more tired, and more tense. However, the correlation between the third negative test-related emotion "anxious" was small and positive. Thus, individuals who are anxious also tend to feel good, energetic, and relaxed.

The correlations between motivation and the two positive test-related emotions were between .44 and .55; thus, they were positive and large. The negative test-related emotions "anxious" and "hopeless" were correlated at .39 (medium effect) and "hopeless" and "angry" were correlated at .50 (large effect), whereas the correlation between "anxious" and "angry" was almost 0 and non-significant. The positive and negative test-related emotions were negatively correlated, but the correlations were low to medium (-.15 to -.44). Thus, positive and negative test-related emotions are not mutually exclusive. The mostly small to medium correlations between emotions can also be interpreted to mean that they represent distinct constructs.

Table 29
Intercorrelations of the Trait Emotions

	Bad vs. good	Tired vs. energetic	Tense vs. relaxed	Motivated	Pos. anticipation	Anxious	Confident	Hopeless
Tired vs. energetic	.67**[a]							
Tense vs. relaxed	.55**[a]	.48**[a]						
Motivated	.20**[b]	.24**[b]	.13**[b]					
Pos. anticipation	.22**[b]	.27**[b]	.25**[b]	.55**[c]				
Anxious	.18**[b]	.24**[b]	.27**[b]	-.19**[c]	-.35**[c]			
Confident	.35**[b]	.36**[b]	.30**[b]	.44**[c]	.45**[c]	-.34**[c]		
Hopeless	-.33**[b]	-.34**[b]	-.26**[b]	-.44**[c]	-.26**[c]	.39**[c]	-.39**[c]	
Angry	-.24**[b]	-.20**[b]	-.21**[b]	-.33**[c]	.04[c]	.09[c]	-.15**[c]	.50**[c]

Note. $N = 428$. Correlations were calculated using the Mplus FIML procedure, which estimates missing values using a maximum likelihood estimator.
[a] Pearson product moment correlation. [b] Polyserial correlation. [c] Polychoric correlation.
** $p < .01$.

Table 30 shows that there were also highly significant correlations between almost all affective states. The correlations between the three mood dimensions were, according to Cohen's (1992) taxonomy, medium (r = .46 between "tired vs. energetic" and "tense vs. relaxed") to large (r = .55 between "bad vs. good" and "tired vs. energetic" and r = .64 between "bad vs. good" and "tense vs. relaxed"). The correlations between the mood dimensions and motivation were between .21 and .33; thus, they were positive and small to medium. The correlations between the mood dimensions and the positive test-related emotions were between .20 and .29; thus, they were positive and small. The correlations between the negative test-related emotions and mood were negative and mostly small (-.19 to -.31). Thus, individuals who experience negative test-related emotions also tend to feel worse, more tired, and more tense.

The correlations between motivation and the two positive test-related emotions were between .63 ("full of positive anticipation") and .77 ("confident") and thus positive and large. The negative test-related emotions were correlated from .44 to .58 (medium to large effects). The positive and negative test-related emotions were negatively correlated, but the correlations were low to medium (-.27 to -.36), and the correlations of "anxious" and "angry" with "full of positive anticipation" were small and nonsignificant (-.12). Thus, positive and negative test-related emotions are not mutually exclusive. The mostly small to medium correlations between emotions can also be interpreted to mean that they represent distinct constructs.

Table 30
Intercorrelations of State Mood and Emotions

	Bad vs. good	Tired vs. energetic	Tense vs. relaxed	Motivated	Pos. anticipation	Anxious	Confident	Hopeless
Tired vs. energetic	.55**[a]							
Tense vs. relaxed	.64**[a]	.46**[a]						
Motivated	.31**[b]	.33**[b]	.21**[b]					
Pos. anticipation	.29**[b]	.31**[b]	.20**[b]	.77**[c]				
Anxious	-.20**[b]	-.17**[b]	-.26**[b]	-.26**[c]	-.12[c]			
Confident	.29**[b]	.29**[b]	.21**[b]	.63**[c]	.59**[c]	-.29**[c]		
Hopeless	-.24**[b]	-.16**[b]	-.26**[b]	-.44**[c]	-.29**[c]	.58**[c]	-.36**[c]	
Angry	-.29**[b]	-.20**[b]	-.31**[b]	-.30**[c]	-.12[c]	.44**[c]	-.27**[c]	.58**[c]

Note. $N = 428$. Correlations were calculated using the Mplus FIML procedure, which estimates missing values using a maximum likelihood estimator.
[a] Pearson product moment correlation. [b] Polyserial correlation. [c] Polychoric correlation.
** $p < .01$.

In Table 31, the correlations between trait moods and emotions and the correponding state moods and emotions are shaded in grey. People's ratings of their own trait emotionality are usually heavily influenced by their current affect (Diener, 2009). From the table, it can be seen that the correlations between each trait and its corresponding state mood or emotion are the highest ones in the table. On the basis of state-trait theories of mood and emotions, this finding is to be expected because mood or emotional states are seen as fluctuations around a stable mood or emotional trait caused by the influences of the current situation (Eid, 1997). Thus, there is usually a high correlation between trait and state, but state and trait are not identical.

Table 31
Intercorrelations of Trait and State Emotions

		State								
		Bad vs. good	Tired vs. energetic	Tense vs. relaxed	Motivated	Pos. anticipation	Anxious	Confident	Hopeless	Angry
Trait	Bad vs. good	.60**	.51**	.48**	.25**	.25**	-.20**	.31**	-.28**	-.21**
	Tired vs. energetic	.39**	.53**	.40**	.25**	.22**	-.10**	.25**	-.17**	-.16**
	Tense vs. relaxed	.40**	.38**	.59**	.20**	.16**	-.17**	.20**	-.23**	-.16**
	Motivated	.24**	.20**	.21**	.57**	.46**	-.13**	.32**	-.23**	-.20**
	Pos. anticipation	.25**	.23**	.19**	.44**	.57**	-.05	.34**	-.12	-.05
	Anxious	-.24**	-.22**	-.31**	-.13**	-.04	.51**	-.15**	.36**	.24**
	Confident	.28**	.26**	.24**	.38**	.36**	-.21**	.58**	-.24**	-.18**
	Hopeless	-.29**	-.28**	-.22**	-.31**	-.13**	.31**	-.18**	.73**	.42**
	Angry	-.25**	-.17**	-.27**	-.34**	-.05	.15	-.11	.46**	.63**

Note. $N = 428$. Correlations were calculated using the Mplus FIML procedure, which estimates missing values using a maximum likelihood estimator.
Correlation coefficients: Between mood scales: Pearson product moment correlation. Between mood and emotion scales: Polyserial correlation. Between emotion scales: Polychoric correlation.
** $p < .01$.

8.3.2 Correlations of Mood and Emotion with Performance on the First Test

Table 32 depicts the intercorrelations between trait and state mood and emotions before the emotion induction and performance on the first test. The correlations between test performance and the mood dimensions and emotions were close to zero and nonsignificant. The only exception was the correlation between Number Wrong and "angry (trait)" (r = -.12). However, when calculating 36 correlations, it is likely that at least one of them will be significant. This is particularly the case when the sample size is large because even very small effects sizes can produce significant results in large samples.

Table 32
Intercorrelations between State and Trait Mood and Emotions and Performance on the First Test

Trait	Number Correct	Number Wrong	State	Number Correct	Number Wrong
Bad vs. good	.00[a]	-.01[a]	Bad vs. good	-.07[a]	-.03[a]
Tired vs. energetic	.01[a]	.03[a]	Tired vs. energetic	-.03[a]	-.01[a]
Tense vs. relaxed	-.01[a]	-.02[a]	Tense vs. relaxed	-.04[a]	-.03[a]
Motivated	-.09[b]	-.09[b]	Motivated	.00[b]	-.02[b]
Pos. anticipation	.02[b]	.06[b]	Pos. anticipation	.02[b]	.03[b]
Anxious	.02[b]	.02[b]	Anxious	-.05[b]	.05[b]
confident	-.05[b]	-.05[b]	Confident	.04[b]	.05[b]
Hopeless	.08[b]	.11[b]	Hopeless	.06[b]	.06[b]
Angry	.07[b]	.12**[b]	Angry	.05[b]	-.01[b]

Note. $N = 428$. Correlations were calculated using the Mplus FIML procedure, which estimates missing values using a maximum likelihood estimator.
[a] Pearson product moment correlation. [b] Polyserial correlation.
** $p < .01$.

In the previous section, intercorrelations between mood and emotions as well as between mood, emotions, and test performance were reported. Results showed that the mood dimensions and the different test-related emotions were related but distinct phenomena. Results also showed that the ratings for trait mood and emotions were not fully determined by participants' current state.

Finally, it was demonstrated that there was no relation between mood and test-related emotions on the one hand and test performance on the other hand. This underscores the need to use a repeated-measures design to tap into the relations between mood, emotions, and test performance.

8.4 Manipulation Check

8.4.1 Changes in Affectivity after the Emotion Induction

The expectation regarding the emotion induction procedure was that it would change participants' current affective state. The following tables present the change in affectivity caused by the emotion induction procedure for each condition. As mood had been measured on an interval level, a t test for dependent samples was calculated. In addition, because the scores were not all normally distributed, a Wilcoxon test was calculated. Motivation and emotions were measured as ordered categories; therefore, a sign test was calculated. Its test statistic S is calculated using the median, and therefore, the test is suitable for data that do not have an underlying continuous distribution (Eid et al., 2010).

Control condition. For mood, the expectation was that individuals' ratings on "bad versus good" would become more neutral but remain positive and that their ratings on "tired versus energetic" and "tense versus relaxed" would remain in a neutral zone or move towards it. The results reflected this expectation: Individuals' ratings were still positive, but their ratings on "bad versus good" had moved towards a more neutral point on the scale. Their ratings on "tired versus energetic" had been neutral before and remained there after the induction, and they were significantly more neutral on "tense versus relaxed" than before the induction (see Table 33).

Table 33
Change in Mood due to the Emotion Induction for the Control Condition

	Before		After			*t* test			Wilcoxon	
	M	*SD*	*M*	*SD*	*d*	*t*	*df*	*p*	*Z*	*p*
Bad vs. good	72.22	21.72	66.23	20.22	-0.29	-2.69	91	.008	-3.02	.003
Tired vs. energetic	48.91	24.75	48.05	26.74	-0.03	-0.39	91	.694	-1.02	.310
Tense vs. relaxed	70.29	22.13	56.28	23.14	-0.62	-5.24	91	<.001	-4.63	<.001

Note. Before = before induction; After = after induction; *d* = Cohen's *d*. The poles of the scales were: "bad versus good": 0 = bad, 100 = good; "tired versus energetic": 0 = tired, 100 = energetic; "tense versus relaxed": 0 = tense, 100 = relaxed. Effect sizes and test statistics were computed on difference scores calculated as: after induction – before induction.

With respect to emotions, the expectation was that individuals would rate themselves lower on motivation and emotions on which they had previously rated themselves high and that their ratings would not change on emotions on which they had previously rated themselves low. In line with expectations, individuals rated themselves slightly but significantly lower on "motivated", "full of positive anticipation", and "confident", but their ratings on "anxious" and "hopeless" did not change significantly. Counter to expectations, their ratings on the emotion "angry" increased (see Table 34).

Table 34
Change in Emotions due to the Emotion Induction for the Control Condition

	Before			After			Sign Test	
	25	*Mdn*	75	25	*Mdn*	75	*S*	*p*
Motivated	3.00	4.00	5.00	2.25	4.00	4.00	8	0.003
Pos. anticipation	3.00	4.00	4.00	2.00	3.00	4.00	11	<.001
Anxious	1.00	1.00	1.00	1.00	1.00	1.75	11	0.648
Confident	3.00	4.00	4.00	2.00	3.00	4.00	5	<.001
Hopeless	1.00	1.00	1.00	1.00	1.00	1.00	9	0.146
Angry	1.00	1.00	1.00	1.00	1.00	2.00	25	0.006

Note. Before = before induction; After = after induction.

Joy condition. For mood, the expectation was that there would be high ratings on all dimensions. This was the case: Ratings on “bad versus good” and “tense versus relaxed” had already been high prior to the induction and thus stayed high, whereas ratings on “tired versus energetic” (which had been neutral before) increased significantly (see Table 35).

Table 35
Change in Mood due to the Emotion Induction for the Joy Condition

	Before		After			*t* test			Wilcoxon	
	M	*SD*	*M*	*SD*	*d*	*T*	*df*	*p*	*Z*	p
Bad vs. good	69.62	21.70	73.64	21.91	0.16	1.81	86	.073	1.94	.053
Tired vs. energetic	53.90	28.73	66.98	23.42	0.49	4.93	86	<.001	4.55	<.001
Tense vs. relaxed	69.00	24.07	68.02	21.64	-0.06	-0.41	86	.681	-0.19	.852

Note. Before = before induction; After = after induction; *d* = Cohen's *d*. The poles of the scales were: "bad versus good": 0 = bad, 100 = good; "tired versus energetic": 0 = tired, 100 = energetic; "tense versus relaxed": 0 = tense, 100 = relaxed. Effect sizes and test statistics were computed on difference scores calculated as: after induction – before induction.

With respect to motivation and emotions, there were specific expectations only for "motivated" and "full of positive anticipation": They were that "motivated" would stay high and that "full of positive anticipation" would increase. However, neither was the case: Motivation decreased significantly, whereas there was no change in positive anticipation. However, the level of anger increased (see Table 36).

Table 36
Change in Emotions due to the Emotion Induction for the Joy Condition

	Before			After			Sign Test	
	25	*Mdn*	75	25	*Mdn*	75	*S*	*p*
Motivated	3.00	4.00	5.00	3.00	4.00	4.00	10	0.007
Pos. anticipation	2.00	3.00	4.00	2.00	3.00	4.00	19	0.119
Anxious	1.00	1.00	2.00	1.00	1.00	2.00	13	0.377
Confident	3.00	3.00	4.00	2.00	3.00	4.00	18	0.144
Hopeless	1.00	1.00	2.00	1.00	1.00	2.00	11	0.210
Angry	1.00	1.00	1.00	1.00	1.00	2.00	14	0.004

Note. Before = before induction; After = after induction.

Sadness condition. For mood, the expectation was that ratings on all three dimensions would decrease. This was the case; there was a significant change in all three dimensions and strong effects for "bad versus good" and "tense versus relaxed" (see Table 37).

Table 37
Change in Mood due to the Emotion Induction for the Sadness Condition

	Before		After			t test			Wilcoxon	
	M	*SD*	*M*	*SD*	*d*	*T*	*df*	*p*	*Z*	*p*
Bad vs. good	74.21	19.45	48.18	24.86	-1.17	-8.54	71	<.001	-6.5	<.001
Tired vs. energetic	57.88	26.01	50.53	23.75	-0.29	-3.07	71	.003	-2.27	.023
Tense vs. relaxed	65.90	25.58	45.82	23.55	-0.82	-5.98	71	<.001	-5.01	<.001

Note. Before = before induction; After = after induction; *d* = Cohen's *d*. The poles of the scales were: "bad versus good": 0 = bad, 100 = good; "tired versus energetic": 0 = tired, 100 = energetic; "tense versus relaxed": 0 = tense, 100 = relaxed. Effect sizes and test statistics were computed on difference scores calculated as: after induction – before induction.

With respect to motivation and emotions, there were expectations for "motivated" and "hopeless", specifically that "motivated" would decrease, whereas "hopeless" would increase. The expectations were met for "motivated", but there was only a slight and marginally significant change in hopelessness. In addition, the ratings for "full of positive anticipation" and "confident" decreased (see Table 38).

Table 38
Change in Emotions due to the Emotion Induction for the Sadness Condition

	Before			After			Sign Test	
	25	*Mdn*	75	25	*Mdn*	75	*S*	*p*
Motivated	3.00	4.00	5.00	2.25	3.00	4.00	4	<.001
Pos. anticipation	3.00	4.00	4.00	2.00	2.00	3.00	5	<.001
Anxious	1.00	1.00	2.00	1.00	1.00	2.00	9	0.524
Confident	3.00	4.00	4.00	2.00	3.00	4.00	4	<.001
Hopeless	1.00	1.00	1.00	1.00	1.00	2.00	16	0.093
Angry	1.00	1.00	1.00	1.00	1.00	2.00	18	0.076

Note. Before = before induction; After = after induction.

Anger condition. For mood, the expectation was that ratings on "bad versus good" and "tense versus relaxed" would decrease, whereas they would increase for "tired versus energetic". The former was the case; however, the latter was not: Individuals became more tired instead of more energetic (see Table 39).

Table 39
Change in Mood due to the Emotion Induction for the Anger Condition

	Before		After			*t* test			Wilcoxon	
	M	*SD*	*M*	*SD*	*d*	*T*	*df*	*p*	*Z*	*p*
Bad vs. good	72.22	21.39	29.03	24.49	-1.88	-14.79	89	<.001	-8.05	<.001
Tired vs. energetic	55.64	25.96	49.54	25.49	-0.24	-2.09	89	.040	-1.80	.072
Tense vs. relaxed	63.40	24.58	24.66	20.52	-1.71	-14.24	89	<.001	-8.00	<.001

Note. Before = before induction; After = after induction; *d* = Cohen's *d*. The poles of the scales were: "bad versus good": 0 = bad, 100 = good; "tired versus energetic": 0 = tired, 100 = energetic; "tense versus relaxed": 0 = tense, 100 = relaxed. Effect sizes and test statistics were computed on difference scores calculated as: after induction – before induction.

With respect to motivation and emotions, there were only three expectations: that "motivated" would stay high and that "angry" and "anxious" would increase. Counter to expectations, the level of motivation sank. However, as expected, anxiety and anger levels rose (see Table 40).

Table 40
Change in Emotions due to the Emotion Induction for the Anger Condition

	Before			After			Sign Test	
	25	*Mdn*	75	25	*Mdn*	75	*S*	*p*
Motivated	3.00	4.00	5.00	2.00	3.00	4.00	4	<.001
Pos. anticipation	3.00	3.50	4.00	1.00	2.00	3.00	4	<.001
Anxious	1.00	1.00	2.00	1.00	2.00	3.00	29	0.003
Confident	3.00	4.00	4.00	2.00	3.00	4.00	8	<.001
Hopeless	1.00	1.00	1.00	1.00	1.00	3.00	27	.034
Angry	1.00	1.00	1.00	1.00	2.00	4.00	43	<.001

Note. Before = before induction; After = after induction.

Contentment condition. For mood, the expectation was that ratings for “bad versus good” and “tense versus relaxed” would remain high, whereas they would remain at an intermediate level for “tired versus energetic”. In line with expectations, ratings on “bad versus good” remained high and ratings on “tired versus energetic” remained at an intermediate level. However, individuals became less relaxed after the induction, a finding that was counter to expectations (see Table 41).

Table 41
Change in Mood due to the Emotion Induction for the Contentment Condition

	Before		After			*t* test			Wilcoxon	
	M	*SD*	*M*	*SD*	*d*	*T*	*df*	*p*	*Z*	*p*
Bad vs. good	72.45	22.19	69.48	20.46	-0.12	-1.81	84	.074	-1.52	.129
Tired vs. energetic	51.33	26.45	51.28	25.52	-0.01	-0.03	84	.979	-0.19	.848
Tense vs. relaxed	70.87	24.23	64.55	25.84	-0.24	-2.89	84	.005	-2.17	.030

Note. Before = before induction; After = after induction; *d* = Cohen's *d*. The poles of the scales were: "bad versus good": 0 = bad, 100 = good; "tired versus energetic": 0 = tired, 100 = energetic; "tense versus relaxed": 0 = tense, 100 = relaxed. Effect sizes and test statistics were computed on difference scores calculated as: after induction – before induction.

With respect to motivation and emotions, there were only two expectations: that ratings on "motivated" would decrease and ratings on "confident" would stay high. The former expectation was met, whereas, counter to expectations, individuals became less confident. In addition, they became more hopeless and angry and less full of positive anticipation after the induction (see Table 42).

Table 42
Change in Emotions due to the Emotion Induction for the Contentment Condition

	Before			After			Sign Test	
	25	*Mdn*	75	25	*Mdn*	75	*S*	*p*
Motivated	3.00	4.00	5.00	3.00	4.00	4.00	10	<.001
Pos. anticipation	3.00	3.00	4.00	2.00	3.00	4.00	13	.001
Anxious	1.00	1.00	2.00	1.00	1.00	2.00	7	.189
Confident	3.00	4.00	4.00	2.00	3.00	4.00	16	.054
Hopeless	1.00	1.00	1.00	1.00	1.00	2.00	15	.002
Angry	1.00	1.00	1.00	1.00	1.00	1.00	16	.004

Note. Before = before induction; After = after induction.

In summary, the emotion induction yielded the expected results in mood change: Individuals in the Control condition moved towards or stayed in a neutral zone on all three mood dimensions and were still above the centre of the scale on “bad versus good”. In the Joy condition, they were in a positive mood, energetic, and relaxed. In the Sadness condition, their mood moved significantly towards a bad mood, and they were more tense and less energetic than before. In the Anger condition, their mood moved considerably towards a bad mood; individuals were more tense, and counter to expectations, they were also less energetic than before. Finally, in the Contentment condition, individuals remained positive in their mood and intermediate on “tired versus energetic”, but counter to expectations, they became more tense.

With respect to motivation, the test-related changes in emotions were small but significant in many cases. In general, the changes were as expected even if they were sometimes smaller. In the Control condition, individuals felt more neutral on all dimensions after the induction than before it. In the Joy condition, counter to expectations, motivation decreased, whereas "full of positive anticipation" did not increase. In the Sadness condition, individuals became less motivated and less "full of positive anticipation" but not more anxious and only slightly more hopeless. In the Anger condition, all positive emotions decreased and negative emotions increased—amongst them, anger, as expected. However, motivation, which had been expected to stay high, decreased. Overall, given the small changes, it seems that test-related emotions are rather stable and not that easy to change.

8.4.2 Comparisons on Affectivity After the Induction

The other question that needed to be answered was whether each experimental condition differed from the Control condition with respect to mood and emotional state after the induction. For mood, three ANOVAs were calculated with "bad versus good", "tired versus energetic", and "tense versus relaxed" as dependent variables and the five conditions as independent variables. They all yielded a significant result; "bad versus good": $F(4, 424) = 60.22$, $p < .05$; "tired versus energetic": $F(4, 424) = 8.19$, $p < .05$; "tense versus relaxed": $F(4, 424) = 50.91$, $p < .05$. A post hoc Dunnett test was calculated to compare each of the four experimental conditions to the Control condition. For motivation and test-related emotions, a Mann-Whitney U test was calculated to compare each of the four experimental conditions to the Control condition. There were four comparisons per dimension; thus, to control the familywise error rate, a Bonferroni correction was applied by dividing .05 by 4 and thus adjusting the significance level from .05 to .0125. In the following sections, the results of both the Dunnett test and the Mann-Whitney U test will be reported condition by condition.

Joy condition. In the Joy condition, the expectation was that individuals would feel better, more energetic, and more relaxed than individuals in the Control condition. Table 43 shows that individuals in the Joy condition were significantly more energetic and more relaxed than those in the Control condition but did not feel significantly better. However, this can be attributed to the fact that individuals in the Control condition were rather high on "bad versus good".

Table 43

Comparisons between the Joy and Control Conditions on the Three Mood Dimensions (Dunnett Test)

	Joy		Control		MD	*SE*	*p*	95% CI		*d*
	M	*SD*	*M*	*SD*				*LL*	*UL*	
Bad vs. good	73.18	22.21	66.23	20.22	6.95	3.34	0.124	-1.26	15.17	0.33
Tired vs. energetic	66.82	23.33	48.05	26.74	18.76	3.74	0.000	9.57	27.96	0.75
Tense vs. relaxed	67.59	21.90	56.28	23.14	11.31	3.43	0.004	2.89	19.73	0.50

Note. MD = mean difference between conditions (Joy – Control); *SE* = standard error; CI = confidence interval for mean difference between conditions; *LL* = lower limit; *UL* = upper limit; *d* = Cohen's *d*. The poles of the scales were: "bad versus good": 0 = bad, 100 = good; "tired versus energetic": 0 = tired, 100 = energetic; "tense versus relaxed": 0 = tense, 100 = relaxed.

For motivation and "full of positive anticipation", the expectation was that both dimensions would be higher in the Joy condition than in the Control condition. However, as Table 44 shows, there were no significant differences in motivation and test-related emotions between the Joy and Control conditions.

Table 44
Comparisons on Motivation and Test-Related Emotions between the Joy and Control Conditions (Mann-Whitney U Test)

	Joy			Control			U test	
	25	*Mdn*	75	25	*Mdn*	75	*Z*	*p*
Motivated	3.00	4.00	4.00	2.25	4.00	4.00	-0.82	.413
Pos. anticipation	2.00	3.00	4.00	2.00	3.00	4.00	-0.01	.995
Anxious	1.00	1.00	2.00	1.00	1.00	1.75	-1.76	.078
Confident	2.00	3.00	4.00	2.00	3.00	4.00	-0.15	.882
Hopeless	1.00	1.00	2.00	1.00	1.00	1.00	-1.64	.101
Angry	1.00	1.00	2.00	1.00	1.00	2.00	-0.18	.861

Note. Mdn = Median. Due to multiple comparisons, a Bonferroni correction was necessary. The alpha level was adjusted from .05 to .0125 because there were four comparisons per emotion.

Sadness condition. In the Sadness condition, the expectation was that individuals would feel worse, more tired, and more tense than subjects in the Control condition. Table 45 shows that individuals in the Sadness condition felt significantly worse and more tense than those in the Control condition. However, there was no difference in energy level.

Table 45

Comparisons between the Sadness and Control Conditions on the Three Mood Dimensions (Dunnett Test)

	Sadness		Control		MD	*SE*	*p*	95% CI		*d*
	M	*SD*	*M*	*SD*				*LL*	*UL*	
Bad vs. good	48.18	24.86	66.23	20.22	-18.05	3.53	0.000	-26.72	-9.38	-0.81
Tired vs. energetic	50.53	23.75	48.05	26.74	2.47	3.95	0.928	-7.23	12.18	0.10
Tense vs. relaxed	45.82	23.55	56.28	23.14	-10.46	3.62	0.015	-19.35	-1.58	-0.45

Note. MD = mean difference between conditions (Sadness – Control); *SE* = standard error; CI = confidence interval for mean difference between conditions; *LL* = lower limit; *UL* = upper limit; *d* = Cohen's *d*. The poles of the scales were: "bad versus good": 0 = bad, 100 = good; "tired versus energetic": 0 = tired, 100 = energetic; "tense versus relaxed": 0 = tense, 100 = relaxed.

For motivation and hopelessness, the expectation was that motivation would be lower and hopelessness would be higher in the Sadness condition than in the Control condition. As Table 46 shows, there were no significant differences in motivation and test-related emotions between the Sadness and Control conditions. Due to the Bonferroni adjustment, significant results were not found for "full of positive anticipation" and "hopeless".

Table 46
Comparisons on Motivation and Test-Related Emotions between the Sadness and Control Conditions (Mann-Whitney U Test)

	Sadness			Control			U test	
	25	*Mdn*	75	25	*Mdn*	75	*Z*	*p*
Motivated	2.25	3.00	4.00	2.25	4.00	4.00	-1.43	.154
Pos. anticipation	2.00	2.00	3.00	2.00	3.00	4.00	-2.36	.019
Anxious	1.00	1.00	2.00	1.00	1.00	1.75	-0.05	.959
Confident	2.00	3.00	4.00	2.00	3.00	4.00	-1.01	.313
Hopeless	1.00	1.00	2.00	1.00	1.00	1.00	-1.97	.049
Angry	1.00	1.00	2.00	1.00	1.00	2.00	-0.09	.930

Note. Mdn = Median. Due to multiple comparisons, a Bonferroni correction was necessary. The alpha level was adjusted from .05 to .0125 because there were four comparisons per emotion.

Anger condition. In the Anger condition, the expectation was that individuals would feel worse, more energetic, and more tense than individuals in the Control condition. Table 47 shows that individuals in the Anger condition felt significantly worse and more tense than in the Control condition. Here, effect sizes were even larger than for the Sadness condition. However, also in this condition, there was no difference in energy level.

Table 47

Comparisons between the Anger and Control Conditions on the Three Mood Dimensions (Dunnett Test)

	Anger		Control		MD	*SE*	*p*	95% CI		*d*
	M	*SD*	*M*	*SD*				*LL*	*UL*	
Bad vs. good	29.03	24.49	66.23	20.22	-37.20	3.33	0.000	-45.36	-29.03	-1.66
Tired vs. energetic	49.54	25.49	48.05	26.74	1.49	3.72	0.985	-7.65	10.63	0.06
Tense vs. relaxed	24.66	20.52	56.28	23.14	-31.63	3.41	0.000	-40.00	-23.26	-1.45

Note. MD = mean difference between conditions (Anger – Control); *SE* = standard error; CI = confidence interval for mean difference between conditions; *LL* = lower limit; *UL* = upper limit; *d* = Cohen's *d*. The poles of the scales were: "bad versus good": 0 = bad, 100 = good; "tired versus energetic": 0= tired, 100 = energetic; "tense versus relaxed": 0 = tense, 100 = relaxed.

For motivation and anger, the expectation was that individuals would feel more motivated and angry in the Anger condition than in the Control condition. In line with expectations, as Table 48 shows, individuals in the Anger condition rated themselves significantly higher on anger, but counter to expectations, also significantly lower on motivation. In addition, individuals were also lower on "full of positive anticipation" but higher on "anxious", "hopeless", and "angry". The rating for "confident" was not significant due to the Bonferroni adjustment.

Table 48
Comparisons on Motivation and Test-Related Emotions between the Anger and Control Conditions (Mann-Whitney U Test)

	Anger			Control			U test	
	25	*Mdn*	75	25	*Mdn*	75	*Z*	*p*
Motivated	2.00	3.00	4.00	2.25	4.00	4.00	-2.63	.009*
Pos. anticipation	1.00	2.00	3.00	2.00	3.00	4.00	-3.84	<.001*
Anxious	1.00	2.00	3.00	1.00	1.00	1.75	-3.51	<.001*
Confident	2.00	3.00	4.00	2.00	3.00	4.00	-2.15	.032
Hhopeless	1.00	1.00	3.00	1.00	1.00	1.00	-3.70	<.001*
Angry	1.00	2.00	4.00	1.00	1.00	2.00	-3.83	<.001*

Note. Mdn = Median. Due to multiple comparisons, a Bonferroni correction was necessary. The alpha level was adjusted from .05 to .0125 because there were four comparisons per emotion.
* $p < .01$.

Contentment condition. Finally, for individuals in the Contentment condition, the expectation was that they would feel significantly better, more tired, and more relaxed than subjects in the Control condition. Table 49 shows that they were significantly more relaxed than individuals in the Control condition. However, there were no significant differences on the other two mood dimensions.

Table 49

Comparisons between the Contentment and Control Conditions on the Three Mood Dimensions (Dunnett Test)

	Content.		Control		MD	*SE*	*p*	95% CI		*d*
	M	*SD*	*M*	*SD*				*LL*	*UL*	
Bad vs. good	69.91	20.47	66.23	20.22	3.68	3.35	0.649	-4.56	11.92	0.18
Tired vs. energetic	51.67	25.76	48.05	26.74	3.61	3.76	0.744	-5.61	12.84	0.14
Tense vs. relaxed	64.89	25.67	56.28	23.14	8.60	3.44	0.044	0.16	17.04	0.35

Note. Content. = Contentment; MD = mean difference between conditions (Contentment – Control); *SE* = standard error; CI = confidence interval for mean difference between conditions; *LL* = lower limit; *UL* = upper limit; *d* = Cohen's *d*. The poles of the scales were: "bad versus good": 0 = bad, 100 = good; "tired versus energetic": 0 = tired, 100 = energetic; "tense versus relaxed": 0 = tense, 100 = relaxed.

For motivation and confidence, the expectation was that motivation would be lower and confidence would be higher in the Contentment than in the Control condition. As Table 50 shows, there were no significant differences in motivation and test-related emotions between the Contentment and Control conditions.

Table 50
Comparisons on Motivation and Test-Related Emotions between the Contentment and Control Conditions (Mann-Whitney U Test)

	Contentment			Control			U test	
	25	*Mdn*	75	25	*Mdn*	75	*Z*	*p*
Motivated	3.00	4.00	4.00	2.25	4.00	4.00	-0.42	.675
Pos. anticipation	2.00	3.00	4.00	2.00	3.00	4.00	-0.42	.677
Anxious	1.00	1.00	2.00	1.00	1.00	1.75	-0.91	.362
Confident	2.00	3.00	4.00	2.00	3.00	4.00	-0.24	.813
Hopeless	1.00	1.00	2.00	1.00	1.00	1.00	-1.65	.098
Angry	1.00	1.00	1.00	1.00	1.00	2.00	-1.11	.267

Note. Mdn = Median. Due to multiple comparisons, a Bonferroni correction was necessary. The alpha level was adjusted from .05 to .0125 because there were four comparisons per emotion.

In summary, for mood, when considering valence, the two positive conditions were similar and did not differ significantly from the Control condition. This may be due to the tendency for baseline mood to generally be slightly positive rather than neutral. The two negative conditions were, as expected, significantly different from the Control condition in both valence and tenseness. Individuals in the two positive conditions were significantly more relaxed in the two positive conditions than in the Control condition. Moreover, energy level was significantly higher in the Joy than in the Control condition. For all other conditions, energy level did not differ significantly from the Control condition.

With respect to motivation and test-related emotions, there were hardly any differences in motivation and test-related emotions. Only in the Anger condition were motivation and all positive test-related emotions significantly lower (except for “confident”) and all negative test-related emotions significantly higher than in the Control condition.

Figure 27 depicts the specific mood state findings for each condition. The significant differences between the Control and the respective experimental conditions were:

- Joy was higher on energy level,
- the two positive conditions were higher on relaxation,
- the two negative conditions were more negative in valence and more tense, and
- Anger was lower on motivation and almost all positive test-related emotions and higher on all negative test-related emotions.

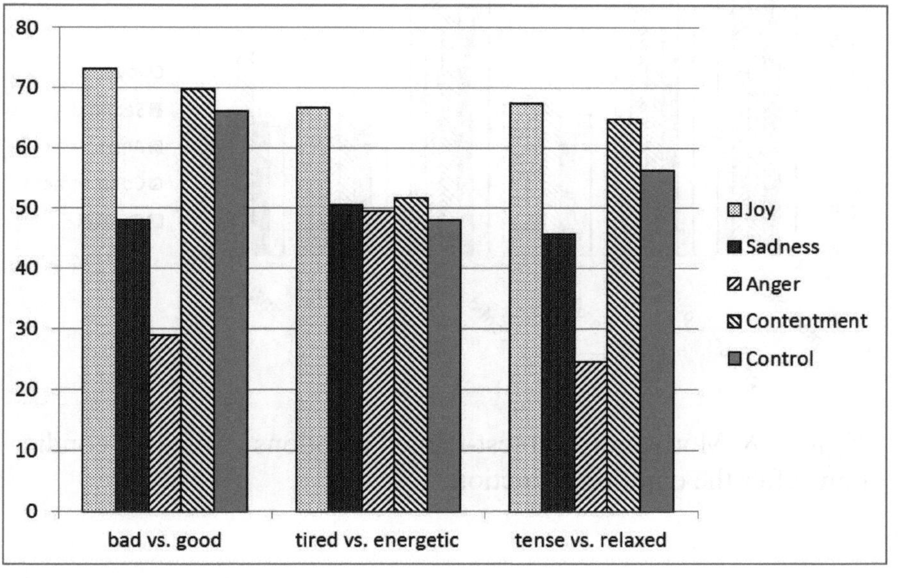

Figure 27. The three mood dimensions in the five conditions after the emotion induction.

Figure 28 depicts the specific motivation and emotional state findings for each condition. The significant differences between the Control and the respective experimental conditions were:

- Sadness was lower on "full of positive anticipation" and "hopeless", and
- Anger was lower on all positive and higher on all negative test-related emotions.

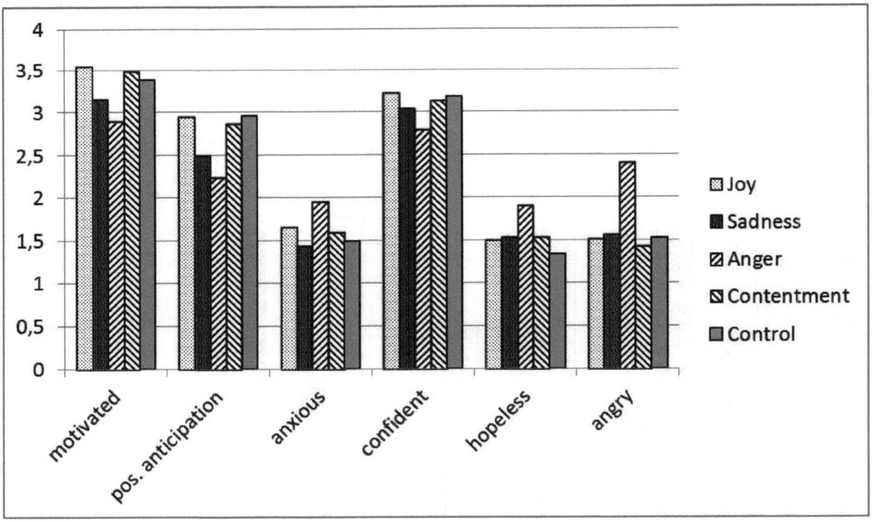

Figure 28. Motivation and test-related emotions in the five conditions after the emotion induction.

8.4.3 *Change in Affectivity During the Test: After Induction versus After Test*

As mentioned previously, one quality criterion for a mood or emotion induction method is how long the effect lasts. In order to test for this, affectivity after the test was compared with affectivity before the test (after the induction). This was possible only for the three mood dimensions because the test-related emotions after the test were different from the test-related emotions before the test.

Control condition. In Table 51, one can see that, just as they had been after the induction, individuals were in a neutral mood state after the test with "bad versus good" slightly in the positive zone.

Table 51
Mood State Comparisons from After the Induction to After the Test for the Control Condition

	After ind.		After test			*t* test			Wilcoxon	
	M	*SD*	*M*	*SD*	*d*	*t*	*df*	*p*	*Z*	*p*
Bad vs. good	66.19	20.33	63.93	23.68	-0.10	-1.35	90	.180	-1.93	.054
Tired vs. energetic	48.42	26.66	49.66	28.54	0.06	0.76	90	.452	0.70	.486
Tense vs. relaxed	56.30	23.27	55.69	23.55	-0.03	-0.33	90	.739	-0.88	.377

Note. After ind. = after induction; *d* = Cohen's *d*. The poles of the scales were: "bad versus good": 0 = bad, 100 = good; "tired versus energetic": 0 = tired, 100 = energetic; "tense versus relaxed": 0 = tense, 100 = relaxed. Effect sizes and test statistics were computed on difference scores calculated as: after test – after induction.

Joy condition. In Table 52, one can see that individuals moved significantly towards a more neutral state in all three mood dimensions.

Table 52
Mood State Comparisons from After the Induction to After the Test for the Joy Condition

	After ind.		After test			t test			Wilcoxon	
	M	*SD*	*M*	*SD*	*d*	*t*	*df*	*p*	*Z*	*p*
Bad vs. good	73.11	22.33	63.34	22.75	-0.44	-5.17	86	<.001	-4.82	<.001
Tired vs. energetic	66.71	23.45	56.66	24.29	-0.43	-4.94	86	<.001	-4.63	<.001
Tense vs. relaxed	67.53	22.01	58.54	23.92	-0.39	-4.41	86	<.001	-3.84	<.001

Note. After ind. = after induction; *d* = Cohen's *d*. The poles of the scales were: "bad versus good": 0 = bad, 100 = good; "tired versus energetic": 0 = tired, 100 = energetic; "tense versus relaxed": 0 = tense, 100 = relaxed. Effect sizes and test statistics were computed on difference scores calculated as: after test – after induction.

Sadness condition. In Table 53, one can see that on the dimension "bad versus good", individuals' scores moved significantly away from the middle of the scale towards a more positive state, which can be viewed as a move towards their baseline mood. They remained in a neutral state on the other two dimensions.

Table 53
Mood State Comparisons from After the Induction to After the Test for the Sadness Condition

	After ind.		After test			*t* test			Wilcoxon	
	M	*SD*	*M*	*SD*	*d*	*t*	*df*	*p*	*Z*	*p*
Bad vs. good	48.18	24.86	58.10	20.26	0.44	3.75	71	<.001	3.97	<.001
Tired vs. energetic	50.53	23.75	50.65	21.99	0.01	0.06	71	.949	0.10	.920
Tense vs. relaxed	45.82	23.55	51.36	21.93	0.24	2.21	71	.030	1.71	.088

Note. After ind. = after induction; *d* = Cohen's *d*. The poles of the scales were: "bad versus good": 0 = bad, 100 = good; "tired versus energetic": 0 = tired, 100 = energetic; "tense versus relaxed": 0 = tense, 100 = relaxed. Effect sizes and test statistics were computed on difference scores calculated as: after test – after induction.

Anger condition. In Table 54, one can see that individuals moved back towards a neutral state on the dimensions "bad versus good" and "tense versus relaxed", whereas they remained in a neutral state on the dimension "tired versus energetic".

Table 54

Mood State Comparisons from After the Induction to After the Test for the Anger Condition

	After ind.		After test			*t* test			Wilcoxon	
	M	*SD*	*M*	*SD*	*d*	*t*	*df*	*p*	*Z*	*p*
Bad vs. good	29.03	24.49	50.08	25.31	0.84	9.62	89	<.001	7.34	<.001
Tired vs. energetic	49.54	25.49	44.89	26.42	-0.18	-1.93	89	.057	-1.50	.134
Tense vs. relaxed	24.66	20.52	42.52	23.81	0.80	9.15	89	<.001	6.91	<.001

Note. After ind. = after induction; *d* = Cohen's *d*. The poles of the scales were: "bad versus good": 0 = bad, 100 = good; "tired versus energetic": 0 = tired, 100 = energetic; "tense versus relaxed": 0 = tense, 100 = relaxed. Effect sizes and test statistics were computed on difference scores calculated as: after test – after induction.

Contentment condition. In Table 55, one can see that individuals moved towards a more neutral state on "bad versus good", but they remained in a neutral state on "tired versus energetic" and slightly above neutral on "tense versus relaxed".

Table 55

Mood State Comparisons from After the Induction to After the Test for the Contentment Condition

	After ind.		After test			t test			Wilcoxon	
	M	*SD*	*M*	*SD*	*d*	*t*	*df*	*p*	*Z*	*p*
Bad vs. good	69.91	20.47	65.07	23.54	-0.22	-3.12	86	.002	-2.99	.003
Tired vs. energetic	51.67	25.76	50.57	26.85	-0.04	-0.77	86	.450	-1.38	.167
Tense vs. relaxed	64.89	25.67	61.85	25.19	-0.12	-1.77	86	.080	-2.07	.039

Note. After ind. = after induction; *d* = Cohen's *d*. The poles of the scales were: "bad versus good": 0 = bad, 100 = good; "tired versus energetic": 0 = tired, 100 = energetic; "tense versus relaxed": 0 = tense, 100 = relaxed. Effect sizes and test statistics were computed on difference scores calculated as: after test – after induction.

The above results indicate that taking the test had an impact on participants' affective states. Their feelings after the test were different from their feelings after the induction: The dimension "bad versus good" returned to or remained at a point slightly above the centre of the scale, which can be viewed as neutral baseline mood in the sense that baseline is slightly positive. The other two dimensions, "tired versus energetic" and "tense versus relaxed", returned to or remained in the neutral zone.

8.4.4 Change in Affectivity During the Test: Before Induction versus After Test

In the section above, it is clear that the effect of the emotion induction was not stable in the sense that mood state was unchanged after the test. It was expected that taking the test would change the mood participants started it. To further tap into the stability of the change induced by the emotion induction procedure, mood state before the induction was compared with mood state after the test. The expectation here was that mood would not return to its initial state.

Control condition. In Table 56, one can see that individuals' states on the dimensions "bad versus good" and "tense versus relaxed" were still significantly different from their initial mood states. None of the three dimensions changed during the test (see Table 51), and thus, mood for the Control condition could be considered stable.

Table 56
Mood State Comparisons from Before the Induction to After the Test for the Control Condition

	Before ind.		After test			*t* test			Wilcoxon	
	M	*SD*	*M*	*SD*	*d*	*t*	*df*	*p*	*Z*	*p*
Bad vs. good	72.30	21.82	63.93	23.68	-0.36	-3.76	90	<.001	-4.05	<.001
Tired vs. energetic	49.31	24.60	49.66	28.54	0.03	0.15	90	.881	0.37	.713
Tense vs. relaxed	70.51	22.16	55.69	23.55	-0.64	-6.21	90	<.001	-5.46	<.001

Note. Before ind. = before induction; *d* = Cohen's *d*. The poles of the scales were: "bad vs. good": 0 = bad, 100 = good; "tired vs. energetic": 0 = tired, 100 = energetic; "tense vs. relaxed": 0 = tense, 100 = relaxed. Effect sizes and test statistics were computed on difference scores calculated as: after test – before induction.

Joy condition. Table 57 shows that individuals' "bad versus good" ratings were higher after the induction than before it but fell below the initial level after the test. Energy level returned to the initial level after the test, and individuals were more tense after the test than they had been before the test; thus, they did not return to their initial state on this dimension.

Table 57
Mood State Comparisons from Before the Induction to After the Test for the Joy Condition

	Before ind.		After test			*t* test			Wilcoxon	
	M	*SD*	*M*	*SD*	*d*	*t*	*df*	*p*	*Z*	*p*
Bad vs. good	69.81	21.75	63.34	22.75	-0.28	-2.94	85	.004	-2.70	.007
Tired vs. energetic	54.01	28.88	56.66	24.29	0.10	1.13	85	.262	0.61	.541
Tense vs. relaxed	69.51	23.73	58.54	23.92	-0.44	-4.46	85	<.001	-4.08	<.001

Note. Before ind. = before induction; *d* = Cohen's *d*. The poles of the scales were: "bad vs. good": 0 = bad, 100 = good; "tired vs. energetic": 0 = tired, 100 = energetic; "tense vs. relaxed": 0 = tense, 100 = relaxed. Effect sizes and test statistics were computed on difference scores calculated as: after test – before induction.

Sadness condition. In Table 58, one can see that individuals' mood state in the Sadness condition did not fully return to its initial state after the test.

Table 58
Mood State Comparisons from Before the Induction to After the Test for the Sadness Condition

	Before ind.		After test			*t* test			Wilcoxon	
	M	*SD*	*M*	*SD*	*d*	*t*	*df*	*p*	*Z*	*p*
Bad vs. good	74.21	19.45	58.10	20.26	-0.81	-6.93	71	<.001	-5.75	74.21
Tired vs. energetic	57.88	26.01	50.65	21.99	-0.30	-3.34	71	.001	-2.74	57.88
Tense vs. relaxed	65.90	25.58	51.36	21.93	-0.61	-5.68	71	<.001	-4.94	65.90

Note. Before ind. = before induction; *d* = Cohen's *d*. The poles of the scales were: "bad vs. good": 0 = bad, 100 = good; "tired vs. energetic": 0 = tired, 100 = energetic; "tense vs. relaxed": 0 = tense, 100 = relaxed. Effect sizes and test statistics were computed on difference scores calculated as: after test – before induction.

Anger condition. Table 59 shows that also in the Anger condition, individuals' mood state did not fully return to its initial state after the test.

Table 59
Mood State Comparisons from Before the Induction to After the Test for the Anger Condition

	Before ind.		After test			*t* test			Wilcoxon	
	M	*SD*	*M*	*SD*	*d*	*t*	*df*	*p*	*Z*	*p*
Bad vs. good	72.22	21.39	50.08	25.31	-0.94	-9.07	89	<.001	-7.04	<.001
Tired vs. energetic	55.64	25.96	44.89	26.42	-0.41	-3.94	89	<.001	-3.60	<.001
Tense vs. relaxed	63.40	24.58	42.52	23.81	-0.86	-8.20	89	<.001	-6.80	<.001

Note. Before ind. = before induction; *d* = Cohen's *d*. The poles of the scales were: "bad vs. good": 0 = bad, 100 = good; "tired vs. energetic": 0 = tired, 100 = energetic; "tense vs. relaxed": 0 = tense, 100 = relaxed. Effect sizes and test statistics were computed on difference scores calculated as: after test – before induction.

Contentment condition. Finally, Table 60 shows that individuals in the Contentment condition did not return to their initial mood states on the dimensions "bad versus good" and "tense versus relaxed", whereas their ratings on "tired versus energetic" did not change significantly from before to after the induction (Table 41) or from before the induction to after the test (Table 60).

Table 60
Mood State Comparisons from Before the Induction to After the Test for the Contentment Condition

	Before ind.		After test			t test			Wilcoxon	
	M	*SD*	*M*	*SD*	*d*	*t*	*df*	*p*	*Z*	*p*
Bad vs. good	72.45	22.19	65.07	23.54	-0.32	-3.68	84	<.001	-3.40	.001
Tired vs. energetic	51.33	26.45	50.57	26.85	-0.03	-0.47	84	.637	-0.65	.517
Tense vs. relaxed	70.87	24.23	61.85	25.19	-0.36	-4.66	84	<.001	-4.16	<.001

Note. Before ind. = before induction; *d* = Cohen's *d*. The poles of the scales were: "bad vs. good": 0 = bad, 100 = good; "tired vs. energetic": 0 = tired, 100 = energetic; "tense vs. relaxed": 0 = tense, 100 = relaxed. Effect sizes and test statistics were computed on difference scores calculated as: after test – before induction.

Thus, after the test, participants did not fully return to the mood states that had been recorded before the emotion induction. This means that the change in mood evoked by the film clips did not peter out right away, but rather persisted for a while.

8.5 Effects of Affective State on Test Performance

8.5.1 *Test Performance After the Emotion Induction*

Table 61 depicts the descriptive statistics for performance on the second test for the five groups and for the entire sample. For the entire sample, there was an overall improvement over the first test (first test: Number Correct: *M* = 9.62, Number Wrong: *M* =

4.09; second test: Number Correct: $M = 11.20$, Number Wrong: $M = 4.66$). The distributions for the two scores for the total sample were, as on the first test, positively skewed and leptokurtic and significantly different from a normal distribution (Kolmogorov-Smirnov test; Number Correct: $Z = 4.24$, $p < .01$; Number Wrong: $Z = 6.04$, $p < .01$). Score distributions can be found in Appendix F.

Table 61
Descriptive Statistics for Performance on the Second Test by Experimental Group and for the Entire Sample

		N	*M*	*SD*	Range	Skew	Kurt
Joy	Number Correct	88	11.91	9.16	3-65	3.17	13.39
	Number Wrong	88	5.40	9.51	0-63	3.65	17.14
Sadness	Number Correct	72	9.76	6.61	1-44	2.92	11.43
	Number Wrong	72	3.74	6.84	0-45	4.28	21.20
Anger	Number Correct	90	10.68	6.94	1-44	2.26	6.72
	Number Wrong	90	3.91	6.13	0-35	2.91	9.61
Contentment	Number Correct	87	11.09	7.65	3-60	3.77	20.23
	Number Wrong	87	4.47	7.93	0-58	4.35	24.73
Control	Number Correct	92	12.27	9.44	4-68	3.30	14.41
	Number Wrong	92	5.60	10.04	0-67	3.74	17.13
Total	Number Correct	429	11.20	8.11	1-68	3.25	14.84
	Number Wrong	429	4.66	8.28	0-67	3.97	20.26

Note. Skew = Skewness. Kurt = Kurtosis.

8.5.2 Differences between the Scores on the Second Test

I tested for whether there were differences between the five groups using an ANOVA. Before calculating the ANOVA, I tested for whether the data met the assumptions for computing an ANOVA. As already mentioned above, independence of residuals is given when individuals are randomly assigned to the conditions (Eid et al., 2010) as was the case here. A Levene test showed that the variances between the five groups were equal; Number Correct: $F(4, 424) = 1.12, p > .05$; Number Wrong: $F(4, 424) = 2.09, p > .05$, but, as mentioned above, the scores were not normally distributed. Therefore, the same procedure that had previously been used to test for group differences on the first test was performed: first an ANOVA with the uncorrected scores, then another one with the Box-Cox transformed scores, and finally a Kruskal-Wallis test. Table 62 shows that there were no significant differences between the five experimental groups in Number Correct, $F(4, 424) = 1.23, p > .05$, and Number Wrong, $F(4, 424) = 0.89, p > .05$.

Table 62
ANOVA Testing for Differences between the Five Experimental Groups on the Second Test for both Number Correct and Number Wrong

								90% CI for η^2	
		SS	*df*	*MS*	*F*	*p*	η^2	*LL*	*UL*
Number Correct	Between	323.97	4	80.99	1.23	0.296	0.011	0.000	0.025
	Within	27849.39	424	65.68					
	Total	28173.36	428						
Number Wrong	Between	243.84	4	60.96	0.89	0.471	0.008	0.000	0.019
	Within	29110.15	424	68.66					
	Total	29353.99	428						

Note. SS = sum of squares; *df* = degrees of freedom; *MS* = mean square; CI = confidence interval; *LL* = lower limit; *UL* = upper limit.

To test the robustness of the ANOVA results, the scores were transformed using the Box-Cox transformation (Box & Cox, 1964) so that they would be more normally distributed. The syntax used for the score transformations and tables with the transformed values along with skewness and kurtosis can be found in Appendix F.

The score that was closest to a normal distribution was used to calculate another ANOVA to check the results of the previously conducted analysis. In line with the results of the first ANOVA, there were no significant differences between the five experimental groups in Number Correct, $F(4, 424) = 1.89$, $p > .05$, or in Number Wrong $F(4, 424) = 0.56$, $p > .05$.

The score transformation yielded an improvement in the score distributions (Number Correct: Skewness = 0.40, Kurtosis = 1.86; Number Wrong: Skewness = 0.49, Kurtosis = -0.20), but the scores were still not normally distributed (Kolmogorov-Smirnov test; Number Correct: $Z = 4.24$, $p < .01$; Number Wrong: $Z = 6.04$, $p < .01$). A normally distributed dependent variable is one of the requirements for an ANOVA, and violations of this requirement affect the power of the test. Therefore, to test the robustness of the results, the differences were once again analysed using a Kruskal-Wallis test (Kruskal & Wallis, 1952). The result was the same: no significant differences between the groups (Number Correct: $\chi^2 = 6.49$, $p > .05$; Number Wrong: $\chi^2 = 2.03$, $p > .05$).

8.5.3 Effects of Emotion on Test Performance

To take into account the group differences in cognitive ability and thus performance on the first test, a two-factorial mixed analysis of variance with one within-subjects factor (performance on the first and second tests) and one between-subjects factor (condition: Joy, Sadness, Anger, Contentment, and Control) was conducted. This was done for Number Correct and Number Wrong.

Number correct. In Table 63, one can see that the analysis yielded a significant main effect of the within-subjects factor, first and second completion of the test, $F(1, 424) = 36.80$, $p < .05$, but no significant main effect of group, $F(4, 424) = 0.81$, $p > .05$, and no significant interaction of the within-subjects factor and the group factor, $F(4, 424) = 1.30$, $p > .05$. The significant effect of the within-subjects factor means that individuals improved significantly from the first to the second completion of the test, but this improvement was not influenced by the condition participants were assigned to; thus, the improvement was not influenced by their emotional state. Medium effects had been expected, but the actual effect sizes were close to 0.

Table 63
Two-Factorial Mixed ANOVA Testing for Differences on Number Correct with One Between-Subjects Factor (Group) and One Within-Subjects Factor (First and Second Test)

	SS	*df*	*MS*	*F*	*p*	η^2_p
Between subjects						
Main effect of condition	304.42	4	76.11	0.81	.518	.008
Residual	39764.49	424	93.78			
Within subjects						
Main effect of retest	512.17	1	512.17	36.80	.000	.080
Interaction Retest * Condition	72.31	4	18.08	1.30	.270	.012
Residual	5901.68	424	13.92			
Total	**46555.06**	**857**	**714.05**			

Note. SS = sum of squares; *df* = degrees of freedom; *MS* = mean square.

A post hoc power analysis on the effects yielded the following values for (1 – β): main effect of condition: 1 – β = .26, main effect of retest: 1 – β = 1.00; interaction effect: 1 – β = .41.

As scores were not normally distributed, in order to back up the results, the same analysis was conducted using the Box-Cox transformed scores. The results in Table 64 point in the same direction as those for the untransformed scores: no significant main effect of condition, $F(4, 424) = 2.08$, $p > .05$, and no significant interaction effect of retest and condition, $F(4, 424) = 0.35$, $p > .05$, but there was a significant main effect of retest $F(1, 424) = 50.62$, $p < .01$. The effect sizes for the two main effects increased slightly (condition: $\eta^2_p = 0.019$; retest: $\eta^2_p = 0.107$) whereas the interaction effect of Retest * Condition became even smaller ($\eta^2_p = 0.003$).

Table 64

Two-Way Factorial Mixed ANOVA Testing for Differences on Number Correct with One Between-Subjects Factor (Group) and One Within-Subjects Factor (First and Second Test) using the Box-Cox Transformed Scores

	SS	*df*	*MS*	*F*	*p*	η^2_p
Between subjects						
Main effect of condition	4.09	4	1.02	2.08	.083	.019
Residual	208.42	424	0.49			
Within subjects						
Main effect of retest	3.95	1	3.95	50.62	.000	.107
Interaction Retest * Condition	0.11	4	0.03	0.35	.846	.003
Residual	33.10	424	0.08			
Total	**249.67**	**857**	**5.57**			

Note. *SS* = sum of squares; *df* = degrees of freedom; *MS* = mean square.

A post hoc power analysis on the effects yielded the following values for (1 – β): main effect of condition: 1 – β = .62, main effect of retest: 1 – β = 1.00; interaction effect: 1 – β = .13.

Number Wrong. Table 65 shows that the mixed analysis of variance for Number Wrong did not yield significant main effects of retest, $F(1, 424) = 2.87$, $p > .05$, or condition, $F(4, 424) = 0.39$, $p > .05$, or a significant interaction effect of retest and condition, $F(4, 424) = 2.00$, $p > .05$.

Table 65
Two-Way Factorial Mixed ANOVA Testing for Differences in Number Wrong with One Between-Subjects Factor (Group) and One Within-Subjects Factor (First and Second Test)

	SS	*df*	*MS*	*F*	*p*	η^2_p
Between subjects						
Main effect of condition	160.22	4	40.06	0.39	.819	.004
Residual	44077.93	424	103.96			
Within subjects						
Main effect of retest	59.27	1	59.27	2.87	.091	.007
Interaction retest * condition	165.04	4	41.26	2.00	.094	.018
Residual	8759.43	424	20.66			
Total	**53221.89**	**857**	**265.20**			

Note. SS = sum of squares; *df* = degrees of freedom; *MS* = mean square.

A post hoc power analysis on the effects yielded the following values for $(1 - \beta)$: main effect of Condition: $1 - \beta = .14$, main effect of retest: $1 - \beta = .39$; interaction effect: $1 - \beta = .60$.

For the Box-Cox transformed scores, the results pointed in the same direction (Table 66): no significant main effect of the within-subjects factor, $F(1, 424) = 0.98$, $p > .05$, or of the between-subjects factor, $F(4, 424) = 0.56$, $p > .05$, and no significant interaction between the two factors, $F(4, 424) = 1.01$, $p > .05$.

Table 66
Two-Way Factorial Mixed ANOVA Testing for Differences on Number Wong with One Between-Subjects Factor (Group) and One Within-Subjects Factor (First and Second test) using the Box-Cox Transformed Scores

	SS	*df*	*MS*	*F*	*p*	η^2_p
Between subjects						
Main effect of condition	2.335	4	.584	0.56	.690	.005
Residual	440.262	424	1.038			
Within subjects						
Main effect of retest	.187	1	.187	0.98	.324	.002
Interaction Retest * Condition	.778	4	.194	1.01	.401	.009
Residual	81.489	424	.192			
Total	**525.05**	**857**	**2.20**			

Note. SS = sum of squares; *df* = degrees of freedom; *MS* = mean square.

A post hoc power analysis on the effects yielded the following values for (1 – β): main effect of condition: 1 – β = .19, main effect of retest: 1 – β = .17; interaction effect: 1 – β = .32.

The results of the ANOVAs showed that there were no differences in test performance between the five groups, neither in Number Correct nor in Number Wrong, even when taking into account performance on the first test. It was expected that there would not be any differences between the five groups when conducting the one-way ANOVA for only the effect of group without taking into account performance on the first test: On an interindividual level, differences in performance seemed to be largely due to differences in underlying cognitive abilities and not so much due to the influence of mood and emotions. In her study, Abele (1995) did not find an impact of mood on test performance until she used a repeated-measures design to control for the large differences between participants in cognitive ability. This was the reason I chose a repeated-measures design here.

However, counter to expectations, there were also no differences when performance on the first test was taken into account by using the two-way factorial mixed ANOVA with one between- and one within-subjects factor. Thus, none of the null hypotheses could be rejected. However, randomisation had not been fully successful: There were differences between the groups on age and on some of the emotional states before the emotion induction. Thus, it was necessary to determine the extent to which this had influenced the results. To test this, the data were further analysed using structural equation modelling.

8.5.4 Structural Equation Models

The purpose of applying structural equation modelling was to test whether there were impacts of mood and emotions on test performance that could not be detected because randomisation had not been fully successful with respect to age and some of the test-related state emotions. Moreover, structural equation modelling allows the user to control for measurement error, a factor that is likely to result in more variance in unsupervised online settings than in laboratory settings, for example. Three structural equation models were tested: The first model comprised only performance on the first and second tests and used the first and second halves of each test as indicators of the latent variables "performance on the first test" and "performance on the second test", respectively. The second model added the five dummy-coded conditions to these variables. The third model added mood and emotional state after the emotion induction to the first model. If there was an effect of mood and emotions on performance, then this third model, which took mood and emotions into account independently of condition, would be likely to detect these differences.

The following restrictions were made to the models: The two tests were parallel versions that measured the same construct; therefore, strong measurement invariance of the test was assumed for all three models. Consequently, the loadings of the first and second halves of the tests were set equal. Furthermore, the intercepts were set to 0 and set equal across time. Finally, the expected values of both the first and second tests were allowed to be free. As test scores were not normally distributed, the MLR estimator was used.

Model 1. Test performance. As already mentioned, Model 1 comprised only performance on the first and second tests as variables. The indicators of the latent variables "Test 1" (performance on the first test) and "Test 2" (performance on the second test) were the number of correct solutions on the first half and the number of correct solutions on the second half of the test. Figure 29 depicts Model 1. The unstandardised loadings of the two test halves on their respective latent trait variables were 1.00 and 1.10, respectively (*ps* $< .01$). The standardised loadings of the two test halves on their respective latent variables were between 0.92 and

0.98 ($ps < .01$). This means that the two test halves were reliable predictors of the underlying latent variables. The test halves were correlate at $r = .91$ (Test 1) and $r = .93$ (Test 2), indicating that the test was reliable.

The unstandardised regression coefficient from regressing Test 2 on Test 1 was 1.00 ($p < .01$) and the standardised regression coefficient was .80 ($p < .01$). This means that performance on the first test was a strong predictor of performance on the second test and that performance was rather stable.

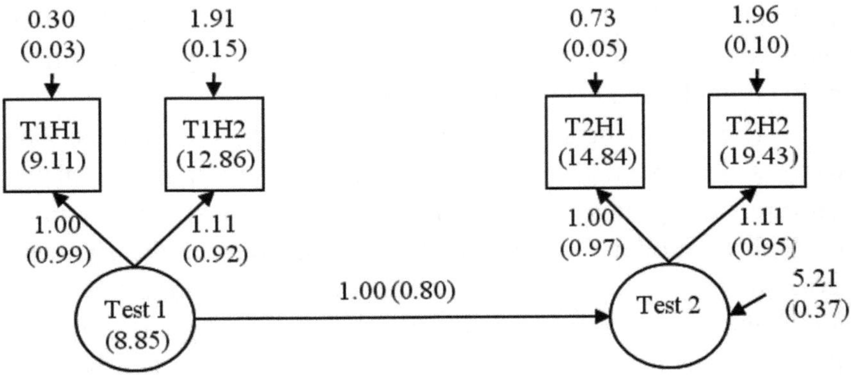

Figure 29. Model 1 with only performance on the first test as the predictor for performance on the second test. T1H1: First half of the first test. T1H2: Second half of the first test. T2H1: First half of the second test. T2H2: Second half of the second test. Unstandardised coefficients do not have parentheses; standardised coefficients are given in parentheses.

Model 2. Test performance and conditions. As already mentioned, Model 2 comprised performance on the first and second tests and the five conditions as variables. As in Model 1, the indicators were the latent variables "Test 1" (performance on the first test) and "Test 2" (performance on the second test) and reflected the number of correct solutions on the first and second halves of the test, respectively. Figure 30 depicts Model 2. The unstandardised loadings of the two test halves on the respective latent variables were between 1.00 and 1.10. The standardised loadings were between .92 and .99. This again means that the two test halves were valid predictors of the underlying latent trait.

As in Model 1, the unstandardised regression coefficient from regressing Test 2 on Test 1 was 1.00, and the standardised regression coefficient was .80, whereas the unstandardised regression coefficients for predicting Test 2 from the conditions were 0. This means that the conditions did not explain additional variance in performance on the second test beyond what could be predicted from the first test.

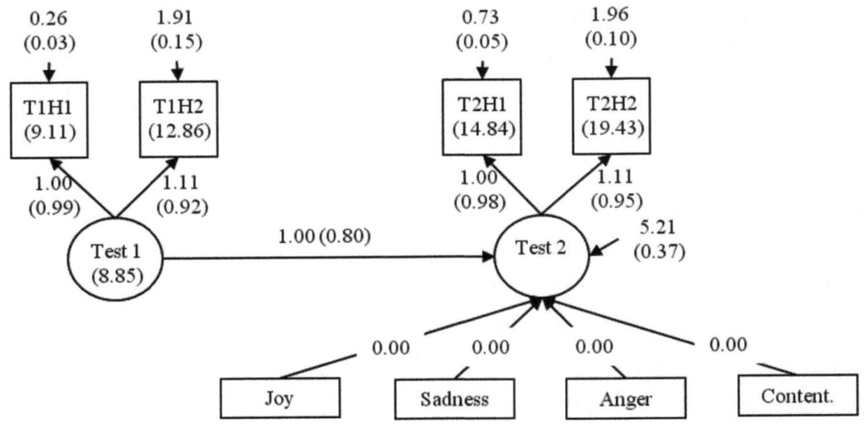

Figure 30. Model 2 with performance on the first test and the experimental conditions as predictors of performance on the second test. T1H1: First half of the first test. T1H2: Second half of the first test. T2H1: First half of the second test. T2H2: Second half of the second test. Unstandardised coefficients do not have parentheses; standardised coefficients are given in parentheses.

Model 3. Test performance, mood, and emotions. As already mentioned, Model 3 comprised performance on the first and second tests and mood and emotions after the induction as variables. As in Model 1, the indicators were the latent variables "Test 1" (performance on the first test) and "Test 2" (performance on the second test) and reflected the number of correct solutions on the first second halves of the test, respectively. It was not possible to create a latent variable for mood and emotions. As mentioned in an earlier section, the three mood dimensions were highly intercorrelated and so were the positive and negative test-related emotions. However, it was also pointed out that the mood dimensions as well as the emotions are distinct. Therefore, no latent variable for mood and emotions was included in the analysis. Rather, mood and emotions were included on a manifest level.

Figure 31 depicts Model 3. The unstandardised loadings of the two test halves on the respective latent variables were between 1.00 and 1.10. The standardised loadings were between .92 and .98. This again means that the two test halves were valid predictors of the underlying latent trait. This time, the unstandardised regression coefficient from regressing Test 2 on Test 1 was 0.99, and the standardised one was .78. The unstandardised regression coefficients for predicting Test 2 from mood and emotions were between -0.38 and 0.30; the standardised regression coefficients were between 0 and .09, and none of them were significant. This means that performance on the first test was the best predictor of performance on the second test, and mood and emotions did not explain a significant amount of additional variance.

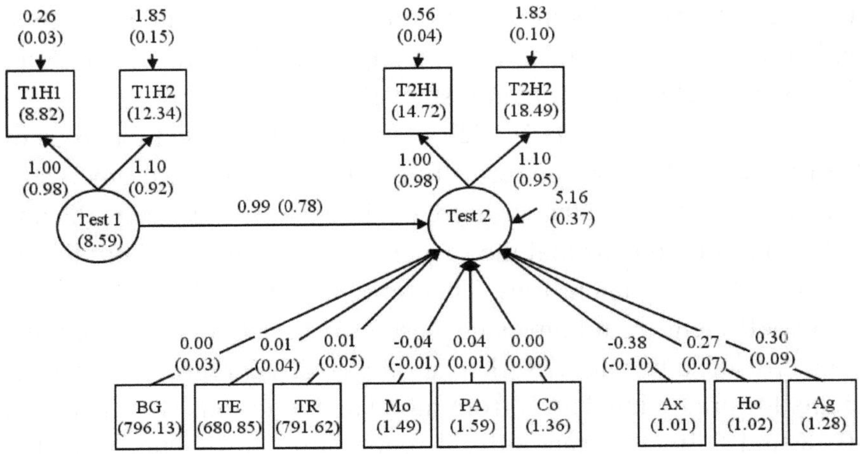

Figure 31. Model 3 with performance on the first test, mood, and emotions after induction as predictors of performance on the second test. T1H1: First half of the first test. T1H2: Second half of the first test. T2H1: First half of the second test. T2H2: Second half of the second test. BG: Mood bad versus good. TE: Mood tired versus energetic. TR: Mood tense versus relaxed. Mo: Motivation. PA: Full of positive anticipation. Co: Confident. Ax: Anxious. Ho: Hopeless. Ag: Angry. Unstandardised coefficients do not have parentheses; standardised coefficients are given in parentheses.

When comparing the variances of the test halves in Model 3 to those shown in Models 1 and 2, one can see that they are different. This is due to missing data in Model 3. All individuals in the data set had been assigned to one of the conditions and had completed both tests. Thus, for Models 1 and 2, all cases were included in the analysis. However, the mood and emotion ratings were not mandatory; therefore, not all participants provided this information, which was needed in the analysis for Model 3. Thus, for Model 3, not all cases were included in the analysis, and the variances in Models 1 and 2 thus differed from the ones in Model 3.

Table 67 contains the fit indices for the three models. All three of them fit the data well. Comparing the three models is not appropriate because each of them comprises a different number of variables and thus fit indices are not comparable. However, from the results presented here, one can conclude that the best predictor of performance on the second test is performance on the first test, and mood and emotions do not explain a significant amount of additional variance.

Table 67
Fit Indices for the Three Models

	Model 1	Model 2	Model 3
$\chi^2 (df)$	6.004(3)	33.672(19)	37.993(30)
$p(\chi^2)$ (Cor. factor for MLR)	0.111 (1.013)	0.0201 (0.970)	0.1499 (0.989)
CFI/TLI	0.998 / 0.996	0.992 / 0.991	0.996 / 0.994
RMSEA	0.048	0.042	0.026
90% CI RMSEA	0.000 0.105	0.017 0.065	0.000 0.048
p(RMSEA $\leq$ .05)	0.435	0.678	0.962
SRMR	0.007	0.025	0.031
AIC	7394.834	7394.834	6778.368

The Mplus outputs for all three models can be found in Appendix G.

8.5.5 Summary

There was no impact of state mood, state test-related motivation, and state test-related emotions on performance on the reasoning test. This result held also when computing a mixed analysis of variance that took into account individual differences in cognitive ability. The result was confirmed by structural equation modelling.

9 Discussion

The experimentally manipulated emotions of joy, sadness, anger, and contentment as well as a neutral emotional state did not impact performance on a test of reasoning ability. This held for the number of correct responses and the number of incorrect responses. The results did not change when individual performance differences were taken into account by using a repeated-measures design as suggested by Abele (1995) on the basis of her experiences with experiments on mood and test performance. Effect sizes were also small. There was a significant effect of only the within-person factor such that performance on the second test was better than performance on the first test. However, there were no differences between the five groups in the amount of improvement. The three structural equation models that were calculated also reflected this result: All three of them fit the data well. Thus, for the present study, it can be concluded that performance on the first test was the strongest predictor of performance on the second test, and there was no significant impact of emotions on test performance.

It was possible to evoke different distinct emotional and mood states using short film clips in an unsupervised online setting. Each affective state had a distinct profile on the three mood dimensions "bad versus good", "tired versus energetic", and "tense versus relaxed". To a lesser degree, it was possible to change test-related emotions, but they appeared to be rather stable and more trait-like.

Participants in this unsupervised online experiment who completed the entire study appeared to be serious and motivated and thus produced interpretable data. The sample was rather diverse and thus can be considered to be more representative of the general population than previous samples that have consisted of only university students. Furthermore, the current study took place in an environment that was identical to the one in which the majority of online assessments in the context of employment testing take place: in front of the home computer. However, due to the unsupervised setting, there were some undesirable effects on the data, particularly drop-out effects but also very likely some self-selection effects.

These findings will be discussed in detail with their implications, limitations, and conclusions below. First, I will present one section on the impact of emotions on test performance, followed by a section on online emotion induction, and then finally by a section on unsupervised online experiments.

9.1 Impact of Emotions on Test Performance

As already mentioned, the experimentally manipulated emotions of joy, sadness, anger, and contentment as well as neutral did not impact performance on a test of reasoning ability. This finding will now be discussed against the backdrop of the present study's four experimental hypotheses. Two of the hypotheses were based on the valence of the emotions and two of them on the activation of the emotions. First, the implications of the results found here will be discussed against the backdrop of theories and findings that are pertinent to the valence component of mood and emotions. Then the same will be done with regard to theories and findings that are pertinent to the arousal component of mood and emotions. Finally, the results will be discussed against the backdrop of theories that claim an interaction of affect and task type on test performance.

9.1.1 Valence of Mood or Emotions and Reasoning Test Performance

The hypotheses on the impact of the valence component of emotions on test performance were:

Hypothesis 1: Activating emotions: Performance on an IQ test will be better for participants in the emotional state of joy than for participants in the emotional state of anger.

Hypothesis 2: Deactivating emotions: Performance on an IQ test will be better for participants in the emotional state of contentment than for participants in the emotional state of sadness.

The backdrop for these hypotheses were theories on (a) mood-induced thinking styles, (b) cognitive capacity and resource allocation, (c) the impact of positive emotions on working memory through certain connections in the brain, and (d) the influence of emotions on task-related motivation. The assumption was that at the same level of activation, the performance of people experiencing positive emotions would be better because (a) positive emotions allow for a more flexible thinking style, faster processing, and the consideration of several aspects at a time; (b) when people experience positive emotions, all of their cognitive resources are available for the task at hand, whereas during the experience of negative emotions, some capacity is allocated towards mood repair processes; (c) working memory, which accounts for a large amount of variance in reasoning tasks, is best for positive affect; and (d) task-related motivation has been found to be higher for people in positive moods in most studies. However, none of these theories could be supported by the present findings. In the following, the results of the present study will be discussed against the backdrop of (a) mood-induced thinking styles, (b) cognitive capacity and resource allocation, (c) results from brain science, and (d) motivation.

Mood-induced thinking styles. Theories on mood-induced thinking styles (Damasio, 1994; Isen, 1984; Kuhl, 1983a, b; Schwarz, 1990) posit that in positive moods, individuals have an intuitive-heuristic thinking style, whereas it is sequential-analytical in negative moods. Proponents of this approach argue that performance on easy tasks is better for people in negative moods because the sequential-analytical mode is less error-prone (Kuhl, 1983b), whereas performance on tasks of intermediate to high difficulty is better for people in positive moods because it allows for faster processing, more efficient allocation of resources (Isen, 2000), and for the consideration of several aspects at a time (Kuhl, 1983b).

Because of the adaptive properties of the test used in the present study, it was not possible to look at different difficulty levels. This issue will be discussed further in the section on limitations. The consequence was that only the overall scores could be examined. It had been predicted that the overall score would be better for positive emotions because the items quickly become increasingly complex, and finding the correct solution requires more intermediate steps the more difficult the item is. Only items from the first difficulty category can be solved in one step. All other difficulty categories require the test-taker to consider several rows and columns at a time. Therefore, it was assumed that being able to consider several aspects at a time and being able to process information more quickly, both of which are related to positive affective states, would contribute to the overall score. This idea was also in line with Abele's (1995) findings that individuals in positive moods had better overall scores on the test than subjects in negative moods. However, her findings could not be replicated here.

On the other hand, on the basis of the tendency for the sequential-analytical processing style to be less error-prone but slower, one could conclude that the individuals in negative moods completed fewer tasks but also gave fewer wrong answers and thus were more accurate (Sinclair, 1988). However, such a tendency could not be found in the present data either.

In their meta-analysis, Lyubomirski and colleagues (Lyubomirski et al., 2005) discussed a few other variables that might moderate the impact of mood-induced thinking styles on performance, amongst them the familiarity versus the novelty of the material. When working with learned material, the heuristic strategy is beneficial because it allows for faster and more efficient problem solving. However, when the material is novel, it requires the problem solver to proceed analytically because heuristic processing may lead to quick but erroneous decisions (Lyubomirski et al., 2005). In the present case, it is likely that the material was rather novel to all participants in the study. However, where is the transition between novel and familiar? In the present study, a repeated-measures design was used, and one could argue that the strategies learned from and used to complete the first test could be heuristics used on the second test. In this case, participants in positive moods would have had an advantage. On the other hand, assuming that a 6-min test is not long enough to allow the test-taker to learn heuristic shortcuts, one could conclude that participants in negative moods had an advantage because they were dealing with novel material, and thus, the analytical thinking style would have been superior. The latter is more likely, but then the results that were found would not have supported the hypothesis (and they would not have supported the other hypothesis of having an advantage in a positive mood due to working with familiar material either). However, this problem also illustrates the fuzzy nature of many of the theories and assumptions on the impact of mood on thinking. It is difficult to operationalise variables and to derive truly falsifiable hypotheses. This was also the reason why this approach was not included when deriving hypotheses for the present study.

To sum up this section, for theories on mood-induced thinking styles, the results found here could mean two things: (a) either the effect of thinking style is—in contrast to other variables that impact performance such as ability level—so small that it does not account for a significant amount of variance; (b) or there is no such thing as mood-induced thinking style, at least when completing an IQ test. However, there are quite a few studies that have found that individuals have a different thinking style in a positive than in a negative mood (Bless et al., 1992; Isen & Means, 1983; Sinclair, 1988; Sinclair & Mark, 1992). The concept of mood-induced thinking style also seems to be backed up by findings from brain science (Kuhbandner et al., 2009). Therefore, it is more likely that thinking style simply accounts for a smaller amount of variance in test scores compared with other variables that impact performance.

Cognitive capacity and resource allocation. Some proponents of resource allocation approaches predict that cognitive performance that requires capacity should be worse for people in negative moods compared with positive or neutral moods (Ellis & Ashbrook, 1988), whereas others predict that it should be worse for people in intense affective states as compared with moderate affective states, independent of the valence of the affect (Riediger et al., 2011).

Those who predict that cognitive capacity should be impaired by negative mood (Ellis & Ashbrook, 1988) claim that individuals in positive moods have fewer self-relevant and thus fewer task-irrelevant thoughts and therefore have more capacity available for the task at hand (Pekrun & Frese, 1992). The theory originated from a clinical setting in which depressed individuals were studied. Thus, perhaps the effect does not hold for nonclinical individuals. However, Knapp (1988) found that the effect was present in his resource dilemma task and found that the effect increased with the intensity of the mood and the difficulty of the task. Others (Riediger et al., 2011) have found that working memory performance is better for people in moderate positive or negative moods than in intense positive or negative moods. Neither effect could be observed here: There was no performance impairment for individuals in negative moods compared with positive or neutral moods, and there was no impairment for subjects in intense moods compared with moderate mood states.

There are three possible explanations for why the effects did not show up here: (a) The test did not require a lot of resources; however, this is unlikely because the test was adaptive and thus always presented the individual with the appropriate level of difficulty; thus, one can assume that it did indeed require cognitive resources; (b) the emotions were not intense enough to require a lot of capacity; however, this is also unlikely because, particularly in the Anger condition, the intensity of the emotion was very high; (c) participants allocated all of their cognitive capacity to the task in all of the five conditions because they became immersed in the test, and thus emotional state no longer played a role. To put it differently, participants probably experienced flow or full immersion and enjoyment in the task (Csikszentmihalyi, 1990).

The characteristics of flow include (Nakamura & Csikszentmihalyi, 2002): (a) full concentration on the present moment, (b) a merging of action and awareness, (c) a loss of self-relevant thoughts, (d) a feeling of being in control of one's actions, (e) a loss of feeling for time, and (f) total intrinsic motivation. This means that a flow experience involves total immersion in the task without allowing other thoughts or feelings to interfere. The loss of self-relevant thoughts is particularly relevant here. Two of the three participants in the test run of the experiment were fully immersed in the task as indicated by their thinking aloud, whereas the third person had a lot of task-irrelevant thoughts. In general, people who take the test that was used in the experiment often report that it is “fun”. Thus, it is possible that the participants experienced flow during the task.

This idea can be further supported by considering the task characteristics that can potentially evoke flow (Czikszentmihalyi, Abuhamdeh, & Nakamura, 2007): (a) The task must have a goal towards which the individual is progressing, (b) there must be clear and immediate feedback, and (c) there must be a balance between the perceived challenge of the task and the individual’s perceived skills. The test used in the current study has a clear goal and it provides feedback in the sense that the item difficulties change in response to the participant’s given answers. Due to the fact that the test is adaptive, individuals are adminstered items that correspond to their ability level or slightly above.

Thus, it is possible that the participants experienced flow while completing the test, and that is why the different emotions did not have an impact on test performance. A finding that can be considered to speak in favour of this idea is the fact that the ratings on the three mood dimensions were located around a neutral point for all five conditions after the test. This is also in line with the finding that mood induction effects disappear when individuals work on a task very intensely or when the task is very difficult (Erber & Tesser, 1992). In any case, the present data do not support the predictions from resource allocation models claiming that performance—particularly on complex tasks—is impaired for people who are in negative or intense moods.

Neuropsychological basis. An approach that takes into account the valence and intensity of emotions is the neuropsychological theory of positive emotions (Ashby et al., 1999), which posits that due to certain connections and mood-related dopamine levels in the brain, working memory is best when people are experiencing moderate positive affect.

In the present study, there were no differences between the conditions even though they differed not only with respect to the type of emotion but also with respect to emotional intensity. This can be taken as evidence against the theory. However, as the test did not measure working memory directly, two alternative explanations come to mind: (1) Perhaps the amount of variance in test performance accounted for by working memory was so small that differences in working memory capacity did not impact overall test performance; or (2) perhaps the amount of variance in working memory capacity that could be explained by affective state was small.

(1) The first possible explanation was that the amount of variance in test performance accounted for by working memory was so small that differences in working memory capacity did not impact overall test performance. In fact, participants can decrease the load placed on working memory from the test by using the option of marking interim stages in the grid. This makes it possible to externalise the manipulations necessary to find a solution instead of manipulating the grid in one's mind. However, the extent to which participants really made use of this option was not clear. During the test run of the experiment, one of the participants did not use this option at all; when asked why she had not used it, she replied that she had forgotten about it. By contrast, the other two participants in the pilot study had used the option. On the other hand, studies have shown that working memory contributes to reasoning performance to a large degree (Callaway & Thompson, 1953; Oberauer, Schulze, Wilhelm, & Süß, 2005); therefore, this was most likely also the case here.

(2) The other possible explanation is that the amount of variance in working memory capacity that could be explained by

affective state was small and that working memory capacity tends to be rather stable unless it is being trained over an extended period of time (Jaeggi et al., 2008). In fact, Ashby, Isen, and Turken (1999) did not provide an effect size for the impact of affect on performance in their theory. Thus, this is the more plausible explanation for the results found here.

In summary, the evidence presented here is not enough to falsify the neuropsychological theory of positive emotions (Ashby et al., 1999), which claims that working memory is best when people are experiencing moderate positive affect. To do so, a direct measure of working memory would be required along with an expected effect size. The most plausible explanation for the findings presented here is that the amount of variance in working memory capacity accounted for by emotional state is too small to have a significant impact compared with other variables.

Motivation. As expected, motivation was quite high in the two positive conditions. However, it was equally high in the Control condition and intermediate in the two negative conditions. Thus, the valence of the emotion had an impact on motivation, but it was smaller than expected. The only condition that differed significantly from the Control condition in its level of motivation was the Anger condition.

This could be taken as evidence against the notion that better performance on cognitive tasks in positive affect is mediated by motivation (Abele, 1995). Given that motivation was almost equal across the five conditions, whereas individuals in the five conditions were rather different in their emotional states, motivation could not be a mediator of the relation between emotion and performance.

It was already mentioned in the literature section that previous findings on the valence of mood and the level of motivation associated with it have been contradictory. Whereas most researchers consider motivation to be higher in positive mood states (e.g., Isen, 1984; Seo et al., 2004), others hold the opinion that it is lower for people experiencing positive affect (e.g., Forgas, 2002; Melton, 1995). Maybe different types of motivation can explain the discrepancies in the findings and also the fact that there was not much of a difference between positive and negative emotional states in the current study. Research on the Rubicon model of action phases (Heckhausen & Gollwitzer, 1986, 1987) has shown that people in positive moods are more likely to have enjoyment goals, whereas people in negative moods are more likely to have performance goals. When given an enjoyment goal (e.g., "stay on the task as long as you enjoy it"), people in positive moods expend more effort on the task and perform better than people in negative moods. When given a performance goal (e.g., "stop when you are satisfied with your performance"), people in negative moods expend more effort and achieve better performance. This could explain why motivation has sometimes been found to be higher and sometimes lower for people experiencing positive affect: It is only high when there is an enjoyment goal.

The present study's results may have been due to a combination of the two factors. On the one hand, all participants were rather motivated when they started working on the test. This motivation was probably kept up for those in positive moods because they enjoyed the test. It has repeatedly been reported that the test is fun even by participants who completed it in a high-stakes setting. Individuals in negative moods were probably motivated by a mood repair motive to perform well on the task in an attempt to get out of their negative mood; thus, they had a performance goal. Indirect feedback on how well they performed was given by the fact that item difficulty increased with every correct answer. In any case, the present data did not support the notion that motivation is considerably higher for people experiencing positive than negative affect and that motivation is therefore a mediator of the relation between emotion and performance.

9.1.2 Activation of Mood or Emotions and Reasoning Test Performance

The hypotheses on the impact of the arousal component of emotions on test performance were:

Hypothesis 3: Positive emotions: Performance on an IQ test will be better for participants in the emotional state of joy than in the emotional state of contentment.

Hypothesis 4: Negative emotions: Performance on an IQ test will be better for participants in the emotional state of anger than in the emotional state of sadness.

The background for this came from studies that had been able to show that (a) performance on cognitive tasks is best under moderate arousal (Lambourne & Tomporowski, 2010; Onyper et al., 2011; Sanders, 1983); (b) higher arousal is associated with higher noradrenalin and dopamine brain levels, which are beneficial for working memory (Flaherty, 2005; Kimberg et al., 1997); and (c) motivation is higher in activating than in deactivating emotions (Bandura & Cervone, 1983; Pekrun, 2006; Sebej et al., 1985). In the following, the results of the present study will be discussed against the backdrop of these three approaches.

Arousal. Participants in the Joy condition were more energetic than participants in the Contentment condition, and participants in the Anger condition were more tense than participants in the Sadness condition. “Tired versus energetic” and “tense versus relaxed” are the two dimensions representing arousal in the three-dimensional model of affect. Thus, participants in the Joy and Anger conditions were more aroused than participants in the Contentment and Sadness conditions. However, this did not lead to any improvements in test performance. Thus, my finding is in contrast to the finding that cognitive performance increases with arousal (Lambourne & Tomporowski, 2010; Onyper et al., 2011). There may be two reasons for this. First, in the cited studies on arousal and cognitive performance, the arousal was purely of a physical nature and was induced by chewing gum (Onyper et al., 2011) or physical exercise (Lambourne & Tomporowski, 2010), respectively. Thus, the arousal was purely a bodily experience with no cognitive component, whereas the arousal in the present study was evoked through a cognitive pathway. Second, the tasks used in the previous experiments were different from the one used in the present study: working memory, episodic memory, and perceptual speed in Onyper et al. (2011), and memory, information processing, and executive function in Lambourne and Tomporowski (2010) versus logical reasoning in the present study.

Thus, the present findings may have one of two implications: Either performance is impacted by only physical but not cognitive arousal, or else arousal does not have an impact on every type of cognitive task. It is not possible to determine which of the two explanations is valid in the current study. To do so would require either a comparison between the impacts of physical and cognitive arousal on the same type of task or a comparison of different types of tasks performed under the same type of arousal.

Motivation. The hypothesis was that motivation would be higher for people experiencing activating emotions than deactivating emotions, and thus, that performance in the two conditions involving activating emotions would be higher than in the two involving deactivating emotions. However, as already mentioned above, the manipulation check showed that motivation was quite high in the two positive conditions and in the Control condition and intermediate in the two negative conditions. Thus, in the present study, motivation appeared to be impacted by the valence of the emotion rather than its activation component, and the effect appeared to be rather small.

The findings here contradict the ones by Pekrun and Hofmann (1999) who saw motivation as a mediator of the relation between emotion and performance. Motivation is high for people experiencing positive emotions (which, to a small extent, was also seen in the present data) and can compensate for the detrimental effect of negative emotions when motivation is high. This effect was not observed in the present study. However, two aspects need to be taken into account here: First, Pekrun and Hofmann's (1999) approach originated from an academic setting in which motivation is relevant for a longer period of time. Not only do students need to be motivated when taking an exam, but they also need to be motivated to study during the days and weeks before the exam; therefore, motivation in this setting has more of the characteristics of a trait than a state. Second, in the present study, differences in motivation between the five conditions were rather small, probably due to the fact that those who participated in the experiment were generally highly motivated. The emotion induction procedure did not change this level of motivation much, and this might point to the fact that test-related motivation is more trait-like and not so much a state.

9.1.3 Task Type, Mood and Emotion, and Reasoning Test Performance

In sum, neither the valence nor the arousal component of emotions had an impact on test performance. This lack of impact is what would be predicted by theories that claim that whether or not and the extent to which emotions have an impact on cognitive processing depend on the type of task; examples of such theories are the affect infusion model (Forgas, 1995), the dual-force model

(Fiedler, 1990a), and the multifactor-system dynamics theory of emotion (Royce & Diamond, 1980).

The affect infusion model (Forgas, 1995) posits that affect will impact only tasks that require simple rule-of-thumb strategies or a generative processing strategy. However, there should be no impact of affect on tasks that require people to retrieve pre-existing information directly or to work towards a pre-defined goal using highly predetermined information search patterns and few generative processes. The test used here would fall into the latter category: There was a pre-defined goal, all the elements to be used were pre-determined, and there was no generative process involved. Thus, the AIM (Forgas, 1995) would predict that emotions would not impact performance on this type of test, and such a prediction is in line with the findings.

Similarly, the dual-force model (Fiedler, 1990) claims that two different forces come into play when tasks are performed, conservation and active transformation, of which only the latter is susceptible to mood influences. Analytical tasks can be identified as consisting of both forces (Fiedler, 1990), and thus, they are somewhat susceptible to mood influences. On the basis of Fiedler's (1990) classification criteria, the test that the participants completed in the present study can be classified as a task that is more reproductive than productive; it is provided by the experimenter rather than self-provided; and it is highly organised, pictorial, and requires almost no knowledge. As a reproductive task, it would thus not be susceptible to affective influences.

The multifactor-system dynamics theory of emotion (Royce & Diamond, 1980) posits that cognitive tasks require people either to perceive (visualise or spatially scan), to conceptualise (generate concepts or work on the basis of logical consistency), or to symbolise (create ideas). Similar to the other two models, it predicts that emotions will have the greatest impact on symbolising, followed by perceiving and then conceptualising. The test that the participants completed in the present experiment required them to conceptualise, and the findings here support the idea that the impact of emotions on a conceptualising task is merely weak or not present at all.

9.1.4 *Impact of Emotions on Test Performance: Limitations*

As already mentioned, it was not possible to investigate the effects of emotions on performance at the different levels of difficulty. The reason for why this was not possible will be discussed in detail now. The test has six categories of difficulty. After a correct answer, the next item comes from the next higher difficulty category, whereas after an incorrect answer, the next item comes from the next lower difficulty category. Therefore, having only a few correct responses in one difficulty category can occur for different reasons: Either the participant gave mostly wrong and only a few correct answers in this category and thus completed mostly items that were below this difficulty category, or else the participant answered the items in this category correctly and thus quickly ascended out of this category and completed mostly items in higher categories. Thus, having only a few correct answers in one category could mean that the participant completed either more items that were easier or more items that were more difficult. Furthermore, participants complete as many items as they can in the time given. This means that the participants have different numbers of items completed in different difficulty categories. Scores in the bottom and top categories are difficult to interpret as well. Therefore, only the overall score was considered in the analyses.

Thus, there may very well be differences between the different emotional states as predicted by theories on mood-induced thinking styles (Bless et al., 1996; Fiedler, 1988; Isen, 2000; Kuhl,

1983a, Kuhl, 1983b) and as found by Abele (1995), but the implications of these theories could not be fully tested. To do so, it would be necessary to administer a nonadaptive test in which all participants complete the same number of items from each difficulty level. However, the analyses presented here showed that participants in the two negative conditions did not give fewer wrong answers as predicted by theories on mood-induced thinking styles.

This raises the question of why an adaptive test was chosen for the experiment given that it did not allow performance to be analysed at different levels of difficulty. The reason for this choice was that study participants should always be faced with items that provide the right amount of challenge in order to prevent them from feeling bored or frustrated, and thus to prevent them from dropping out. It was also necessary to use an instrument that was short so that the entire experiment would not take longer than half an hour. For these reasons, the adaptive test was chosen deliberately.

Moreover, one question pertaining to the scoring model that was used should be addressed. The score "Number Correct" was the sum of correctly solved items, and the score "Number Wrong" was the sum of incorrectly solved items. This kind of scoring assigns the same weight to all categories of difficulty. However, it makes sense to ask whether the result would have been different if a different scoring model had been applied; for example, one that assigns a higher weight to more difficult items. The scoring model used here was chosen to render the overall score comparable to the overall scores from previous studies on mood and test performance. However, a scoring model with different weights assigned to different item difficulties would allow for more differentiation; for example, if two individuals solved the same number of items correctly but one of them was presented with more difficult items, it would make sense to assume that the person administered the more difficult items performed better than the other person. Such differences could not be reflected by the scoring model used in the present study.

Furthermore, I could not test for the impact of the emotional states on working memory or how this in turn impacted test performance. To do so, it would have been necessary to include a test of working memory in the study, and this was not possible due to time limits. A test of working memory would have been necessary to find evidence for or against the neuropsychological theory of positive emotions (Ashby et al., 1999).

Moreover, it was not possible to investigate how emotion (in contrast to mood) and motivation interact to impact test performance. The emotion induction procedure did not change motivation levels enough to result in considerable differences between the groups. The emotion induction procedure also failed to induce considerable differences between the groups. But this lack of difference may also be an artefact of the way in which emotions were assessed. Individuals were asked for their current test-related emotions rather than for their general emotions in that moment. The instructions said: "In the following, you will again complete the logical thinking test that you completed before. How does this make you feel?" Thus, individuals were not asked how they were feeling at the moment, but rather, they were asked for their emotions with respect to the upcoming test. Perhaps their general emotions were different from their test-related ones. An examination the three mood dimensions indicates that this is very likely. Thus, perhaps the emotion induction procedure was successful in the sense that it evoked different emotions across the five groups, but this was not measured because of the way the questionnaire was constructed. In summary, there may be some evidence that the five groups really did differ in their emotions, but we do not know for sure. Therefore, the study's statistical results, which showed no significant impact on test performance from the experimentally induced emotional states, should be interpreted with some caution.

Finally, to test theories on the interaction of mood state and type of task such as the affect infusion model (Forgas, 1995), the dual-force model (Fiedler, 1990), or the multifactor-system dynamics theory of emotion (Royce & Diamond, 1980) it would have been necessary to include two or three types of tests in the experiment.

One last aspect to be taken into consideration is that the present experiment had more sources of variance than the previous studies on mood and test performance presented in the literature section. For example, the current sample was more diverse with respect to age and education, both of which are known to impact test performance. Moreover, due to the rather unstandardised situation, participants' psychological states may have varied more than would have been the case in a laboratory setting (Stanton, 1998).

9.1.5 Summary

To sum this all up, the present study appears to indicate that although emotions have an impact on certain cognitive processes, this does not seem to be the case for all kinds of processes, or at least the impact is too small to change test scores. Again, this idea is in line with models that assume that whether or not and the extent to which emotions have an impact on cognitive performance depends on the type of task and thus on the type of cognitive process involved. Analytical tasks that have a clear goal and do not require any creative or transformative processing might not be susceptible to the impact of state emotions. Moreover, the data also showed that mood changed during the test, and this could be taken as an indicator that the test evoked a state of flow in which emotions do not impact performance. Finally, it is possible that there were some sources of variance that superimposed the effects of affective state onto test performance, such as the diversity of the sample or the rather unstandardised setting relative to a laboratory setting.

9.2 Online Emotion Induction

As already mentioned, this study showed that it is possible to evoke different distinct emotional and mood states using short film clips in an unsupervised online setting. Each affective state had a distinct profile on the three mood dimensions "bad versus good", "tired versus energetic", and "tense versus relaxed". To a lesser degree, it was possible to change the test-related emotions, but they appeared to be rather stable and more trait-like. Changes through the induction procedure were stable only to a certain extent. Mood state changed during the test but did not return to its initial state. These results will now be discussed in more detail.

First, the affective state that participants were in when they started the experiment will be discussed. When participants started the experiment, they were in a rather positive and relaxed mood, and their energy level was at an intermediate level. Test-related positive emotions were also at an intermediate level, whereas test-related negative emotions were low.

Next, the effects of the emotion induction procedure will be discussed, first for mood and then for test-related emotions. The emotion induction procedure caused considerable changes in the three mood dimensions in particular but also smaller changes in the test-related emotions.

Finally, I will discuss the extent to which the changes in mood caused by the emotion induction procedure were stable by comparing mood states after the test to mood states before the test and mood states at the beginning of the experiment. After the test, mood had changed and returned to its initial state.

9.2.1 Affective State Before the Emotion Induction Procedure

The fact that participants' trait mood was rather positive is in line with the finding that human baseline mood state is elevated above a neutral point and is positive (Diener & Diener, 1996; Diener et al., 2006). Participants' state mood when they began the experiment was close to their (self-assessed) normal baseline mood and was rather positive. One can assume that people participate in an experiment only when their mood is rather positive because this is the emotional state in which individuals try out new things and explore their environments (Fredrickson, 1998). Moreover, individuals in the study described themselves as being rather energetic in general (trait) and neither tired nor energetic at the moment (state) as well as rather relaxed in general and at the moment. Also here, it would be logical to expect that someone who is generally low in energy level and rather tense is unlikely to participate in a voluntary online experiment.

Finally, individuals described themselves as medium to high on positive test-related emotions and low on negative test-related emotions for both trait and state emotions. One can assume that those who generally experience high levels of negative test-related emotions are unlikely to voluntarily participate in an experiment involving an IQ test. The same applies to feeling uncomfortable when faced with a testing situation, whereas on the other hand, positive emotions and motivation are more likely to trigger exploratory behaviour.

9.2.2 Changes in Mood States due to the Emotion Induction Procedure

The emotion induction films that were used had been tested for their power to induce specific emotions, but there was no information with respect to their power to change mood states. In the following sections, the mood changes that were due to the emotion induction procedure will be discussed.

Control condition. For the Control condition, there was a significant change from rather positive and rather relaxed towards a more neutral state, whereas participants remained in a neutral state on the dimension "tired versus energetic". This was to be expected. The question is why the affective mood component did not become completely neutral, given that in the study by Gross and Levenson (1995), participants were low on all emotions after watching the film clip "Abstract Shapes". There may be two reasons for this seemingly contradictory result. First, Gross and Levenson (1995) did not assess mood but rather asked only for very specific emotions; therefore, we do not know what their participants' ratings on mood scales would have looked like. Second, considering that baseline mood is not neutral but is actually positive (Diener & Diener, 1996; Diener et al., 2006), as reported before, perhaps the neutral point of the mood continuum is not in the centre of the scale but is instead displaced towards the positive end of the scale such that its midpoint already indicates a depressed mood. Such a finding would be in line with what resulted for the Sadness condition in which the affective component of mood was located at the midpoint of the scale. Thus, perhaps the result found here does not contradict what Gross and Levenson (1995) found. Perhaps they also would have found that mood was slightly positive because the baseline is positive (Diener & Diener, 1996; Diener et al., 2006).

Joy and Contentment conditions. For the two positive conditions, mood remained positive after the induction as expected. In the Joy condition, as anticipated, it remained relaxed and became more energetic because joy is classified as a positive-activating emotion. In the Contentment condition, energy level remained in a neutral zone (as was expected because contentment is a positive-deactivating emotion), but participants became more tense than they had been, which was counter to the hypotheses. It had been hypothesised that participants would be in a rather relaxed state in both positive conditions because they would derive that things were going well from their mood (Schwarz, 1990), whereas individuals in the two negative conditions would be striving for mood repair (Isen, 1984) and would thus be more tense. The fact that individuals in the Contentment condition also became more tense might have something to do with the nature of the film clip "Waves", which was used to induce the emotion. This will be discussed in more detail in the section on the nature of the film clips.

Sadness and Anger conditions. For the two negative conditions, mood became more negative such that it was around the middle of the scale for the Sadness condition and very negative in the Anger condition. The negative direction had been expected, but the great difference between the two had not. Anger had been classified as a negative-activating emotion; therefore, perhaps it is higher in intensity, and this may explain the very negative score. Participants became less energetic in both conditions, which was to be expected for Sadness as a negative-deactivating emotion. However, for Anger as an activating emotion, the expectation had been that the energy level would rise. Finally, in both conditions, individuals became more tense, and the change was greater in the Anger condition. Tenseness versus relaxation seemed to go hand in hand with valence; thus, the more negative the mood, the higher the tenseness. This was in line with expectations because, as already mentioned, the assumption had been that participants in the two negative conditions would be more tense because they would be striving to repair their moods (Isen, 1984). Against the backdrop that mood was a lot worse in the Anger condition than in the Sadness condition, one could argue that the need for mood repair here was greater, and therefore, the tension was also greater.

Summary. Altogether, each condition had a different pattern of characteristics on the three mood dimensions, and all of them were significantly different from the Control condition on at least one dimension. Thus, the fact that the film clips evoked distinct emotions was also reflected in the mood dimensions.

In terms of the affect models that were introduced in the literature section, the respective affective states showed different patterns on all three dimensions of affect. Thus, the three dimensions are not unrelated, but they are distinct. However, further analyses on the structure of the mood states were beyond the scope of this study and should be investigated further in another context.

9.2.3 Changes in Emotional States due to the Emotion Induction Procedure

I predicted that the emotion induction procedure would also change test-related emotions and motivation. The effects here were rather small, and thus, motivation and test-related emotions appear to be rather stable and more trait-like.

For the Control condition, motivation and positive test-related emotions moved towards or remained in a more neutral area after the emotion induction; this finding is in line with what Gross and Levenson (1995) found for the film clip "Abstract Shapes". In the two positive conditions, test-related motivation decreased. Positive test-related emotions remained largely positive in the Joy condition and decreased in the Contentment condition, and negative test-related emotions in these conditions increased. Motivation and positive test-related emotions decreased in the two negative conditions, and negative test-related emotions increased in the Anger condition, probably indicating that a very strong trigger is needed to change these emotions.

The data also showed that each film clip changed the emotional states in different ways, and thus generated very specific responses, just as found by Gross and Levenson (1995).

9.2.4 Changes in Mood States after the Test

After the test, individuals in the Control condition remained in the neutral state that they had been in after the induction; there were no significant changes in either of the mood dimensions. Individuals in the other four conditions approached this more neutral state. In the Joy condition, all three mood dimensions changed significantly, moving from a positive, energetic, and relaxed state into a more neutral one. In the Contentment condition, individuals had already been in a neutral state on "tired versus energetic" and they stayed neutral on this dimension. Along the other dimensions, they moved from rather good and rather relaxed to a more neutral state. Also for the two negative conditions, participants remained in the neutral zone on the dimension "tired versus energetic". With respect to the other two dimensions, after feeling rather negative and tense after the emotion induction, individuals felt better and less tense after the test.

However, a comparison between mood after the test and mood before the induction showed that individuals did not return to their initial mood state. Before the induction, the average mood state was rather positive and relaxed, and it was neutral on the "tired versus energetic" dimension. After the test, individuals were neutral on the "tired versus energetic" dimension again, but they were also neutral on the "tense versus relaxed" dimension. The valence was still more positive than neutral but not quite as positive as before the induction.

Perhaps this mood state after the test can be interpreted as representing an affective state set point to which individuals eventually return after affect-changing events (Brickman & Campbell, 1971; Diener et al., 2006), whereas at the beginning of the experiment, they were still in an elevated state, which motivated them to explore and to try something new (Fredrickson, 1998). The reason why the trait mood they reported at the beginning of the experiment was close to their initial state mood may be the fact that current mood strongly impacts self-ratings on general well-being (Diener, 2009).

In any case, the data showed that mood changed during the test, a finding that is in line with other studies' conclusions that mood changes during a test (Matsumoto & Sanders, 1988) and that mood induction effects may disappear during a difficult test (Erber & Tesser, 1992). However, the fact that mood state does not return to its initial level also shows that the effect of mood induction persists to a certain extent.

9.2.5 Online Emotion Induction: Limitations

Next I will discuss the limitations of the study concerning the measurement of mood and emotions and the emotion induction films that were used.

Measurement of mood and emotions. Trait mood and trait test-related emotions were assessed by asking the participants how they feel in general and what their general emotions are when taking a test. However, it has been shown that when assessing trait affectivity, many effects that distort judgment come into play. For example, memories of past affective states are impacted by current affective state. Furthermore, when thinking about their current affective state, individuals often use heuristics that are likely to bias the measurement of trait affectivity (for an overview, see Diener, 2009). On the other hand, this is not necessarily a distortion. On the basis of state-trait theories of mood and emotions, one would expect substantial correlations between state and trait ratings because mood or emotional states are seen as fluctuations around a stable affective trait caused by influences of the current situation (Eid, 1997). Finally, there are two options for measuring emotions: A questionnaire can ask for frequency or for intensity (Diener et al., 2009). In the present case, participants were asked to indicate the intensity of their affect, which individuals generally tend to overestimate (Diener, 2009). Thus, there were a few sources of bias to consider when interpreting the ratings participants gave on their trait emotions and mood states.

After the emotion induction, a manipulation check was implemented. On the one hand, such a check is necessary to ensure that the manipulation achieved its intended outcome. On the other hand, it may also create demand characteristics. For this reason, participants in Abele's (1995) study did not complete the manipulation check items until after completing the test. However, the present data showed that mood changed substantially during the test, so this would mean that a manipulation check implemented after test completion might not appropriately capture participants' affective state as induced by the manipulation.

Emotion induction. As already mentioned, there were only marginal changes in test-related emotion and motivation. This raises the questions of whether and to what extent it is possible to achieve momentary changes in test-related emotions as this appears to be difficult to do according to the results of the present experiment. Other studies, however, have shown that it is possible to evoke short-term changes. For example, Ramirez and Beilock (2011) had test-anxious individuals write down their worries before taking a test and found that their test scores improved significantly. Lang and Lang (2010) found that a competence intervention weakened the detrimental effect of test anxiety on test scores. Individuals high on test anxiety scored better after the intervention, whereas persons low on test anxiety scored worse after the intervention. This means that test-related emotions can be subject to short-term changes, but material that is directly related to the test itself is probably needed to do this successfully.

Characteristics of the film clips used. Some differences between some of the film clips should be mentioned. Three of the clips were commercial film clips that each had a plot and dialogue between the actors. These were the films "When Harry Met Sally" (Joy), "The Champ" (Sadness), and "Cry Freedom" (Anger). The other two film clips did not comprise a plot, nor were there actors or sound. These clips were "Waves" (Contentment) and "Abstract Shapes" (Control condition). In these two film clips, participants had to watch waves or tubes that multiplied on the screen. Thus, the cognitive processing evoked by these two film clips may differ from the other three. Whereas the commercial film clips required participants to follow conversations and to immerse themselves in the plot, they had only to watch rolling waves or coloured bars on the screen in the other two films. For the two film clips without plots, this could have two implications: First, the plotless film clips provided less control over what participants were thinking or doing, thus reducing the degree of standardisation compared with the other three film clips. Second, it is possible that participants were ruminating about their performance on the test that they had just completed or that they were asking themselves what would come up next. This may account for the fact that participants became more tense in both the Contentment and Control conditions.

The fact that the two film clips without plots were similar to each other in structure might also explain why the two groups who watched these clips were so similar in mood and emotional state after the induction. By contrast, the other three film clips were rather different from each other: completely different plots, different numbers of actors involved, different actors, different sound, and so on. A comparison of the mood states of the participants in the Contentment and Control conditions showed that "tense versus relaxed" was the only dimension that comprised the difference, and this difference was small.

9.2.6 *Online Emotion Induction: Summary*

Participants in the experiment mostly described themselves as positive, energetic, relaxed, and low on negative emotions as well as high on positive emotions towards tests. They began the experiment in rather positive relaxed moods and had an average energy level, again, with rather positive and no negative emotions. All of these findings are in line with the findings that human baseline mood is slightly positive (Diener & Diener, 1996; Diener et al., 2006) and that humans explore new things when in a positive mood rather than when in a negative mood (Fredrickson, 1998).

The emotion induction procedure successfully changed mood for all of the five conditions, and the Contentment and the Control conditions were very similar to each other. The changes were mostly as expected with a few exceptions. By contrast, the induction procedure was able to change test-related emotions and motivation only slightly. Thus, test-related emotions are likely to be more trait-like.

Mood state after the test was more neutral than before the test but still slightly positive, which again can be seen as in line with the findings that human baseline mood is slightly positive (Diener & Diener, 1996; Diener et al., 2006). However, mood state did not return to its initial level, which can be taken as evidence that the effect of the induction procedure persisted to a certain extent.

9.3 Unsupervised Online Experiments

The data were gathered in an unsupervised online experiment. As outlined in the literature section, there are quite a few measures that can be taken in order to ensure good results with respect to sampling, response rate, retention, and in the end, the quality of the data and the generalisability of the results. First, the steps that were taken to ensure that the sample was as diverse as possible and some considerations of the quality of the data will be presented. Afterwards, limitations that originated from drop outs, standardisation, and generalisability will be discussed.

9.3.1 Sampling and Retention

In online studies, the experimenter has no control over who participates in the experiment (Hertel et al., 2002; Tuten et al., 2002). On the one hand, it is not known whether the originally intended subpopulation is reached by the invitation to participate. Even if the intended subpopulation is reached, self-selection effects are likely to occur (but note that these are always a problem when participation in a study is voluntary, even in laboratory studies). Thus, the question is always—and this applies to the present study—to what extent the sample can be considered to be representative of the population. Thus, this is a question that needs to be asked for the results presented here. The intention was to reach a sample that was as diverse as possible with respect to sex, age, education, and occupation.

In order to obtain a diverse sample, several channels were used; that is, I contacted: (a) mentaga GYM programme participants, who are diverse with respect to age, education, and occupation; (b) my social contacts, who are diverse with respect to age and occupation; and (c) other participants who use social media. Once the experiment was set up, inviting people to participate did not require much time and effort. However, a lot of effort was invested to figure out the right way to address them so that they would be motivated to participate. For friends, family, acquaintances, and colleagues, the message was to help me with my Ph.D. study. For participants of the mentaga GYM programme, it was that they could participate in a diverse, interesting experiment and would be helping science to progress. For both groups, a raffle for three Amazon vouchers was given as an incentive. This strategy is in line with research on motives that inspire individuals to participate in online studies: these are, for example, curiosity, opportunity to contribute to research, self-knowledge, and material incentives, with material incentives being the least important motive (Bosnjak & Batinic, 2002). Furthermore, I also followed other recommendations regarding measures for increasing response rates (Fan & Yan, 2010). There was a test run with a small group of respondents; access to the website containing the experiment was easy because it required participants only to click on a link; handling of the tasks during the experiment was intuitive so that only a few instructions were necessary; data safety was ensured by several experienced web programmers who had programmed tests and questionnaires for many years.

Response rates to invitations to online studies can be taken as an indicator of how accurately an online study can estimate the underlying population parameters (Tuten et al., 2002). However, there are only a few studies on this issue, and thus it is difficult to draw a conclusion for the present study. What can definitely be said in general is that self-selection effects come into play whenever volunteers are recruited for a study, even when it is conducted in the laboratory. However, there are a few effects that apply only to online studies. For example, the percentage of internet users differs across age groups, it is significantly lower for internet users above the age of 40 than below the age of 40 (Bandilla, 2002), and internet users are likely to be educated and wealthy (Tuten et al., 2002). Against this backdrop, the fact that participants were rather diverse with respect to age, educational background, and occupation in the present study can be considered encouraging.

For friends, family, acquaintances, and colleagues, the response rate was 75%, whereas amongst participants in the mentaga GYM programme, it was only slightly above 2%. For social media and websites where the experiment was advertised, a response rate cannot be given. But when comparing response rates between the two groups that were invited via email, it appeared that personal commitment played a great role that went far beyond the other motives mentioned with regard to participation. The drop-out rate was slightly lower amongst friends, family, acquaintances, and colleagues (46%) than amongst the mentaga GYM participants (49%) but not much different. Thus, perhaps the mechanisms that made participants persevere during the experiment were likely to be the similar. The greater issue, compared with sampling, was retention. This will be discussed in the section on limitations.

In unsupervised online assessments, it is very difficult to control drop out. As was already outlined in the literature section, studies have indicated the following problems: Participants tend to quit an online study after 25 to 30 items (Krasilovsky, 1996); the longer the questionnaire, the lower the percentage of participants who complete it (Gräf, 2002); not many participants are willing to complete an experiment that takes longer than 30 min (Bosnjak & Batinic, 2002); and web users are accustomed to website contents being appealing, interesting, and diverse (Gräf, 2002). Barriers preventing a participant from aborting an experiment without an experimenter present are a lot lower than in the laboratory where an experimenter is present and to whom one needs to justify why one is leaving. On the other hand, it is possible that participants in laboratory studies stay even though they have lost their motivation for the experiment but do not dare to leave the room, whereas participants in online experiments can be considered to be motivated until the end.

In order to prevent participants from dropping out, the test, the questionnaires, and the instructions were as short as possible, and the tasks and formats were diverse (questionnaires with different response formats, test with symbols, film clip) so that participants would not become bored. Given that the experiment, with a total duration of about 30 min, was rather long, a drop-out rate of less than 50% can be considered encouraging.

9.3.2 Data Quality

The quality of the data can be considered good. There were only two cases that needed to be excluded from further analyses because it was obvious that those participants had only clicked through the two tests. Apart from this, the test data were comparable to the general adult norm for the test. Participants in the experiment worked a bit more slowly but with the same level of accuracy (percentage of correct responses out of all responses given) as the norm sample. The latter consists of people of different ages and occupations from around the world who took the test in a high-stakes situation in which it could be assumed that they were serious about the test. This degree of consistency can be considered to be in line with studies that have shown that data from online experiments are as interpretable as the data from laboratory experiments (McGraw et al., 2000). Moreover, the split-half reliability of the test was high. Thus, as already mentioned, the quality of the data can be considered good.

Missing data for those who had completed both tests were possible only for the ratings on mood and emotion and in the demographic data, for which it was not mandatory to rate every item. The percentages of missing data on these variables ranged from 2% to 7%. Studies comparing missing values between online and paper-and-pencil surveys have found lower percentages of missing values in online data than in paper-and-pencil data (Stanton, 1998) or the same percentage of missing data (Hertel et al., 2002). The extent to which participants were honest about their feelings can only be speculated about. There is evidence for less socially desirable responding on the web than in paper-and-pencil data (Rietz & Wahl, 1999).

9.3.3 Unsupervised Online Experiments: Limitations

There are a few characteristic features of online assessment data that also apply to the results presented here and therefore have to be taken into consideration when interpreting and generalising the findings.

Standardisation and controllability of the situation. As the study was unsupervised, there was no experimenter present. This means that it is not known whether other variables influenced the results or what participants were doing during the experiment. Did they work exclusively on the experiment or did they do other things at the same time, for example, watching a detective story on TV while watching the film clip that was supposed to evoke a state of contentment? Taking this issue into account, the emotion induction procedure worked extremely well. Apparently the film clips were able to attract and maintain participants' attention. The fact that there were significant differences between the groups after the induction speaks in favour of the idea that changes in participants' affective states were due to the induction procedure, but it is not possible to determine this for sure. Thus, it is not known whether the effect was due only to the film clips or whether other factors were involved. This makes it difficult to compare the results to other studies or to classify the results with respect to specific theories. From the perspective of ecological validity, if the results can be replicated, then we will be able to conclude that in unsupervised online assessment, emotions do not impact test performance when all other variables are taken into account.

Furthermore, there was no experimenter present with whom participants could communicate, and therefore, it was not known whether participants understood or followed the instructions (Wilhelm & McKnight, 2002). Thus, a particular issue was to ensure that participants knew what their task was for this online test. Experience in online assessment settings shows that participants tend not to read instructions (Gräf, 2002). Therefore, instructions on the internet need to be short, and the important (but only a few) parts should be highlighted (Nielsen, 1995). Thus, in the present experiment, instructions were kept as brief as possible. The instructions for the test were given step by step. When it was necessary for participants to understand certain actions that they would need to perform, they were forced to try them out before it was possible for them to proceed to the next part of the sequence. Also, an interactive example section allowed them to double check whether they had really understood what they were supposed to do. However, it can only be assumed that participants understood what to do, but it cannot be confirmed.

The fact that instructions are often not read in online studies was also the reason for choosing film clips instead of stories to induce emotion. Stories are, as meta-analyses have shown, just as powerful as film clips in evoking emotions (for an overview, see Otto, 2000). However, there was no way to ensure that the participants would actually read the stories with no experimenter present. Moreover, stories make it necessary for participant to have good reading skills, which cannot always be guaranteed. For these reasons, the film clips were chosen as the stimulus material. However, these have other disadvantages such as advanced technical requirements compared with stories. There were no technical problems in the test run of the experiment. But one cannot rule out the possibility that there were issues in the main study (e.g., in playing the film clips). Another problem is interruptions: If a participant is interrupted while reading a story, he or she can simply reread the story after the interruption. This was not possible for the films. Once the film was over, the manipulation check questionnaire appeared on screen. So if the participant missed the film for some reason, there was no way to repeat the induction procedure.

Generalisability. Generalisability refers to the extent to which the conclusions drawn for a specific sample also apply to a more general population (Brenner, 2002). It is also referred to as external validity. "Generalizability is an empirical issue, determined by the amount of variance in responses caused by confounding factors" (Brenner, 2002, p. 94). When there are factors that represent a threat to generalisability, then the extent to which the results of a study are representative of the underlying population is questionable, and the sample is biased.

Against the backdrop of these findings, to what extent can all of the above-mentioned results be generalised? On the one hand, the sample used in this experiment was more diverse than samples in most other studies reported in the literature section. In previous studies, participants have mostly been university students, whereas here, participants ranged in age from adolescents to old adults and had all kinds of educational and occupational backgrounds. In this sense, one can say that the current sample was more representative of the general population. On the other hand, the sample was biased with respect to (a) sex and (b) mood and emotions.

First, two thirds of the participants were women. There were no significant differences in test performance between the two sexes. However, with respect to the experience of emotions, previous studies have shown a number of different results. For example, it has been found that men and women differ in global descriptions of their emotional experience but not in moment-to-moment emotional experience (Feldman Barrett, Robin, Pietromonaco, & Eyssell, 1998), whereas other studies have found differences in the intensity of momentary emotional experiences between the two sexes (Fujita, Diener, & Sandvik, 1991; Grossman & Wood, 1993), with women expressing more negative emotions but as much happiness as men (Fujita et al., 1991). Gross and Levenson's (1995) findings that women experienced greater levels of the respective target emotions than men did are also in line with these other previous findings. Therefore, it is possible that the effect of the emotion induction was greater in the current sample than it would have been with an equal number of men and women in the sample. Future research should investigate this effect and what it means for the effect of emotions on test performance.

Second, when looking at trait mood and emotion, it can be seen that the participants in the sample were all generally high on positive moods, high on positive test-related emotions, and low on negative test-related emotions. This makes intuitive sense because it is unlikely that someone who is low on positive and high on negative test-related emotions would voluntarily participate in an experiment involving an online test. Therefore, it can be said that the sample represents only those who do not have negative feelings towards tests in general.

Drawing a conclusion from the fact that mood (trait and state) was rather positive in the sample is a bit more difficult. On the one hand, this could mean that only people high on positive mood were part of the sample. On the other hand, considering the fact that baseline mood is generally positive (Diener & Diener, 1996; Diener et al., 2006), it is also possible that the sample is representative of the general population in this aspect. Moreover, the initial mood state did not matter so much because the experiment involved an emotion induction procedure that substantially changed participants' state mood.

Thus, a limitation is that all of the participants were low on negative and relatively high on positive test-related emotions. Perhaps the results would change in a sample of participants who are naturally high on these emotions. However, recruiting them for a voluntary online experiment would likely be a challenge unless there was a good cover story or a powerful incentive targeted towards test-anxious people.

9.3.4 Unsupervised Online Experiments: Summary

A wide range of participants were reached with the experiment. Response rates to invitations tend to depend on the relationships that participants have to the person inviting them, whereas retention is likely to be influenced by other factors. There is evidence that data gathered online is as reliable and valid as data gathered in the lab and even has some advantages (e.g., less socially desirable responding and fewer missing values). Thus, the quality of the data can be considered good. However, representativeness and generalisability are issues in unsupervised online experiments, but also in laboratory studies.

9.4 Summary and Conclusions

Emotions do not impact performance on a reasoning test in internet users who do not have negative test-related emotions such as test anxiety. Within these limitations, the results can be considered representative of different levels of education and different occupations as well as across different age groups and for both sexes. This can be seen as in line with theories claiming that the extent to which affective states impact cognitive tasks depends on the type of task, whereas no evidence for theories on mood-induced thinking styles, capacity theories, and theories that take activation or motivation into account could be found. Moreover, it is likely that in unsupervised online assessments, there are other sources of variance that impact the results of the test apart from mood or emotional state.

Within certain limitations, it was possible to induce different emotional and mood states using film clips. The limitations concern the structure of the film clips: All of them should have a plot that individuals need to follow instead of just presenting movements on a screen. Moreover, test-related emotions seem to be rather stable and not easy to change with an emotion induction procedure such as film clips. Manipulation checks directly after the induction make sense because affective state changes considerably during the test, even though a manipulation check right after the induction might create demand characteristics. To a certain extent, the effect of the manipulation persists after the test.

It is possible to recruit a diverse and motivated sample that can be seen as representative of the two sexes and different age groups, educational backgrounds, and occupations. However, it seems to be difficult to include test-anxious participants in the sample, and women tend to be more apt to participate in such a study. Certainly there are other self-selection effects, which, however, might not always interfere with the constructs measured in the study and are therefore not problematic with regard to the generalisation of the results.

9.5 Outlook and Future Research

The fact that there are only a few and contradictory studies on mood and IQ test performance and no studies on discrete emotions and IQ test performance shows that there are still a lot of open questions. The lack of research on the topic might be a consequence of the contradictory implications the theoretical background provides for deriving hypotheses. It would be desirable to integrate these theoretical claims, which might yield more specific hypotheses that go beyond "IQ test performance is better in one emotional state than in another". Gaining further insight here would be desirable from a scientific but also from a practical point of view. From a scientific point of view, we would gain further insight into how affect, motivation, and cognition interact. From a practical standpoint, we could help test takers find the optimal mental state for showing their best performance on such a test. A side effect that is likely to appear is that error variance caused by different emotional states would be diminished, making the tests more reliable and valid. Moreover, knowledge gained about the optimal emotional state for cognitive performance might then be generalisable to other kinds of cognitive problems. More specifically, future research could address the following issues.

A replication of the study is desirable. There are a few things that should be handled differently from the way they were handled in the present study to gain further insight. It was mentioned that maybe the manipulation check assessing test-related emotions after the emotion induction procedure did not accurately capture individuals' current emotional state. Therefore, in a replication study, it would make sense to ask for general and not test-specific emotions. A manipulation check directly after the induction makes sense, even if there is the threat that it might create demand characteristics. The present data showed that affective state changed considerably during the test; thus, a manipulation check after the test would be unlikely to capture the state individuals are in right after the induction. Using films as an induction method was successful in this study and can be recommended, particularly because the other effective method (i.e., reading stories) is not suitable for the internet due to the fact that internet users do not read online text properly and that reading stories as an induction method requires good reading skills. However, it makes sense to use the same type of film clip for all of the experimental groups, meaning that there should be a plot that individuals need to follow while watching the film clip. This of course requires that study participants use the sound on their computers, but as the data show, this seems to be a minor problem. Furthermore, the assignment of participants to one of the five groups should not take place until the emotion induction film clip so that group sizes will be more equal. This was not possible in the current study for technical reasons, but perhaps in the future it will be.

A replication under supervised conditions would be just as desirable as under unsupervised conditions. The latter would back up (or call into question) the results of the study presented here, whereas the former would shed light on how participants deal with the experiment in general and what happens during the emotion induction in particular. A replication under supervised conditions would also allow for the control of other variables that may possibly impact the result aside from cognitive ability and emotional state, whereas an unsupervised experiment would have higher ecological validity.

The study presented here is the first one to investigate the subject with an online test. It would be interesting to compare online versus paper-and-pencil data. Most likely, intrinsic motivation and enjoyment were greater on an interactive online test such as the one used here than it would be on paper-and-pencil tests that are sometimes perceived as long and not very entertaining. A comparison of the two modes might deliver interesting insights and would allow researchers to analyse additional variables such as familiarity with computers or the internet or enjoyment of the test as a motivator.

In an investigation of the impact of emotions on cognitive performance, it is likely that more than just the type of task plays a role. Motivation seems to moderate this relation, or more specifically, intrinsic versus extrinsic motivation. There seems to be a consensus that performance in positive moods is better when individuals enjoy the tasks (intrinsic motivation) than it is when they do not, whereas it is better in negative moods when coupled with the motivation of doing well on the task (extrinsic motivation; Heckhausen & Gollwitzer, 1986, 1987; Lyubomirski et al., 2005). It would be desirable to further tap into the relations between emotion, intrinsic and extrinsic motivation, and performance.

Also, the differences between men and women in emotional experience should be taken into account. Gross and Levenson (1995) reported that the women in their study experienced more intense emotions than the men did, a finding that is in line with research on the difference in emotional intensity between men and women. This could mean that the impact of emotions on performance is different for men and women. There are theories that predict that the impact of affect on performance increases as the intensity of the affective experience increases (e.g., Ellis

& Ashbrook, 1988; Riediger et al., 2011). In this case, such a relation would imply the differential impact of different emotions on performance. More generally speaking, as the sample in the present study was very diverse, it would be desirable to investigate the effects of mood and emotions on test performance in subsamples such as different age groups or educational backgrounds.

As was mentioned above, it could not be determined why arousal did not impact performance on the test. Was this due to the fact that the studies that had found that arousal impacted performance (Lambourne & Tomporowski, 2010; Onyper et al., 2011) had applied physical arousal as opposed to the cognitive arousal applied in the present study, or was it due to the fact that the other studies used other types of tasks? To answer this question, a study would need either to compare the impact of physical and cognitive arousal on the same type of task or to compare different types of tasks performed under the same type of arousal.

Another moderating variable might be emotional variability or susceptibility to emotional cues. Some people might respond with more intense changes in emotional state than others. To address this issue, a future study could, for example, compare individuals high versus low on mood variability (Allport & Odbert, 1936; Eid & Diener, 1999); that is, individuals whose mood is more consistent across situations and more stable across time versus individuals for whom this is not the case. This variability has been shown to be stable across time (McConville & Cooper, 1997) and to be related to the Neuroticism factor in the Five Factor Model (Eid & Diener, 1999; Murray, Allen, & Trinder, 2002). The hypothesis here would be that individuals higher on mood variability would respond to the emotion induction procedure with stronger changes in emotions and that the impact of the emotional state on performance would be stronger.

Thus, future research should continue to study the topic and integrate the few and contradictory findings on affect and cognitive performance. From a scientific point of view, we would gain further insight into how affect, motivation, and cognition interact. From a practical standpoint, we could help test takers to achieve the optimal mental state for showing their best performance on such a test.

References

Abele, A. (1990). Die Erinnerung an positive und negative Lebensereignisse. Untersuchungen zur stimmungsinduzierenden Wirkung und zur Gestaltung der Texte [The recollection of positive and negative life-events. Studies on the mood effects and descriptions of positive vs. negative life-events]. *Zeitschrift für experimentelle und angewandte Psychologie*, *37*(2), 181–207.

Abele, A. (1992). Alltagsvorstellungen zum Einfluss positiver und negativer Stimmungen auf die aufgabenbezogene Motivation. *Zeitschrift für experimentelle und angewandte Psychologie*, *39*, 345–371.

Abele, A. (1995). *Stimmung und Leistung*. Göttingen: Hogrefe.

Achtziger, A., & Gollwitzer, P. M. (2006). Motivation und Volition im Handlungsverlauf. In J. Heckhausen & H. Heckhausen (Eds.), *Motivation und Handeln* (pp. 277–302). Heidelberg: Springer.

Ackerman, P. L., Beier, M. E., & Boyle, M. O. (2005). Working Memory and Intelligence: The Same or Different Constructs? *Psychological Bulletin*, *131*(1), 30–60. Retrieved from 10.1037/0033-2909.131.1.30

Allport, G. W. (1961). *Pattern and growth in personality. Outstanding books in education and psychology*. New York: Holt, Rinehart and Winston.

Allport, G. W., & Odbert, H. S. (1936). Trait names: a psycholexical study. *Psychological Monographs*, *47*(211), 1–171.

Asendorpf, J. B., & Neyer, F. J. (2012). *Psychologie der Persönlichkeit*. Berlin, Heidelberg: Springer Verlag.

Ashby, F. G., Isen, A. M., & Turken, A. U. (1999). A neuropsychological theory of positive affect and its influence on cognition. *Psychological Review*, *106*, 529–550.

Baas, M., De Dreu, C. K. W., & Nijstad, B. A. (2008). A meta-analysis of 25 years of mood-creativity research: Hedonic tone, activation, or regulatory focus? *Psychological Bulletin, 134*(6), 779–806. doi:10.1037/a0012815

Bandilla, W. (2002). Web Surveys - An Appropriate Mode of Data Collection for the Social Sciences? In B. Batinic, U.-D. Reips, & M. Bosnjak (Eds.), *Online social sciences* (pp. 2–6). Seattle: Hogrefe & Huber Publishers.

Bandura, A., & Cervone, D. (1983). Self-evaluative and self-efficacy mechanisms governing the motivational effects of goal systems. *Journal of Personality and Social Psychology, 45*, 1017–1028.

Bartram, D., & Brown, A. (2004). Online Testing: Mode of Administration and the Stability of OPQ 32i Scores. *International Journal of Selection and Assessment, 12*(3), 278–284. doi:10.1111/j.0965-075X.2004.282_1.x

Bateson, J., Wirtz, J., Burke, E., & Vaughan, C. (2013). When Hiring, First Test, and Then Interview. *Harvard Business Review, 91*(11), 34.

Beauducel, A., & Kersting, M. (2002). Fluid and Crystallized Intelligence and the Berlin Model of Intelligence Structure (BIS). *European Journal of Psychological Assessment, 18*, 97–112.

Binet, A. (1905). New Methods for the Diangnosis of the Intellectual Level of Subnormal. *L'Année Psychologique, 12*, 191–244.

Birney, D. P., Halford, G. S., & Andrews, G. (2006). Measuring the Influence of Complexity on Relational Reasoning. The Development of the Latin Square Task. *Educational and Psychological Measurement, 66*(1), 146–171.

Bless, H., Bohner, G., & Schwarz, N. (1992). Gut gelaunt und leicht beeinflußbar? Stimmungseinflüsse auf die Verarbeitung persuasiver Kommunikationen. *Psychologische Rundschau, 43*, 1–17.

Bless, H., Clore, G. L., Schwarz, N., Golisano, V., Rabe, C., & Wölk, M. (1996). Mood and the use of scripts: Does a happy mood really lead to mindlessness? *Journal of Personality and Social Psychology, 71*(4), 665–679. doi:10.1037/0022-3514.71.4.665

Bless, H., & Fiedler, K. (1999). Förderliche und hinderliche Auswirkungen emotionaler Zustände auf kognitive Leistungen im sozialen Kontext. In M. Jerusalem & R. Pekrun (Eds.), *Emotion, Motivation und Leistung* (pp. 9–29). Göttingen: Hogrefe.

Blomquist, A.-C. (1982). Mood and Performance. *Göteborg Psychological Reports, 12*(7).

Bolte, A., Goschke, T., & Kuhl, J. (2003). Emotion and Intuition: Effects of Positive and Negative Mood on Implicit Judgments of Semantic Coherence. *Psychological Science, 14*(5), 416–421. doi:10.1111/1467-9280.01456

Boring, E. G. (1923). Intelligence as the Tests Test It. *New Republic, 36*, 35–37.

Bortz, J. (2005). *Statistik für Human- und Sozialwissenschaftler* (6th ed.). Heidelberg: Springer.

Bortz, J., & Döring, N. (2006). *Forschungsmethoden und Evaluation für Human- und Sozialwissenschaftler* (4th ed.). Heidelberg: Springer Medizin Verlag.

Bosnjak, M. (1997). *Internetbasierte, computervermittelte psychologische Fragebogenuntersuchungen.* St. Augustin: Gardez.

Bosnjak, M., & Batinic, B. (2002). Understanding the Willingness to Participate in Online-Surveys - The Case of E-Mail Questionnaires. In B. Batinic, U.-D. Reips, & M. Bosnjak (Eds.), *Online social sciences* (pp. 81–92). Seattle: Hogrefe & Huber Publishers.

Bower, G. (1981). Mood and memory. *American Psychologist, 36*, 129–148.

Box, G. E. P., & Cox, D. R. (1964). An analysis of transformations. *Journal of the Royal Statistical Society, B*, *26*, 211–234.

Bradley, M. M., & Lang, P. J. (1994). Measuring emotion: the Self-Assessment Manikin and the Semantic Differential. *Journal of Behavior Therapy and Experimental Psychiatry*, *25*(1), 49–59.

Brehm, J. W. (1999). The Intensity of Emotion. *Personality & Social Psychology Review*, *3*(1), 2.

Brenner, V. (2002). Generalizability Issues in Internet-Based Survey Research: Implications for the Internet Addiction Controversy. In B. Batinic, U.-D. Reips, & M. Bosnjak (Eds.), *Online social sciences* (pp. 91–113). Seattle: Hogrefe & Huber Publishers.

Brickman, P., & Campbell, D. T. (1971). Hedonic relativism and planning the good society. In M. H. Appley (Ed.), *Adaptation-level theory. A Symposium [on Adaptation-Level (AL) Theory held at the University of Massachusetts at Amherst, on May 7 - 9, 1970]* (pp. 287–302). New York: Academic Press.

Burke, E. (2009). Preserving the Integrity of Online Testing. *Industrial and Organizational Psychology*, *2*, 35–38.

Burke, M. J. (1993). Computerized psychological testing: Impacts on measuring predictor constructs and future behavior. In N. Schmitt & W. C. Borman (Eds.), *Frontiers of industrial and organizational psychology. Personnel selection in organizations* (1st ed., pp. 203–239). San Francisco: Jossey-Bass.

Butcher, J. N., Perry, J. N., & Atlis, M. M. (2000). Validity and utility of computer-based test interpretation. *Psychological Assessment*, *12*(1), 6–18.

Callaway, E., & Dembo, D. (1958). Narrowed attention; a psychological phenomenon that accompanies a certain physiological change. *Archives of Neurology and Psychiatry*, *79*(1), 74–90.

Callaway, E., & Thompson, S. V. (1953). Sympathetic Activity and Perception: An Approach to the Relationships between Autonomic Activity and Personality. *Psychosomatic Medicine, 15*(5), 443–455.

Cameron, N. (1947). *The Psychology of Behavior disorders: A biosocial interpretation*. Boston, MA, US: Houghton, Mifflin and Company.

Carroll, J. B. (1993). *Human cognitive abilities: A survey of factor-analytic studies*. Cambridge, New York: Cambridge University Press.

Carver, C. S. (2004). Negative Affects Deriving From the Behavioral Approach System. *Emotion, 4*(1), 3–22. Retrieved from 10.1037/1528-3542.4.1.3

Carver, C. S., & Scheier, M. F. (1998). *On the self-regulation of behavior*. Cambridge: Cambridge University Press.

Cassady, J. C., & Johnson, R. E. (2002). Cognitive Test Anxiety and Academic Performance. *Contemporary Educational Psychology, 27*(2), 270–295. doi:10.1006/ceps.2001.1094

Cattell, R. B. (1941). Some theoretical issues in adult intelligence testing. *Psychological Bulletin, 38*(7), 592.

Cattell, R. B. (1943). The measurement of adult intelligence. *Psychological Bulletin, 40*(3), 153–193. doi:10.1037/h0059973

Cattell, R. B. (1950). *Personality: A systematic theoretical and factorial study*. New York: McGraw-Hill.

Cattell, R. B. (1963). Theory of fluid and crystallized intelligence: A critical experiment. *Journal of Educational Psychology, 54*(1), 1–22. doi:10.1037/h0046743

Chamberlain, S., Müller, U., Blackwell, A., Robbins, T., & Sahakian, B. (2006). Noradrenergic modulation of working memory and emotional memory in humans. *Psychopharmacology, 188*(4), 397-407. doi:10.1007/s00213-006-0391-6

Chuah, S. C., Drasgow, F., & Roberts, B. W. (2006). Personality assessment: Does the medium matter? No. *Journal of Research in Personality*, *40*(4), 359–376. doi:10.1016/j.jrp.2005.01.006

Clark, M. S., & Isen, A. M. (1982). Toward understanding the relationship between feeling states and social behavior. In A. H. Hastorf & A. M. Isen (Eds.), *Cognitive Social Psychology* (pp. 73–108). New York: Elsevier.

Cohen, J. (1992). A power primer. *Psychological Bulletin*, *112*(1), 155–159.

Cohn, J. F., Ambadar, Z., & Ekman, P. (2007). Observer-Based Measurement of Facial Expression With the Facial Action Coding System. In J. A. Coan & J. J. B. Allen (Eds.), *Handbook of emotion elicitation and assessment* (pp. 203–221). Oxford, New York: Oxford University Press.

Coyne, I., Warszta, T., Beadle, S., & Sheehan, N. (2005). The Impact of Mode of Administration on the Equivalence of a Test Battery: A Quasi-Experimental Design. *International Journal of Selection and Assessment*, *13*(3), 220–224. doi:10.1111/j.1468-2389.2005.00318.x

Cropanzano, R., James, K., & Konovsky, M. A. (1993). Dispositional affectivity as a predictor of work attitudes and job performance. *Journal of Organizational Behavior*, *14*(6), 595-606.

Csikszentmihalyi, M. (1990). *Flow: The psychology of optimal experience* (1st ed.). New York: Harper & Row.

Cunningham, M. R. (1988). What do you do when you're happy or blue? Mood, expectancies, and behavioral interest. *Motivation and Emotion*, *12*, 309–331.

cut-e Group. (2008). *scales lst*. Hamburg: cut-e Group.

cut-e Group. (2012). *The cut-e Assessment Barometer 2012/13: The Global Survey of Psychometric Assessment Usage*. Hamburg: cut-e Group.

Czikszentmihalyi, M., Abuhamdeh, S., & Nakamura, J. (2007). Flow. In A. J. Elliot & C. S. Dweck (Eds.), *Handbook of competence and motivation* (pp. 598–608). New York: Guilford Press.

Damasio, A. R. (1994). *Descartes' Error: emotion, reason, and the human brain*. New York: Grosset/Putnam.

Das, J. P., Kirby, J., & Jarman, R. F. (1975). Simultaneous and successive synthesis: An alternative model for cognitive abilities. *Psychological Bulletin, 82*(1), 87–103. doi:10.1037/h0076163

Das, J. P., Naglieri, J. A., & Kirby, J. R. (1993). *Assessment of cognitive processes*. Boston: Allyn and Bacon.

Davis, M. A. (2009). Understanding the relationship between mood and creativity: A meta-analysis. *Organizational Behavior and Human Decision Processes, 108*(1), 25–38. doi:10.1016/j.obhdp.2008.04.001

De Dreu, C. K. W., Baas, M., & Nijstad, B. A. (2008). Hedonic tone and activation level in the mood-creativity link: Toward a dual pathway to creativity model. *Journal of Personality and Social Psychology, 94*(5), 739–756.

Derryberry, D., & Tucker, D. M. (1992). Neural Mechanisms of Emotion. *Journal of Consulting and Clinical Psychology, 60*(3), 329–338.

Derryberry, D., & Tucker, D. M. (1994). Motivating the focus of attention. In P. M. Niedenthal & S. Kitayama (Eds.), *The heart's eye. Emotional influences in perception and attention* (pp. 167–196). San Diego, Calif.: Academic Press.

Diener, E. (2009). Assessing Subjective Well-Being: Progress and Opportunities. In E. Diener (Ed.), *The collected works of Ed Diener: Vol. 3. Assessing Well-Being* (pp. 25–66). Dordrecht, New York: Springer.

Diener, E., & Diener, C. (1996). Most People Are Happy. *Psychological Science*, *7*(3), 181–185. doi:10.1111/j.1467-9280.1996.tb00354.x

Diener, E., & Emmons, R. A. (1984). The independence of positive and negative affect. *Journal of Personality and Social Psychology*, *47*(5), 1105–1117. doi:10.1037/0022-3514.47.5.1105

Diener, E., Lucas, R. E., & Scollon, C. N. (2006). Beyond the hedonic treadmill: Revising the adaptation theory of well-being. *American Psychologist*, *61*(4), 305–314.

Diener, E., Scollon, C. N., & Lucas, R. E. (2009). The Evolving Concept of Subjective Well-Being: The Multifaceted Nature of Happiness. In E. Diener (Ed.), *The collected works of Ed Diener: Vol. 3. Assessing Well-Being* (pp. 67–100). Dordrecht, New York: Springer.

Diener, E., Smith, H., & Fujita, F. (1995). The Personality Structure of Affect. *Journal of Personality and Social Psychology*, *69*(1), 130–141.

Duckworth, A. L., Quinn, P. D., Lynam, D. R., Loeber, R., & Stouthamer-Loeber, M. (2011). Role of test motivation in intelligence testing. *Proceedings of the National Academy of Sciences.* doi:10.1073/pnas.1018601108

Duncker, K., & Lees, L. S. (1945). On problem-solving. *Psychological Monographs*, *58*(5), 1–113. doi:10.1037/h0093599

Easterbrook, J. A. (1959). The effect of emotion on cue utilization and the organization of behavior. *Psychological Review*, *66*(3), 183–201. doi:10.1037/h0047707

Eich, E., Ng, J. T. W., Macaulay, D., Percy, A., & Grebneva, I. (2007). Combining Music With Thought to Change Mood. In J. A. Coan & J. J. B. Allen (Eds.), *Handbook of emotion elicitation and assessment* (pp. 124–136). Oxford, New York: Oxford University Press.

Eid, M. (1997). Happiness and satisfaction: An application of a latent state-trait model for ordinal variables. In J. Rost & R. Langeheine (Eds.), *Applications of latent trait and latent class models in the social sciences* (pp. 145–151). Münster: Waxmann.

Eid, M., & Diener, E. (1999). Intraindividual variability in affect: Reliability, validity, and personality correlates. *Journal of Personality and Social Psychology, 76*(4), 662–676. doi:10.1037/0022-3514.76.4.662

Eid, M., Gollwitzer, M., & Schmitt, M. (2010). *Statistik und Forschungsmethoden: Lehrbuch mit Online-Materialien* (1st ed.). Weinheim [u.a.]: Beltz.

Ekman, P. (1992). An argument for basic emotions. *Cognition & Emotion, 6*(3-4), 169–200. doi:10.1080/02699939208411068

Ekman, P., & Friesen, W. V. (1976). Measuring facial movement. *Environmental Psychology and Nonverbal Behavior, 1*(1), 56-75. doi:10.1007/BF01115465

Ekman, P., & Friesen, W. V. (1978). *Facial Action Coding System.* Palo Alto, CA: Consulting Psychologists Press.

Ekman, P., & Friesen, W. V. (1982). Felt, false, and miserable smiles. *Journal of Nonverbal Behavior, 6*(4), 238-252. doi:10.1007/BF00987191

Ekman, P., Friesen, W. V., & Hager, J. C. (Eds.). (2002). *Facial Action Coding System*. Salt Lake City, UT: Research Nexus.

Ellis, H. C., & Ashbrook, P. W. (1988). Resource allocation model of the effects of depressed mood states on memory. In K. Fiedler & J. Forgas (Eds.), *Affect, cognition and social behavior.* Toronto: Hogrefe.

Erber, R., & Tesser, A. (1992). Task effort and the regulation of mood: The absorption hypothesis. *Journal of Experimental Social Psychology, 28*, 339–359.

Erez, A., & Isen, A. M. (2002). The influence of positive affect on the components of expectancy motivation. *Journal of Applied Psychology*, *87*(6), 1055–1067.

Ergenoglu, T., Demiralp, T., Bayraktaroglu, Z., Ergen, M., Beydagi, H., & Uresin, Y. (2004). Alpha rhythm of the EEG modulates visual detection performance in humans. *Cognitive Brain Research*, *20*(3), 376–383. doi:10.1016/j.cogbrainres.2004.03.009

Estrada, C. A., Isen, A. M., & Young, M. J. (1997). Positive affect facilitates integration of information and decreases anchoring in reasoning among physicians. *Organizational Behavior and Human Decision Processes*, *72*(1), 117–135.

Eysenck, H. J. (1976). Intelligence. In H. J. Eysenck & G. D. Wilson (Eds.), *A Textbook of Human Psychology* (pp. 115–128). Lancaster: MTP Press.

Eysenck, H. J. (1998). *Intelligence: A new look.* New Brunswick, NJ: Transaction Publishers.

Fan, W., & Yan, Z. (2010). Factors affecting response rates of the web survey: A systematic review. *Computers in Human Behavior*, *26*(2), 132–139. doi:10.1016/j.chb.2009.10.015

Feldman Barrett, L., Robin, L., Pietromonaco, P. R., & Eyssell, K. M. (1998). Are Women the "More Emotional" Sex? Evidence From Emotional Experiences in Social Context. *Cognition & Emotion*, *12*(4), 555–578. doi:10.1080/026999398379565

Feldman Barrett, L., & Russell, J. A. (1998). Independence and bipolarity in the structure of current affect. *Journal of Personality and Social Psychology*, *74*(4), 967–984. doi:10.1037/0022-3514.74.4.967

Fiedler, K. (1988). Emotional mood, cognitive style, and behavior regulation. In K. Fiedler & J. Forgas (Eds.), *Affect, cognition and social behavior* (pp. 110–119). Toronto: Hogrefe.

Fiedler, K. (1990). Mood dependent selectivity in social cognition. *European Review of Social Psychology, 1*, 1–32.

Fiedler, K., Nickel, S., Asbeck, J., & Pagel, U. (2003). Mood and the generation effect. *Cognition & Emotion, 17*(4), 585–608. doi:10.1080/02699930302301

Flaherty, A. W. (2005). Frontotemporal and dopaminergic control of idea generation and creative drive. *The Journal of Comparative Neurology, 493*(1), 147–153. doi:10.1002/cne.20768

Forgas, J. P. (1995). Mood and judgment: The affect infusion model (AIM). *Psychological Bulletin, 117*(1), 39–66.

Forgas, J. P. (2002). Feeling and Doing: Affective Influences on Interpersonal Behavior. *Psychological Inquiry, 13*(1), 1–28.

Forgas, J. P. (2008). Affect and Cognition. *Perspectives on Psychological Science, 3*(2), 94–101. doi:10.1111/j.1745-6916.2008.00067.x

Forgas, J. P., Bower, G. H., & Krantz, S. E. (1984). The influence of mood on perceptions of social interactions. *Journal of Experimental Social Psychology, 20*(6), 497–513. doi:10.1016/0022-1031(84)90040-4

Forgas, J. P., & George, J. M. (2001). Affective Influences on Judgments and Behavior in Organizations: An Information Processing Perspective. *Organizational Behavior and Human Decision Processes, 86*(1), 3–34.

Fredrickson, B. L. (1998). What good are positive emotions? *Review of General Psychology, 2*, 300–319.

Fredrickson, B. L. (2001). The role of positive emotions in positive psychology: The broaden-and-build theory of positive emotions. *American Psychologist, 56*(218-226).

Fredrickson, B. L., & Branigan, C. (2005). Positive emotions broaden the scope of attention and thought-action repertoires. *Cognition & Emotion, 19*(3), 313–332. doi:10.1080/02699930441000238

Friedman, R. S., & Förster, J. (2008). Activation and Measurement of Motivational States. In A. J. Elliot (Ed.), *Handbook of approach and avoidance motivation* (pp. 235–250). New York: Psychology Press.

Frijda, N. H. (1994). Varieties of affect: Emotions and episodes, moods, and sentiments. In P. Ekman & R. J. Davidson (Eds.), *The nature of emotion: Fundamental questions* (pp. 59–67). New York: Oxford University Press.

Friswell, R., & McConkey, K. M. (1989). Hypnotically induced mood. *Cognition & Emotion, 3*(1), 1–26. doi:10.1080/02699938908415233

Fujita, F., Diener, E., & Sandvik, E. (1991). Gender differences in negative affect and well-being: The case for emotional intensity. *Journal of Personality and Social Psychology, 61*(3), 427–434. doi:10.1037/0022-3514.61.3.427

Funke, F. (2010). *Internet-Based Measurement With Visual Analogue Scales: An Experimental Investigation* (Doctoral Dissertation). Eberhard-Karls-Universität, Tübingen.

Fuster, J. M. (1989). *The prefrontal cortex*. New York: Raven Press.

Gardner, H. (1983). *Frames of Mind: The Theory of Multiple Intelligences*. New York, NY: Basic Books.

Gardner, H. (1999). *Intelligence reframed: Multiple intelligences for the 21st century*. New York, NY: Basic Books.

Gardner, H., & Hatch, T. (1989). Educational Implications of the Theory of Multiple Intelligences. *Educational Researcher, 18*(8), 4–10. doi:10.3102/0013189X018008004

Gasper, K., & Clore, G. L. (2002). Attending to the Big Picture: Mood and Global Versus Local Processing of Visual Information. *Psychological Science, 13*(1), 34–40. doi:10.1111/1467-9280.00406

Gerrads-Hesse, A., Spies, K., & Hesse, F. W. (1994). Experimental inductions of emotional states and their effectiveness: a review. *British Journal of Psychology*, *85*(1), 55–78.

Gilet, A.-L. (2008). Mood induction procedures: a critical review [Procedures d'induction d'humeurs en laboratoire: une revue critique]. *L'Encephale*, *34*(3), 233–239. doi:10.1016/j.encep.2006.08.003

Goldman-Rakic, P. S. (1995). Cellular basis of working memory. *Neuron*, *14*, 477–485.

Göritz, A. S. (2007). The Induction of Mood via the WWW. *Motivation and Emotion*, *31*(1), 35-47. doi:10.1007/s11031-006-9047-4

Göritz, A. S., & Moser, K. (2006). Web-based mood induction. *Cognition & Emotion*, *20*(6), 887–896. doi:10.1080/02699930500405386

Gottfredson, L. S. (2004). Intelligence: Is It the Epidemiologists' Elusive "Fundamental Cause" of Social Class Inequalities in Health? *Journal of Personality and Social Psychology*, *86*(1), 174–199. doi:10.1037/0022-3514.86.1.174

Gräf, L. (2002). Assessing Internet Questionnaires: The Online Pretest Lab. In B. Batinic, U.-D. Reips, & M. Bosnjak (Eds.), *Online social sciences* (pp. 49–68). Seattle: Hogrefe & Huber Publishers.

Gray, J. A. (1990). Brain systems that mediate both emotion and cognition. *Cognition and Emotion*, *4*, 269–288.

Green, D. P., Goldman, S. L., & Salovey, P. (1993). Measurement error masks bipolarity in affect ratings. *Journal of Personality and Social Psychology*, *64*(6), 1029–1041. Retrieved from 10.1037/0022-3514.64.6.1029

Gross, J. J., & Levenson, R. W. (1995). Emotion elicitation using films. *Cognition and Emotion*, *9*, 87–108.

Grossman, M., & Wood, W. (1993). Sex differences in intensity of emotional experience: A social role interpretation. *Journal of Personality and Social Psychology*, *65*(5), 1010–1022. doi:10.1037/0022-3514.65.5.1010

Guilford, J. P. (1967). *The nature of human intelligence. McGraw-Hill series in psychology*. New York: McGraw-Hill.

Guilford, J. P. (1988). Some Changes in the Structure-of-Intellect Model. *Educational and Psychological Measurement*, *48*(1), 1–4. doi:10.1177/001316448804800102

Halford, G. S. (1993). *Children's understanding: The development of mental models*. Hillsdale, NJ: Lawrence Erlbaum.

Halford, G. S., Wilson, W. H., & Phillips, S. (1998). Processing capacity defined by relational complexity: Implications for comparative, developmental, and cognitive psychology. *Behavioral and Brain Sciences*, *21*, 803–831.

Hanslmayr, S., Aslan, A., Staudigl, T., Klimesch, W., Herrmann, C. S., & Bäuml, K.-H. (2007). Prestimulus oscillations predict visual perception performance between and within subjects. *NeuroImage*, *37*(4), 1465–1473. doi:10.1016/j.neuroimage.2007.07.011

Harmon-Jones, E., Amodio, D. M., & Zinner, L. R. (2007). Social Psychological Methods of Emotion Eliciation. In J. A. Coan & J. J. B. Allen (Eds.), *Handbook of emotion elicitation and assessment* (pp. 91–105). Oxford, New York: Oxford University Press.

Heckhausen, H., & Gollwitzer, P. M. (1986). Information processing before and after the formation of an intent. In F. Klix & H. Hagendorf (Eds.), *In memoriam Hermann Ebbinghaus: Symposium on the structure and function of human memory*. Amsterdam: Elsevier/North Holland.

Heckhausen, H., & Gollwitzer, P. M. (1987). Thought contents and cognitive functioning in motivational versus volitional states of mind. *Motivation and Emotion*, *11*(2), 101–120. doi:10.1007/BF00992338

Hembree, R. (1988). Correlates, causes, effects, and treatment of test anxiety. *Review of Educational Research*, *58*, 47–77.

Hertel, G., Konradt, U., & Orlikowski, B. (2003). Ziele und Strategien von E-Assessment aus Sicht der psychologischen Personalauswahl. In U. Konradt & W. Sarges (Eds.), *Psychologie für das Personalmanagement. E-Recruitment und E-Assessment. Rekrutierung, Auswahl und Beurteilung von Personal im Inter- und Intranet* (pp. 37–54). Göttingen: Hogrefe.

Hertel, G., Naumann, S., Konradt, U., & Batinic, B. (2002). Personality Assessment via Internet. In B. Batinic, U.-D. Reips, & M. Bosnjak (Eds.), *Online social sciences* (pp. 115–133). Seattle: Hogrefe & Huber Publishers.

Hoffman, D. L., & Novak, T. P. (1998). Bridging the Racial Divide on the Internet. *Science*, *280*(5362), 390–391. doi:10.1126/science.280.5362.390

Holling, H., Preckel, F., & Vock, M. (2004). *Intelligenzdiagnostik. Kompendien Psychologische Diagnostik: Vol. 6*. Göttingen: Hogrefe.

Horn, J. L. (1965). *Fluid and crystallized intelligence* (Unpublished doctoral dissertation). University of Illinois, Urbana-Champaign.

Horn, J. L. (1968). Organization of abilities and the development of intelligence. *Psychological Review*, *75*(3), 242–259. doi:10.1037/h0025662

Horn, J. L., & Cattell, R. B. (1966). Refinement and test of the theory of fluid and crystallized general intelligences. *Journal of Educational Psychology*, *57*(5), 253–270. doi:10.1037/h0023816

Hornke, L. F., Küppers, A., & Etzel, S. (2000). Konstruktion und Evaluation eines adaptiven Matrizentests. *Diagnostica, 46*(4), 182–188. doi:10.1026//0012-1924.46.4.182

Huang, H.-M. (2006). Do print and Web surveys provide the same results? *Computers in Human Behavior, 22*(3), 334–350. doi:10.1016/j.chb.2004.09.012

Huff, K. L., & Sireci, S. G. (2001). Validity Issues in Computer-Based Testing. *Educational Measurement: Issues and Practice, 20*(3), 16–25. doi:10.1111/j.1745-3992.2001.tb00066.x

International Test Commission (2005). *The ITC Guidelines on Computer-Based and Internet-delivered Testing*. Downloaded electronically on 08.02.2014 from www.intestcom.org/itc_projects.htm

Isen, A. M. (1984). Toward understanding the role of affect in cognition. In R. Wyer & T. Srull (Eds.), *Handbook of Social Cognition* (pp. 174–236). Hillsdale: Lawrence Erlbaum Assoc.

Isen, A. M. (2000). Positive affect and decision making. In M. Lewis & J. Haviland-Jones (Eds.), *Handbook of Emotions* (2nd ed., pp. 417–435). New York: Guilford Press.

Isen, A. M. (2002). Missing in Action in the AIM: Positive Affect's Facilitation of Cognitive Flexibility, Innovation, and Problem Solving. *Psychological Inquiry, 13*(1), 57–65.

Isen, A. M., & Daubman, K. A. (1984). The influence of affect on categorization. *Journal of Personality and Social Psychology, 47*, 1206–1217.

Isen, A. M., Daubman, K. A., & Gorgolione, J. M. (1984). The influence of positive affect on cognitive organization. In R. Snow & M. Farr (Eds.), *Aptitude, learning, and instruction: Conative and affective factors* (pp. 125–154). Hillsdale, NJ: Lawrence Erlbaum.

Isen, A. M., Daubman, K. A., & Nowicki, G. P. (1987). Positive Affect Facilitates Creative Problem Solving. *Journal of Personality and Social Psychology, 52*(6), 1122–1131.

Isen, A. M., & Geva, N. (1987). The influence of positive affect on acceptable level of risk: The person with a large canoe has a large worry. *Organizational Behavior and Human Decision Processes, 39*, 145–154.

Isen, A. M., Johnson, M. M. S., Mertz, E., & Robinson, G. F. (1985). The influence of positive affect on the unusualness of word associations. *Journal of Personality and Social Psychology, 48*, 1–14.

Isen, A. M., & Means, B. (1983). The influence of positive affect on decision-making strategy. *Social Cognition, 2*, 18–31.

Isen, A. M., Means, B., Patrick, R., & Nowicki, G. P. (1982). Some factors influencing decision-making strategy and risk-taking. In M. S. Clark & S. T. Fiske (Eds.), *Affect and cognition: The 17th Annual Carnegie Symposium on Cognition* (pp. 243–261). Hillsdale, NJ: Erlbaum.

Isen, A. M., Nygren, T. E., & Ashby, F. G. (1988). Influence of positive affect on subjective utility of gains and losses: It is just not worth the risk. *Journal of Personality and Social Psychology, 55*, 710–717.

Isen, A. M., & Patrick, R. (1983). The effect of positive feelings on risk taking: When the chips are down. *Organizational Behavior and Human Performance, 31*, 194–202.

Isen, A. M., Rosenzweig, A. S., & Young, M. J. (1991). The influence of positive affect on clinical problem solving. *Medical Decision Making, 11*(3), 221–227.

Isen, A. M., Shalker, T. E., Clark, M., & Karp, L. (1978). Affect, accessibility of material in memory, and behavior: A cognitive loop? *Journal of Personality and Social Psychology, 36*(1), 1–12.

Izard, C. E. (1977). *Human Emotions*. New York: Plenum.

Izard, C. E. (1991). *The Psychology Of Emotions*. New York: Plenum Press.

Izard, C. E. (1992). Basic emotions, relations among emotions, and emotion-cognition relations. *Psychological Review*, *99*(3), 561–565.

Jaeggi, S. M., Buschkuehl, M., Jonides, J., & Perrig, W. J. (2008). Improving fluid intelligence with training on working memory. *Proceedings of the National Academy of Sciences*. doi:10.1073/pnas.0801268105

Jäger, A. O. (1982). Mehrmodale Klassifikation von Intelligenzleistungen: Experimentell kontrollierte Weiterentwicklung eines deskriptiven Intelligenzstrukturmodells [Multimodal classification of intelligence tests: Experimentally controlled development of a descriptive model of intelligence structure]. *Diagnostica*, *28*, 195–225.

Jäger, A. O. (1984). Intelligenzstrukturforschung: Konkurrierende Modelle, neue Entwicklungen, Perspektiven [Research on intelligence structure: Competing models, new developments, perspectives]. *Psychologische Rundschau*, *35*, 21–35.

Jäger, A. O., Süß, H.-M., & Beauducel, A. (1997). *Berliner-Intelligenz-Struktur-Test: BIS-Test, Form 4 [Berlin-intelligence-structure-test: BIS-test form 4]*. Göttingen: Hogrefe.

Jennings, P. D., McGinnin, D., Lovejoy, S., & Stirling, J. (2000). Valence and Arousal Ratings for Velten Mood Induction Statements. *Motivation and Emotion*, *24*(4), 285–297.

Kahneman, D. (1973). *Attention and effort. Prentice Hall series in experimental psychology*. Englewood Cliffs: Prentice Hall.

Kahneman, D. (2012). *Thinking, fast and slow*. London: Penguin.

Kenealy, P. M. (1986). The Velten Mood Induction Procedure: A Methodological Review. *Motivation and Emotion, 10*(4), 315–335.

Kersting, M., Althoff, K., & Jäger, A. O. (2008). *Wilde-Intelligenz-Test 2*. Göttingen: Hogrefe.

Kihlstrom, J. F. (1985). Hypnosis. *Annual Review of Psychology, 36*(1), 385–418. doi:10.1146/annurev.ps.36.020185.002125

Kimberg, D. Y., D'Esposito, M., & Farah, M. J. (1997). Effects of bromocriptine on human subjects depend on working memory capacity. *NeuroReport, 8*(16).

Klauer, K., Siemer, M., & Stöber, J. (1991). Stimmung und Leistungsniveau bei einfachen Aufgaben. *Zeitschrift für experimentelle und angewandte Psychologie, 38*, 379–393.

Kleinke, C. L., Peterson, T. R., & Rutledge, T. R. (1998). Effects of self-generated facial expressions on mood. *Journal of Personality and Social Psychology, 74*(1), 272–279. doi:10.1037/0022-3514.74.1.272

Klinck, D. (2002). *Computergestützte Diagnostik: Beeinflusst das Medium der Testbearbeitung die Testcharakteristika, die Testfairness oder das Erleben der Testsituation?* Göttingen [u.a.]: Hogrefe.

Klinger, E. (1996). Emotional Influences on Cognitive Processing, with Implications for Theories of Both. In P. M. Gollwitzer & J. A. Bargh (Eds.), *The psychology of action: Linking cognition and motivation to behavior* (pp. 168–189). New York: Guilford.

Knapp, A. (1986). Die Auswirkung emotionaler Zustände auf das Lösen eines sozialen Dilemmas. *Zeitschrift für Sozialpsychologie, 17*, 160–172.

Knapp, A. (1988). *The interaction between task difficulty and mood intensity on performance in a resource dilemma with a time delayed propagation function.* Universität Mainz: Projektbericht Nr. 5.

Knapp, H., & Kirk, S. A. (2003). Using pencil and paper, Internet and touch-tone phones for self-administered surveys: does methodology matter? *Computers in Human Behavior*, *19*(1), 117–134. doi:10.1016/S0747-5632(02)00008-0

Konradt, U., & Sarges, W. (2003). Suche, Auswahl und Förderung von Personal im Intra- und Internet: Strategien, Zielerreichung und Entwicklungspfade. In U. Konradt & W. Sarges (Eds.), *Psychologie für das Personalmanagement. E-Recruitment und E-Assessment. Rekrutierung, Auswahl und Beurteilung von Personal im Inter- und Intranet* (pp. 3–16). Göttingen: Hogrefe.

Krasilovsky, P. (1996). Surveys in cyberspace. *American Demographics*, *Supplement, Nov-Dec*, 18–22.

Kruskal, W. H., & Wallis, W. A. (1952). Use of ranks in one-criterion variance analysis. *Journal of the American Statistical Association*, *47*, 583–621.

Kubinger, K. D. (2009). *Psychologische Diagnostik: Theorie und Praxis psychologischen Diagnostizierens* (2nd ed.). Göttingen [u.a.]: Hogrefe.

Kuhbandner, C., Hanslmayr, S., Maier, M. A., Pekrun, R., Spitzer, B., Pastötter, B., & Bäuml, K.-H. (2009). Effects of mood on the speed of conscious perception: behavioural and electrophysiological evidence. *Social Cognitive and Affective Neuroscience*, *4*(3), 286–293. doi:10.1093/scan/nsp010

Kuhl, J. (1983a). Emotion, Kognition und Motivation: I. Auf dem Weg zu einer systemtheoretischen Betrachtung der Emotionsgenese. *Sprache und Kognition*, *2*, 1–27.

Kuhl, J. (1983b). Emotion, Kognition und Motivation: II. Die funktionale Bedeutung der Emotionen für das problemlösende Denken und für das konkrete Handeln. *Sprache und Kognition*, *4*, 228–253.

Lambourne, K., & Tomporowski, P. (2010). The effect of exercise-induced arousal on cognitive task performance: A meta-regression analysis. *Exercise and the Brain, 1341*, 12–24. doi:10.1016/j.brainres.2010.03.091

Lang, J. W. B., & Lang, J. (2010). Priming Competence Diminishes the Link Between Cognitive Test Anxiety and Test Performance: Implications for the Interpretation of Test Scores. *Psychological Science, 21*(6), 811–819. doi:10.1177/0956797610369492

Lang, P. J. (1980). Behavioral treatment and bio-behavioral assessment: computer applications. In J. B. Sidowski, J. H. Johnson, & T. A. Williams (Eds.), *Technology in mental health care delivery systems* (pp. 119–137). Norwood, NJ: Ablex.

Lang, P. J., Bradley, M. M., & Cuthbert, B. N. (1999). *International affective picture system (IAPS): Technical Manual and Affective Ratings*. Gainesville, FL: The Center for Research in Psychophysiology, University of Florida.

Lang, P. J., Greenwald, M. K., Bradley, M. M., & Hamm, A. O. (1993). Looking at pictures: affective, facial, visceral, and behavioral reactions. *Psychophysiology, 30*(3), 261–273.

Larsen, R. J. (2009). The Contributions of Positive and Negative Affect to Emotional Well-Being. *Psychological Topics, 18*(2), 247–266.

Larsen, R. J., & Diener, E. (1987). Affect intensity as an individual difference characteristic: A review. *Journal of Research in Personality, 21*(1), 1–39. doi:10.1016/0092-6566(87)90023-7

Larsen, R. J., & Diener, E. (1992). Problems and promises with the circumplex model of emotion. In M. S. Clark (Ed.), *Review of personality and social psychology: Emotion* (Vol. 13, pp. 25–59). Newbury Park, CA: Sage.

Larsen, R. J., & Prizmic, Z. (2010). Affect regulation. In R. F. Baumeister & K. D. Vohs (Eds.), *Handbook of self-regulation* (pp. 40–61). New York: Guilford Press.

Latham, G. P., & Locke, E. A. (1991). Self-Regulation through Goal Setting. *Organizational Behavior and Human Decision Processes, 50*, 212–247.

Lefever, S., Dal, M., & Matthíasdóttir, Á. (2007). Online data collection in academic research: advantages and limitations. *British Journal of Educational Technology, 38*(4), 574–582.

Lepper, M. R., Greene, D., & Nisbett, R. E. (1973). Undermining children's intrinsic interest with extrinsic reward: A test of the "overjustification" hypothesis. *Journal of Personality and Social Psychology, 28*(1), 129–137. doi:10.1037/h0035519

Levenson, R. W., Ekman, P., & Friesen, W. V. (1990). Voluntary facial action generates emotion-specific autonomic nervous system activity. *Psychophysiology, 27*(4), 363–384.

Levenson, R. W., & Gottman, J. M. (1983). Marital interaction: Physiological linkage and affective exchange. *Journal of Personality and Social Psychology, 45*(3), 587–597. doi:10.1037/0022-3514.45.3.587

Leventhal, H., & Tomarken, A. J. (1986). Emotion: today's problems. *Annual Review of Psychology, 37*, 565–610.

Liepmann, D., Beauducel, A., Brocke, B., & Amthauer, R. (2007). *Intelligenz-Struktur-Test 2000 R (I-S-T 2000 R). Manual* (2nd ed.). Göttingen: Hogrefe.

Lievens, F., & Burke, E. (2011). Dealing with the threats inherent in unproctored Internet testing of cognitive ability: Results from a large-scale operational test program. *Journal of Occupational and Organizational Psychology, 84*(4), 817–824. doi:10.1348/096317910X522672

Lievens, F., & Harris, M. (2003). Research on Internet Recruiting and Testing: Current Status and Future Directions. In C. L. Cooper & I. T. Robertson (Eds.), *International Review of Industrial and Organizational Psychology* (pp. 131-165). Chichester, UK: Wiley.

Linnenbrink, E. A. (2007). The role of affect in student learning: A multi-dimensional approach to considering the interaction of affect, motivation, and engagement. In P. A. Schutz & R. Pekrun (Eds.), *Emotion in Education* (pp. 107–124). San Diego, CA: Academic Press.

Lischetzke, T., & Eid, M. (2011). Diagnostik affektiver Zustände. In L. F. Hornke, M. Amelang, & M. Kersting (Eds.), *Persönlichkeitsdiagnostik* (pp. 211–265). Göttingen: Hogrefe.

Lottridge, S. M., Nicewander, W. A., & Mitzel, H. C. (2011). A Comparison of Paper and Online Tests Using a Within-Subjects Design and Propensity Score Matching Study. *Multivariate Behavioral Research, 46*(3), 544–566. doi:10.1080/00273171.2011.569408

Lyubomirski, S., King, L., & Diener, E. (2005). The Benefits of Frequent Positive Affect: Does Happiness Lead to Success? *Psychological Bulletin, 131*(6), 803–855.

Mackie, D. M., & Worth, L. T. (1989). Processing deficits and the mediation of positive affect in persuasion. *Journal of Personality and Social Psychology*, *57*, 27–40.

Mandler, G., & Sarason, S. B. (1952). A study of anxiety and learning. *The Journal of Abnormal and Social Psychology*, *47*(2), 166–173. doi:10.1037/h0062855

Marcus, B., & Schütz, A. (2005). Who Are the People Reluctant to Participate in Research? Personality Correlates of Four Different Types of Nonresponse as Inferred from Self- and Observer Ratings. *Journal of Personality*, *73*(4), 959–984. doi:10.1111/j.1467-6494.2005.00335.x

Matsumoto, D., & Sanders, M. (1988). Emotional experiences during engagement in intrinsically and extrinsically motivated tasks. *Motivation and Emotion*, *12*(4), 353-369. doi:10.1007/BF00992359

Matthews, G., Jones, D. M., & Chamberlain, A. G. (1990). Refining the measurement of mood: The UWIST Mood Adjective Checklist. *British Journal of Psychology*, *81*, 17–42.

McConville, C., & Cooper, C. (1997). The temporal stability of mood variability. *Personality and Individual Differences*, *23*(1), 161–164. doi:10.1016/S0191-8869(97)00013-5

McGraw, K. O., Tew, M. D., & Williams, J. E. (2000). The Integrity of Web-Delivered Experiments: Can You Trust the Data? *Psychological Science*, *11*(6), 502–506. doi:10.1111/1467-9280.00296

McGrew, K. S. (2009). CHC theory and the human cognitive abilities project: Standing on the shoulders of the giants of psychometric intelligence research. *Intelligence*, *37*(1), 1–10.

McGrew, K. S., & Flanagan, D. P. (1998). *The intelligence test desk reference (ITDR): Gf-Gc cross-battery assessment*. Boston: Allyn and Bacon.

Mead, A. D., & Drasgow, F. (1993). Equivalence of computerized and paper-and-pencil cognitive ability tests: A meta-analysis. *Psychological Bulletin*, *114*(3), 449–458.

Meade, A. W., Michels, L. C., & Lautenschlager, G. J. (2007). Are Internet and Paper-and-Pencil Personality Tests Truly Comparable? An Experimental Design Measurement Invariance Study. *Organizational Research Methods*, *10*(2), 322–345. doi:10.1177/1094428106289393

Mednick, S. S., & Mednick, M. T. (1967). *Examiner's manual: Remote Associates Test*. Boston: Houghton Mifflin.

Mehrabian, A. (1996). Pleasure-Arousal-Dominance: A General Framework for Describing and Measuring Individual Differences in Temperament. *Current Psychology*, *14*(4), 261–292.

Mehta, E., & Sivadas, R. (1995). Comparing response rates and response content in mail versus electronic mail surveys. *Journal of the Market Research Society*, *37*(4), 429–439.

Melton, R. J. (1995). The role of positive affect in syllogism performance. *Personality and Social Psychology Bulletin, 21*, 788–794.

Mossberger, K., Tolbert, C. J., & Gilbert, M. (2006). Race, Place, and Information Technology. *Urban Affairs Review, 41*(5), 583–620. doi:10.1177/1078087405283511

Murray, G., Allen, N. B., & Trinder, J. (2002). Longitudinal investigation of mood variability and the ffm: neuroticism predicts variability in extended states of positive and negative affect. *Personality and Individual Differences, 33*(8), 1217–1228. doi:10.1016/S0191-8869(01)00217-3

Murray, N., Sujan, H., Hirt, E. R., & Sujan, M. (1990). The Influence of Mood on Categorization: A Cognitive Flexibility Interpretation. *Journal of Personality and Social Psychology, 59*(3), 411–425.

Nakamura, J., & Csikszentmihalyi, M. (2002). Flow theory and research. In C. R. Snyder & S. J. Lopez (Eds.), *Handbook of Positive Psychology* (pp. 195–206). New York: Oxford University Press.

Nasby, W., & Yando, R. (1982). Selective encoding and retrieval of affectively valent information: Two cognitive consequences of children's mood states. *Journal of Personality and Social Psychology, 43*(6), 1244–1253.

Neubauer, A. C., Urban, E., & Malle, B. F. (1991). Raven's Advanced Progressive Matrices: Computerunterstützte Präsentation versus Standardvorgabe. *Diagnostica, 37*(3), 204–212.

Neuman, G., & Baydoun, R. (1998). Computerization of Paper-and-Pencil Tests: When are They Equivalent? *Applied Psychological Measurement, 22*(1), 71–83. doi:10.1177/01466216980221006

Nielsen, J. (1995). *Overview of the 1995 Design of Sun Microsystems' Website, Using Iterative Design and User Testing* [online]. Retrieved from http://www.nngroup.com/articles/1995-design-sun-microsystems-website/ [08.01.2014]

No authorship indicated. (1921). Intelligence and Its Measurement: A Symposium. *Journal of Educational Psychology*, *12*(3), 123–147. doi:10.1037/h0076078

Oberauer, K., Schulze, R., Wilhelm, O., & Süß, H.-M. (2005). Working Memory and Intelligence--Their Correlation and Their Relation: Comment on Ackerman, Beier, and Boyle (2005). *Psychological Bulletin*, *131*(1), 61–65.

Onyper, S. V., Carr, T. L., Farrar, J. S., & Floyd, B. R. (2011). Cognitive advantages of chewing gum. Now you see them, now you don't. *Appetite*, *57*(2), 321–328. doi:10.1016/j.appet.2011.05.313

Osborne, J. W. (2010). Improving your data transformations: Applying the Box-Cox transformation. *Practical Assessment, Research & Evaluation*, *15*(12), 1–9.

Osgood, C. E., Suci, G. J., & Tannenbaum, P. H. (1957). *The measurement of meaning*. Urbana, IL: University of Illinios Press.

Otto, J. H. (2000). Induktionsverfahren. In J. H. Otto, H. A. Euler, & H. Mandl (Eds.), *Emotionspsychologie. Ein Handbuch* (pp. 395–408). Weinheim: Psychologie Verlags Union.

Parrott, W. G. (1991). Mood induction and instructions to sustain moods: A test of the subject compliance hypothesis of mood congruent memory. *Cognition & Emotion*, *5*(1), 41–52. doi:10.1080/02699939108411022

Pearson Assessment (2011). *Raven's Advanced Progressive Matrices: International Technical Manual* [online]. Retrieved from http://www.talentlens.co.uk/assets/resources/raven%27s%20apm%20international%20technical%20manual.pdf [09.02.2014]

Pekrun, R. (2006). The Control-Value Theory of Achievement Emotions: Assumptions, Corollaries, and Implications for Educational Research and Practice. *Educational Psychology Review, 18*(4), 315–341.

Pekrun, R., Elliot, A. J., & Maier, M. A. (2006). Achievement Goals and Discrete Achievement Emotions: A Theoretical Model and Prospective Test. *Journal of Educational Psychology, 98*(3), 583–597.

Pekrun, R., Elliot, A. J., & Maier, M. A. (2009). Achievement Goals and Achievement Emotions: Testing a Model of Their Joint Relations With Academic Performance. *Journal of Educational Psychology, 101*(1), 115–135.

Pekrun, R., & Frese, M. (1992). Emotions in Work and Achievement. In C. L. Cooper & I. T. Robertson (Eds.), *International review of industrial and organizational psychology* (pp. 153–200). Chichester, UK: Wiley.

Pekrun, R., Goetz, T., Perry, R. P., Kramer, K., Hochstadt, M., & Molfenter, S. (2004). Beyond Test Anxiety: Development and Validation of the Test Emotions Questionnaire (TEQ). *Anxiety, Stress, and Coping, 17*(3), 287–316.

Pekrun, R., & Hofmann, H. (1999). Lern- und Leistungsemotionen: Erste Befunde eines Forschungsprogramms. In M. Jerusalem & R. Pekrun (Eds.), *Emotion, Motivation und Leistung* (pp. 247–267). Göttingen: Hogrefe.

Philippot, P. (1993). Inducing and assessing differentiated emotion-feeling states in the laboratory. *Cognition & Emotion, 7*(2), 171–193. doi:10.1080/02699939308409183

Pignatiello, M. F., Camp, C. J., & Rasar, L. A. (1986). Musical mood induction: An alternative to the Velten technique. *Journal of Abnormal Psychology, 95*(3), 295–297.

Plutchik, R. (2001). The Nature of Emotions: Human emotions have deep evolutionary roots, a fact that may explain their complexity and provide tools for clinical practice. *American Scientist*, *89*(4), 344–350. doi:10.2307/27857503

Polivy, J., & Doyle, C. (1980). Laboratory induction of mood states through the reading of self-referent mood statements: Affective changes or demand characteristics? *Journal of Abnormal Psychology*, *89*(2), 286–290.

Pretty, G., & Seligman, M. (1984). Affect and the overjustification effect. *Journal of Personality and Social Psychology*, *46*, 1241–1253.

Radenhausen, R. A., & Anker, J. M. (1988). Effects of depressed mood induction on reasoning performance. *Perceptual and Motor Skills*, *66*, 855–860.

Ramirez, G., & Beilock, S. L. (2011). Writing About Testing Worries Boosts Exam Performance in the Classroom. *Science*, *331*(6014), 211–213. doi:10.1126/science.1199427

Raven, J., Raven, J. C., & Court, J. H. (2003). *Manual for Raven's Progressive Matrices and Vocabulary Scales*. San Antonio, TX: Harcourt Assessment.

Riediger, M., Wrzus, C., Schmiedek, F., Wagner, G. G., & Lindenberger, U. (2011). Is seeking bad mood cognitively demanding? Contra-hedonic orientation and working-memory capacity in everyday life. *Emotion*, *11*(3), 656–665.

Rietz, I., & Wahl, S. (1999). Vergleich von Selbst- und Fremdbild von PsychologInnen im Internet und auf Papier. In B. Batinic (Ed.), *Internet und Psychologie: Vol. 1. Online Research. Methoden, Anwendungen und Ergebnisse* (pp. 77–92). Göttingen [u.a.]: Hogrefe.

Roberts, B. W., Kuncel, N. R., Shiner, R., Caspi, A., & Goldberg, L. R. (2007). The Power of Personality: The Comparative Validity of Personality Traits, Socioeconomic Status, and Cognitive Ability for Predicting Important Life Outcomes. *Perspec-*

tives on Psychological Science, *2*(4), 313–345. doi:10.1111/j.1745-6916.2007.00047.x

Roberts, N. A., Tsai, J. L., & Coan, J. A. (2007). Emotion Elicitation Using Dyadic Interaction Tasks. In J. A. Coan & J. J. B. Allen (Eds.), *Handbook of emotion elicitation and assessment* (pp. 106–123). Oxford, New York: Oxford University Press.

Roid, G. A. (2003). *Stanford-Binet Intelligence Scales, Fifth Edition*. Itasca, IL: Riverside Publishing.

Rottenberg, J., Ray, R. D., & Gross, J. J. (2007). Emotion Elicitation Using Films. In J. A. Coan & J. J. B. Allen (Eds.), *Handbook of emotion elicitation and assessment* (pp. 9–28). Oxford, New York: Oxford University Press.

Royce, J. R., & Diamond, S. R. (1980). A multifactor-systems dynamics theory of emotion-cognitive interaction. *Motivation and Emotion*, *4*, 263–298.

Russell, J. A. (1980). A circumplex model of affect. *Journal of Personality and Social Psychology*, *39*, 1161–1178.

Russell, J. A., & Mehrabian, A. (1977). Evidence for a three-factor theory of emotions. *Journal of Research in Personality*, *11*(3), 273–294. doi:10.1016/0092-6566(77)90037-X

Russell, J. A., Weiss, A., & Mendelsohn, G. A. (1989). Affect Grid: A single-item scale of pleasure and arousal. *Journal of Personality and Social Psychology*, *57*(3), 493–502. doi:10.1037/0022-3514.57.3.493

Russell, M., Goldberg, A., & O'Connor, K. (2003). Computer-based Testing and Validity: a look back into the future. *Assessment in Education: Principles, Policy & Practice*, *10*(3), 279–293. doi:10.1080/0969594032000148145

Ryan, R. M., & Deci, E. L. (2000). Intrinsic and Extrinsic Motivations: Classic Definitions and New Directions. *Contemporary Educational Psychology*, *25*(1), 54–67. doi:10.1006/ceps.1999.1020

Saavedra, R., & Earley, P. (1991). Choice of task and goal under conditions of general and specific affective inducement. *Motivation and Emotion, 15*(1), 45–65.

Sánchez-Fernández, J., Muñoz-Leiva, F., & Montoro-Ríos, F. J. (2012). Improving retention rate and response quality in Web-based surveys. *Computers in Human Behavior, 28*(2), 507–514. doi:10.1016/j.chb.2011.10.023

Sanders, A. F. (1983). Towards a model of stress and human performance. *Acta Psychologica, 53*(1), 61–97. doi:10.1016/0001-6918(83)90016-1

Scherer, K. R. (1990). Theorien und aktuelle Probleme der Emotionspsychologie. In K. R. Scherer (Ed.), *Psychologie der Emotion* (pp. 1–38). Göttingen: Hogrefe.

Scherer, K. R. (2005). What are emotions? And how can they be measured? *Social Science Information, 44*(4), 695–729. doi:10.1177/0539018405058216

Schimmack, U., & Grob, A. (2000). Dimensional models of core affect: A quantitative comparison by means of structural equation modeling. *European Journal of Personality, 14*, 325–345.

Schmidt, F. L., & Hunter, J. E. (1998). The Validity and Utility of Selection Methods in Personnel Psychology: Practical and Theoretical Implications of 85 Years of Research Findings. *Psychological Bulletin, 124*(2), 262–274.

Schneider, F., Gur, R. C., Gur, R. E., & Muenz, L. R. (1994). Standardized Mood Induction With Happy and Sad Facial Expressions. *Psychiatry Research, 51*(1), 19–31.

Schneider, W. (1987). *Ablenkung und Handlungskontrolle: Eine 'kognitiv-motivationale Perspektive' [Distraction and action control: A "cognitive-motivational perspective"]* (Unpublished diploma thesis). University of Bielefeld, Bielefeld.

Schneider, W. J., & McGrew, K. S. (2012). The Cattell-Horn-Carroll Model of Intelligence. In D. P. Flanagan & P. L. Harrison (Eds.), *Contemporary intellectual assessment. Theories, tests, and issues* (3rd ed., pp. 99–144). New York: Guilford Press.

Schuler, H., & Höft, S. (2006). Konstruktorientierte Verfahren der Personalauswahl. In H. Schuler (Ed.), *Lehrbuch der Personalpsychologie* (2nd ed., pp. 101–144). Göttingen: Hogrefe.

Schwarz, N. (1990). Feelings as Information. Informational and motivational functions of affective states. In E. Higgins & R. Sorrentino (Eds.), *Handbook of Motivation and Cognition. Foundations of Social Behavior* (pp. 527–561). New York: The Guilford Press.

Schwarz, N., & Bohner, G. (1996). Feelings and Their Motivational Implications: Moods and the Action Sequence. In P. M. Gollwitzer & J. A. Bargh (Eds.), *The psychology of action: Linking cognition and motivation to behavior* (pp. 119–145). New York: Guilford.

Schwarz, N., & Clore, G. L. (1988). How do I feel about it? The informative function of affective states. In K. Fiedler & J. Forgas (Eds.), *Affect, cognition and social behavior* (pp. 44–62). Toronto: Hogrefe.

Sebej, J., Mullner, J., & Farkas, G. (1985). Cognitive style, emotional characteristics, and sport achievement. *Psychológia a Patopsychológia Diet'at'a, 20*, 399–409.

Seo, M. G., Feldman Barrett, L., & Bartunek, J. M. (2004). The role of affective experience in work motivation. *Academy of Management Review, 29*(3), 423–439.

Sinclair, R. C. (1988). Mood, categorization breadth, and performance appraisal: The effects of order of information acquisition and affective state on halo, accuracy, information retrieval, and evaluations. *Organizational Behavior and Human Decision Processes, 42*, 22–46.

Sinclair, R. C., & Mark, M. M. (1992). The influence of mood state on judgment and action: Effects on persuasion, categorization, social justice, person perception, and judgmental accuracy. In L. L. Martin & A. Tesser (Eds.), *The construction of social judgments* (pp. 165–193). Hillsdale, NJ: Erlbaum.

Spearman, C. (1904). "General Intelligence," Objectively Determined and Measured. *The American Journal of Psychology, 15*(2), 201–292. doi:10.2307/1412107

Spielberger, C. D. (2010). State-Trait Anxiety Inventory. In I. B. Weiner & E. W. Craighead (Eds.), *The Corsini Encyclopedia of Psychology.* Hoboken, NJ: John Wiley & Sons, Inc. doi: 10.1002/9780470479216.corpsy0943

Spieß, K. (1990). Einfluss von Emotionen auf die Ziel- und Handlungsauswahl. *Zeitschrift für experimentelle und angewandte Psychologie, 37*, 124–152.

Stankov, L., & Horn, J. L. (1980). Human abilities revealed through auditory tests. *Journal of Educational Psychology, 72*(1), 21–44. doi:10.1037/0022-0663.72.1.21

Stankov, L., & Lee, J. (2008). Confidence and cognitive test performance. *Journal of Educational Psychology, 100*(4), 961–976. doi:10.1037/a0012546

Stanovich, K. E. (2009). *What intelligence tests miss: The psychology of rational thought*. New Haven: Yale University Press.

Stanton, J. M. (1998). An empirical assessment of data collection using the internet. *Personnel Psychology, 51*(3), 709–725. doi:10.1111/j.1744-6570.1998.tb00259.x

Stemmler, G., Bartussek, D., Hagemann, D., & Amelang, M. (2011). *Differentielle Psychologie und Persönlichkeitsforschung* (7th ed.). *Kohlhammer Standards Psychologie*. Stuttgart: Kohlhammer.

Sternberg, R. J. (1985). *Beyond IQ: A Triarchic Theory of Intelligence*. Cambridge: Cambridge University Press.

Sternberg, R. J. (1991). Death, taxes, and bad intelligence tests. *Intelligence, 15*(3), 257–269. doi:10.1016/0160-2896(91)90035-C

Stern, W. (1912). *Die psychologischen Methoden der Intelligenzprüfung und deren Anwendung an Schulkindern.* Leipzig: Barth.

Steyer, R., Schwenkmezger, P., Notz, P., & Eid, M. (1994). Testtheoretische Analysen des Mehrdimensionalen Befindlichkeitsfragebogens [Test theoretic analyses of the Multi-Dimensional Affectivity Questionnaire]. *Diagnostica, 40*, 320–328.

Steyer, R., Schwenkmezger, P., Notz, P., & Eid, M. (1997). *Der Mehrdimensionale Befindlichkeitsfragebogen (MDBF).* Göttingen: Hogrefe.

Süß, H.-M., Oberauer, K., Wittmann, W. W., Wilhelm, O., & Schulze, R. (1996). Working Memory Capacity and Intelligence: An Integrative Approach Based on Brunswik Symmetry. *Berichte des Lehrstuhls Psychologie II der Universität Mannheim, Heft 8.*

Sutherland, G., Newman, B., & Rachman, S. (1982). Experimental investigations of the relations between mood and intrusive unwanted cognitions. *British Journal of Medical Psychology, 55*(2), 127–138. doi:10.1111/j.2044-8341.1982.tb01491.x

Taylor, S. E., & Brown, J. D. (1988). Illusion and well-being: A social psychological perspective on mental health. *Psychological Bulletin, 103*, 193–210.

Teasdale, J. D., & Fogarty, S. J. (1979). Differential effects of induced mood on retrieval of pleasant and unpleasant events from episodic memory. *Journal of Abnormal Psychology, 88*(3), 248–257.

Tellegen, A., & Watson, D. (1999). On the dimensional and hierarchical structure of affect. *Psychological Science (Wiley-Blackwell), 10*(4), 297.

Thayer, R. E. (1996). *The origin of everyday moods*. New York: Oxford University Press.

Thurstone, L. L. (1921). Intelligence and Its Measurement. *Journal of Educational Psychology, 16*, 201–207.

Thurstone, L. L. (1938). *Primary Mental Abilities*. Chicago: Chicago University Press.

Thut, G., Nietzel, A., Brandt, S. A., & Pascual-Leone, A. (2006). α-Band Electroencephalographic Activity over Occipital Cortex Indexes Visuospatial Attention Bias and Predicts Visual Target Detection. *The Journal of Neuroscience, 26*(37), 9494–9502. doi:10.1523/JNEUROSCI.0875-06.2006

Tippins, N. T., Beaty, J., Drasgow, F., Gibson, W. M., Pearlman, K., Segall, D. O., & Shepherd, W. (2006). Unproctored internet testing in employment settings. *Personnel Psychology, 59*(1), 189–225.

Truell, A. D. (2003). Use of internet tools for survey research. *Information Technology, Learning & Performance Journal, 21*(1), 31–37.

Turner, J. C., Thorpe, P. K., & Meyer, D. K. (1998). Students' reports of motivation and negative affect: A theoretical and empirical analysis. *Journal of Educational Psychology, 90*(4), 758–771. doi:10.1037/0022-0663.90.4.758

Tuten, T. L., Urban, D. J., & Bosnjak, M. (2002). Internet Surveys and Data Quality: A Review. In B. Batinic, U.-D. Reips, & M. Bosnjak (Eds.), *Online social sciences* (pp. 7–26). Seattle: Hogrefe & Huber Publishers.

van Selm, M., & Jankowski, N. W. (2006). Conducting Online Surveys. *Quality & Quantity, 40*(3), 435–456.

Västfjäll, D. (2002). Emotion Induction through Music: A Review of the Musical Mood Induction Procedure. *Musicae Scientiae, 5*(1 suppl), 173–211. doi:10.1177/10298649020050S107

Velten, E. (1968). A laboratory task for induction of mood states. *Behavior Research and Therapy*, *6*(4), 473–482.

Vroom, V. H. (1964). *Work and motivation*. New York: Wiley.

Watkins, M. W., Lei, P.-W., & Canivez, G. L. (2007). Psychometric intelligence and achievement: A cross-lagged panel analysis. *Intelligence*, *35*(1), 59–68. doi:10.1016/j.intell.2006.04.005

Watson, D., & Clark, L. A. (1994). *The PANAS-X: Manual for the Positive and Negative Affect Schedule - Expanded Form*. Iowa City: University of Iowa.

Watson, D., Clark, L. A., & Tellegen, A. (1988). Development and validation of brief measures of positive and negative affect: The PANAS Scales. *Journal of Personality and Social Psychology*, *54*, 1063–1070.

Watson, D., & Tellegen, A. (1985). Toward a consensual structure of mood. *Psychological Bulletin*, *98*, 219–235.

Wechsler, D. (1939). *The Measurement of Adult Intelligence*. Baltimore, MD: Williams & Witkins.

Wechsler, D. (1955). *Manual for the Wechsler Adult Intelligence Scale*. New York: The Psychological Corporation.

Wechsler, D., Coalson, D. L., & Raiford, S. E. (2008). *Wechsler Adult Intelligence Scale—Fourth Edition (WAIS IV)*. San Antonio, TX: Pearson.

Weiss, F., Blum, G., & Gleberman, L. (1987). Anatomically based measurement of facial expressions in simulated versus hypnotically induced affect. *Motivation and Emotion*, *11*(1), 67-81. doi:10.1007/BF00992214

Westermann, R., Spies, K., Stahl, G., & Hesse, F. W. (1996). Relative effectiveness and validity of mood induction procedures: a meta-analysis. *European Journal of Social Psychology*, *26*, 557–580.

Wilhelm, O., & McKnight, P. E. (2002). Ability and Achievement Testing on the World Wide Web. In B. Batinic, U.-D. Reips, &

M. Bosnjak (Eds.), *Online social sciences* (pp. 151–180). Seattle: Hogrefe & Huber Publishers.

Wonderlic, E. F. (1992). *Wonderlic Personnel Test and scholastic level exam user's manual*. Libertyville, IL: Wonderlic Personnel Test.

Woodcock, R. W., & Johnson, M. B. (1977). *Woodcock-Johnson Psycho-Educational Battery*. Itasca, IL: Riverside Publishing.

Woodcock, R. W., & Johnson, M. B. (1989). *WJ-R Tests of Cognitive Ability*. Itasca, IL: Riverside Publishing.

Woodcock, R. W., McGrew, K. S., & Mather, N. (2001). *Woodcock-Johnson III*. Itasca, IL: Riverside Publishing.

Wundt, W. M. (1896). *Grundriss der Psychologie [Outline of Psychology]*. Leipzig: Engelmann.

Yasutake, D., & Bryan, T. (1995). The influence of affect on the achievement behavior of students with learning disabilities. *Journal of Learning Disabilities*, *28*, 329–334.

Yerkes, R. M., & Dodson, J. D. (1908). The relation of strength of stimulus to rapidity of habit-formation. *Journal of Comparative Neurology and Psychology*, *18*, 459–482.

Yik, M. S. M., Russell, J. A., & Feldman Barrett, L. (1999). Structure of self-reported current affect: Integration and beyond. *Journal of Personality and Social Psychology*, *77*(3), 600–619.

Zeidner, M. (1998). *Test Anxiety: The State of the Art*. New York: Erlbaum.

Tables

Table 1 Stratum II Abilities and Descriptions and Examples of Stratum III Abilities in the Carroll (1993) Model (Excerpt of the Table in McGrew, 2009, pp. 5–6) 26
Table 2 Inequalities for Ordering Experimental Tasks with Respect to the Involvement of Productive Task Elements (adapted from Fiedler, 1990, p. 6, Printed With Permission) 103
Table 3 Descriptive Statistics for the Visual Analogue Scale 137
Table 4 Descriptive Statistics for the MDMQ Dimensions 138
Table 5 Intercorrelations between the Visual Analogue Scales (Mood Sliders) and the Mood Scales 139
Table 6 Descriptive Statistics for the Two Slider Versions 145
Table 7 Descriptive Statistics for the Adjectives for "Motivation" 151
Table 8 Descriptive Statistics for the Adjectives for "Joy" 151
Table 9 Descriptive Statistics for the Adjectives for "Anxiety" 151
Table 10 Descriptive Statistics for the Adjectives for "Hope" 152
Table 11 Descriptive Statistics for the Adjectives for "Hopelessness" 152
Table 12 Descriptive Statistics for the Adjectives for "Anger" 152
Table 13 Descriptive Statistics for the Adjectives for "Shame" 153
Table 14 Descriptive Statistics for the Adjectives for "Relief" 153
Table 15 Descriptive Statistics for the Adjectives for "Pride" 153
Table 16 Descriptive Statistics for the Adjectives for "Disappointment" 154
Table 17 Logistic Regression for Predicting Completion of the Experiment (Yes vs. No) from the Demographic Variables 181
Table 18 Descriptive Statistics for Performance on the First Test for the Two Groups (Only First Test Completed vs. Both Tests Completed) 182
Table 19 Number of Participants Assigned to Each of the Five Experimental Conditions and Number of Participants who Completed the Entire Experiment 184
Table 20 Descriptive Statistics for Age across the Five Groups 186
Table 21 Descriptive Statistics for Performance on the First Test by Experimental Group and for the Entire Sample 189
Table 22 Descriptive Statistics for Trait Mood 192
Table 23 Descriptive Statistics for Trait Emotions 193

Table 24 Ordinal Regression Predicting the Ratings on Trait Motivation and Trait Emotions from the Conditions: Results of the Model Fit Test........ 196
Table 25 Ordinal Regression Predicting Angry (Trait) from the Five Experimental Conditions........ 197
Table 26 Descriptive Statistics for State Mood........ 198
Table 27 Descriptive Statistics for State Emotions........ 199
Table 28 Ordinal Regression Predicting State Motivation and State Emotion Ratings from Condition: Results of the Model Fit Test........ 200
Table 29 Intercorrelations of the Trait Emotions........ 203
Table 30 Intercorrelations of State Mood and Emotions........ 205
Table 31 Intercorrelations of Trait and State Emotions........ 206
Table 32 Intercorrelations between State and Trait Mood and Emotions and Performance on the First Test........ 208
Table 33 Change in Mood due to the Emotion Induction for the Control Condition........ 210
Table 34 Change in Emotions due to the Emotion Induction for the Control Condition........ 211
Table 35 Change in Mood due to the Emotion Induction for the Joy Condition........ 212
Table 36 Change in Emotions due to the Emotion Induction for the Joy Condition........ 213
Table 37 Change in Mood due to the Emotion Induction for the Sadness Condition........ 214
Table 38 Change in Emotions due to the Emotion Induction for the Sadness Condition........ 215
Table 39 Change in Mood due to the Emotion Induction for the Anger Condition........ 216
Table 40 Change in Emotions due to the Emotion Induction for the Anger Condition........ 217
Table 41 Change in Mood due to the Emotion Induction for the Contentment Condition........ 218
Table 42 Change in Emotions due to the Emotion Induction for the Contentment Condition........ 219
Table 43 Comparisons between the Joy and Control Conditions on the Three Mood Dimensions (Dunnett Test)........ 221

Table 44 Comparisons on Motivation and Test-Related Emotions between the Joy and Control Conditions (Mann-Whitney U Test) ... 222
Table 45 Comparisons between the Sadness and Control Conditions on the Three Mood Dimensions (Dunnett Test) ... 223
Table 46 Comparisons on Motivation and Test-Related Emotions between the Sadness and Control Conditions (Mann-Whitney U Test) ... 224
Table 47 Comparisons between the Anger and Control Conditions on the Three Mood Dimensions (Dunnett Test) ... 225
Table 48 Comparisons on Motivation and Test-Related Emotions between the Anger and Control Conditions (Mann-Whitney U Test) ... 226
Table 49 Comparisons between the Contentment and Control Conditions on the Three Mood Dimensions (Dunnett Test) ... 227
Table 50 Comparisons on Motivation and Test-Related Emotions between the Contentment and Control Conditions (Mann-Whitney U Test) ... 228
Table 51 Mood State Comparisons from After the Induction to After the Test for the Control Condition ... 231
Table 52 Mood State Comparisons from After the Induction to After the Test for the Joy Condition ... 232
Table 53 Mood State Comparisons from After the Induction to After the Test for the Sadness Condition ... 233
Table 54 Mood State Comparisons from After the Induction to After the Test for the Anger Condition ... 234
Table 55 Mood State Comparisons from After the Induction to After the Test for the Contentment Condition ... 235
Table 56 Mood State Comparisons from Before the Induction to After the Test for the Control Condition ... 237
Table 57 Mood State Comparisons from Before the Induction to After the Test for the Joy Condition ... 238
Table 58 Mood State Comparisons from Before the Induction to After the Test for the Sadness Condition ... 239
Table 59 Mood State Comparisons from Before the Induction to After the Test for the Anger Condition ... 240
Table 60 Mood State Comparisons from Before the Induction to After the Test for the Contentment Condition ... 241
Table 61 Descriptive Statistics for Performance on the Second Test by Experimental Group and for the Entire Sample ... 243

Table 62 ANOVA Testing for Differences between the Five Experimental Groups on the Second Test for both Number Correct and Number Wrong 245
Table 63 Two-Factorial Mixed ANOVA Testing for Differences on Number Correct with One Between-Subjects Factor (Group) and One Within-Subjects Factor (First and Second Test) 247
Table 64 Two-Way Factorial Mixed ANOVA Testing for Differences on Number Correct with One Between-Subjects Factor (Group) and One Within-Subjects Factor (First and Second Test) using the Box-Cox Transformed Scores 249
Table 65 Two-Way Factorial Mixed ANOVA Testing for Differences in Number Wrong with One Between-Subjects Factor (Group) and One Within-Subjects Factor (First and Second Test) 250
Table 66 Two-Way Factorial Mixed ANOVA Testing for Differences on Number Wong with One Between-Subjects Factor (Group) and One Within-Subjects Factor (First and Second test) using the Box-Cox Transformed Scores 251
Table 67 Fit Indices for the Three Models 259

Figures

Figure 1. Integration of Carroll Three-Stratum Model into Cattell-Horn-Carroll (CHC) Model........29
Figure 2. Guilford's Structure-of-Intellect Model (Guilford, 1967)........31
Figure 3. Berlin Model of Intelligence Structure (Jäger, 1982, Jäger, 1984) and how it is implemented in the corresponding test. 32
Figure 4. Sample item from the adaptive matrices test (AMT; Hornke et al., 2000)........39
Figure 5. The four models by Russell (1980), Watson and Tellegen (1985), Larsen and Diener (1992), and Thayer (1996). 46
Figure 6. Two-factor model of affect structure for six emotions. 51
Figure 7. Plutchik's (2001) three-dimensional circumplex model of emotions. 52
Figure 8. The self-assessment manikin (SAM; Lang, 1980)........56
Figure 9. The affect grid (Russell, Weiss, & Mendelsohn, 1989)........57
Figure 10. Visual analogue scale for assessing state mood........57
Figure 11. Some dopamine projections in the human brain........73
Figure 12. Outline of the multiprocess affect infusion model........106
Figure 13. First version of the visual analogue scales........135
Figure 14. Score distributions for the three mood sliders "bad versus good", "tired versus alert", and "tense versus relaxed"........140
Figure 15. The visual analogue scale versions that were compared in the study. 142
Figure 16. The visual analogue scales with the slider present........142
Figure 17. Slider "bad versus good": comparison of the score distributions for when the slider was present (left) and when the slider appeared after the bar was clicked (right). 146
Figure 18. Slider "tired versus energetic": comparison of the score distributions for when the slider was present (left) and when the slider appeared after the bar was clicked (right). 146
Figure 19. Slider "tense versus relaxed": comparison of the score distributions for when the slider was present (left) and when the slider appeared after the bar was clicked (right). 147
Figure 20. The mood questionnaire (state version) before the participant had clicked on the slider bar........162

Figure 21. The mood questionnaire (state version) after the participant had clicked on the slider bar. 163
Figure 22. Screen shot of an item from the test scales lst. 165
Figure 23. Overview of the steps of the experiment. 170
Figure 24. Assessment of mood. 172
Figure 25. Assessment of test-related emotions. 173
Figure 26. Screen shot of a test item. 174
Figure 27. The three mood dimensions in the five conditions after the emotion induction. 229
Figure 28. Motivation and test-related emotions in the five conditions after the emotion induction. 230
Figure 29. Model 1 with only performance on the first test as the predictor for performance on the second test. 254
Figure 30. Model 2 with performance on the first test and the experimental conditions as predictors of performance on the second test. 256
Figure 31. Model 3 with performance on the first test, mood, and emotions after induction as predictors of performance on the second test. 258

Appendix A

ITEM STATISTICS FOR THE THREE MDMQ SUBSCALES

Table A 1

Item Statistics for the MDMQ subscale "Displeasure vs. Pleasure"

	M	*SD*	r_{it}
Zufrieden (satisfied)	3.62	0.92	.75
Schlecht (bad; reversed)	4.14	1.03	.71
Gut (good)	3.70	1.01	.79
Unwohl (unwell; reversed)	4.01	1.14	.73
Wohl (well)	3.61	0.95	.79
Unglücklich (unhappy; reversed)	4.10	1.13	.68
Unzufrieden (dissatisfied; reversed)	3.93	1.10	.75
Glücklich (happy)	3.54	1.00	.7

Note. r_{it} = corrected item-total correlation. Five point rating scale (1 = *not at all*, 5 = *very much*).

Table A 2
Item Statistics for the MDMQ subscale "Tiredness vs. Wakefulness"

	M	SD	r_{it}
Ausgeruht (rested)	3.21	1.14	.75
Schlapp (limp; reversed)	3.62	1.14	.67
Müde (tired; reversed)	3.23	1.15	.72
Munter (lively)	2.99	1.06	.71
Schlaefrig (sleepy; reversed)	3.38	1.13	.68
Wach (awake)	3.16	1.14	.77
Frisch (fresh)	2.96	1.09	.76
Ermattet (weary; reversed)	3.42	1.28	.59

Note. r_{it} = corrected item-total correlation. Five point rating scale (1 = *not at all*, 5 = *very much*).

Table A 3
Item Statistics for the MDMQ subscale "Tenseness vs. Relaxation"

	M	SD	$r_{it}\alpha$
Ruhelos (restless; reversed)	3.93	1.07	.71
Gelassen (serene)	3.47	0.96	.62
Unruhig (uneasy; reversed)	3.97	1.13	.69
Entspannt (relaxed)	3.52	1.09	.74
Ausgeglichen (composed)	3.53	0.95	.69
Angespannt (tense; reversed)	3.76	1.05	.75
Nervös (nervous; reversed)	4.13	0.99	.7
Ruhig (calm)	3.66	0.98	.61

Note. r_{it} = corrected item-total correlation. Five point rating scale (1 = *not at all*, 5 = *very much*).

Appendix B

Screenshots of the Instruction and Example Section of the Test

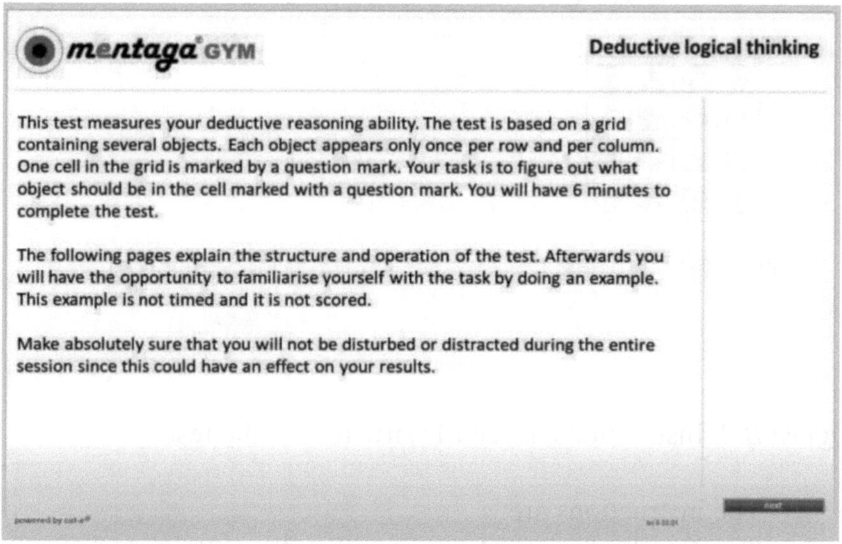

Figure B 1. Starting page of the test.

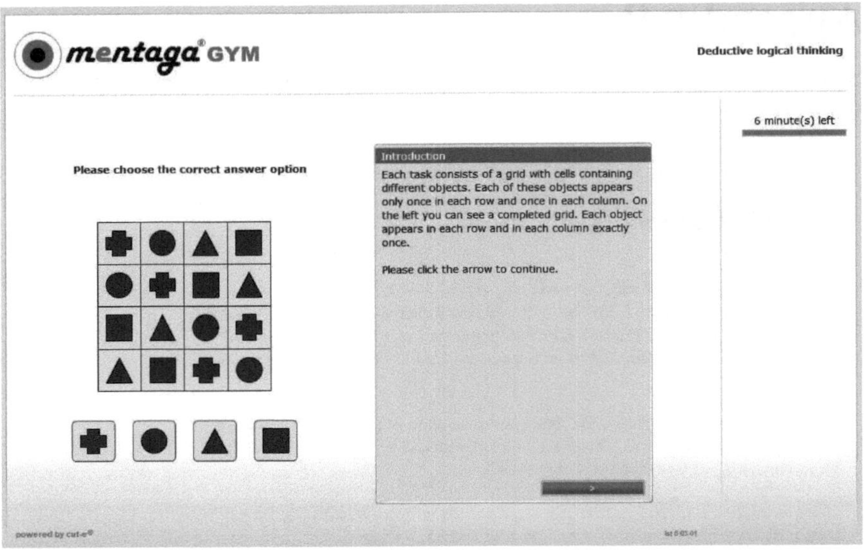

Figure B 2. Instructions, screen 1: structure of the test.

The instructions are:

"Each task consists of a grid with cells containing different objects. Each of these objects appears only once in each row and once in each column. On the left you can see a completed grid. Each object appears in each row and in each column exactly once. Please click the arrow to continue."

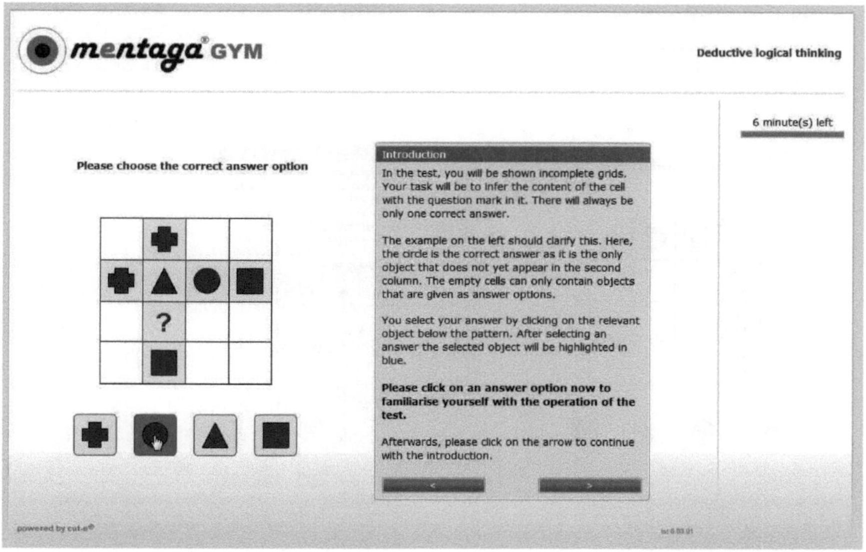

Figure B 3. Instructions, screen 2: operation of the test. Before being able to proceed, participants have to click on one of the answer options (it is not required to click on the correct one).

"In the test, you will be shown incomplete grids. Your taks will be to infer the content of the cell with the question mark in it. There will always be only once correct answer.

"The example on the left should clarify this. Here, the circle in the correct answer as it is the only object that does not yet appear in the second column. The empty cells can only contain objects that are given as answer options.

"You select your answer by clicking on the relevant object below the pattern. After selecting an answer the selected object will be highlighted in blue.

"Please click on an answer option now to familiarise yourself with the operation of the test. Afterwards, please click on the arrow to continue with the instructions."

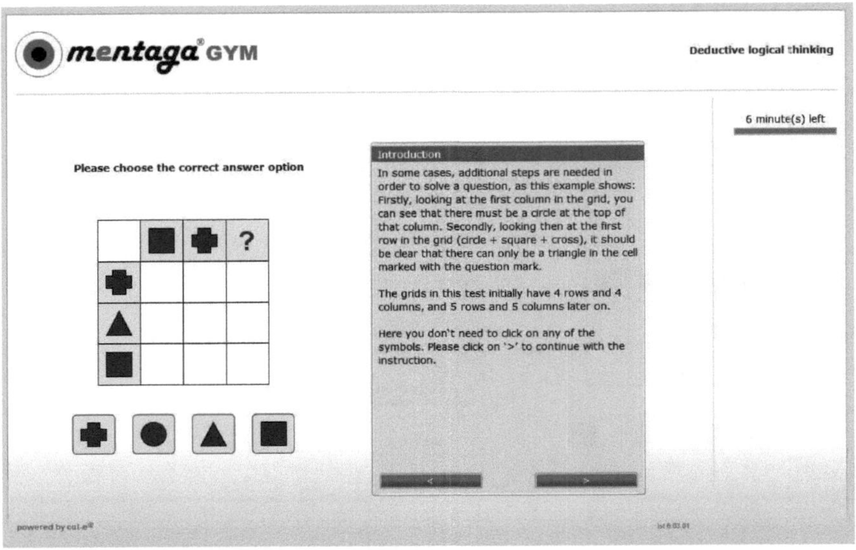

Figure B 4. Instructions, screen 3: explanation of more complex test items.

„In some cases, additional steps are needed in ordert o solve a question, as this example shows: Firstly, looking at the first column in the grid, you can see that there must be a circle at the top of that column. Secondly, looking then at the first rown in the grid (circle + square ü cross), it sould be clear that there can only be a triangle in the cell marked with the question mark.

The grids in this test initially have 4 rows and 4 columns, and 5 rows and 5 columns later on.

Here you don't need to click on any of the symbols. Please click on '>' to continue with the instruction."

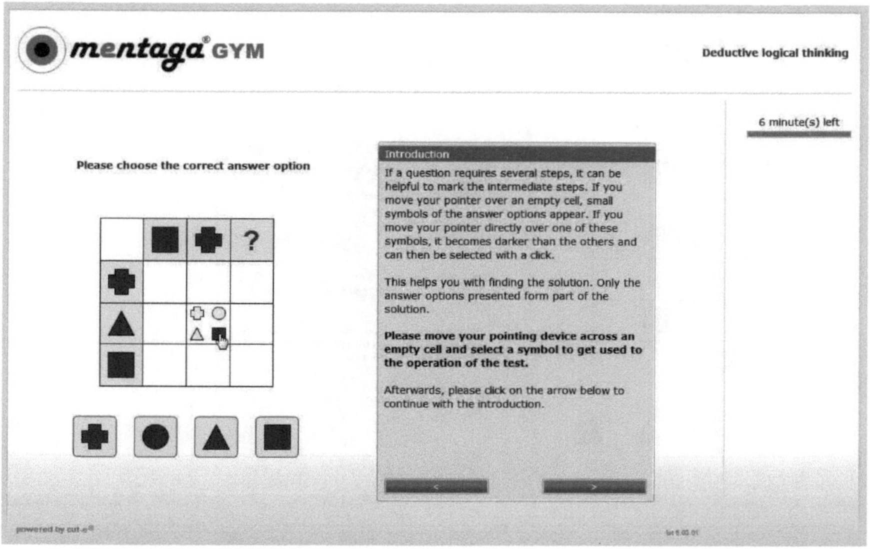

Figure B 5. Instructions, screen 4: how to mark interim solutions. Before being allowed to continue, participants have to mark an interim solution (it is not required to be the correct one).

"If a question requires several steps, it can be helpful to mark the intermediate steps. If you move your pointer over an empty cell, small symbols of the answer options appear. If you move your pointer directly over one of these symbols, it becomes darker than the other and can be selected with a click.

"This helps you with finding the solution. Only the answer options presented form part of the solution.

"Please move your pointing device across and empty cell and select a symbol to get used to the operation of the test.

"Afterward, please click on the arrow below to continue with the introduction."

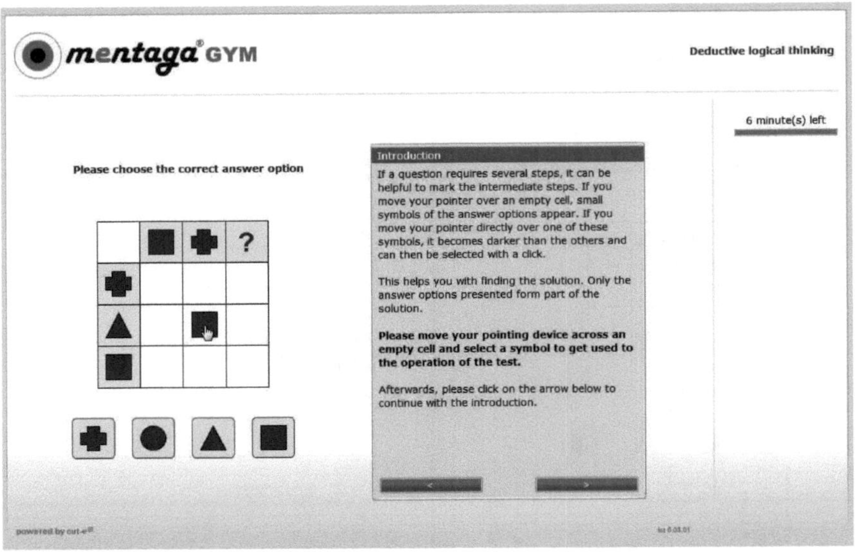

Figure B 6. Instructions, screen 4 (continued): what a marked interim solution looks like. The instruction text is the same as in the previous screen.

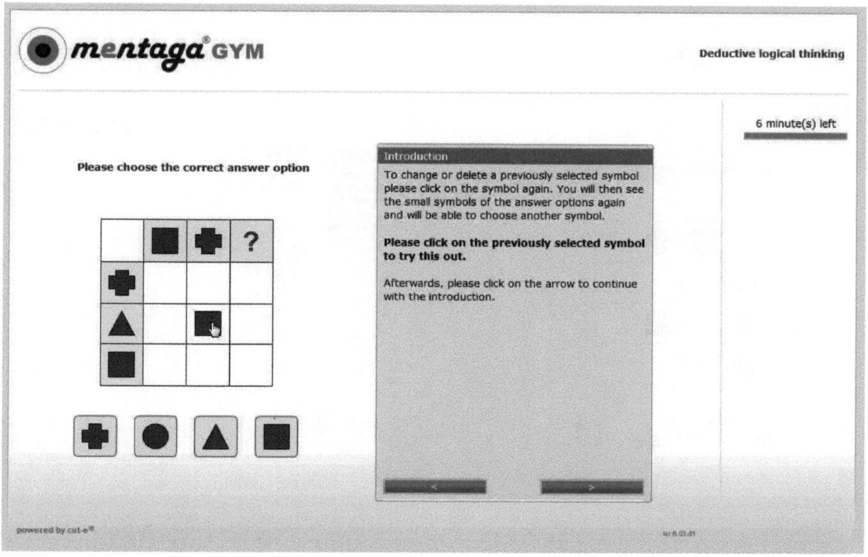

Figure B 7. Instructions, screen 5: how to delete an interim solution. Before being allowed to continue, participants have to delete a previously marked interim solution. The instruction text is the same as in the previous screen.

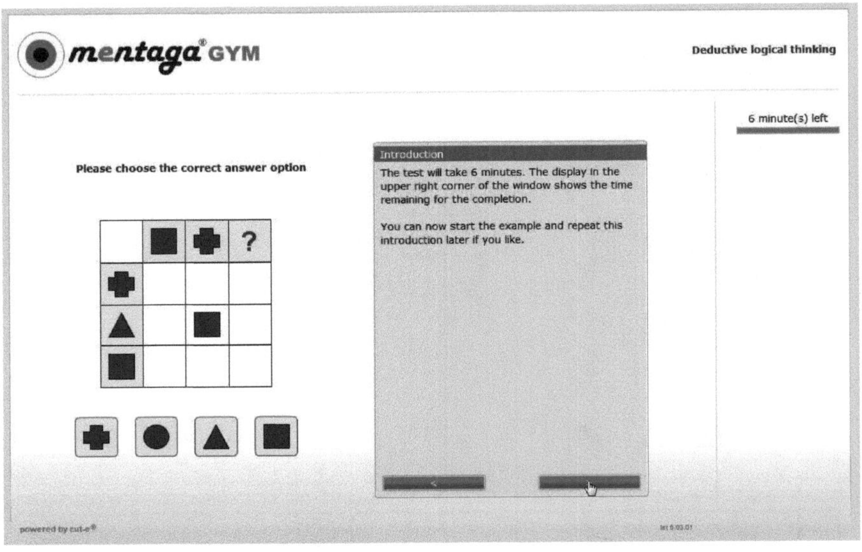

Figure B 8. Instructions, screen 6: explanation of how participants can see how much time they have left.

"The test will take 6 minutes. The display in the upper right corner of the window shows the time remaining for the completion.

"You can now start the example and repeat this introduction later if you like."

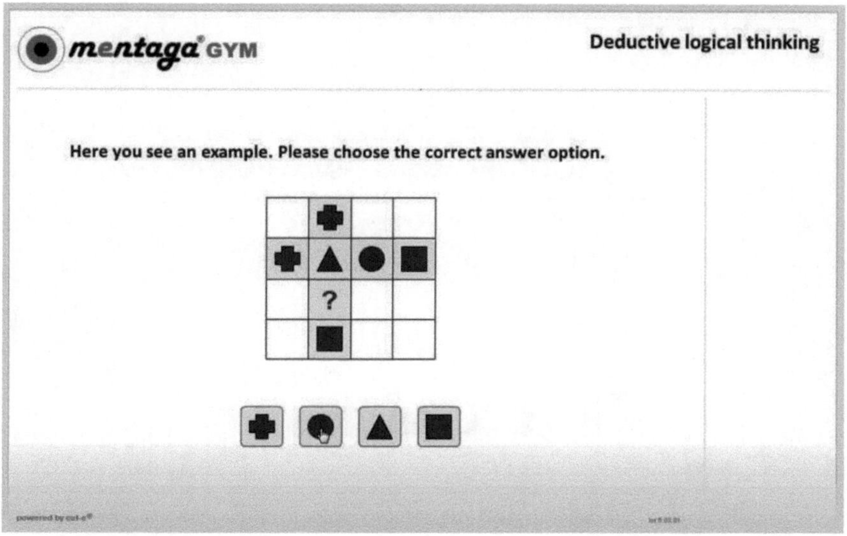

Figure B 9. Interactive example.

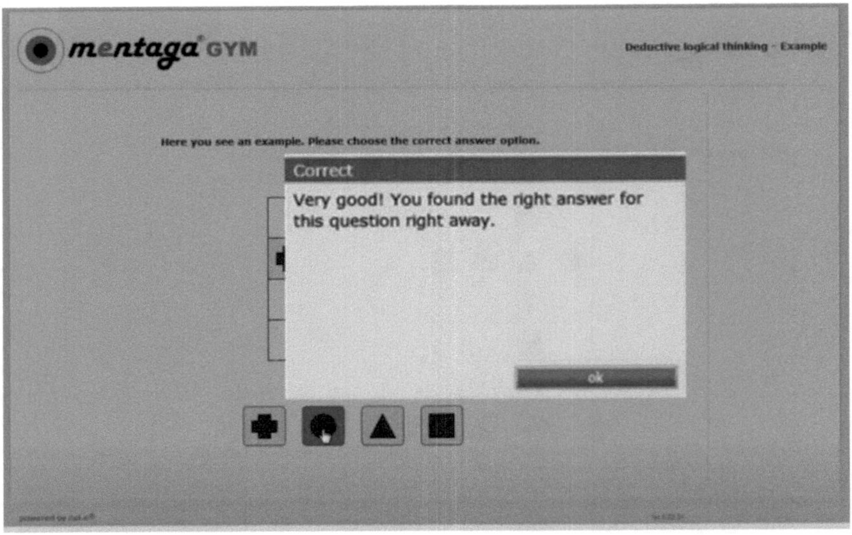

Figure B 10. Interactive example with correct solution marked at the first attempt.

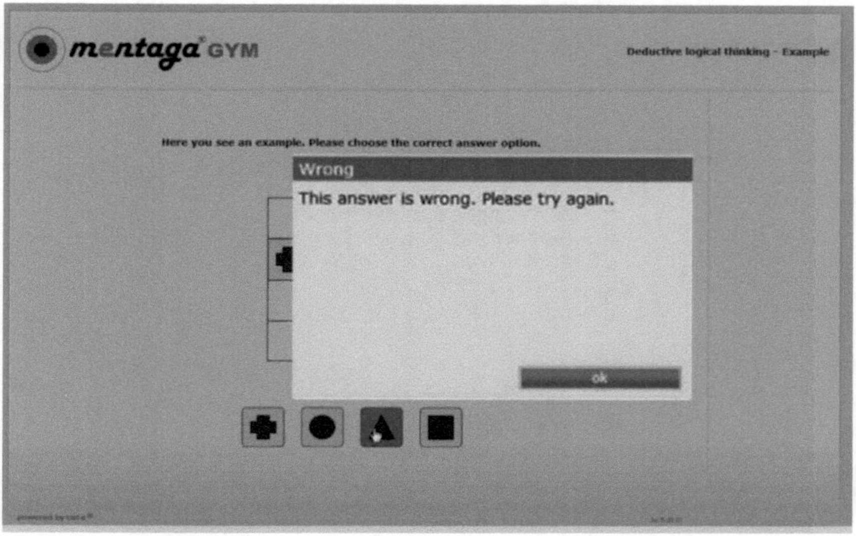

Figure B 11. Interactive example with incorrect solution marked at the first attempt.

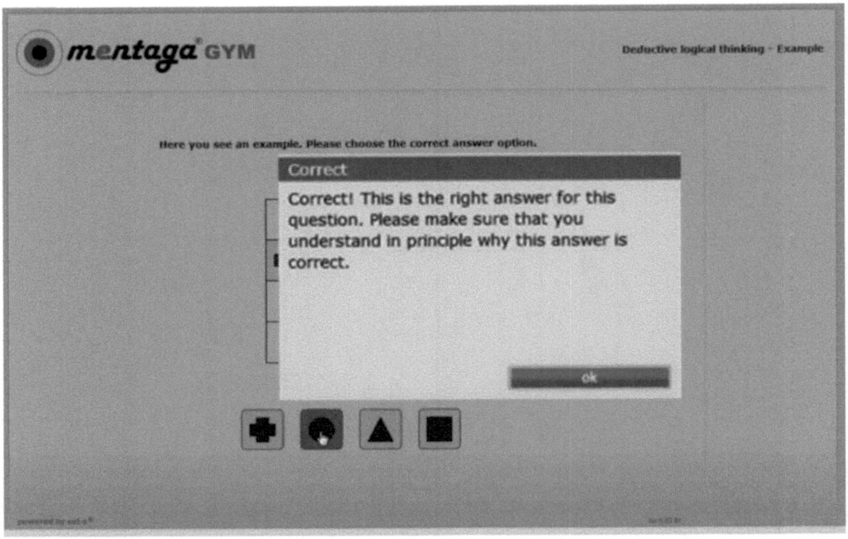

Figure B 12. Interactive example with the correct solution marked at the second attempt.

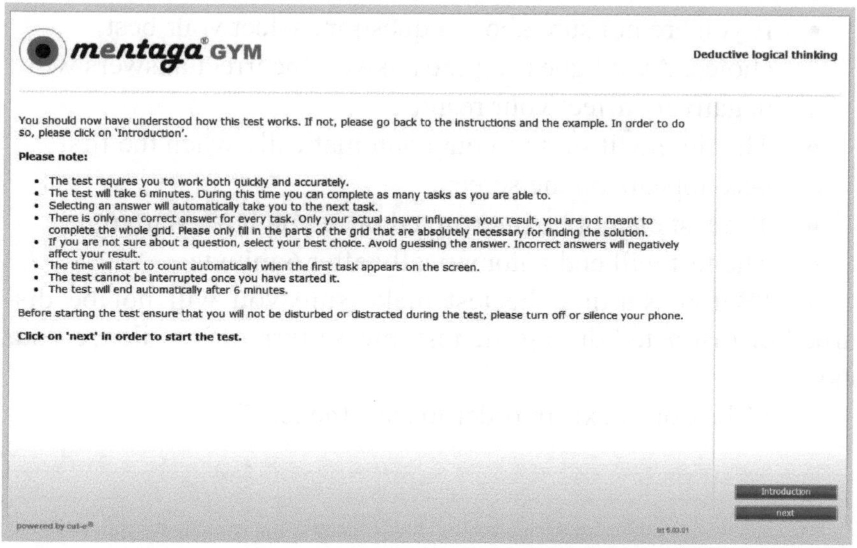

Figure B 13. Instruction page before the actual test.

"You sould now have understood how this test works. If not, please go back to the instructions and the example. In order to do so, please click on 'Introduction'.

"Please note:

- The test requires you to work both quickly and accurately.
- The test will take 6 minutes. During this time you can complete as many tasks as you are able to.
- Selecting an answer will automatically take you to the next task.
- There is only one correct answer for every task. Only your actual answer influences your result, you are not meant to complete the whole grid. Please only fill in the parts of the grid that are absolutely necessary for finding the solution.

- If you are not sure about a question, select your best choice. Avoid guessing the answer. Incorrect answers will negatively affect your results.
- The time will start to count automatically when the first task appears on the screen.
- The test cannot be interrupted once you have started it.
- The test will end automatically after 6 minutes.

"Before starting the test make sure you will not be disturbed or distracted during the test, please turn off or silence your phone.

"Click on 'next' in order to start the test."

Appendix C

Effect Sizes

Table C 1

Effect Sizes for the Key Studies on Affect and Performance

Study	Ability	Score	Comparison	*N*	*d*
Isen, Daubman, & Nowicki (1987)	Creativity	No. of correct solutions	positive vs. control	46	0.25
			positive vs. control	59	0.87
			positive vs. exercise	60	0.58
Abele (1995)	Creativity verbal	No. of solutions	positive vs. negative	60	0.42
			positive vs. control	60	1.07
			negative vs. control	60	0.49
		No. of original solutions	positive vs. negative	60	0.02
			positive vs. control	60	0.62
			negative vs. control	60	0.52
	Creativity figural	No. of solutions	positive vs. negative	56	0.25
			positive vs. control	56	0.86
			negative vs. control	56	0.69
		No. of original solutions	positive vs. negative	56	0.11
			positive vs. control	56	1.01
			negative vs. control	56	0.79
	Processing speed	Time in sec.	positive vs. negative	20	-0.29
			positive vs. control	20	-0.09
			negative vs. control	20	0.16
			negative vs. control	60	0.04
			positive vs. control	56	0.32
			negative vs. control	56	-0.33

Note. *d* = Cohen's *d*.

Table C 2 (continued)
Effect Sizes for the Key Studies on Affect and Performance

Study	Ability	Score	Comparison	*N*	*d*
Abele (1995)	Processing capacity verbal	No. of correct solutions	positive vs. negative	60	1.06
			positive vs. control	60	0.57
			negative vs. control	60	-0.32
		No. of wrong solutions	positive vs. negative	60	-0.79
			positive vs. control	60	-0.47
			negative vs. control	60	0.32
		Items processed	positive vs. negative	60	0.06
			positive vs. control	60	0.10
			negative vs. control	60	0.04
	Processing capacity numerical	No. of correct solutions	positive vs. negative	56	1.18
			positive vs. control	56	0.70
			negative vs. control	56	-0.48
		No. of wrong solutions	positive vs. negative	56	-0.42
			positive vs. control	56	-0.37
			negative vs. control	56	0.08
		Items processed	positive vs. negative	56	0.67
			positive vs. control	56	0.32
			negative vs. control	56	-0.33
Radenhausen & Anker (1988)	Processing capacity verbal	No. of correct solutions	positive vs. negative	38	0.47
			positive vs. control	38	0.37
			negative vs. control	38	-0.09

Note. *d* = Cohen's *d*.

Table C 3

Results of Selected Studies on Affect and Performance: Experiments

Study	Description	N	Results	p
Isen, Daubman & Nowicki (1987)	Performance on			
	Duncker's (1945) candle task			
	Mednick, Mednick & Mednick's (1964) Remote Associates Test			
	Study 1: Duncker's candle task after mood manipulation through			
	positive film vs. neutral film	27	% solutions: 75 vs. 20; $\chi^2 = 8.19$	$p<.01$
	facilitative display vs. no manipulation	36	% solutions: 83 vs. 13; $\chi^2 = 17.62$	$p<.01$
	no significant difference between neutral film and no manipulation		% solutions: 20 vs. 13	
	Study 2: manipulation check (1=positive; 7=negative)			
	film positive vs. neutral vs. negative	33	*M*=3.11;3.90;5.52; *Var*=1.29;1.04;2.12	
	candy bar vs. no manipulation vs. exercise	48	*M*=2.69;3.18;3.10; Var=1.27;2.07;2.88	
	Duncker's candle task:			
	percentage of correct solutions			
	Comedy vs. neutral vs. negative film vs. candy vs. no manip. vs. exercise		58;11;30;25;16;26	
	positive vs. control film		$\chi^2(1)=9.46$	$p<.01$
	exercise vs. no manipulation; negative vs. neutral film		$\chi^2(1)=2.27$	$p<.1$
	positive film vs. exercise, negative film, no manipulation combined / single		$\chi^2(1)=10.41;3.89;3.09;7.24$	$p<.01;.05$
	minutes to solve problem	29		
	Comedy vs. neutral vs. negative film vs. candy vs. no manip. vs. exercise		*M*=4.3;4.2;4.29;5.81;3.06;6.71	

Note. Column "Results" always depicts M and SD or variance for the conditions mentioned in the column "Description" in the respective order.

Table C 2 (continued)

Results of Selected Studies on Affect and Performance: Experiments

Study	Description	N	Results	p
Isen, Daubman &	Study 3: number of correct items in Remote Associates Test	26		
Nowicki (1987)	high difficulty candy vs. control	candy	*M*=.50 vs. .60; *Var*=.66 vs. .36	
(continued)	medium difficulty candy vs. control	20	*M*=4.38 vs. 3.45; *Var*=2.57 vs. 3.00	
	low difficulty candy vs. control	contr	*M*=5.38 vs. 5.10; *Var*=3.45 vs. 3.04	
	main effect of difficulty level		$F(2,88)=174.48$	$p<.0001$
	main effect for affect not significant		$F(1,44)=1.32$	$p<.26$
	positive affect results in improved performance in medium difficulty items		$t(110)=2.13$	$p<.025$
	Study 4: number of correct mod. difficulty items in Remote Associates Test	86		
	comedy film vs. no manipulation vs. exercise		*M*=5.00;3.04;3.81; *Var*=3.69;6.35;4.84	
	main effect of affect		$F(2,83)=5.96$	$p<.01$
	difference between no manipulation and exercise not significant		$t(83)=1.28$	$p>.1$
	positive affect vs. exercise		$t(83)=2.08$	$p<.025$

Note. Column “Results” always depicts M and SD or variance for the conditions mentioned in the column “Description” in the respective order.

Table C 2 (continued)

Results of Selected Studies on Affect and Performance: Experiments

Study	Description	N	Results	p
Knapp (1988)	Induction of a more or less bad vs. neutral mood, then exposure to resource dilemma (fishing); dependent variable: profit gained in dilemma	72		
	2 (bad vs. neutral) x 2 (intense vs. not intense) x 3 (task difficulty) design			
	subjects in bad vs. neutral mood accumulated less profit		$F(24,1440)=2.0$; $\omega^2=.01$	$p=.002$
	the more difficult the task, the less profit subjects made		$F(48,1440)=2.4$; $\omega^2=.03$	$p=.0001$
	no main effect of mood intensity		$F<1$	
	no interaction between mood and task difficulty		$F<1$	
	slight bad mood: performance on moderate and difficult task impaired		$F(24,480)=1.8$; $\omega^2=.03$	$p=.0001$
	intense bad mood: performance on all task difficulties impaired		$F(24,480)=1.8$; $\omega^2=.03$	$p=.008$
Radenhausen & Anker (1988)	Induction of elated vs. depressed vs. neutral mood	57		
	Manipulation check: elated vs. depressed vs. control		BDI: M=2.9;8.1;5.2; SD=1.3;1.5;1.6	
	Performance on syllogism task:			
	- elated vs. depressed		M=75.9;69.5; $t(54)=1.70$	$p<.05$
	- depressed vs. neutral		M=69.6;71.4	n.s.
	recognition of tachistoscopically presented stimulus words			
	elated vs. depressed vs. neutral		no means; $F(2,54)=.33$	n.s.

Note. Column "Results" always depicts M and SD or variance for the conditions mentioned in the column "Description" in the respective order.

Table C 2 (continued)
Results of Selected Studies on Affect and Performance: Experiments

Study	Description	N	Results	p
Melton (1995)	Solving syllogisms after mood induction	61		
	good vs. neutral mood: mood induction via reading cartoons or listening to a comedian on a tape			
	- manipulation check: good mood vs. control		M=33.0 vs. 28.3; $t(55)=3.63$	$p<.001$
	- task performance: good mood vs. control		M=3.24 vs. 5.56; $t(55)=3.58$ ($r=-.43$)	$p<.001$
	- selection of unqualified, universal conclusions; good mood vs. control		M=4.84 vs. 3.4; $t(54)=2.28$	$p<.02$
	- tendency of subjects in good mood to answer according to atmosphere heuristic: good mood vs. control		M=4.2 vs. 3.23; $t(54)=1.74$	$p=.087$

Note. Column "Results" always depicts M and SD or variance for the conditions mentioned in the column "Description" in the respective order.

Table C 2 (continued)

Results of Selected Studies on Affect and Performance: Experiments

Study	Description	N	Results	p
Abele (1995)	Studies on influence of moods on tasks classified according to Royce & Diamond (1980); mood induction and then…			
	Task involving perceptual system (ZVT; Oswald & Roth, 1978); positive vs. negative vs. control	30		
	- manipulation check: positive vs. negative mood		M=7.6;4.67;control?	
	- speed (seconds)		M=56;58.1;56.7; SD=6.27;8.08;9.62	n.s.
	- Correlation self-rated mood-speed: positive vs. negative group		r=-.65;.36	p<.05;n.s.
	Task involving perceptual system (ZVT; Oswald & Roth, 1978); positive vs. negative vs. control, repeated measurements			
	- manipulation check		M=7.8;5.4;6.8	
	- speed 1st vs. 2nd time, positive vs. negative vs. control		M=67.4/55.1;62.3/58.2;67.2/59.6	p<.01
	- Correlation self-rated mood-speed (all groups)		r=.49	

Note. Column "Results" always depicts M and SD or variance for the conditions mentioned in the column "Description" in the respective order.

Table C 2 (continued)

Results of Selected Studies on Affect and Performance: Experiments

Study	Description	N	Results	p
Abele (1995) (continued)	Task involving conceptual system (subtest "Gemeinsamkeiten" from IST; Amthauer, 1970); positive vs. negative vs. control; repeated measurements (1st time without mood induction; 2nd time with mood induction)	55		
	- manipulation check			
	- analysis of variance for repeated measures; independent variable: mood; dependent variable: number of items processed; correct; wrong		M=7.8;6.07;7.07; SD=1.66;2.43;1.41 F<1	n.s.
	- items correct; wrong; processed; 1st vs. 2nd time		F<1;F=2.3 (items processed)	n.s.
	- interaction: mood-repeated measure		F=5.27	p=.009
	number of correct solutions; 1st vs. 2nd time in positive mood		M=3.80 vs. 5.33; t(14)=3.53	p<.01
	number of correct solutions; 1st vs. 2nd time in negative mood		M=5.07 vs. 3.93; t(14)=1.70	p<.08
	number of correct solutions; 1st vs. 2nd time in control group		M=4.33 vs. 4.80; t<1	n.s.
	number of items processed; 1st vs. 2nd time in positive mood		M=6.40 vs. 7.47; t(14)=1.95	p=.07
	number of wrong solutions; 1st vs. 2nd time in negative mood		M=2.00 vs. 2.60; t(14)=1.96	p=.07
	- number of correct solutions in medium difficulty items; 1st vs. 2nd time in positive mood		M=1.13 vs. 1.87; t(14)=2.13	p=.05
	- number of wrong solutions in difficult items; 1st vs. 2nd time in negative mood		M=.87 vs. 1.33; t(14)=2.17	p<.05

Note. Column "Results" always depicts M and SD or variance for the conditions mentioned in the column "Description" in the respective order.

Table C 2 (continued)

Results of Selected Studies on Affect and Performance: Experiments

Study	Description	N	Results	p
Abele (1995) (continued)	Comparison of tasks involving the conceptual (IST subtest "Gemeinsamkeiten"; Amthauer, 1970) and the symbolic system (LPS subtest "Worteinfall); Horn, 1962) (Royce & Diamond, 1980)	90(f)		
	- manipulation check: positive vs. negative vs. neutral		*M*=7.57;6.43;5.93; *F*(2,87)=63.93	*p*<.0001
	- differences between groups: positive vs. negative vs. control			
	Gemeinsamkeiten: number of correct solutions		*M*=4.83;3.33;3.87; *SD*=1.42;1.42;1.91	*p*=.002
	Gemeinsamkeiten: number of wrong solutions		*M*=2.17;3.57;2.97; *SD*=1.61;1.94;1.81	*p*=.01
	Gemeinsamkeiten: items processed		*M*=7.00;6.90;6.83; *SD*=1.62;1.92;1.86	n.s.
	Worteinfall: number of words		*M*=29.47;27.37;25.00; *SD*=4.73;5.56;3.97	*p*=.002
	Worteinfall: number of original words		*M*=1.80;1.77;1.10; *SD*=1.32;1.61;.88	*p*=.07
	- analysis of variance; independent variable: positive vs. negative vs. neutral mood; repeated measures design; dependent variable: number of correct solutions in Gemeinsamkeiten and number of original words in Worteinfall (z values)			
	main effect of mood: positive mood differs from other two conditions			
	interaction effect of mood and task type: performance in Worteinfall in negative mood better than in control; in Gemeinsamkeiten worse in negative mood than in control			

Note. Column "Results" always depicts M and SD or variance for the conditions mentioned in the column "Description" in the respective order.

Table C 2 (continued)

Results of Selected Studies on Affect and Performance: Experiments

Study	Description	N	Results	p
Abele (1995) (continued)	Comparison of tasks involving the conceptual (LPS subtest "Zahlen-Symbol-Test;Horn, 1962) and the symbolic system (AIT subtest "Zeichentest"; Meili, 1966)	84(f)		
	- manipulation check: positive vs. negative vs. control			p<.001
	- Zeichentest: positive vs. negative vs. control		M=7.57;4.79;6.10; F(2,63)=19.85	
	number of drawings (F(2/81)=5.72)			p<.005
	originality of drawings (F(2/81)=7.76)		M=3.61;3.25;2.43; SD=1.59;1.27;1.10	p=.0008
	- Zahlensymboltest: positive vs. negative vs. control		M=1.37;1.32;.95; SD=.39;.49;.44	
	items processed (F(2/81)=2.8)			p<.07
	correct solutions (F(2/81)=9.55)		M=14.32;12.18;13.25; SD=3.22;3.17;3.37	p=.002
	wrong solutions (F(2/81)=1.63)		M=12.64;9.39;10.71; SD=2.74;2.77;2.77	n.s.
	- analysis of variance; repeated measures; independent variable: mood; dependent variable: z-value of number of correct solutions (Zahlensymboltest) and number of correct drawings (Zeichentest)		M=1.68;2.79;2.54; SD=1.70;3.37;2.08	
	main effect of mood			p<.0001
	interaction effect between mood and task		M=0.68;-0.29;-0.39; F(2,81)=12.24 F(2,81)=4.10	p=.02

Note. Column "Results" always depicts M and SD or variance for the conditions mentioned in the column "Description" in the respective order.

Table C 4
Results of Selected Studies on Affect and Performance: Correlational Studies

Study	Description	N	Results	p
Hembree (1988)	Meta-analysis of 562 studies on test anxiety; correlations with			p <.01
	IQ tests	9,430	r=-.10 (grade 1+2) to -.23 (grade 3+)	
	aptitude and achievement tests	6,736	r=-.06 (n.s., gr. 1+2) to -.29 (gr. 3+)	
	problem solving tasks	1,225	r=-.20	
	memory tasks	172	r=-.28	
	course grades	1,664	r=-.15	
	cumulative GPA	4,086	r=-.12 to -.29	
Pekrun & Hofmann (1999)	Correlations of performance in the Abitur with			*p<.05
	learning emotions: joy, anger, anxiety, boredom	251	r=.22***; -.18**; -.13; -.25***	**p<.01
	performance emotions: joy, hope, relief, anger, anxiety, hopelessness	150	r=.13; .11; .12; -.08; -.11; -.20*	***p<.001
	Correlations of performance at university with			
	learning emotions: joy, anger, anxiety, boredom	251	r=.30***; -.36***; -.46***; -.33***	
	performance emotions: joy, hope, relief, anger, anxiety, hopelessness	150	r=.33***; .37***; .17*; -.14; -.15*; -.30***	

Note. Column "Results" depicts correlations. Hembree (1988): correlations of test anxiety with the tests mentioned in the column "Description"; Pekrun & Hofmann (1999): correlations of the German Abitur (corresponds to A-levels) with the emotions mentioned in the column "Description" in the respective order.

Appendix D

DROP-OUT ANALYSIS

Table D 1

Numbers of Participants from Each Data Source

Condition		Data source				Total
		GYM	Email	Soc. media	Other	
Joy	Number	101.00	43.00	3.00	6.00	153.00
	Expected	98.75	42.12	6.16	5.96	153.00
Sadness	Number	99.00	39.00	9.00	7.00	154.00
	Expected	99.40	42.40	6.20	6.00	154.00
Anger	Number	99.00	42.00	7.00	6.00	154.00
	Expected	99.40	42.40	6.20	6.00	154.00
Contentment	Number	98.00	43.00	6.00	8.00	155.00
	Expected	100.05	42.68	6.24	6.04	155.00
Control	Number	100.00	45.00	6.00	3.00	154.00
	Expected	99.40	42.40	6.20	6.00	154.00

Note. Soc. media = social media; Number = total number of participants from each data source; Expected = number of participants expected from each data source given an equal distribution of participants across all data sources

Table D 2 depicts the drop out process during the experiment. It shows each single step participants took during the experiment. A step is usually one single item that participants responded to subsequently. An exception is the two tests where the steps represent only whether the test was started or completed, respectively (so not each single test item responded to). For each condition, the left column ("Participants") depicts how many participants completed the step, whereas the right column ("Drop outs") shows how many dropped out compared to the previous step.

Table D 2

Overview of Drop-Outs during the Course of the Experiment

	Joy		Sadness		Anger		Contentment		Control	
	Participants	Drop outs	Participants	Drop outs	Participants	Drop outs	Participants	Drop outs	Participants	Drop outs
Sex	153		154		154		155		154	
Birth year	153	0	154	0	154	0	155	0	154	0
Marital status	153	0	154	0	154	0	155	0	154	0
Partner (yes/no)	153	0	154	0	154	0	155	0	154	0
Education	153	0	154	0	154	0	155	0	154	0
Occupation	153	0	154	0	154	0	155	0	154	0
Bad vs. good (trait)	149	4	149	5	153	1	152	3	152	2
Tired vs. energetic (trait)	149	0	149	0	153	0	152	0	152	0
Tense vs. relaxed (trait)	149	0	149	0	153	0	152	0	152	0
Motivated (trait)	147	2	145	4	147	6	147	5	151	1
Full of pos. anticipation (trait)	147	0	145	0	147	0	147	0	151	0
Anxious (trait)	147	0	145	0	147	0	147	0	151	0

Note. The table depicts each single step participants took during the experiment. A step is usually one single item, apart from the two tests where it represents only whether the test was started or completed, respectively. For each condition, the left column ("Participants") depicts how many participants completed the step, whereas the right column ("Drop outs") shows how many dropped out compared to the previous step.

Table D 2 (continued)

Overview of Drop-Outs during the Course of the Experiment

	Joy		Sadness		Anger		Contentment		Control	
	Partici-pants	Drop outs	Participants	Drop outs	Participants	Drop outs	Participants	Drop outs	Participants	Drop outs
Confident (trait)	147	0	145	0	147	0	147	0	151	0
Hopeless (trait)	147	0	145	0	147	0	147	0	151	0
Angry (trait)	147	0	145	0	147	0	147	0	151	0
Bad vs. good (state bef. ind.)	146	1	140	5	147	0	143	4	146	5
Tired vs. energetic (state bef. ind.)	146	0	140	0	147	0	143	0	146	0
Tense vs. relaxed (state bef. ind.)	146	0	140	0	147	0	143	0	146	0
Motivated (state bef. ind.)	145	1	138	2	145	2	142	1	145	1
Full of pos. anticipation (state bef. ind.)	145	0	138	0	145	0	142	0	145	0
Anxious (state bef. ind.)	145	0	138	0	145	0	142	0	145	0
Confident (state before ind.)	145	0	138	0	145	0	142	0	145	0
Hopeless (state before ind.)	145	0	138	0	145	0	142	0	145	0
Angry (state before ind.)	145	0	138	0	145	0	142	0	145	0

Note. The table depicts each single step participants took during the experiment. A step is usually one single item, apart from the two tests where it represents only whether the test was started or completed, respectively. For each condition, the left column ("Participants") depicts how many participants completed the step, whereas the right column ("Drop outs") shows how many dropped out compared to the previous step. bef. ind: before induction.

Table D 2 (continued)

Overview of Drop-Outs during the Course of the Experiment

	Joy		Sadness		Anger		Contentment		Control	
	Participants	Drop outs	Participants	Drop outs	Participants	Drop outs	Participants	Drop outs	Participants	Drop outs
Test no. 1 started	128	17	120	18	127	18	121	21	126	19
Test no. 1 completed	105	23	84	36	106	21	102	19	107	19
Bad vs. good (state after induction)	95	10	80	4	99	7	97	5	105	2
Tired vs. energetic (state after induction)	95	0	80	0	99	0	97	0	105	0
Tense vs. relaxed (state after induction)	95	0	80	0	99	0	97	0	105	0
Motivated (state after induction)	94	1	79	1	98	1	97	0	102	3
Full of pos. anticipation (state after induction)	94	0	79	0	98	0	97	0	102	0
Anxious (state after induction)	94	0	79	0	98	0	97	0	102	0
Confident (state after induction)	94	0	79	0	98	0	97	0	102	0
Hopeless (state after induction)	94	0	79	0	98	0	97	0	102	0
Angry (state after induction)	94	0	79	0	98	0	97	0	102	0

Note. The table depicts each single step participants took during the experiment. A step is usually one single item, apart from the two tests where it represents only whether the test was started or completed, respectively. For each condition, the left column (“Participants”) depicts how many participants completed the step, whereas the right column (“Drop outs”) shows how many dropped out compared to the previous step.

Table D 2 (continued)
Overview of Drop-Outs during the Course of the Experiment

	Joy		Sadness		Anger		Contentment		Control	
	Partici-pants	Drop outs	Partici-pants	Drop outs	Partici-pants	Drop outs	Partici-pants	Drop outs	Partici-pants	Drop outs
Test no. 2 started	94	0	77	2	96	2	96	1	101	1
Test no. 2 completed	89	5	74	3	90	6	88	8	93	8
Bad vs. good (state after test)	89	0	75	-1	92	-2	89	-1	92	1
Tired vs. energetic (state after test)	89	0	75	0	92	0	89	0	92	0
Tense vs. relaxed (state after test)	89	0	75	0	92	0	89	0	92	0
Angry (state after test)	89	0	75	0	92	0	89	0	91	1
Ashamed (state after test)	89	0	75	0	92	0	89	0	91	0
Relieved (state after test)	89	0	75	0	92	0	89	0	91	0
Proud (state after test)	89	0	75	0	92	0	89	0	91	0
Disappointed (state after test)	89	0	75	0	92	0	89	0	91	0

Note. The table depicts each single step participants took during the experiment. A step is usually one single item, apart from the two tests where it represents only whether the test was started or completed, respectively. For each condition, the left column ("Participants") depicts how many participants completed the step, whereas the right column ("Drop outs") shows how many dropped out compared to the previous step.

Table D 2 (continued)

Overview of Drop-Outs during the Course of the Experiment

	Joy		Sadness		Anger		Contentment		Control	
	Partici-pants	Drop outs	Partici-pants	Drop outs	Partici-pants	Drop outs	Partici-pants	Drop outs	Partici-pants	Drop outs
Seen film before?	89	0	75	0	92	0	89	0	91	0
Film with sound?	89	0	75	0	92	0	89	0	91	0
Film induced joy	89	0	75	0	92	0	89	0	91	0
Film induced sadness	89	0	75	0	92	0	89	0	91	0
Film induced composure	89	0	75	0	92	0	89	0	91	0
Film induced anger	89	0	75	0	92	0	89	0	91	0

Note. The table depicts each single step participants took during the experiment. A step is usually one single item, apart from the two tests where it represents only whether the test was started or completed, respectively. For each condition, the left column ("Participants") depicts how many participants completed the step, whereas the right column ("Drop outs") shows how many dropped out compared to the previous step.

When looking at the table, the three numbers with a negative sign leap to the eye. There seems to be a negative drop-out after completing the second test: in the Sadness and the Contentment condition there was one participant and in the Anger condition there were two participants who did not complete the test, but then gave their mood state after the test. According to the setup of the experiment, this should not be possible because a certain step can only be taken once the previous step has been completed. In this case it means that participants are not able to fill in their mood state after the test unless they have completed the test. Thus, a negative drop-out is not possible, but happened. A closer look at the data revealed that there were four participants who did in fact complete the second test and then continued with the next steps of the experiment, but their data from the test was not transmitted. This sometimes happens because the test opens in a separate window. It is based on flash, whereas the rest of the experiment is programmed in html. Thus, the data transmission process for the test ran separately from the data transmission of the other experimental data. For this reason, participants could continue with the experiment although their results from the second test had not been transmitted.

Now we turn to the unequal group size. In the table, one can see that during the first steps of the experiment, even before the first test, slightly more participants had dropped out of the Sadness condition, compared to the other four conditions, where the number of participants who had dropped out was almost equal. However, when looking at the number of participants who had completed the first test (line "test no. 1 completed" in the table), there is a rather big difference between the Sadness condition and the other four conditions. This was unexpected because up to this point, the five conditions were exactly the same. Participants had given their biographical data and responded to a number of items assessing their trait and state mood and emotionality, afterwards they had started the test, which was also the same for all groups. Not until watching the emotion induction film clip did the five conditions differ. This film clip, however, was not shown to participants until after the first test. This effect had to be looked at in more detail.

First, it was clarified with the IT expert who had programmed the experiment whether participants could somehow already have watched the film clip before finishing the first test. This was not possible as the film clip did not appear on the screen until the participant had finished the test. Not until then a 'next' button would appear in the window, and only after clicking onto this button, the film clip would appear.

Next, it was checked at which stage of the test participants had dropped out. For the test, it is possible to track what actions participants have taken and at what point they have cancelled their completion of the test.

The test opens in a separate window after clicking onto a link on the page. First, there is an introductory section containing the instructions and an interactive example. When this section is completed, there is one screen that repeats the key parts of the instructions, and from this screen, the actual test can be launched by the participant. The stages recorded are:

- 100: participant got to the page where the test can be launched by clicking onto the link
- 200: participant clicked onto the link in order to launch the test
- 300: player is loaded and window of test is open
- 400: participant completed example
- 500: participant arrived at the final instruction page before launching the test itself

- 1000: participant started test
- 1900: participant completed test

Table D 3 depicts the number of participants who reached the respective stages in each condition and dropped out before completing the test. From the table, it becomes obvious that quite a few participants dropped out after the example section in all conditions. When comparing the dropouts at this stage across conditions, it becomes obvious that there are differences between all five conditions, with the highest dropout in the Sadness condition and the lowest one in the Control condition. Comparing the number of dropouts across all stages, it can also be seen that there are slightly more of them in all stages in the Sadness condition, compared to the other conditions. Summing up this slightly higher dropout in each stage of the test it comes to only 84 completions of the test in the Sadness condition, compared to over 100 in the other four conditions.

Table D 3
Number of Participants at Each Stage of the Test in Each Condition

	100	200	300	400	500	1000	1900
Joy	0	1	1	16	0	5	105
Sadness	0	4	4	21	0	7	84
Anger	0	0	1	12	3	5	106
Contentment	0	0	3	10	1	5	102
Control	0	1	2	3	1	12	107

Note. The table depicts the highest stage participants reached. If they reached 100, they did not get beyond this stage, if they reached 200, they did not get beyond this stage, and so on. If they reached 1000 it means that they completed the test and if they reached 1900 it means that their data were successfully transmitted.

Summing all this up, there is no evidence for a systematic dropout in the Sadness condition, although there appears to be one at first glance.

Appendix E

Randomisation: Ordinal Regression for Motivation and Emotion

As already mentioned in the results section, for motivation and test-related emotions the following steps were performed: (1) display cross tables of group x rating on motivation or the respective emotion; (2) calculate the test of parallel lines; (3) if necessary, accumulate categories; (4) calculate the ordinal regression; and (5) calculate the likelihood ratio test for the model against the null model. The results for both trait and state motivation and test-related emotions will be described in the following sections.

Trait motivation and trait test-related emotions

Motivated (trait). For "motivated (trait)" the test of parallel lines yielded a significant result ($\chi^2(12) = 38.40$, $p < .01$), meaning that the conditional probability functions are not parallel at all levels of the dependent variable ("motivated (trait)"). This again means that the one-equation proportional odds model assuming that the logit coefficients are equal across all levels of "motivated (trait)" is not valid and requires estimating a separate regression weight for each predictor. In such a case the less restrictive exact test can be used (Eid et al., 2010). However, this was problematic because there were 2 cells or 8 percent of cells that did not contain any values (Table E 1). These were at level 1 of "motivated (trait)". Additionally, there were only few cases at level 2. Table E 1 depicts the cross table for "motivated (trait)".

Table E 1
Cross table of Condition x Self-Rating on "Motivated (Trait)"

	motivated (trait)				
	1	2	3	4	5
Joy	0	7	26	33	20
Sadness	3	1	15	39	14
Anger	2	10	13	36	27
Contentment	0	8	18	37	23
Control	1	7	18	43	22

Therefore, levels 1 and 2 of the dependent variable ("motivated (trait)") were aggregated. For the aggregated values, the test of parallel lines yielded a non-significant result, $\chi^2(8) = 11.15$, $p > .05$. Table E 2 shows the result of the linear regression. The model is not significantly better than the null model, $\chi^2(4) = 1.62$, $p > .05$. This means that there are no significant differences between the five groups with respect to "motivated (trait)".

Table E 2
Ordinal Regression from Motivated (Trait) onto the Five Experimental Conditions

		β	SE β	Wald test	*df*	*p*	95% CI for β LL	95% CI for β UL	e^{β}
Threshold	Motivated = 1 or 2	-2.32	0.24	92.97	1	<.001	-2.79	-1.85	0.10
	Motivated = 3	-0.85	0.20	17.96	1	<.001	-1.25	-0.46	0.43
	Motivated = 4	1.07	0.20	27.66	1	<.001	0.67	1.47	2.93
Location	Joy	-0.23	0.28	0.71	1	.399	-0.78	0.31	0.79
	Sadness	-0.03	0.29	0.01	1	.921	-0.60	0.54	0.97
	Anger	0.12	0.28	0.18	1	.672	-0.42	0.66	1.12
	Contentment	0.02	0.28	0.00	1	.945	-0.52	0.56	1.02

Note. CI = confidence interval; LL = lower limit; UL = upper limit; e^{β} = odds ratio.

Full of positive anticipation (trait). For "full of positive anticipation (trait)", there were no cells with zero (Table E 3). The test of parallel lines did not yield a significant result ($\chi^2(12) = 19.08$, $p > .05$), thus the conditional probability functions are parallel at all levels of the dependent variable ("full of positive anticipation (trait)").

Table E 3
Cross Table: Frequencies of Ratings per Condition on "Full of Positive Anticipation (Trait)"

	full of positive anticipation (trait)				
	1	2	3	4	5
Joy	10	17	39	12	8
Sadness	9	17	29	11	6
Anger	10	22	26	26	4
Contentment	11	15	26	25	8
Control	10	25	23	26	6

Table E 4 shows the result of the linear regression. The model is not significantly better than the null model, $\chi^2(4) = 2.09$, $p > .05$. This means that there are no significant differences between the five groups with respect to "full of positive anticipation (trait)".

Table E 4

Ordinal Regression from Full of Positive Anticipation (Trait) onto the Five Experimental Conditions

		β	SE β	Wald test	*df*	*p*	95% CI for β LL	95% CI for β UL	e^{β}
Threshold	Pos. anticipation = 1	-2.01	0.23	79.34	1	<.001	-2.45	-1.57	0.13
	Pos. anticipation = 2	-0.64	0.20	10.53	1	.001	-1.02	-0.25	0.53
	Pos. anticipation = 3	0.79	0.20	15.82	1	<.001	0.40	1.17	2.2
	Pos. anticipation = 4	2.51	0.25	101.34	1	<.001	2.02	3.00	12.29
Location	Joy	-0.07	0.27	0.06	1	.801	-0.60	0.46	0.93
	Sadness	-0.17	0.28	0.34	1	.558	-0.72	0.39	0.85
	Anger	-0.01	0.27	0.00	1	.985	-0.53	0.52	0.99
	Contentment	0.23	0.27	0.71	1	.398	-0.30	0.76	1.26

Note. CI = confidence interval; LL = lower limit; UL = upper limit; e^{β} = odds ratio.

Anxious (trait). For "anxious (trait)" there were no cells with zero frequencies (Table E 5). The test of parallel lines did not yield a significant result ($\chi^2(12) = 7.55$, $p > .05$), thus the conditional probability functions are parallel at all levels of the dependent variable ("anxious (trait)").

Table E 5

Cross Table: Frequencies of Ratings per Condition on "Anxious (Trait)"

	anxious (trait) 1	2	3	4	5
Joy	19	22	23	17	3
Sadness	13	27	20	10	2
Anger	15	30	18	20	4
Contentment	18	23	20	17	5
Control	19	28	24	13	5

Table E 6 shows the result of the linear regression. The model is not significantly better than the null model, $\chi^2(4) = 1.04$, $p > .05$. This means that there are no significant differences between the five groups with respect to "anxious (trait)".

Table E 6
Ordinal Regression from Anxious (Trait) onto the Five Experimental Conditions

							95% CI for β		
		β	SE β	Wald test	*df*	*p*	LL	UL	e^{β}
Threshold	Anxious = 1	-1.30	0.21	39.48	1	<.001	-1.70	-0.89	0.27
	Anxious = 2	0.14	0.19	0.48	1	.486	-0.25	0.52	1.15
	Anxious = 3	1.28	0.21	38.57	1	<.001	0.87	1.68	3.58
	Anxious = 4	3.12	0.29	115.36	1	<.001	2.55	3.69	22.57
Location	Joy	0.09	0.27	0.10	1	.750	-0.45	0.62	1.09
	Sadness	-0.06	0.28	0.04	1	.839	-0.61	0.50	0.94
	Anger	0.18	0.27	0.46	1	.496	-0.35	0.71	1.2
	Contentment	0.15	0.27	0.30	1	.582	-0.38	0.69	1.16

Note. CI = confidence interval; LL = lower limit; UL = upper limit; e^{β} = odds ratio.

Confident (trait). For "confident (trait)", there was one cell with zero frequency (Table E 7). However, the test of parallel lines did not yield a significant result, $\chi^2(12) = 12.04$, $p > .05$, thus the conditional probability functions are parallel at all levels of the dependent variable ("confident (trait)").

Table E 7
Cross Table: Frequencies of Ratings per Condition on "Confident (Trait)"

	confident (trait)				
	1	2	3	4	5
Joy	5	12	27	33	10
Sadness	1	5	27	31	8
Anger	1	8	33	39	7
Contentment	1	10	30	35	9
Control	0	11	28	38	14

Table E 8 shows the result of the linear regression. The model is not significantly better than the null model, $\chi^2(4) = 2.56$, $p > .05$. This means that there are no significant differences between the five groups with respect to "confident (trait)".

Table E 8
Ordinal Regression from Confident (Trait) onto the Five Experimental Conditions

		β	SE β	Wald test	*df*	*p*	95% CI for β LL	95% CI for β UL	e^{β}
Threshold	Confident = 1	-4.16	0.40	109.07	1	<.001	-4.94	-3.38	0.02
	Confident = 2	-2.13	0.23	86.58	1	<.001	-2.58	-1.68	0.12
	Confident = 3	-0.32	0.20	2.66	1	.103	-0.71	0.07	0.72
	Confident = 4	1.86	0.23	67.41	1	<.001	1.41	2.30	6.41
Location	Joy	-0.43	0.28	2.39	1	.122	-0.97	0.11	0.65
	Sadness	-0.11	0.29	0.14	1	.704	-0.68	0.46	0.9
	Anger	-0.24	0.28	0.75	1	.386	-0.78	0.30	0.79
	Contentment	-0.25	0.28	0.79	1	.373	-0.79	0.30	0.78

Note. CI = confidence interval; LL = lower limit; UL = upper limit; e^{β} = odds ratio.

Hopeless (trait). For “hopeless (trait)” there were three cells with zero frequency (Table E 9). The test of parallel lines did not yield a significant result, $\chi^2(12) = 11.31, p > .05$, thus the conditional probability functions are parallel at all levels of the dependent variable.

Table E 9

Cross Table: Frequencies of Ratings per Condition on "Hopeless (Trait)"

	hopeless (trait)				
	1	2	3	4	5
Joy	50	20	8	2	2
Sadness	54	9	4	3	0
Anger	50	22	10	2	1
Contentment	53	16	10	0	1
Control	63	13	8	1	0

Table E 10 shows the result of the linear regression. The model is not significantly better than the null model, $\chi^2(4) = 8.50$, $p > .05$. This means that there are no significant differences between the five groups with respect to "hopeless (trait)".

Table E 10
Ordinal Regression from Hopeless (Trait) onto the Five Experimental Conditions

		β	SE β	Wald test	*df*	*p*	95% CI for β LL	95% CI for β UL	e^{β}
Threshold	Hopeless = 1	1.04	0.24	18.14	1	<.001	0.56	1.52	2.84
	Hopeless = 2	2.25	0.27	69.82	1	<.001	1.72	2.78	9.51
	Hopeless = 3	3.83	0.37	106.91	1	<.001	3.10	4.56	46.09
	Hopeless = 4	4.95	0.55	80.68	1	<.001	3.87	6.03	141.3
Location	Joy	0.59	0.33	3.16	1	.075	-0.06	1.23	1.8
	Sadness	-0.14	0.37	0.14	1	.705	-0.87	0.59	0.87
	Anger	0.65	0.32	4.06	1	.044	0.02	1.29	1.92
	Contentment	0.37	0.34	1.19	1	.276	-0.29	1.03	1.44

Note. CI = confidence interval; LL = lower limit; UL = upper limit; e^{β} = odds ratio.

Angry (trait). For "angry (trait)", 5 cells or 20 percent of cells did not contain any values (Table E 11). Four out of five cells not containing any values were at level 5 of the dependent variable and the fifth one at level 4 of the dependent variable. When conducting the ordinal regression, the test of parallel lines yielded a significant result, $\chi^2(12) = 62.44$, $p < .01$, meaning that the conditional probability functions are not parallel at all levels of the dependent variable ("angry (trait)"). This means that the one-equation proportional odds model assuming that the logit coefficients are equal across all levels of "angry (trait)" is not valid. As already mentioned above, an exact test that can be calculated when lines are not parallel is problematic in this case because of the cells with zero frequencies. Therefore, levels 4 and 5 of the dependent variable were aggregated. For the aggregated values, the test of parallel lines yielded a non-significant result, $\chi^2(8) = 4.58$, $p > .05$).

Table E 11

Cross Table: Frequencies of Ratings per Condition on "Angry (Trait)"

	angry (trait)				
	1	2	3	4	5
Joy	55	18	8	3	0
Sadness	59	8	2	0	1
Anger	66	9	6	3	0
Contentment	51	20	4	4	0
Control	71	9	4	2	0

Table E 12 shows the result of the linear regression. The model is not significantly better than the null model, $\chi^2(4) = 1.62$, $p > .05$. This means that there are no significant differences between the five groups with respect to "angry (trait)".

Table E 12
Ordinal Regression from Angry (Trait) onto the Five Experimental Conditions

		β	SE β	Wald test	*df*	*p*	95% CI for β LL	UL	e^{β}
Threshold	Angry = 1	1.54	0.28	29.89	1	<.001	0.99	2.09	4.67
	Angry = 2	2.77	0.31	77.69	1	<.001	2.15	3.38	15.91
	Angry = 3	3.88	0.39	101.10	1	<.001	3.13	4.64	48.60
Location	Joy	0.89	0.36	6.09	1	.014	0.18	1.60	2.44
	Sadness	-0.15	0.43	0.12	1	.730	-1.00	0.70	0.86
	Anger	0.28	0.38	0.55	1	.460	-0.47	1.04	1.33
	Contentment	0.90	0.37	6.01	1	.014	0.18	1.61	2.45

Note. CI = confidence interval; LL = lower limit; UL = upper limit; e^{β} = odds ratio.

State motivation and test-related emotions

Motivated (state). For “motivated (state)”, 2 cells or 8 percent of cells did not contain any values (Table E 13). When conducting the ordinal regression, the test of parallel lines yielded a significant result, $\chi^2(12) = 40.17, p < .01$), meaning that the conditional probability functions are not parallel at all levels of the dependent variable (“motivated (state)”). Like in “motivated (trait)”, the two cells not containing values were at level 1 of the dependent variable. Additionally, like the case with “motivated (trait)”, there were only few cases at level 2. Therefore, calculating an exact test would have been problematic and thus levels 1 and 2 of the dependent variable were aggregated. For the aggregated values, the test of parallel lines yielded a non-significant result, $\chi^2(8) = 2.88, p > .05$).

Table E 13

Cross Table: Frequencies of Ratings per Condition on "Motivated (State)"

	motivated (state)				
	1	2	3	4	5
Joy	0	9	16	37	25
Sadness	1	7	11	29	24
Anger	0	12	13	36	29
Contentment	5	4	15	35	27
Control	2	4	17	39	29

Table E 14 shows the result of the linear regression. The model is not significantly better than the null model, $\chi^2(4) = 0.50$, $p > .05$. This means that there are no significant differences between the five groups with respect to "motivated (state)".

Table E 14

Ordinal Regression from Motivated (State) onto the Five Experimental Conditions

							95% CI for β		
		β	SE β	Wald test	*df*	*p*	LL	UL	e^{β}
Threshold	Motivated = 1 or 2	-2.24	0.23	91.10	1	<.001	-2.70	-1.78	0.11
	Motivated = 3	-1.06	0.20	27.31	1	<.001	-1.46	-0.66	0.35
	Motivated = 4	0.70	0.20	12.31	1	<.001	0.31	1.09	2.01
Location	Joy	-0.18	0.28	0.41	1	.524	-0.71	0.36	0.84
	Sadness	-0.02	0.29	0.01	1	.933	-0.59	0.54	0.98
	Anger	-0.10	0.27	0.14	1	.713	-0.64	0.43	0.90
	Contentment	-0.10	0.28	0.12	1	.727	-0.64	0.44	0.91

Note. CI = confidence interval; LL = lower limit; UL = upper limit; e^{β} = odds ratio.

Full of positive anticipation (state). For "full of positive anticipation (state)" there were no cells with zero frequencies (Table E 15). The test of parallel lines did not yield a significant result, $\chi^2(12) = 12.94$, $p > .05$, thus the conditional probability functions are parallel at all levels of the dependent variable.

Table E 15

Cross Table: Frequencies of Ratings per Condition on "Full of Positive Anticipation (State)"

	full of positive anticipation (state)				
	1	2	3	4	5
Joy	7	19	29	23	8
Sadness	3	14	16	26	13
Anger	5	16	24	32	13
Contentment	6	14	29	17	19
Control	6	13	21	37	14

Table E 16 shows the result of the linear regression. The model is not significantly better than the null model, $\chi^2(4) = 6.72$, $p > .05$. This means that there are no significant differences between the five groups with respect to "full of positive anticipation (state)".

Table E 16

Ordinal Regression from Full of Positive Anticipation (State) onto the Five Experimental Conditions

		β	SE β	Wald test	*df*	*p*	95% CI for β LL	95% CI for β UL	e^{β}
Threshold	Pos. anticipation = 1	-2.91	0.26	121.89	1	<.001	-3.43	-2.40	0.05
	Pos. anticipation = 2	-1.36	0.20	43.73	1	<.001	-1.76	-0.95	0.26
	Pos. anticipation = 3	-0.11	0.19	0.31	1	.577	-0.49	0.27	0.9
	Pos. anticipation = 4	1.49	0.21	50.03	1	<.001	1.08	1.90	4.43
Location	Joy	-0.62	0.27	5.18	1	.023	-1.15	-0.09	0.54
	Sadness	-0.01	0.28	0.00	1	.964	-0.57	0.54	0.99
	Anger	-0.16	0.27	0.36	1	.551	-0.68	0.36	0.85
	Contentment	-0.20	0.27	0.55	1	.459	-0.73	0.33	0.82

Note. CI = confidence interval; LL = lower limit; UL = upper limit; e^{β} = odds ratio.

Anxious (state). For “anxious (state)”, 2 cells or 8 percent of cells did not contain any values (Table E 17). When conducting the ordinal regression, the test of parallel lines yielded a significant result, $\chi^2(12) = 37.54, p < .01$, meaning that the conditional probability functions are not parallel at all levels of the dependent variable (“anxious (state)”). Because of the cells with zero frequencies calculating an exact test would have been problematic and thus levels 4 and 5 of the dependent variable were aggregated. For the aggregated values, the test of parallel lines yielded a non-significant result, $\chi^2(8) = 12.65, p > .05$).

Table E 17
Cross Table: Frequencies of Ratings per Condition on "Anxious (State)"

	anxious (state)				
	1	2	3	4	5
Joy	49	15	13	5	1
Sadness	50	10	6	3	1
Anger	56	17	16	0	0
Contentment	49	15	12	3	1
Control	67	9	6	2	2

Table E 18 shows that all thresholds were significant. This indicates that the rating scale is interpreted in the way that higher categories correspond with higher degrees of the pertaining state.

Here the conditions Joy, Anger, and Contentment were significant predictors of the rating of "anxious (state)". Effect sizes eβ for these conditions as predictors of the rating on "anxious (state)" are 1.44 ("Joy"), 1.91 ("Anger"), and 2.15 ("Contentment"), see Table E 18. However, for this model the Pseudo R2 is still rather small: Cox-Snell-Index = .022, Nagelkerke-Index = .016, and McFadden-Index = .012. However, the model is only better than the null model with marginal significance and not at 5% level, $\chi^2(4) = 9.19$, $p = .06$.

This means that there are slight differences between the five groups in "anxious (state)". Compared to the Control condition (reference group), individuals in the Joy, Anger, and Contentment condition are slightly higher on state anxiety.

Table E 18

Ordinal Regression from Anxious (State) onto the Five Experimental Conditions

		β	SE β	Wald test	*df*	*p*	95% CI for β LL	95% CI for β UL	e^{β}
Threshold	Anxious = 1	1.23	0.26	23.19	1	<.001	0.73	1.74	3.43
	Anxious = 2	2.13	0.27	61.27	1	<.001	1.59	2.66	8.37
	Anxious = 3	3.65	0.34	114.65	1	<.001	2.99	4.32	38.62
Location	Joy	0.89	0.33	7.10	1	.008	0.24	1.54	2.44
	Sadness	0.33	0.36	0.84	1	.358	-0.38	1.05	1.40
	Anger	0.65	0.33	3.75	1	.053	-0.01	1.30	1.91
	Contentment	0.77	0.34	5.09	1	.024	0.10	1.43	2.15

Note. CI = confidence interval; LL = lower limit; UL = upper limit; e^{β} = odds ratio.

Confident (state). For “confident (state)”, there were no cells with zero frequencies (Table E 19). The test of parallel lines did not yield a significant result, $\chi^2(12) = 14.35$, $p > .05$), thus the conditional probability functions are parallel at all levels of the dependent variable.

Table E 19
Cross Table: Frequencies of Ratings per Condition on "Confident (State)"

	confident (state)				
	1	2	3	4	5
Joy	5	11	29	27	15
Sadness	2	5	21	29	15
Anger	2	9	25	39	15
Contentment	10	5	23	31	17
Control	1	6	25	41	18

Table E 20 shows the result of the linear regression. The model is not significantly better than the null model, $\chi^2(4) = 5.40$, $p > .05$. This means that there are no significant differences between the five groups with respect to "confident (state)".

Table E 20

Ordinal Regression from Confident (State) onto the Five Experimental Conditions

		β	SE β	Wald test	*df*	*p*	95% CI for β LL	95% CI for β UL	e^{β}
Threshold	Confident = 1	-3.28	0.29	128.31	1	<.001	-3.85	-2.71	0.04
	Confident = 2	-2.15	0.23	89.76	1	<.001	-2.60	-1.71	0.12
	Confident = 3	-0.57	0.20	8.29	1	.004	-0.96	-0.18	0.57
	Confident = 4	1.23	0.21	35.49	1	<.001	0.83	1.64	3.42
Location	Joy	-0.57	0.27	4.40	1	.036	-1.11	-0.04	0.56
	Sadness	-0.09	0.29	0.09	1	.762	-0.65	0.48	0.92
	Anger	-0.22	0.27	0.66	1	.418	-0.75	0.31	0.8
	Contentment	-0.37	0.27	1.79	1	.181	-0.90	0.17	0.69

Note. CI = confidence interval; LL = lower limit; UL = upper limit; e^{β} = odds ratio.

Hopeless (state). For “hopeless (state)”, the test of parallel lines did not yield a significant result, $\chi^2(12) = 16.08, p > .05$, thus the conditional probability functions are parallel at all levels of the dependent variable. However, as there was only one single rating on level 5 of “hopeless (state)” (Table E 21), levels 4 and 5 were collapsed into one category. For this model, the test of parallel lines also did not yield a significant result, $\chi^2(8) = 13.64, p > .05$, thus the conditional probability functions are parallel at all levels of the dependent variable.

Table E 21
Cross Table: Frequencies of Ratings per Condition on "Hopeless (State)"

	hopeless (state)				
	1	2	3	4	5
Joy	62	11	7	2	1
Sadness	54	10	3	2	0
Anger	69	12	4	1	0
Contentment	68	6	4	0	0
Control	76	1	4	3	0

Table E 22 shows that all thresholds were significant. This indicates that the rating scale is interpreted in the way that higher categories correspond with higher degrees of the pertaining state.

Here the Joy condition is a significant predictor of the rating on "hopeless (state)". The Sadness condition is a marginally significant predictor ($\beta = 0.89$, $p = .06$). The effect size eβ for the Joy condition as predictor of the rating on "hopeless (state)" is 3.06 and it is 2.43 for the Sadness condition, see Table E 22. However, for this model the *Pseudo* R^2 is still rather small: Cox-Snell-Index = .022, Nagelkerke-Index = .031, and McFadden-Index = .018. The model is better than the null model only with marginal significance, $\chi^2(4) = 9.06$, $p = .06$.

Thus, individuals in the Joy condition differ from the others in their level of "hopeless (state)" and there is a tendency for individuals in the Sadness condition to be different from the others as well. They are slightly higher on this state.

Table E 22
Ordinal Regression from Hopeless (State) onto the Five Experimental Conditions

		β	SE β	Wald test	*df*	*p*	95% CI for β LL	95% CI for β UL	e^{β}
Threshold	Hopeless = 1	2.20	0.36	36.58	1	<.001	1.48	2.91	8.98
	Hopeless = 2	3.15	0.39	65.44	1	<.001	2.39	3.92	23.42
	Hopeless = 3	4.45	0.48	85.48	1	<.001	3.51	5.40	85.83
Location	Joy	1.12	0.44	6.47	1	.011	0.26	1.98	3.06
	Sadness	0.89	0.47	3.64	1	.056	-0.02	1.80	2.43
	Anger	0.76	0.45	2.79	1	.095	-0.13	1.65	2.13
	Contentment	0.27	0.50	0.29	1	.588	-0.70	1.24	1.31

Note. CI = confidence interval; LL = lower limit; UL = upper limit; e^{β} = odds ratio.

Angry (state). For "angry (state)", there were no ratings on level 5 and three cells with zero ratings on level 4 (Table E 23). Therefore levels 3 to 5 were aggregated. The test of parallel lines did not yield a significant result, $\chi^2(4) = 3.82$, $p > .05$, thus the conditional probability functions are parallel at all levels of the dependent variable.

Table E 23
Cross Table: Frequencies of Ratings per Condition on "Angry (State)"

	angry (state)				
	1	2	3	4	5
Joy	71	9	2	2	0
Sadness	65	3	0	1	0
Anger	78	7	1	0	0
Contentment	68	4	5	0	0
Control	80	3	1	0	0

Table E 24 shows the result of the linear regression. The model is not significantly better than the null model, $\chi^2(4) = 7.44$, $p > .05$. This means that there are no significant differences between the five groups with respect to "angry (state)".

Table E 24
Ordinal Regression from Angry (State) onto the Five Experimental Conditions

							95% CI for β		
		β	SE β	Wald test	*df*	*p*	LL	UL	e^{β}
Threshold	Angry = 1	3.00	0.51	34.18	1	<.001	1.99	4.00	20.05
	Angry = 2	4.23	0.57	55.58	1	<.001	3.12	5.35	69.01
Location	Joy	1.30	0.59	4.76	1	.029	0.13	2.46	3.66
	Sadness	0.21	0.73	0.08	1	.776	-1.22	1.63	1.23
	Anger	0.70	0.63	1.22	1	.269	-0.54	1.95	2.02
	Contentment	1.01	0.62	2.64	1	.104	-0.21	2.22	2.74

Note. CI = confidence interval; LL = lower limit; UL = upper limit; e^{β} = odds ratio.

Appendix F

Test Scores, Test Score Distributions, and Test Score Transformations

First Test

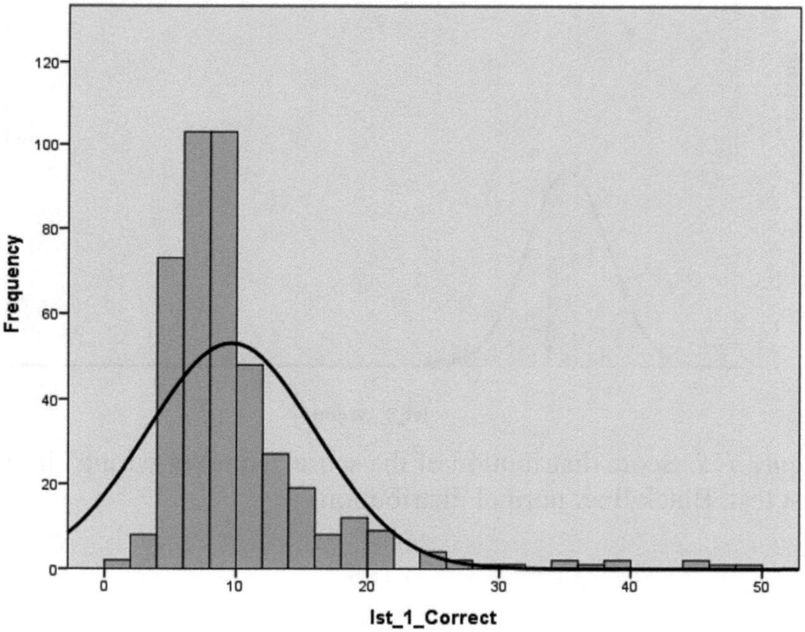

Figure F 1. Score distribution of the score "Number correct" in the first test. Black line: normal distribution.

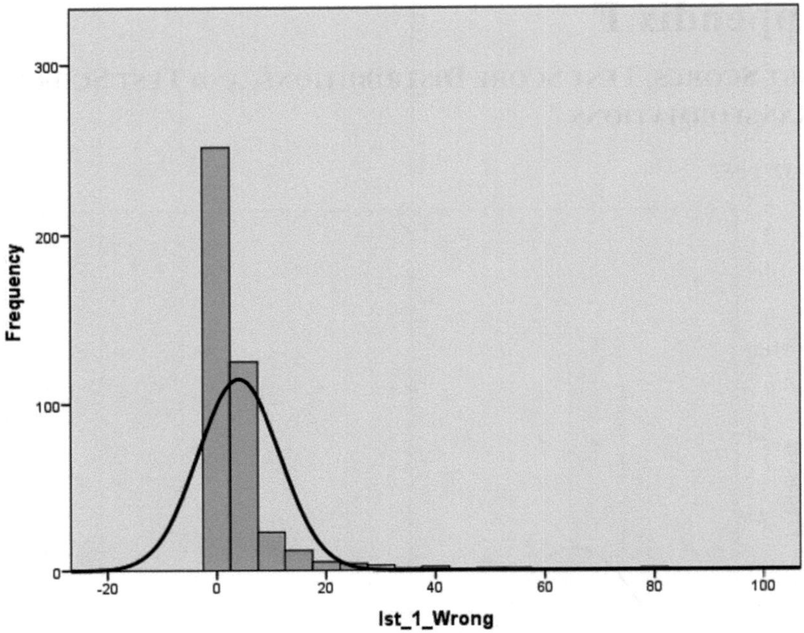

Figure F 2. Score distribution of the score "Number wrong" in the first test. Black line: normal distribution.

Syntax 1

SPSS Syntax Used to Calculate the Lambda Parameters and Transform the Score "Number Correct" of the First Test to Approximate a Normal Distribution

```
VECTOR lam(31) /x1(31).
LOOP idx=1 TO 31.
  COMPUTE lam(idx)=-2.1 + idx*.1.
  DO IF lam(idx)=0.
    COMPUTE x1(idx)=LN(1st_1_Correct).
  ELSE.
    COMPUTE   x1(idx)=   (1st_1_Correct**lam(idx)-
1)/lam(idx).
  END IF.
END LOOP.
EXECUTE.
```

Table F 1
Skewness and Kurtosis of the Score "Number Correct" in the First Test for Different Lambda Parameters Using the Box-Cox Transformation

	N	Skewness	Kurtosis	Min	Max
lst_1_Correct	429	2.971	11.741	1	49
x11	429	-12.539	170.943	0.00	.50
x12	429	-12.112	162.689	0.00	.53
x13	429	-11.607	153.094	0.00	.56
x14	429	-11.020	142.126	0.00	.59
x15	429	-10.348	129.844	0.00	.62
x16	429	-9.592	116.424	0.00	.66
x17	429	-8.762	102.174	0.00	.71
x18	429	-7.873	87.532	0.00	.76
x19	429	-6.948	73.028	0.00	.83
x110	429	-6.013	59.221	0.00	.90
x111	429	-5.098	46.617	0.00	.98
x112	429	-4.229	35.598	0.00	1.08
x113	429	-3.427	26.373	0.00	1.19
x114	429	-2.705	18.972	0.00	1.33
x115	429	-2.067	13.273	0.00	1.51
x116	429	-1.512	9.059	0.00	1.71
x117	429	-1.031	6.072	0.00	1.97
x118	429	-.614	4.055	0.00	2.30
x119	429	-.248	2.783	0.00	2.70

Note. Score x121 was used for the further analyses in the results section.

Table F 1 (continued)
Skewness and Kurtosis of the Score "Number Correct" in the First Test for Different Lambda Parameters Using the Box-Cox Transformation

	N	Skewness	Kurtosis	Min	Max
x120	429	.077	2.077	0.00	3.22
x121	429	.374	1.800	0.00	3.89
x122	429	.650	1.855	0.00	4.76
x123	429	.913	2.178	0.00	5.89
x124	429	1.169	2.728	0.00	7.38
x125	429	1.421	3.481	0.00	9.36
x126	429	1.673	4.422	0.00	12.00
x127	429	1.927	5.544	0.00	15.55
x128	429	2.184	6.843	0.00	20.35
x129	429	2.444	8.312	0.00	26.87
x130	429	2.706	9.948	0.00	35.78
x131	429	2.971	11.741	0.00	48.00

Note. Score x121 was used for the further analyses in the results section.

Syntax 2

SPSS Syntax used to Calculate the Lambda Parameters and Transform the Score "Number Wrong" of the First Test to Approximate a Normal Distribution

```
COMPUTE lst_1_Wrong_1 = lst_1_Wrong+1.
EXECUTE.

VECTOR lam(31) /xx1(31).
LOOP idxx=1 TO 31.
  COMPUTE lam(idxx)=-2.1 + idxx*.1.
  DO IF lam(idxx)=0.
    COMPUTE xx1(idxx)=LN(lst_1_Wrong_1).
  ELSE.
    COMPUTE                              xx1(idxx)=
(lst_1_Wrong_1**lam(idxx)-1)/lam(idxx).
  END IF.
END LOOP.
EXECUTE.
```

Note. The scores have to be anchored at 1.00. As the minimum score for "Number Wrong" had been 0, a transformation was necessary.

Table F 2

Skewness and Kurtosis of the Score "Number Wrong" in the First Test for Different Lambda Parameters Using the Box-Cox Transformation

	N	Skewness	Kurtosis	Min	Max
lst_1_Wrong_1	429	5.128	36.750	1.00	82.00
xx11	429	-1.407	.305	0.00	.50
xx12	429	-1.376	.255	0.00	.53
xx13	429	-1.342	.200	0.00	.56
xx14	429	-1.302	.140	0.00	.59
xx15	429	-1.258	.073	0.00	.62
xx16	429	-1.208	.000	0.00	.67
xx17	429	-1.153	-.079	0.00	.71
xx18	429	-1.091	-.163	0.00	.77
xx19	429	-1.021	-.252	0.00	.83
xx110	429	-.944	-.344	0.00	.90
xx111	429	-.858	-.436	0.00	.99
xx112	429	-.762	-.525	0.00	1.09
xx113	429	-.656	-.606	0.00	1.21
xx114	429	-.538	-.673	0.00	1.36
xx115	429	-.408	-.717	0.00	1.55
xx116	429	-.263	-.726	0.00	1.78
xx117	429	-.103	-.683	0.00	2.07
xx118	429	.074	-.570	0.00	2.44
xx119	429	.272	-.356	0.00	2.93

Note. Score xx120 was used for the further analyses in the results section.

Table F 2

Skewness and Kurtosis of the Score "Number Wrong" in the First Test for Different Lambda Parameters Using the Box-Cox Transformation

	N	Skewness	Kurtosis	Min	Max
xx120	429	.491	-.008	0.00	3.56
xx121	429	.735	.522	0.00	4.41
xx122	429	1.007	1.294	0.00	5.54
xx123	429	1.310	2.384	0.00	7.07
xx124	429	1.648	3.887	0.00	9.17
xx125	429	2.024	5.917	0.00	12.07
xx126	429	2.440	8.603	0.00	16.11
xx127	429	2.897	12.090	0.00	21.78
xx128	429	3.396	16.523	0.00	29.80
xx129	429	3.937	22.040	0.00	41.21
xx130	429	4.515	28.757	0.00	57.53
xx131	429	5.128	36.750	0.00	81.00

Note. Score xx120 was used for the further analyses in the results section.

Second Test

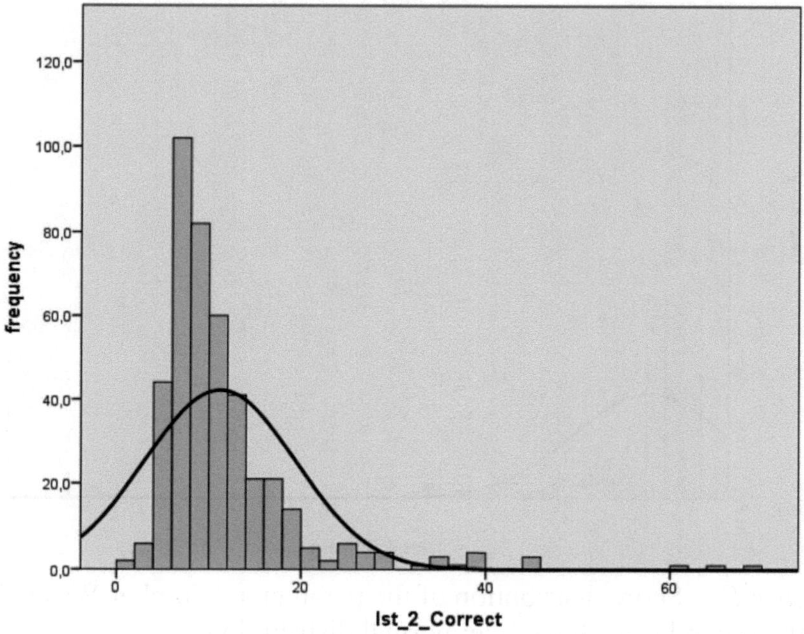

Figure F 3. Score distribution of the parameter “Number Correct” in the second test. Black line: normal distribution.

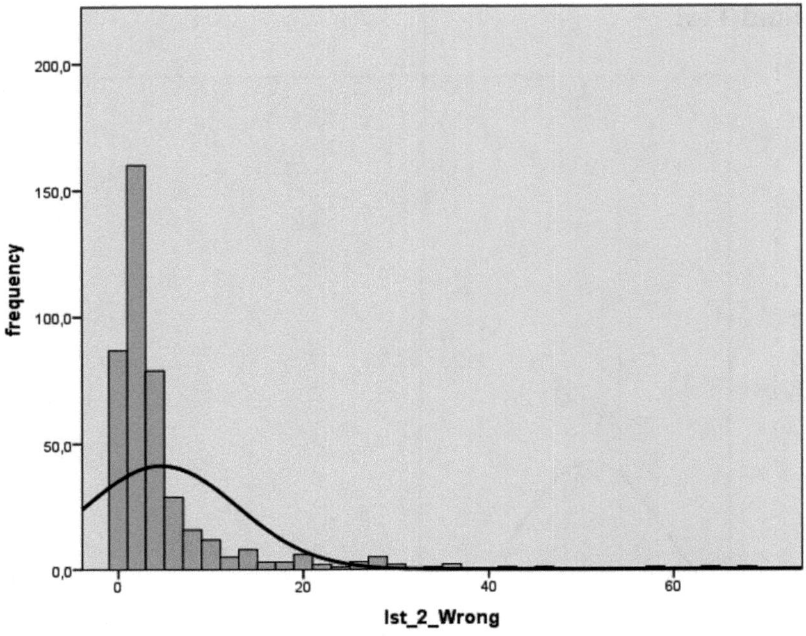

Figure F 4. Score distribution of the parameter "Number Wrong" in the second test. Black line: normal distribution.

Syntax 3

SPSS Syntax Used to Calculate the Lambda Parameters and Transform the Score "Number Correct" of the Second Test to Approximate a Normal Distribution

```
VECTOR lam(31) /y1(31).
LOOP idy=1 TO 31.
  COMPUTE lam(idy)=-2.1 + idy*.1.
  DO IF lam(idy)=0.
    COMPUTE y1(idy)=LN(lst_2_Correct).
  ELSE.
    COMPUTE  y1(idy)=  (lst_2_Correct**lam(idy)-
1)/lam(idy).
  END IF.
END LOOP.
EXECUTE.
```

Table F 3
Skewness and Kurtosis of the Score "Number Correct" in the Second Test for Different Lambda Parameters Using the Box-Cox Transformation

	N	Skewness	Kurtosis	Min	Max
lst_2_Correct	429	3.25	14.84	1.00	68.00
y11	429	-13.27	185.78	0.00	0.50
y12	429	-12.93	179.13	0.00	0.53
y13	429	-12.51	171.03	0.00	0.56
y14	429	-12.00	161.33	0.00	0.59
y15	429	-11.39	149.92	0.00	0.62
y16	429	-10.68	136.82	0.00	0.67
y17	429	-9.86	122.22	0.00	0.71
y18	429	-8.95	106.47	0.00	0.77
y19	429	-7.97	90.16	0.00	0.83
y110	429	-6.94	73.98	0.00	0.90
y111	429	-5.90	58.68	0.00	0.99
y112	429	-4.90	44.93	0.00	1.09
y113	429	-3.96	33.20	0.00	1.21
y114	429	-3.10	23.68	0.00	1.35
y115	429	-2.35	16.34	0.00	1.53
y116	429	-1.70	10.93	0.00	1.76
y117	429	-1.15	7.14	0.00	2.04
y118	429	-0.68	4.62	0.00	2.39
y119	429	-0.27	3.05	0.00	2.85

Note. Score y121 was used for the further analyses in the results section.

Table F 3 (continued)

Skewness and Kurtosis of the Score "Number Correct" in the Second Test for Different Lambda Parameters Using the Box-Cox Transformation

	N	Skewness	Kurtosis	Min	Max
y120	429	0.08	2.19	0.00	3.44
y121	429	0.40	1.86	0.00	4.22
y122	429	0.69	1.92	0.00	5.25
y123	429	0.97	2.29	0.00	6.63
y124	429	1.23	2.94	0.00	8.49
y125	429	1.50	3.84	0.00	11.02
y126	429	1.77	4.98	0.00	14.49
y127	429	2.05	6.39	0.00	19.29
y128	429	2.33	8.06	0.00	25.97
y129	429	2.63	10.01	0.00	35.30
y130	429	2.94	12.27	0.00	48.44
y131	429	3.25	14.84	0.00	67.00

Note. Score y121 was used for the further analyses in the results section.

Syntax 4
SPSS Syntax Used to Calculate the Lambda Parameters and Transform the Score "Number Wrong" of the Second Test to Approximate a Normal Distribution

```
COMPUTE lst_2_Wrong_1 = lst_2_Wrong+1.
EXECUTE.

VECTOR lam(31) /yy1(31).
LOOP idyy=1 TO 31.
  COMPUTE lam(idyy)=-2.1 + idyy*.1.
  DO IF lam(idyy)=0.
    COMPUTE yy1(idyy)=LN(lst_2_Wrong_1).
  ELSE.
    COMPUTE                          yy1(idyy)=
(lst_2_Wrong_1**lam(idyy)-1)/lam(idyy).
  END IF.
END LOOP.
EXECUTE.
```

Note. The scores have to be anchored at 1.00. As the minimum score for "Number Wrong" had been 0, a transformation was necessary.

Table F 4

Skewness and Kurtosis of the Score "Number Wrong" in the Second Test for Different Lambda Parameters Using the Box-Cox Transformation

	N	Skewness	Kurtosis	Min	Max
lst_2_Wrong_1	429	3.974	20.259	1.00	68.00
yy11	429	-1.302	-.057	0.00	.50
yy12	429	-1.277	-.093	0.00	.53
yy13	429	-1.248	-.133	0.00	.56
yy14	429	-1.215	-.178	0.00	.59
yy15	429	-1.178	-.227	0.00	.62
yy16	429	-1.135	-.282	0.00	.67
yy17	429	-1.087	-.341	0.00	.71
yy18	429	-1.032	-.405	0.00	.77
yy19	429	-.970	-.473	0.00	.83
yy110	429	-.900	-.544	0.00	.90
yy111	429	-.821	-.616	0.00	.99
yy112	429	-.731	-.685	0.00	1.09
yy113	429	-.630	-.748	0.00	1.21
yy114	429	-.517	-.799	0.00	1.35
yy115	429	-.389	-.829	0.00	1.53
yy116	429	-.247	-.828	0.00	1.76
yy117	429	-.088	-.784	0.00	2.04
yy118	429	.088	-.678	0.00	2.39
yy119	429	.281	-.491	0.00	2.85

Note. Score yy120 was used for the further analyses in the results section.

Table F 4 (continued)
Skewness and Kurtosis of the Score "Number Wrong" in the Second Test for Different Lambda Parameters Using the Box-Cox Transformation

	N	Skewness	Kurtosis	Min	Max
yy120	429	.492	-.198	0.00	3.44
yy121	429	.722	.228	0.00	4.22
yy122	429	.970	.821	0.00	5.25
yy123	429	1.237	1.617	0.00	6.63
yy124	429	1.520	2.657	0.00	8.49
yy125	429	1.822	3.983	0.00	11.02
yy126	429	2.140	5.641	0.00	14.49
yy127	429	2.475	7.677	0.00	19.29
yy128	429	2.827	10.130	0.00	25.97
yy129	429	3.195	13.034	0.00	35.30
yy130	429	3.578	16.409	0.00	48.44
yy131	429	3.974	20.259	0.00	67.00

Note. Score yy120 was used for the further analyses in the results section.

Appendix G

Mplus Outputs

Model 1

```
  analysis:          type = general;
                     estimator = mlr;

  model:             lst1 by lst1H1 lst1H2 (1);
                     lst2 by lst2H1 lst2H2 (1);

                     lst2 on lst1*1;
                     [lst1H1@0 lst2h1@0];
                     [lst1H2 lst2H2] (2);
                     [lst1* lst2*];


  output:            sampstat standardized stdyx residual
modindices (all);



INPUT READING TERMINATED NORMALLY



Regression on latent level
from lst 2 onto lst 1
Indicators = number of correct solutions per test half
Estimator MLR

SUMMARY OF ANALYSIS

Number of groups 1
Number of observations 429

Number of dependent variables 4
Number of independent variables 0
Number of continuous latent variables 2

Observed dependent variables

  Continuous
   LST1H1      LST1H2      LST2H1      LST2H2

Continuous latent variables
```

```
   LST1         LST2


Estimator MLR
Information matrix OBSERVED
Maximum number of iterations 1000
Convergence criterion 0.500D-04
Maximum number of steepest descent iterations 20
Maximum number of iterations for H1 2000
Convergence criterion for H1 0.100D-03

Input data file(s)
  Models.dat

Input data format  FREE


SUMMARY OF DATA

     Number of missing data patterns           1


COVARIANCE COVERAGE OF DATA

Minimum covariance coverage value   0.100


     PROPORTION OF DATA PRESENT


           Covariance Coverage
        LST1H1        LST1H2        LST2H1        LST2H2
        ________      ________      ________      ________
 LST1H1 1.000
 LST1H2 1.000         1.000
 LST2H1 1.000         1.000         1.000
 LST2H2 1.000         1.000         1.000         1.000


SAMPLE STATISTICS


     ESTIMATED SAMPLE STATISTICS


           Means
   LST1H1        LST1H2        LST2H1        LST2H2
```

```
                ________      ________      ________      ________
 1               5.103         4.513         5.925         5.277


              Covariances
              LST1H1        LST1H2        LST2H1        LST2H2
              ________      ________      ________      ________
 LST1H1         9.108
 LST1H2         9.845        12.856
 LST2H1         8.882         9.826        14.838
 LST2H2         9.867        11.163        15.704        19.427


              Correlations
              LST1H1        LST1H2        LST2H1        LST2H2
              ________      ________      ________      ________
 LST1H1         1.000
 LST1H2         0.910         1.000
 LST2H1         0.764         0.711         1.000
 LST2H2         0.742         0.706         0.925         1.000


     MAXIMUM LOG-LIKELIHOOD VALUE FOR THE UNRESTRICTED (H1)
MODEL IS   -3683.376


THE MODEL ESTIMATION TERMINATED NORMALLY



MODEL FIT INFORMATION

Number of Free Parameters                       11

Loglikelihood

          H0 Value                       -3686.417
          H0 Scaling Correction Factor       3.469
            for MLR
          H1 Value                       -3683.376
          H1 Scaling Correction Factor       2.942
            for MLR

Information Criteria

          Akaike (AIC)                    7394.834
          Bayesian (BIC)                  7439.510
```

```
          Sample-Size Adjusted BIC          7404.602
            (n* = (n + 2) / 24)

Chi-Square Test of Model Fit

          Value                                6.004*
          Degrees of Freedom                       3
          P-Value                             0.1114
          Scaling Correction Factor            1.013
            for MLR

*   The chi-square value for MLM, MLMV, MLR, ULSMV, WLSM
and WLSMV cannot be used
    for chi-square difference testing in the regular way.
MLM, MLR and WLSM
    chi-square difference testing is described on the Mplus
website.  MLMV, WLSMV,
    and ULSMV difference testing is done using the DIFFTEST
option.

RMSEA (Root Mean Square Error Of Approximation)

          Estimate                             0.048
          90 Percent C.I.                      0.000  0.105
          Probability RMSEA <= .05             0.435

CFI/TLI

          CFI                                  0.998
          TLI                                  0.996

Chi-Square Test of Model Fit for the Baseline Model

          Value                             1344.374
          Degrees of Freedom                       6
          P-Value                             0.0000

SRMR (Standardized Root Mean Square Residual)

          Value                                0.007


MODEL RESULTS

                                                Two-Tailed
                Estimate       S.E.  Est./S.E.    P-Value
```

```
 LST1      BY
    LST1H1            1.000        0.000      999.000    999.000
    LST1H2            1.110        0.032       34.511      0.000

 LST2      BY
    LST2H1            1.000        0.000      999.000    999.000
    LST2H2            1.110        0.032       34.511      0.000

 LST2      ON
    LST1              1.004        0.105        9.606      0.000

 Means
    LST1              5.111        0.146       35.053      0.000

 Intercepts
    LST1H1            0.000        0.000      999.000    999.000
    LST1H2           -1.217        0.165       -7.393      0.000
    LST2H1            0.000        0.000      999.000    999.000
    LST2H2           -1.217        0.165       -7.393      0.000
    LST2              0.771        0.470        1.640      0.101

 Variances
    LST1              8.853        1.540        5.750      0.000

 Residual Variances
    LST1H1            0.261        0.232        1.123      0.261
    LST1H2            1.906        0.374        5.099      0.000
    LST2H1            0.729        0.278        2.621      0.009
    LST2H2            1.956        0.405        4.824      0.000
    LST2              5.209        1.298        4.013      0.000


STANDARDIZED MODEL RESULTS


STDYX Standardization

                                                        Two-Tailed
                   Estimate          S.E.  Est./S.E.     P-Value

 LST1      BY
    LST1H1            0.986        0.013       74.861      0.000
    LST1H2            0.923        0.019       48.253      0.000

 LST2      BY
    LST2H1            0.975        0.010       95.934      0.000
```

```
   LST2H2          0.948      0.014     65.960      0.000

 LST2     ON
   LST1            0.795      0.050     15.869      0.000

 Means
   LST1            1.718      0.117     14.714      0.000

 Intercepts
   LST1H1          0.000      0.000    999.000    999.000
   LST1H2         -0.340      0.043     -7.893      0.000
   LST2H1          0.000      0.000    999.000    999.000
   LST2H2         -0.277      0.035     -7.990      0.000
   LST2            0.205      0.136      1.507      0.132

 Variances
   LST1            1.000      0.000    999.000    999.000

 Residual Variances
   LST1H1          0.029      0.026      1.102      0.271
   LST1H2          0.149      0.035      4.214      0.000
   LST2H1          0.049      0.020      2.473      0.013
   LST2H2          0.101      0.027      3.704      0.000
   LST2            0.369      0.080      4.631      0.000


R-SQUARE

   Observed                                        Two-Tailed
   Variable        Estimate       S.E.  Est./S.E.    P-Value

   LST1H1          0.971      0.026     37.430      0.000
   LST1H2          0.851      0.035     24.127      0.000
   LST2H1          0.951      0.020     47.967      0.000
   LST2H2          0.899      0.027     32.980      0.000

    Latent                                         Two-Tailed
   Variable       Estimate       S.E.  Est./S.E.     P-Value

   LST2            0.631      0.080      7.934      0.000


QUALITY OF NUMERICAL RESULTS

     Condition Number for the Information Matrix  0.497E-03
       (ratio of smallest to largest eigenvalue)
```

```
RESIDUAL OUTPUT


     ESTIMATED MODEL AND RESIDUALS (OBSERVED - ESTIMATED)


           Model Estimated Means/Intercepts/Thresholds
              LST1H1        LST1H2        LST2H1        LST2H2
              ________      ________      ________      ________
 1               5.111         4.457         5.902         5.335


           Residuals for Means/Intercepts/Thresholds
              LST1H1        LST1H2        LST2H1        LST2H2
              ________      ________      ________      ________
 1              -0.008         0.056         0.024        -0.057


           Standardized Residuals (z-scores) for
Means/Intercepts/Thresholds
              LST1H1        LST1H2        LST2H1        LST2H2
              ________      ________      ________      ________
 1             999.000         1.109         0.688        -5.408


           Normalized Residuals for
Means/Intercepts/Thresholds
              LST1H1        LST1H2        LST2H1        LST2H2
              ________      ________      ________      ________
 1              -0.058         0.323         0.128        -0.269


           Model Estimated Covari-
ances/Correlations/Residual Correlations
              LST1H1        LST1H2        LST2H1        LST2H2
              ________      ________      ________      ________
 LST1H1         9.114
 LST1H2         9.828        12.817
 LST2H1         8.888         9.867        14.860
 LST2H2         9.867        10.954        15.688        19.372


           Residuals for Covariances/Correlations/Residual
Correlations
              LST1H1        LST1H2        LST2H1        LST2H2
              ________      ________      ________      ________
```

```
 LST1H1     -0.005
 LST1H2      0.017          0.039
 LST2H1     -0.006         -0.041          -0.022
 LST2H2      0.000          0.209           0.016          0.055


          Standardized Residuals (z-scores) for Covari-
ances/Correlations/Residual Corr
           LST1H1         LST1H2          LST2H1          LST2H2
          ________       ________        ________        ________
 LST1H1    999.000
 LST1H2      0.061          0.081
 LST2H1     -0.069         -0.113          -0.104
 LST2H2    999.000          1.002         999.000          0.247


          Normalized Residuals for Covari-
ances/Correlations/Residual Correlations
           LST1H1         LST1H2          LST2H1          LST2H2
          ________       ________        ________        ________
 LST1H1     -0.004
 LST1H2      0.009          0.017
 LST2H1     -0.004         -0.020          -0.008
 LST2H2      0.000          0.084           0.005          0.014


MODEL MODIFICATION INDICES

Minimum M.I. value for printing the modification index
10.000

                  M.I.     E.P.C.  Std E.P.C.  StdYX E.P.C.

No modification indices above the minimum value.
```

Model 2

```
  analysis:         type = general;
                    estimator = mlr;

  model:            lst1 by lst1H1 lst1H2 (1);
                    lst2 by lst2H1 lst2H2 (1);
```

```
                    lst2 on lst1*1 d_joy@0 d_sad@0 d_anger@0
d_cont@0;
                    [lst1H1@0 lst2h1@0];
                    [lst1H2 lst2H2] (2);
                    [lst1* lst2*];

  output:           sampstat standardized stdyx residual
modindices;



INPUT READING TERMINATED NORMALLY



Regression on latent level
from lst 2 onto lst 1 and conditions
Indicators = number of correct solutions per test
half
Estimator: MLR

Schätzer: MLR

SUMMARY OF ANALYSIS

Number of groups 1
Number of observations 429

Number of dependent variables 4
Number of independent variables 4
Number of continuous latent variables 2

Observed dependent variables

  Continuous
   LST1H1      LST1H2      LST2H1      LST2H2

Observed independent variables
   D_JOY       D_SAD       D_ANGER     D_CONT

Continuous latent variables
   LST1        LST2


Estimator MLR
Information matrix OBSERVED
```

```
Maximum number of iterations 1000
Convergence criterion 0.500D-04
Maximum number of steepest descent iterations 20
Maximum number of iterations for H1 2000
Convergence criterion for H1 0.100D-03

Input data file(s)
  Models.dat

Input data format  FREE


SUMMARY OF DATA

     Number of missing data patterns             1


COVARIANCE COVERAGE OF DATA

Minimum covariance coverage value   0.100


     PROPORTION OF DATA PRESENT


           Covariance Coverage
           LST1H1    LST1H2    LST2H1    LST2H2    D_JOY
           ________  ________  ________  ________  ________
 LST1H1    1.000
 LST1H2    1.000     1.000
 LST2H1    1.000     1.000     1.000
 LST2H2    1.000     1.000     1.000     1.000
 D_JOY     1.000     1.000     1.000     1.000     1.000
 D_SAD     1.000     1.000     1.000     1.000     1.000
 D_ANGER   1.000     1.000     1.000     1.000     1.000
 D_CONT    1.000     1.000     1.000     1.000     1.000


           Covariance Coverage
              D_SAD         D_ANGER       D_CONT
              ________      ________      ________
 D_SAD         1.000
 D_ANGER       1.000         1.000
 D_CONT        1.000         1.000         1.000


SAMPLE STATISTICS
```

```
     ESTIMATED SAMPLE STATISTICS


           Means
              LST1H1       LST1H2       LST2H1       LST2H2       D_JOY
              ________     ________     ________     ________     ________
 1           5.103        4.513        5.925        5.277        0.205


           Means
              D_SAD        D_ANGER      D_CONT
              ________     ________     ________
      1      0.168        0.210        0.203


           Covariances
              LST1H1       LST1H2       LST2H1       LST2H2       D_JOY
              ________     ________     ________     ________     ________
 LST1H1         9.108
 LST1H2         9.845       12.856
 LST2H1         8.882        9.826       14.838
 LST2H2         9.867       11.163       15.704       19.427
 D_JOY          0.033       -0.040        0.08         0.064        0.163
 D_SAD         -0.059       -0.03        -0.158       -0.08        -0.034
 D_ANGER       -0.024       -0.010       -0.054       -0.056       -0.043
 D_CONT         0.010       -0.001       -0.006       -0.01        -0.042


           Covariances
              D_SAD        D_ANGER      D_CONT
              ________     ________     ________
 D_SAD          0.140
 D_ANGER       -0.035        0.166
 D_CONT        -0.034       -0.043        0.162


           Correlations
              LST1H1       LST1H2       LST2H1       LST2H2       D_JOY
              ________     ________     ________     ________     ________
 LST1H1         1.000
 LST1H2         0.910        1.000
 LST2H1         0.764        0.711        1.000
 LST2H2         0.742        0.706        0.925        1.000
 D_JOY          0.027       -0.028        0.052        0.036        1.000
 D_SAD         -0.052       -0.022       -0.110       -0.051       -0.228
```

```
 D_ANGER -0.019   -0.007   -0.035   -0.031   -0.262
 D_CONT   0.008   -0.001   -0.004   -0.009   -0.256


           Correlations
              D_SAD          D_ANGER        D_CONT
              ________       ________       ________
 D_SAD         1.000
 D_ANGER      -0.231          1.000
 D_CONT       -0.227         -0.260          1.000


    MAXIMUM LOG-LIKELIHOOD VALUE FOR THE UNRESTRICTED (H1)
MODEL IS   -4374.878


THE MODEL ESTIMATION TERMINATED NORMALLY



MODEL FIT INFORMATION

Number of Free Parameters                       11

Loglikelihood

          H0 Value                        -3686.417
          H0 Scaling Correction Factor        3.469
            for MLR
          H1 Value                        -3670.088
          H1 Scaling Correction Factor        1.886
            for MLR

Information Criteria

          Akaike (AIC)                     7394.834
          Bayesian (BIC)                   7439.510
          Sample-Size Adjusted BIC         7404.602
            (n* = (n + 2) / 24)

Chi-Square Test of Model Fit

          Value                              33.672*
          Degrees of Freedom                     19
          P-Value                            0.0201
          Scaling Correction Factor           0.970
            for MLR
```

```
*   The chi-square value for MLM, MLMV, MLR, ULSMV, WLSM
and WLSMV cannot be used
    for chi-square difference testing in the regular way.
MLM, MLR and WLSM
    chi-square difference testing is described on the Mplus
website.  MLMV, WLSMV,
    and ULSMV difference testing is done using the DIFFTEST
option.

RMSEA (Root Mean Square Error Of Approximation)

          Estimate                           0.042
          90 Percent C.I.                    0.017  0.065
          Probability RMSEA <= .05           0.678

CFI/TLI

          CFI                                0.992
          TLI                                0.991

Chi-Square Test of Model Fit for the Baseline Model

          Value                           1819.994
          Degrees of Freedom                    22
          P-Value                           0.0000

SRMR (Standardized Root Mean Square Residual)

          Value                              0.025



MODEL RESULTS

                                                Two-Tailed
                  Estimate       S.E.  Est./S.E.    P-Value

 LST1     BY
    LST1H1           1.000      0.000    999.000    999.000
    LST1H2           1.110      0.032     34.511      0.000

 LST2     BY
    LST2H1           1.000      0.000    999.000    999.000
    LST2H2           1.110      0.032     34.511      0.000

 LST2     ON
```

```
    LST1              1.004       0.105       9.606       0.000

 LST2      ON
    D_JOY             0.000       0.000     999.000     999.000
    D_SAD             0.000       0.000     999.000     999.000
    D_ANGER           0.000       0.000     999.000     999.000
    D_CONT            0.000       0.000     999.000     999.000

 Means
    LST1              5.111       0.146      35.053       0.000

 Intercepts
    LST1H1            0.000       0.000     999.000     999.000
    LST1H2           -1.217       0.165      -7.393       0.000
    LST2H1            0.000       0.000     999.000     999.000
    LST2H2           -1.217       0.165      -7.393       0.000
    LST2              0.771       0.470       1.640       0.101

 Variances
    LST1              8.853       1.540       5.750       0.000

 Residual Variances
    LST1H1            0.261       0.232       1.123       0.261
    LST1H2            1.906       0.374       5.099       0.000
    LST2H1            0.729       0.278       2.621       0.009
    LST2H2            1.956       0.405       4.824       0.000
    LST2              5.209       1.298       4.013       0.000


STANDARDIZED MODEL RESULTS


STDYX Standardization

                                                    Two-Tailed
                    Estimate       S.E.  Est./S.E.    P-Value

 LST1      BY
    LST1H1            0.986       0.013      74.861       0.000
    LST1H2            0.923       0.019      48.253       0.000

 LST2      BY
    LST2H1            0.975       0.010      95.934       0.000
    LST2H2            0.948       0.014      65.960       0.000

 LST2      ON
    LST1              0.795       0.050      15.869       0.000
```

```
 LST2     ON
    D_JOY            0.000       0.000     999.000     999.000
    D_SAD            0.000       0.000     999.000     999.000
    D_ANGER          0.000       0.000     999.000     999.000
    D_CONT           0.000       0.000     999.000     999.000

 Means
    LST1             1.718       0.117      14.714       0.000

 Intercepts
    LST1H1           0.000       0.000     999.000     999.000
    LST1H2          -0.340       0.043      -7.893       0.000
    LST2H1           0.000       0.000     999.000     999.000
    LST2H2          -0.277       0.035      -7.990       0.000
    LST2             0.205       0.136       1.507       0.132

 Variances
    LST1             1.000       0.000     999.000     999.000

 Residual Variances
    LST1H1           0.029       0.026       1.102       0.271
    LST1H2           0.149       0.035       4.214       0.000
    LST2H1           0.049       0.020       2.473       0.013
    LST2H2           0.101       0.027       3.704       0.000
    LST2             0.369       0.080       4.631       0.000


R-SQUARE

    Observed                                           Two-Tailed
    Variable        Estimate       S.E.  Est./S.E.    P-Value

    LST1H1           0.971       0.026      37.430       0.000
    LST1H2           0.851       0.035      24.127       0.000
    LST2H1           0.951       0.020      47.967       0.000
    LST2H2           0.899       0.027      32.980       0.000

     Latent                                            Two-Tailed
    Variable        Estimate       S.E.  Est./S.E.    P-Value

    LST2                0.631      0.080       7.934       0.000


QUALITY OF NUMERICAL RESULTS

     Condition Number for the Information Matrix 0.497E-03
```

```
      (ratio of smallest to largest eigenvalue)


RESIDUAL OUTPUT


     ESTIMATED MODEL AND RESIDUALS (OBSERVED - ESTIMATED)


           Model Estimated Means/Intercepts/Thresholds
              LST1H1        LST1H2        LST2H1        LST2H2        D_JOY
              ________      ________      ________      ________      ________
 1              5.111         4.457         5.902         5.335         0.205


           Model Estimated Means/Intercepts/Thresholds
              D_SAD         D_ANGER       D_CONT
              ________      ________      ________
 1              0.168         0.210         0.203


           Residuals for Means/Intercepts/Thresholds
              LST1H1        LST1H2        LST2H1        LST2H2        D_JOY
              ________      ________      ________      ________      ________
 1             -0.008         0.056         0.024        -0.057         0.000


           Residuals for Means/Intercepts/Thresholds
              D_SAD         D_ANGER       D_CONT
              ________      ________      ________
 1              0.000         0.000         0.000


           Standardized Residuals (z-scores) for
Means/Intercepts/Thresholds
              LST1H1        LST1H2        LST2H1        LST2H2        D_JOY
              ________      ________      ________      ________      ________
 1            999.000         1.109         0.688        -5.408         0.000


           Standardized Residuals (z-scores) for
Means/Intercepts/Thresholds
              D_SAD         D_ANGER       D_CONT
              ________      ________      ________
 1              0.000         0.000         0.000
```

```
           Normalized Residuals for
Means/Intercepts/Thresholds
       LST1H1      LST1H2      LST2H1      LST2H2      D_JOY
      ________    ________    ________    ________    ________
1      -0.058      0.323       0.128      -0.269       0.000


           Normalized Residuals for
Means/Intercepts/Thresholds
                D_SAD          D_ANGER         D_CONT
              ________        ________        ________
      1         0.000           0.000           0.000


           Model Estimated Covari-
ances/Correlations/Residual Correlations
       LST1H1      LST1H2      LST2H1      LST2H2      D_JOY
      ________    ________    ________    ________    ________
 LST1H1   9.114
 LST1H2   9.828      12.817
 LST2H1   8.888       9.867      14.860
 LST2H2   9.867      10.954      15.688      19.372
 D_JO     0.000       0.000       0.000       0.000       0.163
 D_SAD    0.000       0.000       0.000       0.000      -0.034
 D_ANGER  0.000       0.000       0.000       0.000      -0.043
 D_CONT   0.000       0.000       0.000       0.000      -0.042


           Model Estimated Covari-
ances/Correlations/Residual Correlations
                D_SAD          D_ANGER         D_CONT
              ________        ________        ________
 D_SAD          0.140
 D_ANGER       -0.035           0.166
 D_CONT        -0.034          -0.043           0.162


           Residuals for Covariances/Correlations/Residual
Correlations
           LST1H1      LST1H2      LST2H1      LST2H2      D_JOY
          ________    ________    ________    ________    ________
 LST1H1   -0.005
 LST1H2    0.017       0.039
 LST2H1    0.006      -0.041      -0.022
 LST2H2    0.000       0.209       0.016       0.055
 D_JOY     0.033      -0.040       0.081       0.064       0.000
 D_SAD    -0.059      -0.030      -0.158      -0.084       0.000
```

D_ANGER	-0.024	-0.010	-0.054	-0.056	0.000
D_CONT	0.010	-0.001	-0.006	-0.017	0.000

Residuals for Covariances/Correlations/Residual Correlations

	D_SAD	D_ANGER	D_CONT
D_SAD	0.000		
D_ANGER	0.000	0.000	
D_CONT	0.000	0.000	0.000

Standardized Residuals (z-scores) for Covariances/Correlations/Residual Corr

	LST1H1	LST1H2	LST2H1	LST2H2	D_JOY
LST1H1	99.000				
LST1H2	0.061	0.081			
LST2H1	-0.069	-0.113	-0.104		
LST2H2	999.000	1.002	999.000	0.247	
D_JOY	0.576	-0.608	0.957	0.705	0.000
D_SAD	-0.957	-0.414	-2.610	-1.223	0.000
D_ANGER	-0.411	-0.150	-0.810	-0.713	0.000
D_CONT	0.159	-0.019	-0.084	-0.197	0.000

Standardized Residuals (z-scores) for Covariances/Correlations/Residual Corr

	D_SAD	D_ANGER	D_CONT
D_SAD	0.000		
D_ANGER	0.000	0.000	
D_CONT	0.000	0.000	0.000

Normalized Residuals for Covariances/Correlations/Residual Correlations

	LST1H1	LST1H2	LST2H1	LST2H2	D_JOY
LST1H1	-0.004				
LST1H2	0.009	0.017			
LST2H1	-0.004	-0.020	-0.008		
LST2H2	0.000	0.084	0.005	0.014	
D_JOY	0.576	-0.608	0.957	0.705	0.000
D_SAD	-0.957	-0.414	-2.610	-1.223	0.000
D_ANGER	-0.411	-0.150	-0.810	-0.713	0.000

```
 D_CONT       0.159    -0.019     -0.084     -0.197      0.000


           Normalized Residuals for Covari-
ances/Correlations/Residual Correlations
             D_SAD          D_ANGER        D_CONT
             ________       ________       ________
 D_SAD        0.000
 D_ANGER      0.000          0.000
 D_CONT       0.000          0.000          0.000


MODEL MODIFICATION INDICES

NOTE:  Modification indices for direct effects of observed
dependent variables
regressed on covariates may not be included.  To include
these, request
MODINDICES (ALL).

Minimum M.I. value for printing the modification index
10.000

                             M.I.     E.P.C.  Std E.P.C.
StdYX E.P.C.

No modification indices above the minimum value.
```

Model 3

```
  analysis:         type = general;
                    estimator = mlr;

  model:            lst1 by lst1H1 lst1H2 (1);
                    lst2 by lst2H1 lst2H2 (1);

                    lst2 on lst1*1 mspre_1 mspre_2*1
mspre_3*1
                    espre_1 espre_2 espre_3
                    espre_4 espre_5 espre_6;
                    [lst1H1@0 lst2H1@0];
                    [lst1H2 lst2H2] (2);
                    [lst1* lst2*];
```

```
  output:          sampstat standardized stdyx residual
modindices;



Regression on latent level
from lst 2 onto lst 1 and mood and emotions
Indicators = number of correct solutions per test half
Estimator: MLR

SUMMARY OF ANALYSIS

Number of groups 1
Number of observations 397

Number of dependent variables 4
Number of independent variables     9
Number of continuous latent variables 2

Observed dependent variables

  Continuous
   LST1H1      LST1H2      LST2H1      LST2H2

Observed independent variables
   MSPRE_1     MSPRE_2     MSPRE_3     ESPRE_1     ESPRE_2
ESPRE_3
   ESPRE_4     ESPRE_5     ESPRE_6

Continuous latent variables
   LST1        LST2


Estimator MLR
Information matrix OBSERVED
Maximum number of iterations 1000
Convergence criterion 0.500D-04
Maximum number of steepest descent iterations 20
Maximum number of iterations for H1 2000
Convergence criterion for H1 0.100D-03

Input data file(s)
  Models.dat

Input data format  FREE
```

```
SUMMARY OF DATA

     Number of missing data patterns             1


COVARIANCE COVERAGE OF DATA

Minimum covariance coverage value   0.100


     PROPORTION OF DATA PRESENT
```

Covariance Coverage

	LST1H1	LST1H2	LST2H1	LST2H2	MSPRE_1
LST1H1	1.000				
LST1H2	1.000	1.000			
LST2H1	1.000	1.000	1.000		
LST2H2	1.000	1.000	1.000	1.000	
MSPRE_1	1.000	1.000	1.000	1.000	1.000
MSPRE_2	1.000	1.000	1.000	1.000	1.000
MSPRE_3	1.000	1.000	1.000	1.000	1.000
ESPRE_1	1.000	1.000	1.000	1.000	1.000
ESPRE_2	1.000	1.000	1.000	1.000	1.000
ESPRE_3	1.000	1.000	1.000	1.000	1.000
ESPRE_4	1.000	1.000	1.000	1.000	1.000
ESPRE_5	1.000	1.000	1.000	1.000	1.000
ESPRE_6	1.000	1.000	1.000	1.000	1.000

Covariance Coverage

	MSPRE_2	MSPRE_3	ESPRE_1	ESPRE_2	ESPRE_3
MSPRE_2	1.000				
MSPRE_3	1.000	1.000			
ESPRE_1	1.000	1.000	1.000		
ESPRE_2	1.000	1.000	1.000	1.000	
ESPRE_3	1.000	1.000	1.000	1.000	1.000
ESPRE_4	1.000	1.000	1.000	1.000	1.000
ESPRE_5	1.000	1.000	1.000	1.000	1.000
ESPRE_6	1.000	1.000	1.000	1.000	1.000

Covariance Coverage

	ESPRE_4	ESPRE_5	ESPRE_6

```
 ESPRE_4          1.000
 ESPRE_5          1.000          1.000
 ESPRE_6          1.000          1.000          1.000


SAMPLE STATISTICS


     ESTIMATED SAMPLE STATISTICS


           Means
              LST1H1        LST1H2        LST2H1        LST2H2        MSPRE_1
              ________      ________      ________      ________      ________
 1              5.060         4.471         5.887         5.204        57.305


           Means
              MSPRE_2       MSPRE_3       ESPRE_1       ESPRE_2       ESPRE_3
              ________      ________      ________      ________      ________
 1             53.441        51.814         3.290         2.683         1.640


           Means
              ESPRE_4       ESPRE_5       ESPRE_6
              ________      ________      ________
 1              3.043         1.554         1.693


           Covariances
              LST1H1        LST1H2        LST2H1        LST2H2        MSPRE_1
              ________      ________      ________      ________      ________
 LST1H1         8.818
 LST1H2         9.473        12.335
 LST2H1         8.642         9.587        14.720
 LST2H2         9.340        10.501        15.361        18.485
 MSPRE_1       -2.227        -5.950         3.339         2.205       796.126
 MSPRE_2       -4.208        -3.349         1.347         2.039       373.845
 MSPRE_3        0.515        -4.063         6.261         7.381       624.311
 ESPRE_1       -0.274        -0.330        -0.259        -0.240        15.972
 ESPRE_2       -0.132        -0.072        -0.038        -0.099        16.366
 ESPRE_3        0.120         0.187        -0.061        -0.141        -8.482
 ESPRE_4       -0.139        -0.028        -0.076         0.009        13.833
 ESPRE_5        0.284         0.301         0.415         0.343       -10.522
 ESPRE_6        0.303         0.402         0.469         0.461       -15.264
```

Covariances

	MSPRE_2	MSPRE_3	ESPRE_1	ESPRE_2	ESPRE_3
MSPRE_2	680.846				
MSPRE_3	272.291	791.623			
ESPRE_1	12.487	12.072	1.485		
ESPRE_2	12.848	12.913	1.170	1.587	
ESPRE_3	-2.108	-9.017	-0.228	-0.155	1.006
ESPRE_4	10.906	11.383	0.904	0.981	-0.335
ESPRE_5	-3.834	-9.154	-0.415	-0.346	0.520
ESPRE_6	-6.542	-13.808	-0.556	-0.513	0.474

Covariances

	ESPRE_4	ESPRE_5	ESPRE_6
ESPRE_4	1.356		
ESPRE_5	-0.457	1.018	
ESPRE_6	-0.488	0.533	1.281

Correlations

	LST1H1	LST1H2	LST2H1	LST2H2	MSPRE_1
LST1H1	1.000				
LST1H2	0.908	1.000			
LST2H1	0.759	0.712	1.000		
LST2H2	0.732	0.695	0.931	1.000	
MSPRE_1	-0.027	-0.060	0.031	0.018	1.000
MSPRE_2	-0.054	-0.037	0.013	0.018	0.508
MSPRE_3	0.006	-0.041	0.058	0.061	0.786
ESPRE_1	-0.076	-0.077	-0.055	-0.046	0.464
ESPRE_2	-0.035	-0.016	-0.008	-0.018	0.460
ESPRE_3	0.040	0.053	-0.016	-0.033	-0.300
ESPRE_4	-0.040	-0.007	-0.017	0.002	0.421
ESPRE_5	0.095	0.085	0.107	0.079	-0.370
ESPRE_6	0.090	0.101	0.108	0.095	-0.478

Correlations

	MSPRE_2	MSPRE_3	ESPRE_1	ESPRE_2	ESPRE_3
MSPRE_2	1.000				
MSPRE_3	0.371	1.000			
ESPRE_1	0.393	0.352	1.000		
ESPRE_2	0.391	0.364	0.762	1.000	
ESPRE_3	-0.081	-0.319	-0.187	-0.122	1.000

```
 ESPRE_4  0.359      0.347      0.637      0.669     -0.287
 ESPRE_5 -0.146     -0.322     -0.337     -0.272      0.513
 ESPRE_6 -0.222     -0.434     -0.403     -0.360      0.417


           Correlations
              ESPRE_4       ESPRE_5       ESPRE_6
              ________      ________      ________
 ESPRE_4         1.000
 ESPRE_5        -0.389         1.000
 ESPRE_6        -0.370         0.467         1.000


     MAXIMUM LOG-LIKELIHOOD VALUE FOR THE UNRESTRICTED (H1)
MODEL IS  -11803.969


THE MODEL ESTIMATION TERMINATED NORMALLY



MODEL FIT INFORMATION

Number of Free Parameters                       20

Loglikelihood

          H0 Value                       -3369.184
          H0 Scaling Correction Factor       2.315
            for MLR
          H1 Value                       -3350.393
          H1 Scaling Correction Factor       1.519
            for MLR

Information Criteria

          Akaike (AIC)                    6778.368
          Bayesian (BIC)                  6858.047
          Sample-Size Adjusted BIC        6794.586
            (n* = (n + 2) / 24)

Chi-Square Test of Model Fit

          Value                             37.993*
          Degrees of Freedom                    30
          P-Value                           0.1499
          Scaling Correction Factor          0.989
```

```
           for MLR

*   The chi-square value for MLM, MLMV, MLR, ULSMV, WLSM
and WLSMV cannot be used
    for chi-square difference testing in the regular way.
MLM, MLR and WLSM
    chi-square difference testing is described on the Mplus
website.  MLMV, WLSMV,
    and ULSMV difference testing is done using the DIFFTEST
option.

RMSEA (Root Mean Square Error Of Approximation)

          Estimate                           0.026
          90 Percent C.I.                    0.000  0.048
          Probability RMSEA <= .05           0.962

CFI/TLI

          CFI                                0.996
          TLI                                0.994

Chi-Square Test of Model Fit for the Baseline Model

          Value                           1898.001
          Degrees of Freedom                    42
          P-Value                           0.0000

SRMR (Standardized Root Mean Square Residual)

          Value                              0.031



MODEL RESULTS

                                                Two-Tailed
                 Estimate       S.E.  Est./S.E.    P-Value

 LST1     BY
    LST1H1          1.000      0.000    999.000    999.000
    LST1H2          1.091      0.030     36.453      0.000

 LST2     BY
    LST2H1          1.000      0.000    999.000    999.000
    LST2H2          1.091      0.030     36.453      0.000
```

```
 LST2      ON
    LST1            0.996       0.113       8.847       0.000

 LST2      ON
    MSPRE_1         0.004       0.007       0.565       0.572
    MSPRE_2         0.006       0.005       1.349       0.177
    MSPRE_3         0.007       0.007       0.956       0.339
    ESPRE_1        -0.042       0.143      -0.293       0.770
    ESPRE_2         0.043       0.119       0.358       0.721
    ESPRE_3        -0.377       0.215      -1.753       0.080
    ESPRE_4         0.004       0.131       0.031       0.975
    ESPRE_5         0.273       0.271       1.009       0.313
    ESPRE_6         0.299       0.194       1.543       0.123

 Means
    LST1            5.071       0.150      33.909       0.000

 Intercepts
    LST1H1          0.000       0.000     999.000     999.000
    LST1H2         -1.129       0.159      -7.092       0.000
    LST2H1          0.000       0.000     999.000     999.000
    LST2H2         -1.129       0.159      -7.092       0.000
    LST2           -0.399       1.027      -0.389       0.698

 Variances
    LST1            8.591       1.545       5.560       0.000

 Residual Variances
    LST1H1          0.263       0.242       1.087       0.277
    LST1H2          1.853       0.373       4.971       0.000
    LST2H1          0.563       0.273       2.062       0.039
    LST2H2          1.827       0.351       5.204       0.000
    LST2            5.164       1.189       4.341       0.000


STANDARDIZED MODEL RESULTS


STDYX Standardization

                                                   Two-Tailed
                    Estimate       S.E.  Est./S.E.    P-Value

 LST1      BY
    LST1H1          0.985       0.014      69.975       0.000
    LST1H2          0.920       0.020      45.545       0.000
```

```
 LST2     BY
    LST2H1              0.980      0.010     96.742      0.000
    LST2H2              0.949      0.014     66.786      0.000

 LST2     ON
    LST1                0.782      0.058     13.571      0.000

 LST2     ON
    MSPRE_1             0.029      0.052      0.569      0.570
    MSPRE_2             0.043      0.031      1.394      0.163
    MSPRE_3             0.053      0.054      0.977      0.329
    ESPRE_1            -0.014      0.047     -0.292      0.770
    ESPRE_2             0.014      0.040      0.357      0.721
    ESPRE_3            -0.101      0.056     -1.823      0.068
    ESPRE_4             0.001      0.041      0.031      0.975
    ESPRE_5             0.074      0.071      1.037      0.300
    ESPRE_6             0.091      0.056      1.613      0.107

 Means
    LST1                1.730      0.122     14.196      0.000

 Intercepts
    LST1H1              0.000      0.000    999.000    999.000
    LST1H2             -0.325      0.041     -7.945      0.000
    LST2H1              0.000      0.000    999.000    999.000
    LST2H2             -0.263      0.032     -8.143      0.000
    LST2               -0.107      0.268     -0.398      0.690

 Variances
    LST1                1.000      0.000    999.000    999.000

 Residual Variances
    LST1H1              0.030      0.028      1.072      0.284
    LST1H2              0.153      0.037      4.126      0.000
    LST2H1              0.039      0.020      1.955      0.051
    LST2H2              0.099      0.027      3.677      0.000
    LST2                0.371      0.082      4.510      0.000


R-SQUARE

    Observed                                            Two-Tailed
    Variable        Estimate       S.E.  Est./S.E.    P-Value

    LST1H1              0.970      0.028     34.988      0.000
    LST1H2              0.847      0.037     22.772      0.000
    LST2H1              0.961      0.020     48.371      0.000
```

```
    LST2H2             0.901      0.027      33.393      0.000

    Latent                                            Two-Tailed
    Variable        Estimate          S.E.  Est./S.E.    P-Value

    LST2               0.629      0.082       7.660      0.000


QUALITY OF NUMERICAL RESULTS

     Condition Number for the Information Matrix
0.286E-05
       (ratio of smallest to largest eigenvalue)


RESIDUAL OUTPUT


     ESTIMATED MODEL AND RESIDUALS (OBSERVED - ESTIMATED)


           Model Estimated Means/Intercepts/Thresholds
              LST1H1        LST1H2        LST2H1        LST2H2        MSPRE_1
              ________      ________      ________      ________      ________
 1               5.071         4.404         5.864         5.270        57.305


           Model Estimated Means/Intercepts/Thresholds
              MSPRE_2       MSPRE_3       ESPRE_1       ESPRE_2       ESPRE_3
              ________      ________      ________      ________      ________
 1              53.441        51.814         3.290         2.683         1.640


           Model Estimated Means/Intercepts/Thresholds
              ESPRE_4       ESPRE_5       ESPRE_6
              ________      ________      ________
 1               3.043         1.554         1.693


           Residuals for Means/Intercepts/Thresholds
              LST1H1        LST1H2        LST2H1        LST2H2        MSPRE_1
              ________      ________      ________      ________      ________
 1              -0.010         0.067         0.022        -0.066         0.000


           Residuals for Means/Intercepts/Thresholds
              MSPRE_2       MSPRE_3       ESPRE_1       ESPRE_2       ESPRE_3
```

```
1        ________   ________   ________   ________   ________
          0.000      0.000      0.000      0.000      0.000


           Residuals for Means/Intercepts/Thresholds
              ESPRE_4          ESPRE_5          ESPRE_6
              ________         ________         ________
      1        0.000            0.000            0.000


           Standardized Residuals (z-scores) for
Means/Intercepts/Thresholds
           LST1H1     LST1H2     LST2H1     LST2H2     MSPRE_1
          ________   ________   ________   ________   ________
1          999.000      1.111      0.529    999.000      0.000


           Standardized Residuals (z-scores) for
Means/Intercepts/Thresholds
           MSPRE_2    MSPRE_3    ESPRE_1    ESPRE_2    ESPRE_3
          ________   ________   ________   ________   ________
1          0.000      0.000      0.000      0.000      0.000


           Standardized Residuals (z-scores) for
Means/Intercepts/Thresholds
              ESPRE_4          ESPRE_5          ESPRE_6
              ________         ________         ________
      1        0.000            0.000            0.000


           Normalized Residuals for
Means/Intercepts/Thresholds
           LST1H1     LST1H2     LST2H1     LST2H2     MSPRE_1
          ________   ________   ________   ________   ________
1          -0.070      0.380      0.115     -0.306      0.000


           Normalized Residuals for
Means/Intercepts/Thresholds
           MSPRE_2    MSPRE_3    ESPRE_1    ESPRE_2    ESPRE_3
          ________   ________   ________   ________   ________
1          0.000      0.000      0.000      0.000      0.000


           Normalized Residuals for
Means/Intercepts/Thresholds
```

```
             ESPRE_4        ESPRE_5        ESPRE_6
             ________       ________       ________
 1             0.000          0.000          0.000


           Model Estimated Covari-
ances/Correlations/Residual Correlations
          LST1H1    LST1H2    LST2H1    LST2H2    MSPRE_1
          ________  ________  ________  ________  ________
 LST1H1   8.854
 LST1H2   9.374     12.081
 LST2H1   8.553      9.332    14.498
 LST2H2   9.332     10.182    15.204    8.416
 MSPRE_1  0.000      0.000     5.599     6.109    796.126
 MSPRE_2  0.000      0.000     5.410     5.902    373.845
 MSPRE_3  0.000      0.000     6.491     7.083    624.311
 ESPRE_1  0.000      0.000     0.021     0.023     15.972
 ESPRE_2  0.000      0.000     0.066     0.072     16.366
 ESPRE_3  0.000      0.000    -0.203    -0.221     -8.482
 ESPRE_4  0.000      0.000     0.065     0.071     13.833
 ESPRE_5  0.000      0.000     0.114     0.124    -10.522
 ESPRE_6  0.000      0.000     0.153     0.167    -15.264


           Model Estimated Covari-
ances/Correlations/Residual Correlations
          MSPRE_2   MSPRE_3   ESPRE_1   ESPRE_2   ESPRE_3
          ________  ________  ________  ________  ________
 MSPRE_2  680.846
 MSPRE_3  272.291   791.623
 ESPRE_1   12.487    12.072     1.485
 ESPRE_2   12.848    12.913     1.170     1.587
 ESPRE_3   -2.108    -9.017    -0.228    -0.155     1.006
 ESPRE_4   10.906    11.383     0.904     0.981    -0.335
 ESPRE_5   -3.834    -9.154    -0.415    -0.346
0.520
 ESPRE_6   -6.542   -13.808    -0.556    -0.513     0.474


           Model Estimated Covari-
ances/Correlations/Residual Correlations
                ESPRE_4       ESPRE_5       ESPRE_6
                ________      ________      ________
 ESPRE_4          1.356
 ESPRE_5         -0.457         1.018
 ESPRE_6         -0.488         0.533         1.281
```

```
          Residuals for Covariances/Correlations/Residual
Correlations
        LST1H1     LST1H2     LST2H1     LST2H2     MSPRE_1
       ________   ________   ________   ________   ________
 LST1H1  -0.037
 LST1H2   0.099      0.254
 LST2H1   0.089      0.255      0.222
 LST2H2   0.008      0.319      0.156      0.069
 MSPRE_1 -2.227     -5.950     -2.260     -3.904      0.000
 MSPRE_2 -4.208     -3.349     -4.062     -3.864      0.000
 MSPRE_3  0.515     -4.063     -0.231      0.298      0.000
 ESPRE_1 -0.274     -0.330     -0.281     -0.264      0.000
 ESPRE_2 -0.132     -0.072     -0.105     -0.171      0.000
 ESPRE_3  0.120      0.187      0.142      0.081      0.000
 ESPRE_4 -0.139     -0.028     -0.141     -0.062      0.000
 ESPRE_5  0.284      0.301      0.301      0.218      0.000
 ESPRE_6  0.303      0.402      0.316      0.294      0.000


          Residuals for Covariances/Correlations/Residual
Correlations
        MSPRE_2    MSPRE_3    ESPRE_1    ESPRE_2    ESPRE_3
       ________   ________   ________   ________   ________
 MSPRE_2  0.000
 MSPRE_3  0.000      0.000
 ESPRE_1  0.000      0.000      0.000
 ESPRE_2  0.000      0.000      0.000      0.000
 ESPRE_3  0.000      0.000      0.000      0.000      0.000
 ESPRE_4  0.000      0.000      0.000      0.000      0.000
 ESPRE_5  0.000      0.000      0.000      0.000      0.000
 ESPRE_6  0.000      0.000      0.000      0.000      0.000


          Residuals for Covariances/Correlations/Residual
Correlations
              ESPRE_4       ESPRE_5       ESPRE_6
             ________      ________      ________
 ESPRE_4        0.000
 ESPRE_5        0.000         0.000
 ESPRE_6        0.000         0.000         0.000


          Standardized Residuals (z-scores) for Covari-
ances/Correlations/Residual Corr
        LST1H1     LST1H2     LST2H1     LST2H2     MSPRE_1
       ________   ________   ________   ________   ________
```

```
LST1H1 999.000
LST1H2   0.263      0.368
LST2H1   0.562      0.495      0.250
LST2H2 999.000      0.800      0.173      0.074
MSPRE_1 -0.486     -1.108     -0.453     -0.693      0.000
MSPRE_2 -1.054     -0.693     -0.891     -0.752      0.000
MSPRE_3  0.119     -0.798     -0.050      0.057      0.000
ESPRE_1 -1.427     -1.454     -1.579     -1.264      0.000
ESPRE_2 -0.684     -0.319     -0.535     -0.783      0.000
ESPRE_3  0.763      1.046      1.181      0.505      0.000
ESPRE_4 -0.762     -0.130     -0.747     -0.295      0.000
ESPRE_5  1.770      1.537      1.502      0.840      0.000
ESPRE_6  1.751      1.978      1.494      1.119      0.000


          Standardized Residuals (z-scores) for Covari-
ances/Correlations/Residual Corr
        MSPRE_2    MSPRE_3    ESPRE_1    ESPRE_2    ESPRE_3
        ________   ________   ________   ________   ________
MSPRE_2  0.000
MSPRE_3  0.000      0.000
ESPRE_1  0.000      0.000      0.000
ESPRE_2  0.000      0.000      0.000      0.000
ESPRE_3  0.000      0.000      0.000      0.000      0.000
ESPRE_4  0.000      0.000      0.000      0.000      0.000
ESPRE_5  0.000      0.000      0.000      0.000      0.000
ESPRE_6  0.000      0.000      0.000      0.000      0.000


          Standardized Residuals (z-scores) for Covari-
ances/Correlations/Residual Corr
              ESPRE_4        ESPRE_5        ESPRE_6
              ________       ________       ________
ESPRE_4        0.000
ESPRE_5        0.000          0.000
ESPRE_6        0.000          0.000          0.000


          Normalized Residuals for Covari-
ances/Correlations/Residual Correlations
        LST1H1     LST1H2     LST2H1     LST2H2     MSPRE_1
        ________   ________   ________   ________   ________
LST1H1  -0.024
LST1H2   0.054      0.111
LST2H1   0.049      0.117      0.075
LST2H2   0.004      0.125      0.046      0.017
MSPRE_1 -0.486     -1.108     -0.372     -0.576      0.000
```

```
 MSPRE_2 -1.054      -0.693     -0.738     -0.628       0.000
 MSPRE_3  0.119      -0.798     -0.039      0.044       0.000
 ESPRE_1 -1.427      -1.454     -1.175     -0.970       0.000
 ESPRE_2 -0.684      -0.319     -0.424     -0.626       0.000
 ESPRE_3  0.763       1.046      0.809      0.381       0.000
 ESPRE_4 -0.762      -0.130     -0.582     -0.232       0.000
 ESPRE_5  1.770       1.537      1.083      0.652       0.000
 ESPRE_6  1.751       1.978      1.105      0.873       0.000


          Normalized Residuals for Covari-
ances/Correlations/Residual Correlations
       MSPRE_2    MSPRE_3    ESPRE_1    ESPRE_2    ESPRE_3
      ________   ________   ________   ________   ________
 MSPRE_2  0.000
 MSPRE_3  0.000      0.000
 ESPRE_1  0.000      0.000      0.000
 ESPRE_2  0.000      0.000      0.000      0.000
 ESPRE_3  0.000      0.000      0.000      0.000      0.000
 ESPRE_4  0.000      0.000      0.000      0.000      0.000
 ESPRE_5  0.000      0.000      0.000      0.000      0.000
 ESPRE_6  0.000      0.000      0.000      0.000      0.000


          Normalized Residuals for Covari-
ances/Correlations/Residual Correlations
             ESPRE_4       ESPRE_5       ESPRE_6
            ________      ________      ________
 ESPRE_4       0.000
 ESPRE_5       0.000         0.000
 ESPRE_6       0.000         0.000         0.000


MODEL MODIFICATION INDICES

NOTE:  Modification indices for direct effects of observed
dependent variables
regressed on covariates may not be included.  To include
these, request
MODINDICES (ALL).

Minimum M.I. value for printing the modification index
10.000

                              M.I.     E.P.C.  Std E.P.C.
StdYX E.P.C.
No modification indices above the minimum value.
```

MIX
Papier aus verantwortungsvollen Quellen
Paper from responsible sources
FSC® C105338

If you have any concerns about our products,
you can contact us on
ProductSafety@springernature.com

In case Publisher is established outside the EU,
the EU authorized representative is:
Springer Nature Customer Service Center GmbH
Europaplatz 3, 69115 Heidelberg, Germany

Printed by Libri Plureos GmbH
in Hamburg, Germany